# COMMANDOS AND RANGERS
## OF WORLD WAR II

# COMMANDOS AND RANGERS
## OF WORLD WAR II

### JAMES LADD

ST. MARTIN'S PRESS
NEW YORK

*'A green beret does not make you bullet-proof.'*

Major-General J.L. Moulton CB, DSO, OBE in conversation
with the author.

Copyright © 1978 by James D. Ladd

All rights reserved.    For information, write:
St. Martin's Press, Inc., 175 Fifth Ave., New York, N.Y. 10010
Printed in Great Britain

Library of Congress Catalog Card Number: 78–3125

First published in the United States of America in 1978


Design: Judy Tuke

Maps and diagrams: Alec Spark


Library of Congress Cataloging in Publication Data
Ladd, J. D.
    Commandos and rangers of World War II.

    Bibliography: p.
    Includes index.
    1. World War, 1939–1945—Regimental histories—
Great Britain—Combined Operations Command.
2. Great Britain.    Combined Operations Command.
3. World War, 1939–1945—Regimental histories—
United States—1st Ranger Battalion.    4. United
States.    Army.    1st Ranger Battalion.    5. World
War, 1939–1945—Amphibious operations.    I. Title.
D760.C63L32        940.54′12        78–3125
ISBN 0–312–15167–5

# CONTENTS

Commandos and rangers on the road from Anzio to Rome.

# FOREWORD

by Admiral of the Fleet the Earl Mountbatten of Burma, KG, PC, GCB, OM, GCSI, GCIE, GCVO, DSO, FRS

This book tells the story of the men who carried out the raids in World War II, mostly in the Landing Craft described by James Ladd in his book *Assault from the Sea 1939/45*.

Armed conflict invariably brings forth acts of great courage, but I believe that nobody showed the superb quality of our fighting men better than the volunteers for the highly dangerous task of raiding enemy held strong points from the sea.

When I relieved Admiral of the Fleet Lord Keyes in charge of Combined Operations these volunteers had had their title finally settled as Commandos. I extended the entry to include our European allies, Norwegians, French, Belgians, Dutch, Danish and Polish in No. 10 Commando. We eventually recruited some Germans who were bitterly opposed to Hitler and his Nazis, and they became X Troop of 10 Commando. These men of X Troop showed quite exceptional courage by risking death by torture if captured and identified as Germans and for this reason we created new English identities for them.

When General Marshal visited me in the Combined Operations Headquarters in April 1942 we discussed, among other matters, the highly successful Commando Training Centre at Achnacarry. He was so impressed he asked if he could send American soldiers over to be trained there in the raiding technique. These American soldiers became the 1st United States Ranger Battalion.

I was proud when President Roosevelt agreed that I should present the first award for gallantry won by the U.S. Army in Europe in World War II to Corporal Koons of the 1st Ranger battalion. He won the British Military Medal with No. 4 Commando at Dieppe in August 1942. King George VI gave me the authority to make the presentation at a large U.S. Military Parade under General George Patton at Casablanca in January 1943.

On two occasions I summoned men who had volunteered for particularly hazardous but important small scale raids to my Headquarters and warned them that the odds were heavily against more than about two men in a dozen getting back alive, for those captured would be summarily shot by personal command of Hitler who had issued special orders against the Commandos. I then gave them the chance to withdraw their names and let others volunteer to take their place before revealing the objectives. No one withdrew their name. Nearly all were lost. I felt quite emotionally overcome by their courage as I wished them good luck.

Today we are used to the daring exploits of 007, James Bond, but the story of these gallant raiders, Commandos, Rangers and those associated with them, is even more exciting and gripping for these were real men facing real live dangers. It is time their story was told and James Ladd has done it well.

Mountbatten of Burma

A. F.

# ACKNOWLEDGEMENTS

The author would like to thank all those individuals and organisations who have helped in the preparation of this book and in particular: the Australian War Memorial Trust; Mr S. J. (Sonnie) Bissell; Mr Henry Brown, MBE, secretary of the Commando Association; Mr T. Charman; Captain N. Clogstoun-Willmott, DSO, DSC,* RN; Major-General E. C. Cole, CB, CBE; Miss S. K. Connett for secretarial work; Mr J. Davidson; Mr Brian L. Davis for use of the commando knife featured on the jacket; Major A. J. Donald RM, Royal Marines archivist and his staff; Major-General H. D. Fellowes, CB, DSO; Mr D. J. Flunder, MC; Mr Geoffrey V. Galwey; General Sir Campbell R. Hardy, KCB, CBE, DSO**; the Historical Branch, United States Marine Corps; the Hisorical Services Division, United States Army; Major-General G. C. Horton, CB, OBE; the Imperial War Museum, London; Colonel A. J. Leahy, OBE, Royal Signals (retd); Major-General J. L. Moulton, CB, DSO, OBE; Admiral of the Fleet the Earl Mountbatten of Burma, KG, PC, GCB, OM, GCSI, GCIE, GCVO, DSO; the National Maritime Museum, London; the National Archives and Records Service, Washington; Mr J. W. Nicholson and Camper & Nicholsons Ltd; Nottingham Central Library; Mr Bruce Ogden-Smith, DCM, MM; Brigadier D. W. O'Flaherty, CBE, DSO; Colonel J. F. Parsons, OBE, MC, RM; Mr Harold Perlmutter, Ranger Bn Association; Mr A. M. Preston, historian; the Public Records Office, London; Ranger Department, United States Army, Fort Benning, Georgia; the Royal Engineers Corps library; the Royal Navy Submarine Museum; Mr A. Spark, the artist; Mr Michael Stevens, the editor, for his encouragement and advice; Rev Dr Albert T. Tovey, DD, Executive Secretary of the Ranger Bn Association; Ms Judy Tuke, the book's designer; Mr S. Weatherall; the Wilkinson Sword Company Ltd; Brigadier P. Young, DSO, MC, MA, FRGS.

Grateful acknowledgement is made to the following for permission to reproduce photographs and drawings: Australian War Memorial Trustees, pages 70-81; Canadian Forces Photo, page 153; Commando Association, pages 33, 82, 93, 231, 233; Illustrated London News, pages 46, 115, 181; Imperial War Museum, pages 3-30, 35-43, 51, 92, 119-142, 149, 155-170, 184-6, 189, 192, 193, 214, 244; Ministry of Defence (Navy), page 174; Royal Navy Submarine Museum, page 173; Public Archives, Canada, pages 145, 154; Royal Marines Museum, pages 64, 230; Mr J. W. Nicholson, page 219; United States Army Signal Corps, pages 108-112, 188, 197, 205, 221, 227; United States Marine Corps, pages 94-103; Mr S. Weatherall, page 213.

# PREFACE

'A steel hand from the sea' is Sir Winston Churchill's description of Commandos. For they plucked the enemy from his seaboard defences in the early days of World War II, and later became - with their close allies, the American Rangers - the spearheading force in amphibious assaults.

Throughout their existence these elite troops were controversial with arguments against the concentration of talent in Special Forces that rumbles on in the 1970s, but in the 1940s their operations heartened their fellow countrymen through freedom's darkest hours. The discomfort and confusion these raiders caused to their enemies is seen in the history of German dispositions along the coasts of Europe in 1944 and the Japanese reactions to Pacific raids. Commandos probed the German defences north of the Arctic Circle, fought alongside partisans in the Balkans, swam ashore on secret missions against the enemies' Atlantic, Mediterranean, and Pacific coasts, and were in action in almost every theatre of the war. Rangers saw action in Africa, through Italy and on the beaches of Normandy, landed in the Philippines, and fought alongside the Commandos on occasions.

Trained to fight without the support of artillery and other heavy weapons, the early commandos depended entirely on their own resources and skill with small arms. But the changing nature of the war as it moved from coastal raids to continental campaigns led to the reorganisation of the Commando and Ranger forces as flank guards and spearheaders of invasion landings: a role involving all the complexities of amphibious assault with the coordination of fire support from ships and tactical air strikes against beach defences, as the later chapters show. The raiding traditions continued, however, in the sabotage parties of the Special Boat Section, in assault pilotage reconnaissance, and other special work of Commando units in the van of invasions.

The fighting skills of these superb infantry are explained by examples showing their talents at all levels of command. In the appendices are details of their organisations, weaponry, and equipment, with brief details of each unit's history. Their story unfolds to show what sort of men they were, something of their robust humour, their tactics and ingenious use of conventional weapons, their achievements and limitations. A story of courage and tenacity dedicated to all who served with these Special Forces in the hope that their example will not be forgotten, and to the defenders - some gallant, many tenacious in their resistance on the beaches.

James D. Ladd                    London      March 1977

An explosion catches men on a toggle bridge in realistic battle training, January 1943 at Achnacarry.

# EUROPE AND AFRICA: SEPTEMBER 1939 TO DECEMBER 1940

After German forces invaded Poland on 1 September 1939, the British and French declared war on 3 September, and in mid-September the Russians occupied the eastern Polish provinces. Through the winter of 1939-40 there followed the 'phoney war' of patrolling on the Franco-German border and leaflet raids by Allied bombers. But in Finland a Russian invasion was held until March 1940, when the main Finnish defence line was breached. British and French plans to send a force of 100,000 men to aid the Finns were deferred when Norway and Sweden refused to allow the Allies to cross their countries.

The war at sea, fought mainly between convoys and U-boats, led the Germans to include Norway in their plans for the domination of Europe, and they needed the port of Narvik (north Norway) for Swedish iron-ore shipments. Allied forces, including men raised for the intended Finnish Campaign, landed in three areas including Narvik to fight separate battles rather than a coordinated campaign, but without adequate air strength the Allies could not prevent the German occupation of Norway being virtually complete before the Germans' main thrust in the west. The Swedes remained neutral with an element of pro-German sentiment among their people.

The main German offensive began on 10 May 1940, rapidly overrunning Belgium and Holland, the momentum of its success carrying the Germans by 24 May to within 15 miles (24km) of Dunkirk on the French Channel coast, splitting the Allied armies. Some 330,000 Allied troops escaped through this port when Hitler stopped the German advance for several days.

On 10 June the Italians invaded southern France and by the time France surrendered (23 June), British forces were preparing to meet attacks from the Italian African colonies - Tripoli, Libya, Somaliland, and Ethiopia. These east African lands soon fell to the British, but in the deserts of North Africa the war ebbed and flowed for two years.

At home the British suffered their first serious air raid on London docks (7 September 1940). Despite the loss of nearly all their guns and tanks in France they prepared to fight off a German invasion. They convoyed food and weapons across the Atlantic and reinforced their North African armies.

# 1 THE COMMANDO IDEA - 1940

Feet firmly on the ground, the stocky Private Donkin methodically swung his tommy-gun, firing from left to right. Some 15 Germans, startled by his sudden appearance in the doorway, were cut down. In another action, the speed marchers stretched their stride to cover the last 6 of 20 desert miles after a sharp night action. Ignoring their thirst and the ache of hunger after two nights and a day in the enemy's hills, they pushed on, fearing his tanks might encircle them. Elsewhere a lone swimmer fought off a chilling exhaustion, his senses dulled by three hours of silent reconnaissance swimming and crawling among the enemy's beach defences. He felt pangs of doubt: would his fellow canoeist see the flickering torch among the waves before an enemy patrol boat caught sight of it?

Men in these situations need more than courage; they need a rare determination, extreme physical fitness, and great skill in their profession of raiding, as this commando, these rangers, and the Royal Navy navigator turned canoeist showed in typical actions of the Commando and American Ranger units (see diagram p. 14). In their amphibious war were all the hazards of land patrols and raids, with the added uncertainty of a seaborne approach all too easily foundering on an adverse change in the weather or some unexpected shoal.

In preparing for a raid on a beach there was less opportunity to see the lie of the land than before conventional military raids. At best the amphibious raiders might have panoramic shots from aerial reconnaissance, or be given a flight over the target beach. Neither of these showed the sea-level view from an assault craft, when the 'white house' reference point for a beach could be hidden by trees. From a canoe the view was even more restricted: the looming hinterland was there, but was the beach below it the right landfall? Or was this the bay with a mined shore west of the intended landing point? This was just one of the many problems in getting ashore.

The general reconnaissance raid, mounted to find out what enemy defences if any stood along a stretch of coast, developed into the assault pilotage surveys of 1943 and 1944, secretly landing for specific intelligence of beach conditions and defences. Would the exit road from the beach not only carry tanks but could a matting road be laid beside this route to carry wheeled vehicles? Were the peat workings of Roman times now impassable mud holes behind that beach? Would this island's coral make an airstrip for fighters? Whatever the answers, the enemy must not discover these questions were being asked, for this would give away the landing areas of a future invasion. The assault pilotage parties, therefore, carried other people's secrets which could betray an invading army.

Sabotage raids were no less difficult to execute than recces, although these raiders carried no one else's secrets. Throughout all these Commando and Ranger operations, however, the raiders wore military uniform, although often without their commando shoulder flashes for reasons that will become obvious.

As the war moved towards amphibious invasions and a clash of continental armies, the Commandos' numbers increased but there were proportionately fewer involved in small-scale raids. The strength of a full Commando varied with some reorganisation from time to time (see Appendix 2) but in November 1942 the establishment was 24 officers and 435 other ranks (enlisted men). At other times in action there were up to 630 men in a Commando. Each Commando had a headquarters and several Troops, the equivalent of platoons in infantry companies, the usual arrangement being six Troops, one of which was - after late 1942 - the Heavy Weapons Troop armed with medium machine-guns and heavy mortars. A Commando was therefore not unlike an infantry battalion but had only five small rifle or fighting Troops by comparison with the battalion's four companies, each with over 120 all ranks. At full strength a rifle Troop with its three officers 'was handled like a strong platoon', to quote Major General J.L. Moulton, CB, DSO, OBE who in 1944 was the colonel commanding 48 Royal Marine Commando. When the 60-strong Troop was reduced through casualties to the 38 or so of an infantry platoon, their handling was very similar. However, the

Rugged Norway suited commando raids.

official composition of these rifle Troops, each having two 30-man Sections with their sub-sections of 15 men, was not strictly followed; and a number of Royal Marine Commandos deployed five rifle sub-Sections rather than two Sections and the headquarters in each Troop.

There was a higher proportion of officers and NCO's in Special Forces than in regular formations (a term used in this book to distinguish Special Forces from other units), particularly in the specialised reconnaissance and raiding parties. But the essence of Commando organisation was its flexibility, and a Heavy Weapons Troop, for example, might be strengthened from its established two Vickers machine-guns and two 3 inch (76mm) mortars to twice that number for a particular operation. (Metric and Imperial measure comparison of all weapon sizes in this book are mathematical and do not take account of slight variations in different countries' measurements of bore sizes, etc.)

The choice of target beaches could be critical. General Holland M. Smith, USMC, has written of one Pacific raid that 'it was a spectacular performance by (the) 2nd Marine Raider Battalion but it was a pure piece of folly. The raid had no useful military purpose and served only to alert the Japanese. . . the intensive fortifications of Tarawa dates from that raid.' Although speaking of the Gilbert Islands in the Pacific, where the Raiders had landed on Makin Island in August 1942 leaving nine men behind to an undeserved fate, the General's stricture could apply to several amphibious operations. When the US Marine Corps' 2 Division stormed ashore at Tarawa in November 1943, a third of the 5,000 marines landing on the first day were casualties because the Japanese were well prepared and the tide played fateful tricks over the reefs.

There are arguments for suggesting the landings at Tarawa were unnecessary, much in the way the Dieppe raid on the French coast the previous summer is considered by some historians to have been a waste of many Canadian and other lives. Yet in Europe, as in the Pacific, a great deal of the art of amphibious warfare was learnt from

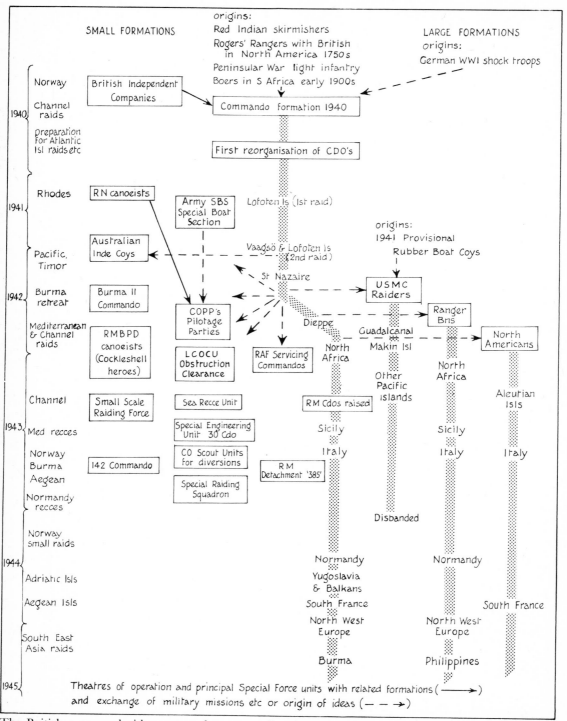

**SMALL FORMATIONS**

origins:
Red Indian skirmishers
Rogers' Rangers with British
  in North America 1750s
Peninsular War light infantry
Boers in S Africa early 1900s

**LARGE FORMATIONS**
origins:
German WWI shock troops

Norway

Channel raids

1940

preparation for Atlantic Isl raids etc

British Independent Companies

Commando formation 1940

First reorganisation of CDO's

Rhodes

1941

RN canoeists

Army SBS Special Boat Section

Lofoten Is (1st raid)

origins:
1941 Provisional
  Rubber Boat Coys

Pacific, Timor

Australian Inde Coys

Vaagsö & Lofoten Is (2nd raid)

St Nazaire

1942

Burma retreat

Burma II Commando

USMC Raiders

Ranger Bns

Mediterranean & Channel raids

RMBPD canoeists (Cockleshell heroes)

COPP's Pilotage Parties

Dieppe

Guadalcanal

North Americans

North Africa

Makin Isl

North Africa

Channel

Small Scale Raiding Force

LCOCU Obstruction Clearance

RAF Servicing Commandos

Other Pacific islands

Aleutian Isls

1943

Med recces

Sea Recce Unit

Special Engineering Unit 30 Cdo

RM Cdos raised

Sicily

Sicily

Italy

Italy

Italy

Norway
Burma
Aegean

142 Commando

CO Scout Units for diversions

RM Detachment '385'

Normandy recces

Special Raiding Squadron

Norway small raids

Disbanded

1944

Adriatic Isls

Normandy

Normandy

Aegean Isls

Yugoslavia & Balkans

South France

South France

North West Europe

North West Europe

South East Asia raids

Burma

Philippines

1945

Theatres of operation and principal Special Force units with related formations (———➤)
and exchange of military missions etc or origin of ideas (— — —➤)

The British commando idea spawned many small units and military missions between the Allies that led to the formation of Australian, American and other nations' Special Forces.

these two operations. The Allies modified their strategy, as readers will see in chapter 11, while the Germans - satisfied they had repulsed a possible invasion attempt - did not modify their posture defending major ports and paid the price in defeat at Normandy. In 1940, however, there were many lessons to be learnt, for little thought had been given to *major* amphibious assault. The British hardly conceived the French could be defeated and few Americans expected to be embroiled in a global war. What work was done in the United Kingdom on raiding and amphibious operations had been mainly carried out by the Inter-Service Training and Development Centre (ISTDC) and the Royal Marines' Mobile Naval Base Defence Organisation (MNBDO), the Royal Navy being responsible for amphibious operations. The Centre - with raids in mind - had devised plans for a relatively silent, low silhouette landing craft that became the LCA (Landing Craft, Assault), and produced some other worthwhile ideas, including methods for supplying troops by air. The MNBDO, more concerned with landing heavy guns for harbour defences, did not

include an assault force to capture a naval base because economies prevented this planned development. The US Marine Corps was responsible for the United States inter-war plans for amphibious operations; and although they did a number of landing exercises in the 1930s, not until 1940 were they joined in these by the US Army's 1 Division.

The British, in late 1940, began to integrate command for all three services deployed in what became Combined Operations. (Allied planners, however, used this term to describe a campaign by forces of several countries and 'Joint Operations' for actions involving three services.) Combined operations became the commando's *métier* and he would become as accustomed to calling up a battleship's gunnery officer or the leader of a flight of rocket firing Typhoon aircraft as he might be radioing for mortar fire from his own Heavy Weapons Troop. The call to the Navy or RAF might be made indirectly through Forward Observation Officers or others but the effect was the same, if not more devastating.

Long before they reached this degree of sophistication, however, in the main stream of Commando forces (see diagram p. 14) were spawned many small fry. The administrative problems were solved, for the early Commando units were without 'a tail' of cooks, cobblers, and others so essential in keeping a fighting unit in the field. At least sufficient

The landing craft carrier ship HMS *Princess Beatrix* on 6 March 1941 with LCAs in davits and an LCM in special davit fitted to only this ship and her sister (LCMs usually launched by derricks), summer 1941. Commandos and Ranger Battalions were put ashore from these Landing Ships in the Mediterranean, Normandy and other operations.

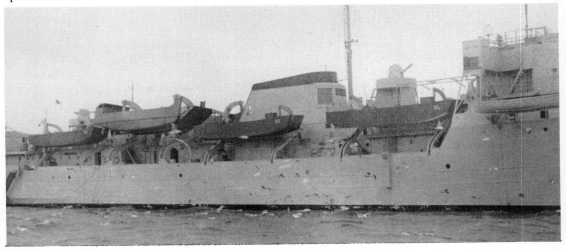

transport was found to carry these Special Forces from one action to another in a land battle, a far cry from 1940 when one or two trucks might be the only vehicles a Commando had on its strength. Transport nevertheless remained a major problem, and as Commandos' equipment for raiding roles did not include those infantryman's delights of defensive wire and mines - not, that is, in the normal course - they always had problems in battles of attrition. Nevertheless, as their story does not follow the usual path of military organisation, it was not particularly surprising to find later commandos coming ashore with anti-tank mines strapped to their equipment. However, they were not normally set up for the heavy infantryman's tactics of prolonged defence before a steady advance, although they were misused in these roles at times. They were nimble-footed, lightly equipped for the in-and-out thrust over terrain where others might not be expected to beach or march. But all the speed of foot is no substitute for an anti-tank gun to beat off armoured attack, 'nor does a Green Beret make you bullet-proof' (again to quote General Moulton).

That Commandos and other Special Forces of World War II were superb light infantry, is a fact all too often forgotten in the fashion of the 1970s when every political cut-throat wants to be called a 'commando'.

From the Independent Companies - forerunners of the Commandos - who landed in Norway in 1940, to the Rangers in 1945 who landed in the Philippines, the Special Forces' story is full of interest and paradox. How were those Independent Companies to operate from a ship as their base if the enemy had air superiority? Might the Rangers in the Philippines have saved the fleet if the approaches to Leyte Gulf had been studded with mines controlled from the shore? This book is not concerned, however, with might-have-beens but with the facts as they were, so far as can be told.

Four Independent Companies were the first British special service forces in action in World War II. They came ashore at the small fishing ports of Mo i Rana and Bodö; their headquarters group landing from their parent ship HMS *Royal Ulsterman* on 13 May 1940. In skirmishes on the rugged Norwegian mountains made dangerous by an early thaw, these companies screened the Allied operations a hundred or so miles to the north around Narvik. Among the companies' officers were 20 experts on mountain warfare, flown home from the Indian north-west frontier, who put to good use their knowledge of Pathan tribesmen's tactics, ambushing some 60 Germans who came ashore to probe northward.

Despite such setbacks, the Germans continued their infantry frontal attacks with supporting parachute infantry outflanking Allied positions, and after nearly a month of confused fighting the Independent Companies were withdrawn through Bodö along with elements of the 24th Guards Brigade and Norwegian troops.

The operations in Norway showed clearly one of the paradoxes of the commando idea. These special forces were used as infantry, although the Independent Companies had been hurriedly raised for guerrilla operations, an idea fostered by Major Holland, an engineer who, by a lucky chance, was appointed head of the general staff's research section, then known as GS(R), in 1938. His research into the possible use of guerrillas led him to champion preparations for all types of irregular operations, although he could make little headway against the traditional thinking of those directing military operations. However, a study dated 1 June 1939 concluded that 'if guerrilla warfare is coordinated ... (with the) main operations, it should, in favourable circumstances ... present decisive opportunities to the main forces'. Holland was joined by (Sir) Collin Gubbins and the GS(R) section - renamed MIR (Military Intelligence Research) - became a powerhouse of ideas, including escape organisations, deception techniques, and commando-like formations. These guerrillas - Collin Gubbins had pointed out in 1939 - would be in actions usually fought 'at point-blank range as the result of an ambush or raid'. By the spring of 1940 the War Office had been persuaded to put some of these ideas into practice and a number of companies were raised to act independently in guerrilla roles.

In April 1940 Colonel Holland put Collin Gubbins in charge of the Independent Companies and he went with them to Norway, where through no fault of Collin Gubbins much - if not all - of his and the ISTDC's teachings were ignored. The Independent Companies were intended to be a ship-based force slipping ashore to harass German communications and cut the supply line of Swedish ore, but they often fought as infantry because the Allies had no other troops available; an unavoidable reason for deploying special forces in this role in Norway. Their successor units were misused with less reason. An added paradox to the Narvik actions was the Germans' own demolitions that destroyed much of the port's facilities, reducing iron-ore shipments to little more than a quarter of the pre-war level.

Ten Independent Companies, each with 20 officers and 270 men (see Appendix 2) had been formed from Territorial Army volunteers with a leavening of regular and reservist soldiers.

While the Independent Companies were returning from Norway, an extension of the idea for independent forces was being shaped in Whitehall. The first amphibious raid - three officers landing between Boulogne and Etaples - had been mounted on 2-3 June by MI R with informal contacts in the Royal Navy, who provided a trawler. These first raiders successfully fired 200,000 tons of fuel near Harfleur and then rowed 13 miles back to safety on 10 June bringing a lone straggler. However, the Prime Minister was pressing for even more positive action. On 4 June, the day the Dunkirk evacuation ended, he wrote to the Chiefs of Staff: 'if it is so easy for the Germans to invade us . . . why should it be . . . impossible for us to do anything of the same kind to him?' That evening Lieutenant-Colonel Dudley Clarke set down his thoughts in brief notes on raiding parties carried by ship to the French coast and drawn from a special force. Aware of the way 25,000 Boer farmers had been defeated only by ten times their number in the war of 1899-1902, during his boyhood in South Africa, Dudley Clarke was able to interest his chief, Sir John Dill, Chief of the Imperial General Staff, in the idea and it was put to the Prime Minister. A few days later, on 8 June, the scheme was approved on two conditions: no unit was to be diverted from the essential defence of the British Isles; and the new force must make do with a minimum of arms. Dudley Clarke was also instructed to mount a raid across the Channel 'at the earliest possible moment'. The War Office Section MO 9 came into being that afternoon and began steps to raise the special force of commandos named after those Boer farmers of the South African war. Before the 1939-45 War was over, many soldiers and marines wore the commando shoulder flashes or rangers' badges but the green beret was not introduced until late in 1942.

The activities of MIR and others associated with clandestine operations were to take a separate, but not unrelated, course mainly from the activities of the Special Operations Executive (SOE). Their paths were to cross quite frequently with commando raids, but Commando formations were uniformed military forces - as mentioned earlier - if not always treated as such by their enemies.

Before the commandos could begin their raiding, links had to be forged with the Navy. Captain G.A. Garnons-Williams RN, an enthusiastic supporter of the raiding idea, found some 'crash' air-sea rescue boats for Dudley Clarke's first raid, which was mounted on the night France surrendered, 23 June, with four landings along a 20-mile stretch of French coast around Boulogne. The 115 raiders were drawn from the Independent Companies as No.11 Independent Company carrying half the British stock of Thompson sub-machine guns: 20 tommy-guns. Dudley Clarke went on the raid as an observer; no doubt it appealed to his swash-buckling sense of adventure.

Faces blackened with grease paint, a cosmetic replaced in later years by burnt cork or mud daubs, the men crouched on the boat's decks, going inshore at three points. At the fourth landing the boat almost ran into Boulogne harbour, despite earlier reconnaissance of the target beaches by her skipper, Lieutenant-Commander J.W.F. Milner-Gibson RN. An enemy searchlight lit

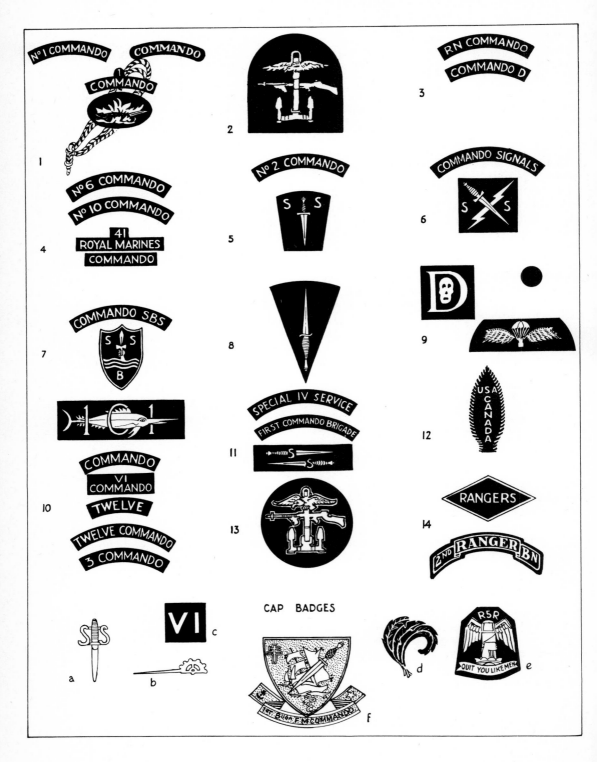

CAP BADGES

Commando and Ranger shoulder flashes:
1. From 1940-2 varying styles of flash were worn and use of identifying numbers was 'not likely to be approved for security reasons'. After May 1943, however, numbers were incorporated in the printed flashes (see below) replacing the then forbidden red on blue variety of flashes including red embroidery on worsted. Early in the war some commando officers wore a white and black lanyard and 1 Commando had a salamander badge - green salamander with red tongue, in red and yellow flames, on khaki background.
2. Red details on black background (sometimes a roundel) of the Combined Operations badge was issued in matching pairs with guns facing forward on upper arms; in addition to commandos the landing craft crews and other Combined Operations personnel wore these badges.
3. Royal Navy Commando in white lettering on dark blue ground and Commando Depot flash of red on dark blue.
4. Examples of printed red on dark blue background of army-style flashes worn by 1 to 14 Commando and of Royal Marine commando flashes. These RM red on blue flashes were Cash's tapes and added to existing flashes worn by RMs. 43 (RM) Commando also wore a red and yellow lanyard.
5. 2 Commando flash and dagger badge (silver on black) with dagger downwards - a point of some discussion but eventually the dagger of the general badge pointed upwards as in 8 below.
6. Commando signals badge of white on dark blue with white lightning streak.
7. Special Boat Section red on blue and badge of 101 Troop with white swordfish passing through red figures on blue ground. Some 'swordfish' badges were of metal.
8. Red dagger on navy blue ground worn by Commandos from late in 1944.
9. Black spot of No. 5 Troop (Commando not identified), black square with white D and skull worn by Depot staff, and wings of para-trained commandos (worn by Frenchmen of 10 Commando - among others - on right shoulder between commando and combined operations flashes but SBS paras wore these wings on the left breast of tropical shirts).
10. Examples of unauthorised Commando flashes usually red lettering on dark blue ground.
11. SS and Commando Brigade flashes and the double daggers of Brigade Headquarters' personnel (c.1943 probably). The HQ flash had red 'SS' with silver daggers marked in black on a black ground.
12. 1st Special Service Force (the North Americans) badge of a Red Indian arrowhead, their red flag carried a black dagger on a white shield.
13. The American Combined Operations badge in yellow on a blue ground worn by US *army* amphibious forces.
14. Ranger diamond with gold lettering and edges on blue ground, worn on left shoulder by 2nd and 5th Rangers in training 1943. The diamond was replaced by the authorised scroll badge of white lettering with red outline on black ground and appropriate number for 1st to 6th Ranger Battalion. Any badges were unauthorised that identified so-called 'rangers' within infantry divisions.

Cap badges - commandos wore the badge of their regiments on a green beret but several badges were used from time to time or by units associated with commandos. *a.* the dagger-SS badge of 2 Commando and probably the badge rejected by the War Office for general use; *b* the knuckle-duster knife badge of 50-52 Commandos in the Middle East; *c* black square with red (?) VI of 6 Commando; *d* a black hackle worn for a time by 9 Commando; *e* the badge of the Raiding Support Regiment 1943-5; and *f* the badge of the 1er Bataillon Fusilier Marin Commando with 10 (Inter Allied) Commando. Frenchmen and other nationalities with 10 Cdo also wore a national flash above their commando flashes. Royal Marine commandos wore appropriate officers' or other ranks' cap badge, except for 41(RM) Commando who wore an officer's full-dress collar badge as their cap badge.

---

the danger and the boat sheered off to beach further up the coast on sand dunes, 'a dark outline showing against the sky'. Led by Major Ronnie Tod, 30 men went ashore and had hardly been gone a few minutes when Dudley Clarke and the commander saw the dark outline of a boat coming in from the sea. This spectre anchored some 100 yards away, a small mysterious vessel that prompted Dudley Clarke - as such uncertainties would concern future raiders - to move quietly to the bow and warn the men ashore. A Very light flickered into the sky away to the south: other raiders were in action. As a figure appeared on the beach - it was Ronnie Tod - a German cycle patrol rode up. However, Ronnie Tod's one-man ambush failed when he dropped his tommy-gun magazine as he cocked the gun, and there was a burst of fire from the Germans. The long silence that followed would become a familiar feature of night raids filled with uncertainty and pregnant with disaster. But this night, after being ashore an hour or so, the raiders waded back out to the boat arm-pit deep in the rising tide. By dawn they were eight miles off shore under fighter aircraft's escort. Dudley Clarke had been the only casualty, hit in the ear, which had been sewn back in place by a petty officer as the boat left the beach.

The other landings that night had varied success: two Germans killed south of Le Touquet; a seaplane stalked in its anchorage near Boulogne, but it took off - no doubt unaware of the intruders - before they reached it; and the other party saw nobody after landing on a waste of dunes. Arriving back at Dover the raiders were cheered, and later the whole country was heartened by their exploits. But having tippled some extra rum ration, the men on the boat entering Folkestone were threatened with arrest as deserters before their identity was established.

Three lessons came from this raid: the need for means to identify friend from foe, always difficult in night actions but particularly so for a small party on a hostile shore; the problems of coordinating secret operations with regular forces - friendly Spitfires had delayed the boats for an hour in mid-Channel on their outward voyage before establishing their true identity; the difficulty of pin-point navigation, the third point, was the most crucial of all. Milner-Gibson had made nine solo landings in recces of the beaches during the three weeks before the raid, but on *the* night his boat's compass proved faulty and others lost their way. Nevertheless the raid, like the one made earlier in June, had proved landings were possible. No men had been lost, and a sentry's body might have been brought back to identify his unit had not overcrowded conditions aboard forced the raiders to tow the body, which sank.

MO 9 had plans to raise 10 Commandos, each with 10 50-man Troops, and called for volunteers for unspecified hazardous duties who must also be prepared to work and train for longer hours than regular formations. These Commandos intended to mount successive small raids in lightening strikes, keeping the Germans off balance and fearful of more serious threats. Before this force of 5,000 commandos could be raised, however, Churchill's enthusiasm for special forces was tempered by reality. He had seen all the commando-like forces, including Storm-Troops and Leopard Units for guerrilla actions in the event of a German invasion, drawn from existing formations. But these regiments, which included reservists and conscripts with some company commanders over 40, were unlikely to provide the aggression needed in a commando action.

On 22 June, when the Prime Minister was asking for a corps of at least 5,000 parachutists, the commando idea was moving in a number of directions. Men of 2 Commando were originally to be parachute troops, but the RAF had even greater difficulty in finding planes than the Royal Navy had in finding craft. The proposal was therefore dropped, but the 500 men who had started their parachute training became the nucleus of 1 Airborne Division formed in November 1941. However, some years would pass before selected commandos were trained as parachutists.

These changes of direction were confused by Admiral Sir Roger Keyes, who had much of the Churchillian spirit but no gift for cooperation with ministries. He had been a World War I hero in the Gallipoli and Zeebrugge landings, and in 1940, aged 68, was the Member of Parliament for Portsmouth. On his appointment as head of combined operations, he embarked on endless controversy over hypothetical command of raids by 5,000 men, although there were no more than 500 trained commandos and some 750 men in the Independent Companies. Only one more raid was mounted in 1940 and that in July, when Lieutenant-General Alan Bourne of the Royal Marines was temporarily running Combined Operations Headquarters (the name used throughout this book for the directorate, although in fact having some variations of title) before Keyes's appointment.

This raid, on Guernsey in the Channel Islands, by some 100 men from 3 Commando and No. 11 Independent Company (sometimes referred to as No. 11 Commando) was well rehearsed, and after last-minute changes of plan, literally within half an hour of setting out, the raiders boarded two destroyers to transfer to motorboats refuelled from the parent ships they accompanied.

These crash boats made a great noise, and part of the plan was to fly Anson aircraft overhead as the run was made to the beach, this being timed to a nicety. Nevertheless, the raid was later described by its leader, Colonel John Durford-Slater, as a 'very amateurish affair'. Nothing was achieved and several men had to be left ashore as they were unable to swim to the boats, whose RNVR crews would not beach for fear of damage to the crafts' hulls.

Through the rest of that summer and autumn the Prime Minister's demands for major raids by 5,000 to 10,000 men could not be met because there were no craft to land them. Proposals for two 'invasion corps' came to nothing; each needed 380 LCAs and 180 Landing Craft, Tank (LCTs), the first LCT having her trials in landing five or six tanks only that November. Convoy protection and aircraft had to take priority over raiding forces' equipment, but, as the name 'invasion corps' suggests the British were considering ways of getting a more permanent foothold in Europe. However, this conflict between preparation for an invasion and the immediate raiding of the enemy coasts was never clearly resolved; and a force of Royal Marines and Commandos was held on the Clyde forever preparing for landings against the possible need to capture an Atlantic island base should Gibraltar fall.

However, this 'Puma' force - code-named as the largest cat - was never launched against the Canaries or the Azores. The Royal Marine elements - a division without a 'tail' although the establishment list shows some support units - sailed to Dakar in September 1940 but did not land. This and other abortive moves brought frustration and some despondency to the commandos who had been gathered by Keyes into large groups to train with their landing force from the Royal Navy.

During the winter of 1940-41, the days of what had become Keyes's private army were over when the War Office reasserted their authority and the command of the Special Service Brigade passed to Brigadier (later Major-General) J.C. Haydon. A small man whose charm belied his determination, he had proved his abilities in action in France, and - what was probably more important at this stage of the commandos' ill-fortunes - he knew his way around the Whitehall ministries.

The Commando idea was established but would continue to have its critics, including the colonels of regiments resenting the poaching - as they saw it - of some of their best men. The reasons for the Special Forces not proving more effective in this desperate year of 1940, lay as much in the political problems and strategy as in shortages of equipment. But many of their future commanders - John Durnford-Slater, Peter Young, Mike Calvert among them - were preparing their men for a new type of soldiering. The Royal Marines had not landed at Dakar because, without adequate craft for an overwhelming initial assault, any piecemeal landing could have led to prolonged fighting with potential allies. A proposed landing in Pantelleria was aborted when German dive-bombers arrived in Sicily. The Canaries were no longer considered essential once Spanish political pressures eased on Gibraltar. Whether or not the commandos might have landed in strength on the French coast, there seems little likelihood that they would have achieved any worthwhile military objective, and every possibility the force would have been destroyed. To land a large, lightly armed force was dodging the realities of amphibious warfare when the difficulty of landing supporting weapons must be faced squarely.

On the other hand, the idea of small, general reconnaissance and sabotage raids was to prove practical and effective to a limited extent, as the next chapter illustrates. Once the British had been driven from the European mainland, they had lost virtually all of the general intelligence that armies gather on their enemy's positions, his deployment, and his defences. Regaining this knowledge involved a long and hazardous series of amphibious raids in which the clandestine activities of SOE and the Secret Intelligence Service (SIS), as well as the commandos, became involved.

# EUROPE, JANUARY 1941 TO DECEMBER 1943

During these years a number of small and some large Allied raids were made against Norway, and the French Channel and Biscay coasts. In March 1941, the first of the major raids landed unopposed in the Lofoten Islands (north Norway). The following month a German army advanced into the Balkans and in three weeks occupied Yugoslavia and Greece, drawing British forces from North Africa into battles in Greece and Crete, which was captured by 1 June 1941 (see page 113). On 22 June, 136 German divisions with 3,000 tanks invaded the USSR, the Germans believing that the quality of their war machine would defeat the Russian masses. Moscow, 700 miles (1,000km) from the border, was almost reached but the first snows slowed the Germans who, at the end of November, froze 20 miles (30+km) west of Moscow, and by December the Russian front ran 2,000 miles (3,200km) from Leningrad to the Caucasus.

On 7 December 1941, the Japanese bombed Pearl Harbour and America entered the now global war. The war in North Africa saw further Allied setbacks. In Europe, the British mounted their first opposed raid against Vaagsö Island (central Norway) that December. In the spring of 1942 they carried out the most effective sabotage raid of modern times, destroying the St Nazaire (French coast) battleship dock and preventing the *Tirpitz* - the most powerful battleship then afloat - from moving to this possible base for raids on American troop and weapon convoys. That summer there was the Canadian raid on the French Channel port of Dieppe, with its consequent tragedies and subsequent lessons (see Chapter 5).

The British Isles became, in 1941-43, a giant aircraft-carrier punished by German raids but giving more than was received as the air war was intensified by 1943. Amphibious raiding along the Channel coast and elsewhere became a coordinated intelligence gathering operation in preparation for the opening of a Second Front by the invasion of Europe, plans for which entailed amphibious training for large armies, pre-empting men and equipment from possible large raids.

Sword in hand Colonel Jack Churchill leads his commandos ashore from an LCP(L) in an arduous training exercise.

# 2  GENERAL RECONNAISSANCE AND SABOTAGE

Stan Weatherall and 'Darkie' A. Harrison paddled their two-man canoe from Salen down the broad, rocky loch Sunart into the open sea on a clear day in February 1941. Their civilian Folbot canoe had no added buoyancy of Mae-West lifebelts, no navigation aids, not even a spray cover as they crossed the sound from the Scottish mainland to land on the isle of Mull. Anyone using the double-paddle of these canoes for the first time finds his (or her) chest expanded in a strain on shoulder muscles he never knew were there until he started canoeing. With legs stretched out and with no space to flex a muscle - or so it seems to the beginner - a sneeze might unbalance the boat. With practice, however, the canoe becomes an extension of the canoeist although his muscles never quite adjust to hours in its cramped confines. Nor, as these raiders paddled towards an enemy shore, was there more than a canvas skin on its wooden frame between them and a hostile reception.

The men of No. 1 Troop, all volunteers, included Territorials (men who had been civilians doing part-time army training), some regulars, and reservists like Lance-Corporal Weatherall who were recalled to the colours. Having served with the Duke of Wellington's Regiment in two campaigns on the north-west frontier of India, the Corporal was recalled briefly in 1938, went to France in 1939, and spent five days coming out over the Dunkirk beaches. In the summer of 1940 he was volunteered for parachute training by friends who added his name to a list for this course. But to stay with two friends, he and half a dozen of his regiment were recruited for sea raiding with 6 Commando ('No.6') on its formation in July 1940. For some months this Commando, with their small arms, a few petrol bombs, and an old 4.7 inch gun, stood between the Germans and their possible foothold on the Kent coast near New Romney. The invasion scare passed and the Troop went north to do independent training, as all Troops did at that time.

Toughening their endurance by frequent climbs to nearly 3,000 feet (900m) up the crags of Goat Fell on Arran they saw, when it was not raining - a rare occasion in west Scotland - Lieutenant Roger Courtney at sea, training his canoeists around the island's choppy waters where a short sharp sea comes up with little warning. The broad Firth of Clyde runs north from the island, with Goat Fell on the east shore appearing to fall in a sheer drop into the sea, making ideal conditions for commando training.

Courtney's canoeists with ten Folbots (see diagram p. 25) were the first of what became the Special Boat Section, formed after their leader had given a practical demonstration of the canoe's military potential, a potential doubted by even the adventurous characters in Combined Operations headquarters until Courtney paddled out one summer night in 1940 to a carrier ship moored in the Clyde. Stealing a gun cover undetected, he brought it ashore and presented it dripping wet to the ship's captain in a conference. The gift

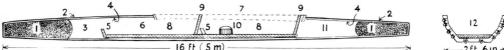

16 ft (5 m)   —   2 ft 6 in

Not to scale

1   Buoyancy air bags or table tennis balls in netting/bags
2   Rubberised canvas cover
3   Stowage forward
4   Frame in assembled sections
5   Footrests adjustable for leg length
6   Thompson sub m/c gun between knees of 'swimmer' (the front paddler) on floor boards
7   Coaming about 3in deep hard wood
8   Cockpit
9   Back rests
10  P8 compass—as in Spitfire aircraft
11  Stowage for limpets etc. (some might also go forward to 3)
12  Approximate cross-section showing ribs taped to frame (ferrule-ends of rib joints also taped into sockets)

Note: other canoes had Mae West life-jackets for smaller buoyancy at bow and stern and an inflated collar around cockpit, allowing more space forward for rucksack and a 'deck' load could be carried behind the aft (no. 1) paddler. A map case with attached parallel rule usually mounted behind forward backrest, and mugs for bailers on hooks under coaming. SBS crews carried a hand compass to port of No. 1 paddler, two grenades on floor beside each man, used square bungey rubber to hold T-gun etc. The cockpit cover—secured by bulldog clips in early Mks—fitted around paddlers.

was accepted and plans made - although never fulfilled - to have some 30 canoeists with each Commando, and in July 1940 the first Special Boat Section was formed. They, among others, would gather intelligence on enemy strengths and fortifications. Although descriptions of these defences on Atlantic and North Sea coastlines could in part be gleaned from aerial photographs, much lay hidden; as the Canadians were to find at Dieppe.

Through the winter of 1940-41, Lieutenant Courtney trained his Special Boat Section attached to 8 Commando, and with a second-in-command and 15 men he went to the Middle East in February 1941. For Courtney this was a return to Africa, for he had been a big-game hunter and had once canoed down the Nile from Lake Victoria. A big man in every sense of the word, with a bellow of a laugh, he displayed irrepressible confidence. (His Section's Mediterranean operations, where his cheerful courage discomforted the Germans and Italians, are dealt with in later chapters.)

Through most of 1940 and 1941, a complex command system made raids from the United Kingdom difficult to organise, for each Army Command was responsible for raiding shores opposite their area in the United Kingdom, and the Navy had a final say on any seaborne raid. Only Norway, the reserve of the C-in-C Home Fleet, escaped

Two-man Folbot canoe of 101 Troop from 6 Commando.

this web of conflicting red tape. Thus, while Corporal Weatherall and a growing force of commandos were on interminable training exercises, or standing by for operations that were cancelled before they got afloat, very few slipped the mesh of authority. The only significant raid, apart from some SOE operations, was a sortie in the early spring of 1941 by some 500 men of 3 and 4 Commandos with 52 Royal Engineers and a like number of Free Norwegian forces.

They sailed in comparatively mild weather for the Lofoten Islands (see map p. 28) aboard two carrier ships with assault landing craft (LCAs) on their davits, and escorted by five destroyers although without air cover once in North Norwegian waters. The ships were ex-Channel ferries, now Landing Ships, Infantry (LSIs) HMS *Princess Beatrix* and HMS *Queen Emma*. The force met the submarine HMS *Sunfish* stationed as a navigation check for the assault force, and at 0400 hours on 4 March the ships were piloted into Stamsund, as at other landing points, by local seamen of the Free Norwegian Navy.

At least one landing craft commander was for 'giving her the gun' to speed the tense minutes as they approached the enemy shore, but Lieutenant-Colonel John Durnford-Slater (Commanding Officer of 3 Commando) made him maintain a steady speed. The sequence of landing was planned to put the raiders ashore in a fighting formation, and although all went to plan at Stamsund, indiscipline among boats' crews would on other occasions cause difficulties for commandos landed late or ahead of their supporting Troops. Even the fishing fleet came down the harbour as expected from intelligence reports, and might have choked the narrow 100 yards wide entrance if a burst of tracer from a destroyer had not turned them aside as they grasped the situation. They hauled up their Norwegian colours, forbidden by the Germans whose only presence was an armed trawler, pulling away from a jetty and prepared to fight. She was quickly set on fire by the destroyer HMS *Somali* and the LCAs came alongside the quay. The town seemed deserted until a postman appeared and willingly explained that the only Germans there were Gestapo

and a few businessmen. The small party of Norwegians with each commando Troop acted as interpreters for this and other intelligence, leading to the Gestapo chief - a fat man in a dark suit - squealing his protest at capture within a quarter of an hour of the landing. Men set off in a local bus commandeered to take them to the factories on the edge of the town. The telephone exchange was occupied, Lieutenant Richard Wills using its land-line to the mainland to send a telegram to A. Hitler, Berlin: 'You said in your last speech German troops would meet the English wherever they landed stop where are your troops? - Signature Wills 2-Lieut.' Such direct communication, if not with Hitler, might have summoned German naval reinforcements, but no aircraft was available north of Trondheim, more than 400 miles and two flying hours to the south, because all the northern airfields early that spring were operational only for transport aircraft fitted with skis.

The commandos landed at three harbours besides Stamsund - Henningsvaer, Svolvar, and Brettesnes - each on a different island in this compact group. None of the landings was opposed except by the gallant action of the armed trawler *Krebbs*, and by midday the oil factories were burning. Demolition charges had also been carefully set on machinery in the fish meal and other factories; these small charges of gun cotton being placed so that they destroyed equipment without the risk of causing needless casualties. Electric installations were smashed with sledgehammers and then switched on, melting connexions in complete destruction. Some 800,000 gallons (3.5 million litres) of oil and petrol burned fiercely and 11 small ships, totalling more than 20,000 tons, were sunk.

They gathered in 315 volunteers for the Norwegian forces, 60 followers of the Norwegian traitor Quisling with Nazi sympathies, and 225 German prisoners. The only commando casualty before the Force set sail for an uneventful passage home, was an officer accidentally shot in the foot. They were not to learn of the German reaction for some nine months, when the commandos again visited the Lofoten Islands, but the world heard for the first time of British commandos that night in German broadcasts: 'Light naval forces destroyed several fishing boats and landed commandos in the Norwegian skerries where they took prisoner some Germans and Norwegians.' The word was out, for until then the British had kept secret their special raiding forces.

Lofoten was chosen for this first large raid because it offered a chance to hit back at the enemy as well as such economic targets as the destruction of fish oil supplies, which might impair German manufacture of nitro-glycerine and would reduce supplies of vitamin A and B capsules issued to German troops. And as an undefended or so-called 'soft' target it offered a chance of a much-needed success. Lofoten apart, though, Keyes's private armies were to chafe at the bit of ministry reins throughout the summer of 1941, while remaining dependent on these masters for the very shoe-string of their existence as Commandos.

There were nevertheless plenty of suggestions for targets: St Nazaire was considered but dismissed because shoal waters were thought to make a sea approach impractical; Dieppe appeared too heavily defended; and many suggested moves to occupy distant islands were ruled out by the impossibility of maintaining garrisons. In the last category was a proposal from Sir Stafford Cripps, British Ambassador in Moscow, for the occupation of the coal-mining and strategic island of Spitsbergen (see map p. 28), but Allied sea power would not stretch to convoying supplies for a garrison so far from home waters. Instead a raid was mounted. Canadian troops trained with the British amphibious forces at Inverary (Argyll) and were then taken in SS *Empress of Canada* to land on the island, 600 miles from the North Pole on 24 August 1941. The eventual landing force was smaller than planned because naval air reconnaissance showed the Germans had not garrisoned the island. The Canadians' ship then took 2,000 local Russian miners and their families to Archangel, returning nine days later on 2 September to take off the men of the Edmonton Regiment and Saskatoon Light Infantry who, with

sappers and some Norwegians, had destroyed the mines. The raiders' principal memory, however, is the smell of Eau de Cologne drunk by the miners who were allowed no spirits on the island. By the time the Canadians were safely back in a British port, the ship had sailed 7,000 miles (13,000km) on the round trip.

Another commando raid that summer was mounted by 12 Commando; 16 men led by 2nd Lieutenant Pinkney landing near Ambleteuse where they made a general reconnaissance returning safely to England, although a stoker on the naval craft was killed by enemy action, probably during the withdrawal.

In October 1941 Sir Roger Keyes was replaced by the 41-year old naval Commodore Lord Louis Mountbatten, cousin of King George VI. Lord Mountbatten's orders from the Prime Minister made the invasion of Europe the main objective with 'a programme of raids in ever-increasing intensity'. After a service lifetime in the Royal Navy, the Commodore quickly established the essential liaison with the Chiefs-of-Staff, ministries, and others whom the Commandos depended on for weapons as well as shoestrings. Within weeks Combined Operations headquarters were to take on a new vitality.

One final raid was made from plans conceived under the old management, 100 men from 9 Commando attempting to capture a gun battery near Houlgate. Two Rob Roy canoes had been in ahead of the main raiding force on the night of 22/3 November, one pair of these canoeists were caught - described later - and the second missed their rendezvous, paddling back to England. The main force came ashore the next night and followed a strict timetable. This prevented them fully exploiting their initial landings as they had to start their withdrawal before an assault could be mounted on the naval guns installed behind Houlgate. On their return to the beach, an hour's flashing of torches was needed to catch the attention of the landing craft crews who had withdrawn too far from the beach according to one report. This pantomime aroused the defenders and

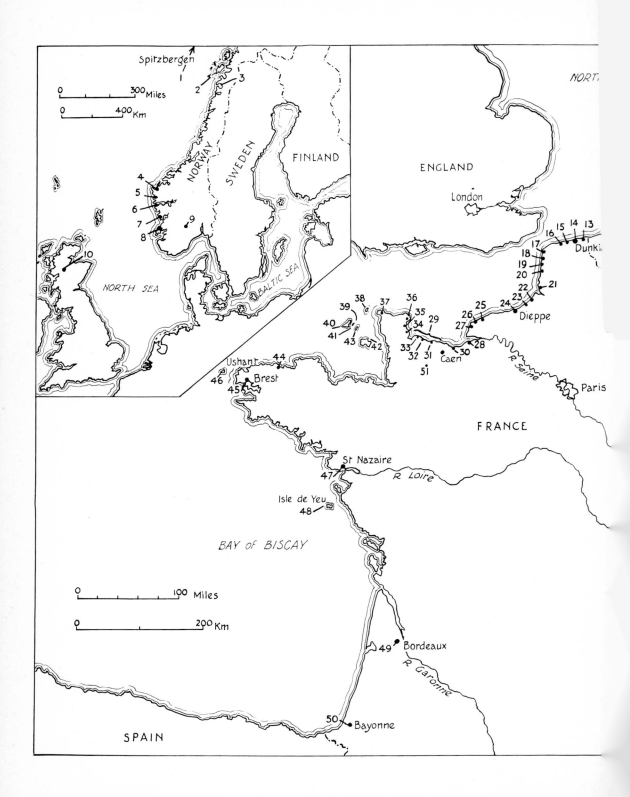

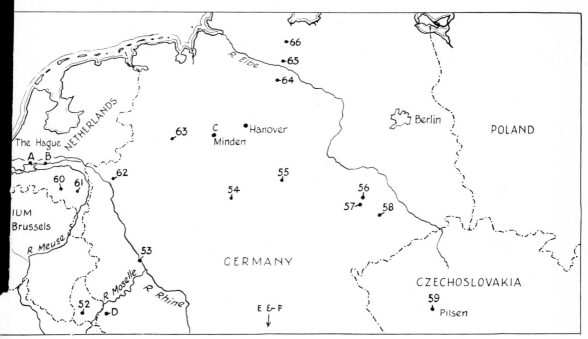

Locations of Special Forces' European operations showing large forces' actions in capitals (date and *code name*) in alphabetical order by year. Coastal raids are shown (with the Depot) by numbered locations from north to south:

**1940**

| | |
|---|---|
| Boulogne & Berch (23/4 June, *Collar*) | 18 |
| Guernsey (14/5 July, *Ambassador*) | 40 |

**1941**

| | |
|---|---|
| Ambleteuse (27/8 July, *Chess*) | 17 |
| Courselles (27/8 Sept, *Chopper*) | 30 |
| Houlgate (E of, 22/3 Nov, *Sunstar*) | 28 |
| Les Hemmes (12/3 Nov, *Astrakhan*) | 16 |
| LOFOTEN Isl (4 Mar, *Claymore*) | 2 |
| LOFOTEN Isl (26 Dec, *Anklet*) | 2 |
| Merlimont Plage (30/1 Aug. *Cartoon-Aciddrop*) | 20 |
| St Vaast (27/8 Sept) | 35 |
| SPITZBERGEN (17 Aug-8 Sept, *Gauntlet*) | 1 |
| VAAGSO (27 Dec, *Archery*) | 5 |

**1942**

| | |
|---|---|
| Achnacarry Depot | 10 |
| BAYONNE (5 Apr, *Myrmidon*) | 50 |
| Bordeau (7 Dec, *Franklin*) | 49 |
| Boulogne (11/2 Apr, *JV*) | 18 |
| BRUNEVAL (27/8 Feb, *Biting*) | 26 |
| DIEPPE (18 Aug, *Jubilee*) | 24 |
| Glomfjord (20/1 Sept, *Musketoon*) | 3 |
| HARDELOT (21/2 Apr, *Abercrombie*) | 19 |
| Isle Burhou (probably Isle Brechou, 7/8 Sept, *Branford*) | 41 |
| Isle Casquets (2/3 Sept, *Dryad*) | 38 |
| Omonville (SE of, 15/6 Nov, *Batman*) | 37 |

| | |
|---|---|
| Pointe de Plouezec (11/2 Nov, *Farenheit*) | 44 |
| Pointe de Saire (14/5 Aug, *Barricade*) | 36 |
| St Cecily—probably an Anglicised Ste Cécile—(3/4 June, *Bristle*) not numbered | |
| Ste Honorine (12/3 Sept, *Aquatint*) | 31 |
| St Laurent (11 Jan, *Curlew*) | 33 |
| St NAZAIRE (27/8 Mar, *Chariot*) | 47 |
| Sark (3/4 Oct, *Basalt*) | 43 |
| Vermork (19 Nov, *Freshman*)—approx location | 9 |

**1943**

| | |
|---|---|
| Biville (5/6 July, *Forfar Dog*) | 23 |
| Biville (24/7 Nov, *Hardtack Dog*) | 23 |
| Biville (26/7 Dec, *Hardtack 4*) | 23 |
| Dunkirk pier (3/4 Aug, *Forfar Love*) | 14 |
| Eletot (3/5 Aug, 1/2 Sept & 3/4 Sept, *Forfar Beer*) | 27 |
| Gravelines (24/5 Dec, *Hardtack 2*, repeated 25/6 Dec) | 15 |
| Haugesund (27 Apr, *Checkmate*) | 8 |
| Herm (27/8 Feb, *Huckaback*) | 39 |
| Jersey (25/6 Dec, *Hardtack 28*) | 42 |
| Landet (22/3 Mar, *Roundabout*) | 4 |
| Normandy beaches (31 Dec by COPP) | 29 |
| Onival (3/4 July, *Forfar Easy*) | 22 |
| Onival (26/7 Dec, *Hardtack 5*) | 22 |
| Quineville (26/7 Dec, *Hardtack 21*) | 34 |
| St Valery en Caux (2/3 Sept, *Forfar Item*) | 25 |
| Sark (25/6 Dec, *Hardtack 7*, repeated 27/8 Dec) | 43 |
| Sognefjord (22 Feb-3 Mar, *Crackers*) | 6 |
| Stord Isl (23/4 Jan, *Cartoon*) | 7 |
| Ushant (3/4 Sept *Pound*) | 46 |

**1944**

| | |
|---|---|
| Bray-Dunes Plage (16/7 May, *Tarbrush 3*) | 13 |
| Isle de Yeu (25/6 Aug, *Rumford*) | 48 |
| Less Hemmes (15/6 May, *Tarbrush 5*) | 16 |
| Les Moulens (18/9 Jan, *Postageable*) | 32 |
| NORMANDY (6 June, *Overlord*) | 29 |
| Norway—see also diagram on Norway | |
| Onival (17/8 May, *Tarbrush 10*) | 22 |
| Quend Plage (15/6 May, *Tarbrush 8*) | 21 |
| Schevneningen (24/5 Feb, *Premium*) | 11 |
| Walcheren (15 to 26 Oct, *Tarbrush* recces failed) | 12 |
| WALCHEREN (1 Nov, *Infatuate*) | 12 |

**1944/5**

| | |
|---|---|
| Route of 2nd Rangers numbered from Vire (51) to Brest (45) and then eastward to Pilsen (59): | |
| NORMANDY (6 June 1944) | 29 |
| Vire | 51 |
| BREST (20 Aug to 17 Sept 1944) | 45 |
| Paris—not numbered | |
| Luxemburg | 52 |
| Sinzig | 53 |
| KASSEL | 54 |
| Gottingen | 55 |
| Leipzig | 56 |
| Merseburg | 57 |
| MULDE RIVER | 58 |
| Pilsen | 59 |

**1945**

| | |
|---|---|
| Route of 1 Commando Brigade numbered from west to east (60-66): | |
| Asten (16 Jan) | 60 |
| Venraij (20 Feb) | 61 |
| WESEL (25 Mar) | 62 |
| OSNABRUCK (5 Apr) | 63 |
| LAUENBURG (29 Apr) | 64 |
| LUNEBURG | 65 |
| Neustadt (3 May) | 66 |

**1945**

| | |
|---|---|
| Other locations lettered from west to east: | |
| BIESBOSCH (4 Cdo Bde) | A |
| Maas River (4 Cdo Bde) | B |
| Minden (4 Cdo Bde) | C |
| RIED (5th Rangers) | F |
| WEHINGEN (5th Rangers) | E |
| Zerf (5th Rangers) | D |

showed clearly the need for better ship-to-shore communications.

The organisation for all but very small raids was now formulated, with Lord Mountbatten as Chief of Combined Operations (CCO) having adequate staff to prepare outline plans for raids. Any Commander-in-Chief in a theatre where raiding forces would be involved was asked to comment on the outline plan, which was then put to the Chiefs of Staff. On their approval of the scheme, a force commander was appointed with responsibility for detailed planning and coordinating the army, navy, and air force units involved. He also issued the detailed orders, arranged training, and led the raid. Any extra equipment or special materials he required could be obtained through the agency of the headquarters' staff. CCO was responsible for obtaining final approval of the force commander's plan from the Chiefs of Staff Committee of which he was a member, and the plans were always subject to the naval Commander-in-Chief's blessing for no major dispositions of ships were made without his say-so.

The organisation was more complex than may appear from this summary. Liaison with the RAF Chiefs in various theatres, for instance, was made through their representatives on CCO's staff. But the success of the organisation lay in the men who ran it as much as in the formal orders (set down in a minute of July 1942). The Prime Minister gave Lord Mountbatten a free hand and he selected six brilliant senior officers who, like the Commodore - soon promoted Vice-Admiral - had a flair for cutting red tape and reconciling different services' points of view. Also on the new team were two scientists, Professors J.D. Bernal and Solly Zuc-

HM King George VI watches commandos assemble a Goatley boat, Admiral Sir Roger Keyes stands on the right of the picture.

kerman, chosen for their original minds by the Chief Government Scientist. They worked on the plans for future operations. Later Geoffrey Pyke, whose snow vehicle is described in Chapter 9, joined COHQ on the recommendation of a Government minister. Targets would now be more specific, equipment more deadly, and the whole Combined Operations' set-up run like a taut ship in the fashion of the destroyer HMS *Kelly*, which the CCO had sunk beneath him off Crete earlier that year.

For men like Stan Weatherall, whom we left experiencing his first long journey by canoe, this reorganisation swept away the frustrations of the summer of 1941. He was recruited into the second Special Boat Section operating across the Channel from Dover, after the second-in-command of No.1 Troop had called for volunteers - duties unspecified - as the Troop walked by his chair in the middle of a field. This way there was no pressure to volunteer.

The SBS had been established in Dover to help naval forces attack shipping as well as to make beach reconnaissances. In November 1941 they became 101 Troop of 6 Commando, with Lieutenant Smith in command, and were attached to the naval shore base HMS *Lynx*, from which they operated, with MTBs, submarines, or other carriers taking them to the area of their target beaches. They were joined by their former Troop commander, Captain G.C.S. Montanaro (Royal Engineers). Lieutenant Smith failed to return from one recce, and it was later learnt that he and his companion, Lance-Corporal C. Woodhouse, had capsized in heavy surf, losing their paddles. They made their way inland, but Lieutenant Smith, without badges of rank, and Corporal Woodhouse, wearing sergeant's stripes, were taken prisoner. Fortunately this confusion of ranks also foxed the Germans, for 'Lieutenant Smith' was a *nom de guerre*. He survived four years as a prisoner of war and after the war returned to run the family business in the north of England. A second canoe on this mission was paddled back to be safely picked up five miles from the English coast. Although the two canoeists who were ashore

had been barely 200 yards inland they had gathered sufficient information to confirm that LACs could land on the beach at Houlgate.

In December 1941, under the new management, Combined Operations headquarters promoted three major raids. The first, planned for 9 December, was by the full 6 Commando and half of 'No.12'. But on the passage to Norway, an accidental explosion killed six men and wounded 11 others. Although the loss would not have affected the landing, doubts about the Force's navigation caused the senior naval officer to call off the raid. The second raid was a diversion, for now that raiding was becoming more organised, full use could be made of feints and diversions to distract defenders from intended targets, and in a wider strategy the whole policy of raiding would involve a major distraction of the enemy towards an invasion of Norway, not France.

On Boxing Day, 26 December, 300 men of 12 Commando under Lieutenant-Colonel S.S. Harrison went ashore on the Lofoten Islands in a diversion raid. They landed at 0600 hours, unopposed by a German garrison satiated on Christmas fare; the commando planners picking times for a strike force to land when the enemy were likely to be off-guard. In white hooded overalls and trained for snow warfare, the Commando quickly occupied the two harbours on the westerly island of Moskenesöy, where they found the local Norwegians anxious they should stay in case there were German reprisals. How much intimidation took place after the previous raid is hard to gauge, but in 1955 Charley Head, who had been signals officer with 3 Commando in March 1941, revisited the islands and learnt that no one was shot after the March raid, although some houses had been burnt down. Nevertheless there was a fear of greater reprisals, and many hostages were shot in Europe, sometimes in the mistaken belief that commando actions were the work of local resistance fighters.

In December 1941 there were risks of Allied ships being bombed now that the Germans had improved their Norwegian airfields. However, the Arctic night, with no

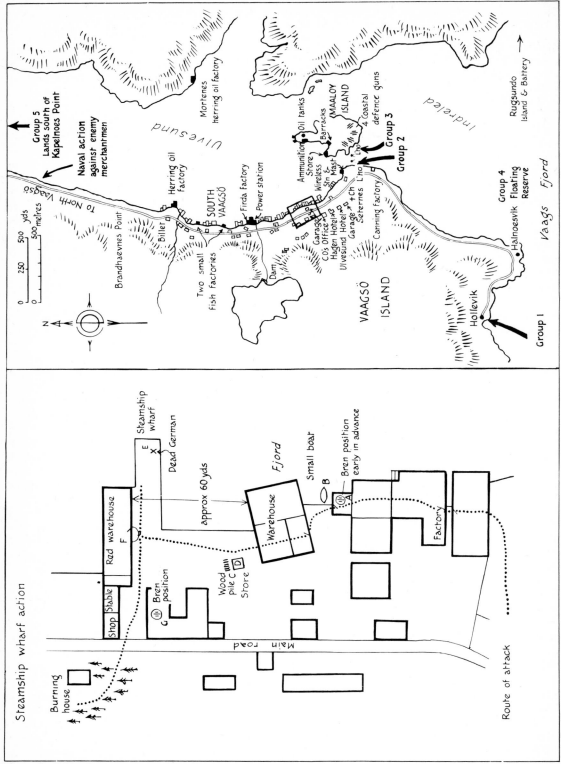

Vaagsö raid by 3 Commando, 27 December 1941.

Vaagsö and Maaloy island in the rugged Norwegian fjord surrounded by steep mountains.

sunrise from 10 December to 3 January in these latitudes, tempted Admiral Hamilton to keep the strike force of eight destroyers and the cruiser HMS *Arethusa* in support of a prolonged visit, until a German bomb fell close to the cruiser, forcing the decision to withdraw after two days' occupation.

While 12 Commando were creating their diversion, Vaagsö Island was the main commando target that Christmas (see map p. 28). This first raid against a defended port was regarded by Lord Mountbatten as a 'test pilot run'. 'For nobody knows quite what is going to happen and you are the ones who are going to find out', he told the raiders.

The way this raid was organised, the commando landing, and street battles make this a classic of fighting raids. There were five assault groups (see diagram). Group 1 was to land at Hollevik on the island's south shore, to clear a known defence point and villages a mile to a mile and a half from the town of South Vaagsö, and then move in support of Group 2, which was to land just south of the town and capture it. Group 3 was to capture Maaloy, an island 500 yards (450m) long and only 200 yards (180m) wide lying not far from the town quays. Group 4 was a floating reserve lying offshore in their landing craft until required to reinforce one of the other Groups. This practice became common in the Pacific, but later British major assaults usually had a timetable for landing reserves. The fifth Group at Vaagsö was to be carried by the destroyer HMS *Oribi* up the Ulvesund, part of the Indreled Channel, for a landing near Kapelnoes point north of the town, to cut the road in order to prevent reinforcements from North Vaagsö reaching South Vaagsö.

The southern town was thought to be defended by 150 men from the 181 Division, with a solitary tank and 100 men of a labour corps building defences. There were known to be four coastal guns, mounted with anti-aircraft batteries, on Maaloy to defend the Ulvesund anchorage where convoys sheltered in bad weather or gathered before crossing more open waters not protected by outer islands. A twin-tube torpedo battery covered the entrance to the fjord, and away to the north was a German mobile battery of 105mm guns at Halsor. No German warships were thought to be in the immediate area and only some four squadrons of fighters and bombers - an estimated 37 planes - were flying from Herdia, Stavanger, and Trondheim.

Brigadier Charles Haydon was military commander, and with Admiral Burrough, commanding the naval force, he sailed in the 6-inch gun cruiser HMS *Kenya*. Ashore the troops were commanded by Colonel John Durnford-Slater, the Commanding Officer of 3 Commando, who did most of the detailed planning for the raiding force which was made up from the entire 3 Commando, reinforced by two Troops from 'No.2' with additional Royal Engineers from 'No.6', Royal Army Medical Corps (RAMC) personnel from 'No.4', intelligence officers from the War Office, and a Press Unit. Photographers from this Unit were to take some of the finest action shots of the war.

Troop commanders and the men were briefed from a model with each house's position shown and other fine details except place names, so avoiding the possibility of literally fatal slips of the tongue. Once aboard two LSIs, the raiders carried out successful rehearsals at Scapa Flow (north Scotland), despite the navy's understandable challenge to the carrier ships' small craft bobbing about in the night. On Christmas Eve these two LSIs, HMS *Prince Leopold* and HMS *Prince Charles*, sailed for Shetland with a screen of four destroyers, taking a rough pounding in force 8 to 9 gales that put 14 feet of water in the forward part of *Prince Charles*. At the Sollum Voe anchorage this 145 tons of sea water was pumped out and the ships patched up, causing a day's delay but also giving time for Christmas dinner and a night's sleep with everyone fully recovered from sea sickness, a malady with no respect for rank or courage.

Sailing on the night on 26 December - the day Colonel Harrison's men landed in the Lofoten Islands - the Vaagsö force met the submarine HMS *Tuna* on station as their navigation check at 0700 hours off Vaagsfjord and steamed up the fjord between spectacular snow-covered hills glinting in the dark. Although reveille had been at 0400 hours, the landing would not be made until first light at 0850. The LSIs anchored in a bay beyond the sight of and direct fire from the Maaloy batteries, giving the assault craft a run down the coast round a headland before heading for the beaches, while the cruiser bombarded Maaloy and destroyers engaged other targets.

Colonel John Durnford-Slater led in 200 men of Troops 1, 2, 3, and 4 (Group 2) from 3 Commando, and 100 yards from the beach he fired 10 Very lights, signalling the navy to stop their bombardment. As he stepped ashore, three RAF Hampden bombers made a low-level attack, placing their smoke bombs in so close a screen for the landing that phosphorous from a sheet of flame set fire to the Colonel's tunic. One bomber, hit by fire from a German trawler went out of control and dropped a bomb among the landing craft, while the other bombers had to climb sharply in a stream of tracer to avoid the cliff behind the town. One landing craft was set on fire by the bombs that fell short, and many commandos suffered terrible burns from the phosphorous. Ammunition, grenades, and demolition explosives went off in a deadly firework display. The wounded were treated by the Commando's calm Irish doctor, Captain Sam Corry RAMC, who remained unruffled by the turmoil, and the casualties were sent out to the ships.

This landing by Group 2 was deliberately made at the base of some sheer, snow-covered rocks 30 feet high, for no German machine-guns were likely to cover such an apparently impossible landing point, the enemy unaware the commandos had developed their techniques for such rough landings. They got ashore dry shod - as they described those landings in which you do not get your feet wet - but in these harsh conditions, Lieutenant Arthur Komrower suffered severe back and leg injuries when he was crushed between a rock and the 10-ton assault craft that had been on fire.

More aircraft provided cover, with Coastal Command Blenheims dropping smoke to screen landings and fighter-bombers - again Blenheims and Beaufighters - putting a protective umbrella over the raiding force for the next seven hours by flying 400 miles (650km) from Wick, north Scotland, or 250 miles (400km) from Shetland.

Group 3, 105 men of Troops 5 and 6 under 3 Commando's second-in-command Major Jack Churchill, were waiting for the Maaloy batteries to open up as the craft ran towards the beach. Major Churchill, affectionately known as 'Mad Jack', stood in the leading LCA playing 'The march of the Cameron men' on his bagpipes. This Group were only 50 yards from the shore when the *Kenya's* bombardment lifted, her job well done with the German guncrews keeping in their dugouts, and before the batteries could come into action Jack Churchill's men had overrun Maaloy. Captain Peter Young came with his men through a gap in the wire cut by shells from *Kenya*, with nobody stepping on a mine, although these were expected. One German clerk, rather foolishly perhaps, tried to disarm this Troop officer and was shot for his indiscretion; other Germans were captured and a few shot during the brisk action.

The 50 men of Group 1 had landed without opposition; eight of the Germans defending the strongpoint at Hellevik having gone to Vaagsö for breakfast. The villages were cleared and two wounded Germans made prisoner. The leader of this Group, Lieutenant R. Clement, having signalled the colonel by way of HMS *Kenya* - communications by radio were always difficult in this or any other hilly country - was then told to move up the coast road and form a reserve for the Troops attacking the town. By now, about 1030, they needed reinforcement, even though they had lodged a foothold from their beach headquarters in spite of meeting fiercer opposition than expected: some 50 men of a crack regiment were spending Christmas in the town.

South Vaagsö lies on a narrow strip of shoreline beneath a sheer rock face several hundred feet high, the town's unpainted wooden buildings straggling along the three-quarters of a mile of main road running parallel to and some 50 yards from the shoreline. Down this road No.3 Troop were led by their Troop officer, a giant of a man, making a series of wild charges. They had taken several houses when the Troop officer - Captain Johnny Giles - was working his way room by room through another. He and his men had killed three Germans in this house when he burst into a back room and was probably killed by a fourth German hiding there, although he may have been hit from across the street. Such is the confusion of street fighting that bullets can appear to come from anywhere and everywhere.

No.4 Troop had caught a section of German defenders early in the battle as they ran to their alarm posts, but other Germans,

3-inch mortar team firing at minimum(?) range in the town, Vaagsö.

many of whom had seen action in Norway in 1940, tenaciously defended the strongpoints, including the improvised fortifications of the Ulvesund Hotel. Headquarters personnel were pressed into this defence, in Peter Young's words, 'to give it a bit of depth'.

No.4 Troop followed Captain Algy Forrester as he charged on down the high street. Along with Lieutenant Bill Lloyd he had perfected the techniques for getting ashore among rocks; but now Bill Lloyd was badly wounded, hit in the neck almost as soon as they began their grenade-tossing dash, firing tommy-guns from the hip. Algy Forrester, something of a fire-eater, stormed on, reaching the hotel, now the centre of German resistance, where he was about to throw a grenade when a shot from the hotel knocked him down and he fell on his own grenade, which exploded to kill him. No.4 Troop was stalled for only a moment. Captain Martin Linge, a Norwegian intelligence officer with the Troop, kept up the momentum of the attack, leading a second assault on the hotel, until he, too, was killed trying to force open a door.

During the fighting around the hotel, Sergeant Johnny Dowling and Sergeant Cork of No.1 Troop went to find the tank known to be nearby, for had this been brought into action, its 12 tons or more could have tipped the scales against the commandos. Sergeant Cork made more than sure it would not enter the battle: setting off a large demolition charge, he was killed in the blast.

For a while No.4 Troop were held up, but Corporal 'Knocker' White took charge and was awarded the DCM for his part in the action. The Colonel, from his open air headquarters on the beach, called over reinforcements from the Maaloy Group and Peter Young, with 18 men of his No.6 Troop, came across to the rock-shielded beach where Group 2 had landed some two hours before. He was sent along the quayside to keep the attack moving, and Brigadier Haydon committed the floating reserve (Group 4) in a landing at the north end of the town.

No.1 Troop had acquired a 3-inch (76mm) mortar which increased the Troop's firepower beyond its establishment. The mortar men were not trained as Heavy Weapons Troops would be later in the war, but this did not prevent Sergeant Ramsey from getting off a bomb that appeared to go down the hotel chimney, reportedly causing a dozen or more casualties. This was the turning-point at the hotel, and with grenades and tommy-gun fire Corporal White led the remains of No.4 Troop and a few Norwegians into the blazing building. Resistance at this strongpoint was over.

The radios of the 1940s being comparatively delicate valve affairs prone to water damage, radio contact had been lost with the forward Troops, so the Colonel walked boldly down the road to see the position for himself. A daring horseman, whose racing and pig-sticking had developed strong nerves in his robust frame, he scorned Charley Head's suggestion - and the signals officer was not battle-shy - of looking out for snipers. The Colonel was in a hurry, realising how essential it was to keep the momentum of the attack rolling; otherwise the resistance might become coordinated into a strong, interlocked series of defence positions. He reached the hotel unscathed, although the burns on his jacket showed where he had beaten out the phosphorous splashes with his leather gloves, and as he followed Peter

Young there were, as he later described, 'different sounds, from the various calibres of small arms, artillery exchanges between *Kenya* and a coast defence battery somewhere down the fjord, anti-aircraft fire from the ships against attacking Messerschmitts, the demolitions, and the crackling roar of flames'. There were also those smells of battle: the sharp tang of cordite, choking smoke, and the sickly whiff of death.

With the advantage of hindsight, we can take stock of the position at this point, but at the time the Colonel had only runners to keep him in touch with his headquarters and forward Troops, whose wirelesses had been knocked out. He had, however, seen his demolition squads begin their work at a cod-meal(?) factory and had had its Quisling owner arrested. Group 1, as we have seen, had cleared the south coast villages and were in positions on the south side of the town. Group 3 had cleared Maaloy and sent a party of sappers, men of 6 Commando attached to 'No.3' for this raid, over to Mortenes on the east shore of the fjord, where they landed unopposed and destroyed a fish processing factory. The demolition squad from No.6 Troop were blowing up the guns, four Belgian 75mm field pieces, their wheels shackled to turntables for anti-ship fire. This squad also exploded a store of mines which the Germans had not laid behind the beach - an extraordinary piece of dilatoriness for them, although they were probably complacent, in part at least, because their propaganda had written off the British. Group 4 - 65 men - were landing at the north end of the town, putting the defenders under pressure from two sides, while 30 men of Group 5 had landed from HMS *Oribi* at about 1000 hours. This Section from 2 Commando had set up a road-block ambush, while the destroyer joined others in her flotilla in attacking an armed tug and other ships. The German defences north of South Vaagsö had been bombed by three Blenheims an hour or so earlier, no doubt adding to the confusion at the German 181 Division's headquarters for they had no clear picture of events and a patrol sent down from the northern defences lost two men at the road-block. These commandos then blew a gap in the road and withdrew under covering fire from HMS *Oribi* and HMS *Onslow*, the former picking them up in her ship's boats as they came off the beach. Far away from this foray, Blenheim bombers were heading for Herdia airport, which they attacked at midday, cratering its timbered runway, while others bombed Stavanger.

The Colonel's force (Group 2) was down to probably 100 men as their reinforcements arrived. He came up to Peter Young's men who had advanced, after some losses, through a quayside warehouse and reached a yard (see diagram p. 32). There, cramped between a store house ('D' on the diagram) and a woodpile ('C'), the party had to move to get space so that they could reorganise. This meant capturing the red warehouse ('F') across a bare patch of snow and some 60 yards north of the woodpile. A rifleman hit two men crouching near the Colonel, who later wrote that 'this was the first time in warfare that I truly felt fear. I didn't like it.' Whenever there was a movement by the woodpile, the sniper fired, and soon he hit a third man. Everyone fired back. Sergeant George Herbert slipped into the storehouse and found some petrol. The small party - Peter Young by now had about half the men he had brought from Maaloy - opened fire on the warehouse, the Colonel having already emptied his revolver in firing at a sniper's window, and they kept the German from the window long enough for George Herbert to splash a bucket of petrol over the wooden walls. A couple of grenades then set a nearby house alight. Meanwhile Lieutenant Denis O'Flaherty and Trooper Sherington made a determined effort to reach the warehouse ('F') with Peter Young, who saw three stick grenades flung towards him in quick succession; the first two missed and the third did not go off. Both O'Flaherty and Sherington were severely wounded as they got into the warehouse, but with grim determination they staggered clear, leaving a few equally determined Germans in an inner room of the building. There were a few moments' stalemate, then more petrol was thrown, this time into the warehouse, and two men with a bren gun were left to cover the building as Peter Young led his men on.

The Colonel went towards the road to press forward the attack down the main street, a grenade that fell between his feet putting a few splinters in his hand, after he had dived for cover, and seriously wounding his runner. The next minute the grenade thrower appeared with his hands up. John Durnford-Slater would have accepted this sailor's surrender, but a more angry commando shot the bomber dead. The Colonel's cool compassion showed his command of the situation: no moment of fury distorted his fearless and level-headed view.

The commandos had been able to keep up their grenade-throwing sorties because civilian volunteers from the town carried sacks of grenades forward to the men in action. With this help, No.1 Troop had fought their way from building to building up the landward side of the road and were attacking a house when Sergeant Culling was hit in the face and killed by a percussion grenade exploding on impact. Sergeant Ramsey's 3-inch mortar was again brought into action, and a direct hit on the building's roof with the third round was followed by a score of bombs through the resulting hole which set the place ablaze. This ended the most severe part of the operation, although the air battles overhead continued to keep enemy bombers from the ships.

By now, 1345 hours, the Colonel had been up with the leading Troops for more than two hours, and as the short Arctic day was drawing to a close he ordered the withdrawal to begin. No.2 Troop led the way back down the road towards the beach headquarters, followed by No.6 with No.1 as rearguard. Many buildings along the road were burning fiercely and, as he counted 12 dead Germans around the house just destroyed by mortar fire, Colonel Durnford-Slater encouraged the men to run through the flames by leading the way. Apparently they feared the burning timbers more than the bullets, but no doubt they were feeling some reaction after more than four hours in action: four hours of dodging snipers' bullets and bursting open doors that all too often concealed a rifleman who fired, while around the houses a grenade could be dropped from any window.

Walking wounded being evacuated by LCA from Vaagsö.

Throughout the fighting, the intelligence section had been searching houses and the German headquarters, and naval parties had boarded ships in similar searches - a dangerous task because several were killed as they rowed towards the quays in ships' whalers. After an exchange of rifle shots with the crew of the *Föhn*, Lieutenant-Commander A.N.F. de Costabadic DSC got aboard this armed trawler.

Sam Corry and his medics carried the wounded who could not walk to the top of the rock above the landing beach, to which they were then lowered, down the rock face, on stretchers. Moreover, between tending the wounded, the doctor managed to loose off a few shots at snipers. Despite them the withdrawal went smoothly, with the Colonel, who had been the first man ashore, the last man off, just behind Charley Head, who, as signals officer, had kept up a stream of messages, 40 an hour at one point, that included reassuring but unproven 'going well' reports. He later explained that he had not wished to distract the Colonel during the fighting with enquiries on its actual progress.

Back in Britain, the Norwegian government exiled there felt this raid had done nothing to ease Norway's plight; a problem for any raiders attacking an ally's occupied shore. But against this destruction must be set some solid achievements, including the Press Unit's making as much as censorship would allow in a morale-boosting report. German reaction after the raid was to later over-stretch their Atlantic Wall, with some 30,000 extra troops and material being deployed in Norway, which Hitler took to be 'the zone of destiny in this war'. There was also a small bonus, for among the documents captured - when the Lieutenant-Commander from CCO's planning headquarters boarded *Föhn* - was part of the German navy's master code which the Allies added to their information in breaking its secrets.

The raids against Norway continued through the next three years, 1942-44, and were mounted in other theatres as more raiding parties were trained. The Vaagsö raid had proved that a landing was possible against a defended port, while Lord Mountbatten's test pilots, as he called them, had proved the mettle of his command. A modest naval force, a dozen squadrons of aircraft, and 600 commandos with their Norwegian allies, had favourably influenced the strategy of the war at comparatively minor cost - five aircraft were lost with their crews, and 19 other raiders killed and 52 wounded. Some, like Denis O'Flaherty, who was in hospital for two years, would be a long time returning to the fight. But the days of aimlessly wandering on enemy beaches were over and specific targets could be raided despite their defences: targets the scientists and planners calculated as most likely to influence the war.

Among these targets were small components whose size bore no relation to their great importance in the technology of war,

and great installations considered indestructible by the air bombardment of those years. Many of the smaller technological targets were in the province of SOE, but one, the new components in radar equipment of a German site some hundred yards from the top of a 300-foot cliff near Bruneval (see

The plan of the successful raid on the radar station at Bruneval, this called for one parachute party to take the beach while the main force dropped to take the isolated house and the RDF installation. Half the beach party were dropped 2½ miles (4km) from their intended assembly area and arrived late but in time to clear the pill boxes before 12 Commandos' LCAs came in, and Major J. D. Frost and his men could be evacuated.

THE RAID ON BRUNEVAL

BRUNEVAL

MISSING SECTIONS OF BEACH

M.G.

M.G.

XXXX M.G.

M.G.
M.G.

M.G.

ROAD BLOCK

ASSEMBLY POINT

PARATROOPS LANDED HERE

RDF M.G.

ISOLATED HOUSE

PRESBYTÈRE

M.G.

PARATROOPS
XXXX BARBED WIRE
---- BURIED CABLE
M.G. M.G. POST
P PILL BOX

| YARDS | 0 | 500 | 1000 | 1500 | 2000 | 2500 |
| METRES | 0 | 500 | 1000 | 1500 | 2000 | |

map p. 28), was attacked by a small force of paratroops supported by a seaborne commando party covering the withdrawal. Although the Germans had used a warning radar since before 1939, the Bruneval station included a new Würzburg set with its 20-foot (6m) dish aerial able to range guns and direct planes on to a single aircraft. It was protected by 15 machine-gun posts along the cliff top and had, therefore, to be entered by the 'back door'. A hundred parachute troops from the 2nd Parachute Battalion made this entrance on 27 February 1942, fighting their way into the station and coming out with the vital gear dismantled by Flight-Sergeant Cox, a radar expert.

They withdrew down a gulley to the beach under fire that intensified as they remained below the cliffs, a sea mist shrouding their signals to the landing craft. However, three LCA crews saw a Very light above the mist and came in with three motor gun boat escorts. Each LCA had the added firepower of four brens manned by men from 12 Commando, and in their fight with the Germans on the cliff top the commandos kept the defenders at bay until 0330 hours - some two and a half hours after the paras had landed - when the last craft left the beach under heavy fire. The equipment enabled scientists to develop 'window', a successful counter to radar. After the War General Student who had commanded German airborne forces congratulated Lord Mountbatten on the raid as the 'best example of the use of airborne forces with other forces', and Lord Mountbatten considers this raid 'the most 100% perfection of any raid I know'.

The CCO's position underwent a fundamental change in March 1942 when Lord Mountbatten 'was made an Acting Vice-Admiral, an Honorary Lieutenant-General, an Honorary Air Marshal, with a seat on the Chiefs of Staff Committee itself, and was thus one of the four military leaders in charge of the higher direction of the War as a whole and in my case Combined Operations in particular' - to quote Lord Mountbatten. He goes on to explain that this change was fundamental to the development of Combined Operations as he was then able to order the ships and craft, and requisition bases among the other resources controlled by the Minister of Defence (Winston Churchill).

The successes of December 1941 and February 1942 were crowned in March by the most profitable amphibious raid of modern times, in terms of effective damage with an economy of force. The achieved aim was to destroy the dry-dock at St Nazaire, a success in no small part due to the bond between officers and men. A hallmark of Commandos, such relationships avoided the discourtesies of familiarity lapsing into slackness in command. Moreover, in 2 Commando which carried out this raid, there was, in its commanding officer's words 'an extra scruple of endurance' that turned the seemingly impossible into the possible. Like almost all commando colonels, Colonel A.C. Newman was a man with technical as well as military ability: a civil engineer of cheerful but quiet character, seldom seen without his pipe. He was 38 years old at the time of this raid. His second-in-command - Major W.O. Copland - was, at 44, getting on in years for commando work, but as a works manager in civilian life he had the experience of technical organisation needed for such ventures. Indeed they required as much brain as brawn, and among the demolition parties at St Nazaire, drawn from eight different Commandos, were a curator of a fine arts museum, a member of the London Stock Exchange, a

---

St Nazaire raid by 2 Commando, 28 March 1942, naval forces included: 2 Hunt-class destroyers as escorts; the destroyer HMS *Campbeltown* stripped for shallow draught; 16 Fairmile 'B' Motor Launches (MLs) mahogany skin hulls 112 by 19½ft beam with 2 650hp engines and each manned by 2 officers and 13 ratings (3 extra) for raid - 12 carried 20mm fore and aft, 4 had 18-inch torpedo tubes in case there were guardships and with usual MLs' 3pdr Hotchkiss - all had wireless but no radar; MTB No 74 with foredeck tubes for delayed action torpedoes; MGB No 314 Fairmile 'C' mahogany hard-chine hull 110 by 17½ft beam with 3 850hp engines (max 25 knots), Vickers 2pdr hand operated pom-pom forward, aft 2 pdr in Rolls Royce semi-automatic turret, and amidships 2 twin-.5in m/c guns in powered mountings, she carried a fixed fore-and-aft radar, wireless and navigation equipment.

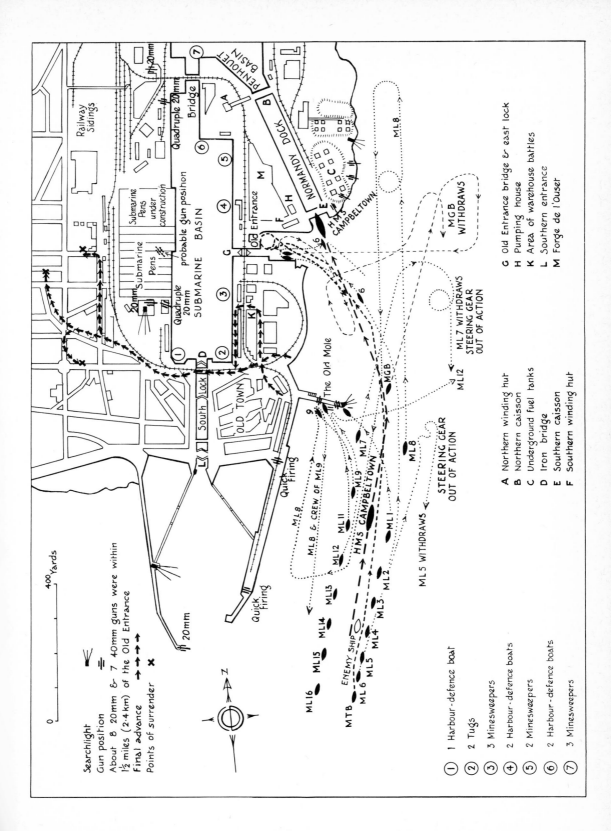

Nottingham miner, an economist, and several regular soldiers. These last included Sergeant Tom Durrant, Royal Engineers, one-time butcher's boy and, although only 23, a man with granite determination.

Earlier plans for a purely commando raid had been abandoned, as mentioned earlier, because St Nazaire stands on the Loire estuary with only one deep-water channel which was covered by coastal batteries in 1942. The river's broad mud-flats were thought impassable. However, Captain John Hughes-Hallet RN of the Planning Staff turned these shallows to the raiders' advantage, because on the extra-high water of a spring tide it was possible that lightly laden ships and boats might scrape over these flats. Aerial photographs showed there was no boom protecting the dry-dock gate (the caisson 'E' on diagram p. 41) nor were there any barbed-wire entanglements ashore on the quays. The Captain also knew that mining the shallows was an unlikely precaution and technically difficult, thus leaving open a side entrance to the port. When they were ashore, Lord Mountbatten suggested, the raiders 'might do something different'. This they did.

The destroyer HMS *Campbeltown* was given an explosive warhead to ram against the outer caisson. As big as a block of flats, this steel gate was 167ft x 54ft x 35ft thick (about 50m x 15m x 10m). Commandos would land from the destroyer and from coastal forces motorboats in small assault parties, demolition squads, and protection parties. Their part in the plan was to demolish the lock gates ('L' and 'G') so making the submarine basin tidal, and preventing U-boats passing freely into their eight bomb-proof pens on the west side of this basin, where five additional pens were being built. The raiders would also attack the inner (northern 'B') caisson, setting charges if possible inside its box sections. Other installations would be demolished, including the gates' winding gear ('A' and 'F') which hauled the caissons aside to allow ships of up to 85,000 tons to enter the 1,148 feet (351m) dock. Also to be destroyed were the pumps used to empty it, these being in a deeper chamber below the dock level.

The commando parties were to come ashore at three points: over the bows of *Campbeltown*; on the Old Entrance quays; and on the Old Mole. Their first objective would be to capture quick-firing 20mm and 40mm guns around these positions: secondly, they would hold perimeter bridges leading to the south and west sides of the submarine basin and the dry-dock while others gave close protection to the demolition parties. These squads were armed only with automatic pistols as each man carried a 60lb (27kg) rucksack of explosives and some had as much as 90lb (40kg) loads. The raid would truly be 'the sauciest since Drake'.

The Elizabethan admiral was 'war' and wakin'' on that March weekend in 1942 when the navy's little ships - lightly built wooden craft designed for high-speed attacks rather than close-quarters work - stormed into St Nazaire with their landing parties. The crews included many officers and men in for the duration, the 'Hostilities only' (HO) personnel like Able Seaman William Savage who manned the forward 2-pounder pom-pom on the motor gun boat. Although he had all the appearance of an old hand with his beard and sea-salt's pipe, he was a brewery worker by trade. The little fleet's senior officer was Commander R.E.D. Ryder RN, who had spent four days alone in the Atlantic after his Q-ship was sunk before she could bring her hidden guns into action. A dedicated professional seaman, he practised his motor launches (MLs), the motor gun boat (MGB), and the modified motor torpedo boat (MTB 74) operating in close company, manoeuvres they did not normally execute and only had a few weeks to learn. Indeed, MTB 74, with her torpedo tubes on the foredeck instead of amidships, was ready for sea only a few hours before the raid, her crew having changed one of her five engines. Details on these craft are shown in the caption to the diagram on page 41, but MTB 74 was an unusual ship even among these fast midgets. Her individualist skipper - Sub-Lieutenant R.C.M.V. Wynn RNVR - had devised an engineless torpedo with 2,200lb (over 450kg) of explosive to be launched at close range. The torpedo then sank under a moored target and was fired by

Royal Engineer commandos landed with all manner of demolition equipment, one method of carrying this was the Yukon pack with a frame to hold sledge hammer, pick and other heavy tools, February 1943.

a time fuse which allowed MTB 74 time to get clear.

The commandos rehearsed their demolition exercises to the point of boredom, believing they were merely on another training course. But after a couple of weeks around Cardiff and Southampton docks - where there was a similar dry-dock to the battleship dock at St Nazaire - they could each carry out almost every demolition in under 10 minutes. The raiding force were then assembled at Falmouth, and on the afternoon of 26 March, a Thursday, they sailed with the khaki uniforms of the soldiers out of sight below decks.

At sea the force rolled south-westward in a light breeze, making 13 knots (24kph) with the MTB and MGB towed by destroyers. The crew of the explosive blockship HMS *Campbeltown* had been reduced to 75 hands; the four funnels she had carried as the USS

*Buchanan*, old *Buck*, had been replaced by two raked-back stacks to resemble a German Möwe-class destroyer. She rode light in the water despite the extra armour-plate around her bridge and forming fences amidships to protect her commando landing parties where they would crouch on her final run, but she was carrying a minimum of fuel and water and her guns were gone except for a 12-pounder forward and oerlikons on the bridge wings. Below decks were 24 Mark VII depth-charges each of 400lb (180kg) concreted into a steel box. Placed abaft the column of her forward gun, the warhead would be protected from the impact of ramming the caisson as the bows crumpled, and the eight-hour delay chemical fuses would give the raiders time to get clear before the acid ate through copper discs. Alternative two-and-a-half-hour fuses were available, but all who might know if these were also used were killed in the action.

During Thursday night the force changed course, and hoisted German colours. Next morning they sighted U-593 and attacked her; about midday they came on a fleet of French trawlers but were satisfied they carried no German radio operators. News from Plymouth of five *Wolfe/Möwe* destroyers in the estuary caused some concern, but these ships were sent to investigate what mines had been laid by the force - mistakenly thought to be sailing *west* when U-593 signalled her base. There was little for the crews to do. They smeared grease or paint to prevent the MLs' bridge windows glinting and on *Campbeltown* the commandos mounted their two 3-inch (76mm) mortars forward of the gun and the last rehearsal was held.

The success of their final run depended on a diversionary air raid. But the possibility of French casualties, with cloud at 3,000 feet (1,000m) obscuring the docks, led to only four of the bombers dropping their loads, while some 30 other Whitleys and 25 Wellingtons flew around above the clouds. The activity was unusual enough to cause Captain Mecke, commanding the naval Flak Brigade's anti-aircraft guns, to guess 'some devilry was afoot' when the air raid petered out before midnight.

An hour before then, at 2300 hours,

Lieutenant Nigel T.B. Tibbetts RN set the fuses on *Campbeltown's* warhead. An expert on explosives he had been responsible for the design and building of this 4½ tons charge. Its fuses were expected to blow the lot about five o'clock next morning, Saturday, or at the latest by nine o'clock.

The ships had some 10 miles to go; the MLs had used their extra fuel and filled the spare tanks with seawater as they stole into the estuary in two columns, headed by MGB 314:

MGB 314
Ryder and Newman

(7) ML 270
with torpedoes
Irwin RN

(8) ML 160
with torpedoes
Boyd RN

HMS *Campbelton*
Beattie RN
Copland directing landing
Roy assault
Roderick assault
Chant, Smalley, Burtenshaw,
Brett, Purdon—demolition
Proctor 3-in mortars

(9) ML 447
Platt RN
Birney assault

(1) ML 192
Stephens RN
Burn assault

(15) ML 446
Falconer RN
Hodgson assault

(2) ML 262
Burt RN
Woodcock demolition
Morgan protection

(11) ML 457
Collier RN
Pritchard demolition
Walton demolition
Watson protection

(3) ML 267
Beart RN
Moss HQ party

(12) ML 307
Wallis RN
Bradley demolition

(4) ML 268
Tillie RN
Pennington demolition
Jenkins protection

(13) ML 443
Horlock RN
Basset-Wilson demolition
Bonvin demolition
Houghton protection

(5) ML 156
with torpedoes
Fenton RN
Hooper assault

(14) ML 306
Henderson RN
Savayne demolition
Vanderwerve protection

(6) ML 177
with torpedoes
Rodier RN
Haines assault

(10) ML 447
Brault RN
cdo to (15)
before action

(16) ML 446
Nock RN
spare boat

(17) MTB 74
with special torpedoes
Wynn RN

*Note:* References in () are operational numbers for the St Nazaire raid.

These motorboats are difficult to handle at slow speed and *Campbeltown* was sluggish, but at speed she drew an extra foot aft and every inch counted as she came towards the mud. They passed the old wreck of the SS *Lancastria*, *Campbeltown* steering 050 degrees to offset the tide's strong northerly set, and reduced speed to 10 knots, the MGB's echo-sounder probing for some depth of water as the destroyer twice churned over mud-bars. Two German boats away to port challenged them but could not report the intrusion as these harbour patrol boats had no wireless.

Bill Copland ordered action stations at midnight, when the German searchlights were going out as the anti-aircraft defences stood down. Only the murmur of ships' engines and swish of bows cutting the tide could be heard across the calm sea. In the port column heading for the Old Mole, an ML skipper caught the distinct smell of countryside, sweet traces of grass scents among the more pervasive exhaust fumes.

The clouds were parting and the moon showed dimly at first when the 12-pounder gun's crew of cooks and stewards closed up aboard the destroyer. The commandos moved forward to man the 3-inch mortars. The destroyer passed a disused tower in midstream, but already the ships had been spotted at 0115 hours and Mecke signalled: *Achtung Landegfahr* - Beware landings. There was an unexplained delay of five or ten minutes - perhaps while the searchlight crews came back to their action stations on the great lights, including the five-foot beam on the west bank a mile or so downstream from the port, and the light commanding the river from the end of the Old Mole. German radar at St Marc or lookouts at about this time reported 17 ships, so the coastal batteries were closed up for action against ships.

The columns of MLs led by the destroyer riding high out of the water were suddenly caught in the harsh glare of the west bank searchlight. Other searchlights came on, but the German-looking silhouette of *Campbeltown* and some other confusions of identity enabled the intruders to bluff their way for another five minutes and about 2,000 yards (1,800m) nearer the harbour. Ryder fired some German Very recognition signals but these were the wrong shade of red for that night, and at 0127 the defence opened fire in its full fury.

*Campbeltown* struck her German colours and hoisted her battle ensign: she had about a mile to go. The 12-pounder exposed on a turntable mounting, the mortars and the oerlikons all fired at the flashes of German guns, as did the commandos in the MLs, firing brens in a pre-arranged fire-plan that helped conserve ammunition. As if to escape from the great pool of light, the destroyer gathered speed, but it moved with her, red, green, and orange tracer streaming into her sides. Occasionally there was the heavier judder as larger shells struck. Forward on the MGB's exposed foredeck, Able Seaman Savage racked the *Sperrbrecher* with his 2-pounder pom-pom, knocking out this mine destroyer's 88mm (3.5in) gun and setting fire to its ready-use ammunition lockers on deck. But the *Sperrbrecher*, unidentified before the raid although moored a few hundred yards from the east jetty (see diagram p. 41) was a strong ship. Nevertheless, for some five minutes the British guns seemed to gain a temporary advantage.

*Campbeltown* took the brunt of the shot and shell, her captain - Lieutenant-Commander S. (Sam) H. Beattie RN - blinded by searchlights yet making last-minute corrections to her course when a rift in the smoke showed she was not heading for the caisson, still 700 yards upriver. The coxswain and the quartermaster were killed at the wheel, and Nigel Tibbets took the helm. MLs 7 and 8 drove ahead, firing at the Mole and dockgate batteries. At the last moment a heavy incendiary bomb - from an RAF plane - hit the foredeck of *Campbeltown* but the ship forged ahead, ripped over the anti-torpedo nets, and rammed the caisson. Sam Beattie swung her stern to starboard as she hit, leaving clear the Old Entrance for the MLs' landing. It was 0134 hours, just four minutes behind the planned time of impact.

The columns of MLs were now under heavy fire, the port group of MLs making for the Mole to land their commandos, the starboard group intending to slip under the stern of *Campbeltown* into the Old Entrance. Something of the MLs' agony as they fought their way towards the quays can be seen in the diagram on page 41. Most of them were so badly damaged that they sank or were forced to withdraw as shell splinters cut their steering lines and tracer set fire to fuel tanks, but they gave a good account of themselves because the port was defended by well-sited, quick-firing guns used for anti-aircraft or anti-ship fire. Some of these guns were on the top of the submarine pens, others were on concrete towers as large as a couple of houses but far more strongly built. The tower near the south caisson received more than a hundred hits from the British motor launches and other Royal Navy guns, but the strongpoint on the Old Mole, some 400 yards downstream from the Old Entrance, still commanded the river despite the raiders' fire. The 20mm and 40mm quick-firing guns here were in or on concrete emplacements, and although the crew of the outer guns were knocked out for a time the

HMS *Campbeltown* rams the battleship dock gate at St. Nazaire.

Germans got this battery firing again, and the searchlight on the Mole's tip was never put out.

A few commandos struggled ashore, among them Captain Michael Burn, who went alone threequarters of a mile across the docks to near the northern bridge where he did what he could to destroy an unmanned battery and was visited by Bill Copland doing a round of the northern positions. Many of the commandos, though, died out on the river: Regimental Sergeant-Major A. Moss leading the tiny reserve of 2 Commando's assault troops was killed swimming in the river after giving his place on a life-raft to a young soldier; many were burnt in the pools of flaming petrol.

Despite the heavy fire and German infantry dropping grenades from the Mole, ML11 got Captain Bill Pritchard, Lieutenant Philip Walton, and Lieutenant W.H. (Tiger) Watson ashore with their squads. Bill Pritchard hurrying them on towards their objectives around the south entrance bridge ('D') beyond the old town, although Tiger Watson wanted to clear the Mole first. Two other MLs got men ashore under *Campbeltown's*

stern and the MGB landed Charles Newman with his fighting headquarters - two tommy-gunners and a signaller - about the time *Campbeltown* rammed the lock. Landing the headquarters at the Old Entrance was itself a miracle of seamanship among the blazing wrecks and heavy fire directed at the MGB.

The destroyer's forward gun crew and mortarmen were all dead or wounded, her bow a cauldron of smoke and thermite fumes, even though the incendiary bomb was put out before it set fire to *Campbeltown's* warhead of depth charges. Her oerlikons blazed at the batteries on the harbour wall as Bill Copland calmly marshalled the assault parties. Dressed for easy recognition in white blancoed webbing, with clean (at the start) faces, and with every second man carrying a blue-lensed pencil-beamed torch, the assault parties dropped their scaling-ladders over the bow and plunged ashore. John Roderick's party attacked the guns off the starboard bow, the 12 men capturing the first gun's sandbagged emplacement in a grenade-throwing rush along the dock wall. They knocked out the next emplacement, but then came to one of those house-like ack-ack towers. Unable to get up its outside flight of steps, they lobbed grenades on to the gun platform, killing the gun commander and men drawing ammunition inside the tower, before moving on along the harbour wall to take a 40mm gun position. Then they returned to the destroyer. Beyond this last position was a fourth gun and a searchlight which were also destroyed, although not by Roderick's men. Possibly some men from an ML or maybe the boats' gunfire did this damage.

Within a couple of minutes of going over the destroyer's port side, Donald Roy's kilted Scotsmen were attacking the pumphouse 50 yards from the caisson ('H' on diagram p. 41). The gun crews on its roof fled, and the commandos doubled on to the bridge ('G') across the Old Entrance lock into the submarine basin, holding this exposed position for half an hour under fire from 20mm guns on the roof of the submarine pens and other buildings on the west side of the basin.

For the demolition parties the days of scheming and planning were over: now they needed steady nerves and physical strength. The five squads aboard *Campbeltown* had several targets. Stuart Chant (5 Commando), with four sergeants, would destroy the pumping station. Robert Burtenshaw (also from 'No.5'), with six NCOs, had a reserve of explosives to place inside the southern caisson if the destroyer had failed to ram. Christopher Smalley and four NCOs would demolish the winding-house for this caisson. The other two squads had further to go in attacking similar installations around the northern or inner caisson. All these men were encumbered with their heavy loads and had only automatic pistols. Some were wounded before they left the destroyer, including Stuart Chant and Sergeant Chamberlain. Many of these squads also carried sledge-hammers, axes, and incendiaries.

Carrying Chamberlain and with Stuart Chant limping, his team followed Donald Roy's assault, reaching the pump-house and ignoring the Germans who fled. The commandos blew in its steel door, and, leaving Chamberlain, who could hardly help himself along, to guard it, they ran down the long stairway to the pumps 40 feet below. Their torches barely penetrated the gloom, but they could have laid the charges by feel in complete darkness: all their training was paying off. The charges, linked by two rings of cordtex, were set to fire and the squad ran for cover clear of the building. Captain R.K. Montgomery RE - an old friend of Bill Pritchard and like him a coordinator of demolition squads in the raid - moved them further away. The windows of the pump-house blew out with a roar of debris and crashing concrete blocks, one falling where they had first taken cover. Inside the pump-house there was little more to do, but they smashed the transformer oil pipes with sledge-hammers and threw down some tar baby incendiaries. Christopher Smalley's men had already destroyed the great wheels in the winding-house. As these squads withdrew, Montgomery threw an incendiary into a shed, sending it up 'in a colossal sheet of continuous flame'.

The three squads making for the northern caisson, including Bob Burtenshaw's men who were not needed at the southern caisson, were less fortunate. Corran Purdon and four corporals, including 'Johnny' Johnson, a Gordon Highlander of 12 Commando who carried through his task although severely wounded before leaving the destroyer, made for the northern winding-house ('A' on diagram). They were closely followed by Gerard Brett with a largely Irish squad from 12 Commando. The giant Bob Burtenshaw, sporting a borrowed naval cap (Commander Beattie's), swung his walking-stick, his monocle firmly in place, unconcerned by the frenzy of gunfire as they came over the destroyer's bows. He hummed softly 'There'll always be an England' and joked as he shifted the weight of his rucksack 'as if on a walking holiday'. Moving along a dockside with its crane-tracks, bollards, and railway lines is no jaunt in daylight; at night the going can be grim.

The tiny protection parties for these three squads were down to 10 men through casualties before landing, but they led the way, stifling small arms fire from near the burning Forge de l'Ouest, then clearing an enemy trench in a skirmish round a dockside crane. Padding behind them were the demolition squads, Corran Purdon's men held for a tense few moments in the open when every second might draw more fire as they smashed the northern winding-hut door ('A'). Inside they placed their charges and sledge-hammered the electric gear. All was ready for demolition, but in going to report this, the burly Corporal Chung was wounded, the two parties on the caisson being under heavy fire.

Gerard Brett, wounded in both legs, had been dragged to the protection of a low wall before his team slipped across the caisson, killing two Germans who appeared out of the gloom on the east side. The hatch trap-door into the caisson would not come open and fire was coming from all sides, including the north where three ships were moored beyond the caisson on the Penhouet Basin's south quay. Burtenshaw took charge and 12 18lb (8kg) charges were lowered against the outside (north) underwater face of the caisson, the cords tied to the guard rail. Tarred timbers covered in grit - unlike the gates at Southampton - protected the caisson's sides, and the men took some cover behind these timbers' projections when the Penhouet ships opened accurate fire with their 20mm guns. No doubt these gunners had seen Sergeant Carr's two further attempts to blow open the hatch. Bob Burtenshaw, realising they must at least silence the ships lying inside the dry-dock, south of the caisson, took several men with him along the wall, firing their pistols down into a tanker undergoing a refit. More effective was the rush by two of the protection squad firing their tommies as they ran down the ship's steep gangplank. When Germans appeared on the west dockside, Bob Burtenshaw - still humming 'There'll always be an England ...' ran at them firing his pistol, despite his wounds. The Germans scattered, but the Lieutenant and a corporal were killed. Sergeant Carr - a tall regular Royal Engineer - went back along the caisson, found the hatch still unopened, and decided the wreath of underwater charges at least must be blown. Coming back from this explosion he checked the damage - in the tradition of his Corps - and heard the gurgle of water flowing into the dry-dock.

The machinery in the winding house was blown before the parties withdrew carrying Gerard Brett. All the possible demolitions north and south of the dry-dock were now complete, but attempts to damage the submarine basin's southern lock had failed. Bill Pritchard, whom we left going ashore at the Old Mole with his demolition control party and Philip Walton's demolition squad, protected by Tiger Watson's men, moved into the Old Town in commando fashion : each party, indeed each man, when alone, moved towards the target without waiting for support. Bill Pritchard got within sight of the steel lattice bridge ('D') before heavy fire forced his corporals to take cover in a concrete hut. Pritchard and one corporal then nipped back across the open roadway to drop a 10lb charge between two tugs moored in the basin, and their dash back to the hut, a mere 60 yards or less from the approaching enemy, was achieved without mishap. They heard the muffled thud as the charge blew before they set off to see how others were faring on this southern lock.

The three corporals left in the hut were told 'to do what you can' for no one had appeared to blow the bridge. Meanwhile Captain Bill Pritchard and his corporal - a Scots engineer apprentice, Mac, I.L. Maclagan - jogged silently down the lock's east wall but found none of the expected demolitions at its gates. They heard the tramp of boots but saw no one, although the enemy appears to have marched boldly but sometimes indiscreetly into the area. There was no one at the pumping station in the Old Town, so the two of them headed back through the dockside streets to find out what was happening. Rounding a corner Bill Pritchard ran into a German. No shot was fired before Mac killed the rifleman with a tommy-gun burst, but the captain had been wounded, and his last order, gasped through heavy breathing, '. . . report to HQ' was followed by the lone corporal. Threading his way past the echoing warehouses, boarded shop fronts, and silent cafes, he returned to the concrete hut, only to find there the body of Philip Walton. Undeterred, Mac now made his way down the side of the now dangerous Old Town Place back to Colonel Newman's headquarters.

Watson's party, with some of Walton's squad, had fought a firefight around this *place* and had been forced northward between buildings on the basin wharf which was where their Colonel appeared. Cheerful, and unaware of the failures at the southern lock, he urged on young Watson, who steeled himself for another attempt at breaking through the *place*. However, before a further attack could be made they were told to withdraw, because the Colonel needed all his little force regrouped.

Next day the Germans found that the one-time schoolmaster and lieutenant of 2 Commando Philip Walton, and maybe one of the corporals from Pritchard's squad, had laid charges on the bridge, but this brave effort had been foiled by lethal fire at close range.

Regrouping at the Colonel's command post began around 0300 hours, 90 minutes after landing. On coming ashore Charles Newman had set up his headquarters near the bridge ('G') across the lock leading from the Entrance. Bumping into a German, the Colonel, with natural politeness, said 'Sorry' before the man surrendered and persuaded his mates to do the same. The Colonel then made his rounds of the southern parties while Bill Copland, landing from the destroyer, visited those to the north. But as they checked their tiny forces - a hundred or so ashore - the first German *Stosstruppen*, Thrust Troops, were moving into the docks over the bridges of the submarines' basin's southern lock ('D') at 0150 hours. There was more to come: about 5,000 troops and seamen were in the area, including the crews of the five minesweepers and four harbour defence boats and the technicians of the naval Works Companies Nos 2 and 4. The *Stosstruppen* of 703 and 705 naval flak battalions moved into the Old Town, while the Works Companies came towards the north caisson from both east and west.

Troop Sergeant-Major Haines - landed from ML 6 - reported to Newman and early in the fight lay out in the open with a 2-inch (51mm) mortar firing on the guns across the submarine basin. When a ship shifted position to silence him, Sergeant-Major Haines drove it off with a bren gun! The headquar-

ters' 38-set (see Appendix 5) could not contact Ryder on the MGB and Newman did not at first realise how few men were ashore. Donald Roy's assault party joined him and John Roderick's men came back, crossing a now silent *Campbeltown's* bow. Chris Smalley had earlier come upon ML 2 alongside in the Entrance and scrambled aboard with his squad, but in trying to get her forward guns firing he was killed before she was afire and had to be abandoned about 0245 hours. Other commandos may have got ashore for - as mentioned earlier - some German guns were silenced beyond John Roderick's objectives, but after landing no other commandos got away in the MLs.

Crouching behind some railway trucks the commandos formed a tiny perimeter facing the Old Mole's landward side and around the buildings just south of the Entrance. They were being attacked on every side but the northward quay towards the destroyer. Newman and Copland walked to the edge of the entrance, a grenade silencing one post a mere 25 yards away; over the water the searchlight of the Mole could be seen beamed on the river. The entrance was an inferno of petrol fires as flames flared and flickered across the water, sending a black column of heavy smoke mixed with the MLs' white smoke-screens slowly rolling north-west on the still night air above the wrecked boats. Most of the other searchlights were out now, and only the fires lit the quays and the gaunt dockside warehouses that echoed to the sharp burst of a tommy-gun's fire and the sharper answering rent of a German Schmeisser's more rapid fire. The Colonel checked with Bill Copland whether they should call it a day: 'Certainly not' was the Major's assured reply, for all felt the confidence of success.

Some two hours after landing they moved out of the perimeter in parties of 20 or so, with Michael Burn lopping in the van followed by Donald Roy with the strongly armed assault parties. Behind these came the demolition squads. Troop Sergeant Haines brought up the rear as the raiders moved towards the Old Entrance lock bridge ('G') but had first to swing north round the buildings on the east of the basin. In the next few minutes the small parties moved in quick spurts from the deep shadow of one warehouse to the next black patch of cover. Donald Roy led the way when contact was lost with Mike Burn, for in these dark moments a dash for cover could plunge men into enemy defences. One party supported another with covering fire as best they could. There were unexplained hold-ups, enemy strongpoints catching the leaders in heavy fire perhaps, or a few moments' loss of direction as they probed forward. Sergeant-Major Haines was sent forward at one point and with Donald Roy got the column moving. Tiger Watson was wounded; Donald Roy killing his friend's attacker, for this was a personal battle of man against man in the shadows, even though at the same time there was the impersonal hammer from machine-guns and 20mm cannons firing from beyond the basin and its locks. This more distant fire let up long enough, however, for the column to make its way beside the buildings on the east side of the basin. The German gunners no doubt feared firing on their own men in these warehouses.

The Colonel at one point was firing his revolver over Donald Roy's shoulder, and reaching the *place* they could see the bridge ('D') 70 yards off. 'Away you go lads' sent the leading squad dashing for the bridge literally under a hail of fire, for the startled Germans were shooting too high. Those minutes of fighting in the shadows had extended to an hour or more. But once over the bridge they met the first vehicles of a German column and the Commando force were scattered. They left the streets, making their way across gardens and by back ways into the town to hide in buildings. Most were captured: a few, with the inevitable brutality of war, were killed needlessly - one young soldier was shot as he surrendered, another, with his head between kilted knees, died with a knot of Germans looking on.

Out on the river earlier in the battle, Commander Ryder had ordered the MGB back alongside *Campbeltown* and gone ashore with Leading Seaman Pike - an expert in German signals, part of the bluff - to make sure the destroyer was locked into the southern caisson, but he did not know how the battle was going ashore. He came away from the Old Entrance, having collected those of the destroyer's crew not taken off by ML 6, and as Micky Wynn came up with his special MTB, Robert Ryder told him to fire the torpedoes at the outer lock gate in the Old Entrance. These time-fused torpedoes fired, Micky Wynn set off at 0230 for the sea down river, while Commander Ryder moved into midstream to check the position, coming between the wrecks - five MLs were now blazing hulks - to within 250 yards (230m) of the Mole's batteries as Able Seaman Savage and his mate, AB F.A. Smith, fired into the outer emplacement, silencing its 20mm gun. However, the Mole was still held by Germans, and moving back to the Old Entrance Bob Ryder saw that somebody - a party from an ML? Germans? - had manned *Campbeltown*'s oerlikons and was firing across the entrance. The MGB's decks and meagre cabin spaces were covered with wounded, many being hit for a second and third time, and so the Commander decided the MGB must withdraw, although he was reluctant to leave.

There were six miles of gauntlet to run before reaching the open sea, and some damaged craft limped through this passage while others were still able to set off at some speed, making smoke cover with their special equipment. Micky Wynn used all his 3,000hp to make over 40 knots (75kph) until, with a neat piece of boat handling, he stopped alongside two men on a Carley float life-raft. This few seconds' pause was all the German gunners needed to set MTB 74 on fire. ML 6, caught in a searchlight, was also hit and afire, and survivors from the two craft drifted down river on rafts, many of them badly wounded - Micky Wynn had lost an eye and been rescued unconscious from the MTB's charthouse. Later that Saturday afternoon, about 1400 hours, three of them, including Micky Wynn, were picked up by German patrol boats; a fourth man, Able Seaman Len Denison, swam to a concrete pile in the river. They were the only survivors from the 36 aboard the MTB and ML 6.

ML 14 which had not landed her commandos because their leader and the boat's skipper were both badly wounded, was one of the last boats to reach the Old Mole. A little after 0530 hours she was 45 miles (72km) from the estuary, when she crossed the tracks of the Wolfe-Möwe destroyers, sent out earlier that night to sweep for mines that the Germans thought had been laid by the British force. The first two passed the ML in the dark but *Jaguar* came to investigate, snapping on her searchlight as she closed on the ML in the start of an hour-long ship-to-ship fight. The ships struck in a glancing blow that rolled some men off the ML's deck, and on the next pass the small destroyer came within 100 yards, firing two of her three 105mm (4.1in) guns and her 20mm guns into the ML. Sergeant Tom Durrant, Royal Engineers and 1 Commando, was badly wounded in the first exchange of fire as the ML's commandos and naval crew brought their light weapons to bear on the German destroyer. When the gunner on the after twin-Lewis was killed, Tom Durrant took over although he already had several serious wounds, and he collapsed still firing these guns at the German destroyer on her third or fourth attempt to approach the ML.

Before the wooden boat sank, however, her crew were taken off and treated with the utmost courtesy by Kapitän Leutnant F.K. Paul, who accepted the ML's surrender: a tribute he paid to a gallant foe, and evidence if this is needed that chivalry is the prerogative of individuals, not nations. Tom Durrant died aboard the destroyer, honoured by his enemies as well as his friends.

As the MGB came out of the river, Able Seaman Bill Savage was found dead at his gun before the boat reached her destroyer escorts waiting at sea. These had already had a brief clash with the German destroyers and now headed north with the MGB were MLs 5 and 15, but ML 15 had to be abandoned. Four other MLs reached England - ML 8 made the passage on one engine and MLs 6, 12 and 13 had some damage and casualties.

About 1030 on Saturday morning, HMS *Campbeltown's* warhead blew up, bursting the caisson: the river poured into the dry dock. There is no reason to believe any of the raiders were aboard at the time, although

Men of 6 Commando return from raid north of Plage St. Cecily (France) 4 June 1942.

two rumours have persisted through the years. The French believed there were British officers aboard, and others think someone came back to fire the explosive, for there was more than an hour's delay on the set time. However, the only unauthorised visitors appear to have been souvenir hunters and men foraging among the stores. By 1030 all those with the knowledge to blow up the warhead were dead or prisoners. There seems every likelihood that faulty fuses caused the delay.

Throughout the day the Germans were unusually jittery, and several French men and women were killed in mistake for commandos. But by Sunday night order was restored, although at least one German officer was shot at while driving through the town - probably by Germans of another unit. On Monday the docks were re-opened and the stevedores were at work when Micky Wynn's first torpedo exploded at 1600 hours; an hour later the second one went off. French workmen fleeing from the dock were fired on because the Germans thought this was an organised rising, the explosions coming so long after the raid that they took them to be the work of the Free French Resistance Movement and threatened reprisals if the 'revolt' did not stop. There is little doubt that some Frenchmen fired on Germans during the raid and afterwards, although on this occasion no hostages were shot. Nevertheless, already 16 French were dead, including a child of five and a man of 76.

In addition to this price for their success, the Allies had lost 169 raiders killed and about 200 taken prisoner. Comparisons in blood are an inadequate measure of courage or military achievement, but these raiders' losses were a far greater proportion of their force - 369 from 611 army and naval personnel - than were lost in the World War I blocking of Zeebrugge when 195 men were killed from a force of 1,784.* But whereas the submarine pens were re-opened within four days in 1918, after the St Nazaire raid this dry-dock was not repaired until the 1950s - one reason perhaps why the British were not popular with all the townsfolk for many years afterwards.

*Figures given in the detailed study of the raid by C.E. Lucas Phillips: *The Greatest Raid of All* - William Heinemann Ltd., London, 1958.

Large and small raids continued, with the SBS 101 Troop sending a canoe into Boulogne on the night of 11-12 April, three weeks after the St Nazaire raid. Originally Stan Weatherall and Guardsman R. Sidlow were to accompany Captain Gerald Montanaro RE with Trooper Freddie Preece RAC, in two canoes. But as the weather was rough, the Troop commander went with his paddler and the other canoe team stayed ashore. Launched from ML 102, the two raiders had a mile or so to paddle on a compass course through choppy water into the harbour where, as the canoe surged on the swell alongside a large ship, they reached down underwater to fix their eight limpet mines. Tightening the butterfly nuts on these magnet limpets broke the glass phials, so setting chemical time-fuses (see Appendix 3) before the raiders turned their canoe back to sea on a reciprocal course for the motor launch. They barely reached it, for the seas had got up and the waterlogged canoe was foundering as they were hauled to safety. A few days later the Troop were shown aerial photographs of five tugs towing the sinking ship towards a sandbank, where she settled with her cargo of 5,000 tons of copper. The Germans are said to have shot 100 French hostages in reprisal for this sinking which they thought was the work of the Resistance.

Raiding was now growing apace with Lord Mountbatten's wish for 'a raid every fortnight' in addition to the smaller raids of the SBS and other units who were joining the ranks of the commandos. On 21-22 April, 100 men of 4 Commando, with 50 Canadians, landed from six LCAs at the village of Hardelot (see map p. 28) in a reconnaissance in force. Their leader Lord Lovat thought their safe return was due to 'the opposition being half-hearted or badly trained' and not to any skill on the raiders' part. Three sailors were killed nevertheless by the defenders.

In May, following these forays, Hitler had his first top-level meeting to discuss the western defences with the Todt Organisation, and plans were begun for the so-called Atlantic Wall, although there already existed a series of defended ports and the original defence arrangements set up when fleets of craft were being assembled for an invasion

Crossing the beach defences of 1942 needed the guts to dive at a stake holding concertina wire, flatten it, and let the rest of the Section run over the resulting gap - if not over the back of the man who made it.

of England. The Wall itself never became a complete line of defences.

Among those who would join the commandos in probing these defences were the men of the Small Scale Raiding Force (SSRF), responsible jointly to Lord Mountbatten and SOE. In the spring of 1942, Major Gus March-Phillips, Major J. Geoffrey Appleyard, who served with 7 Commando in the autumn of 1940, and Captain Graham Hayes had the SSRF in training at Wareham (Dorset), where they did a lot of boat work, especially in dories. They trained to land in various numbers, although in later years some nine men made up the team in a powered dory. With their SOE connexions, the SSRF found a dory more suitable than canoes when landing an agent who wanted to melt into the local scene rather than stagger ashore dripping wet from a canoe. In collecting agents, however, canoes were quite suitable and Geoffrey Appleyard made several 'collections' from enemy beaches. Once, landing from the submarine HMS *Tigris*, his fellow canoeist - a Free French soldier - lost his boat in rough water, but they managed to get back to the submarine. The next night Geoffrey Appleyard went in alone, and after scouting round for the two agents he was to meet, he abandoned all caution, running up and down the beach shouting for them and waving his torch. They appeared at last and

he got them safely off in one canoe. The Germans could not man every half-mile - never mind every yard - *and* campaign in Russia. However, the ambiguities under the SOE cloak of secrecy had repercussions for all commandos, for they were strictly uniformed troops, even if they sometimes appeared off enemy coasts under flags of convenience.

Two of these raids, however, had special significance to our story. On the night of 12/13 September 1942, Gus March-Phillips and Graham Hayes, with nine men, were landed in a Goatley boat (see Appendix 4) at St Honoriné near the Cherbourg peninsula. Geoff Appleyard was in the MTB - he had an injured leg from a previous raid - when he heard the landing party ambush some seven Germans in a patrol before the raiders were in turn ambushed by a larger force. They reached their boat, but the Germans were there before them and Gus March-Phillips was killed along with three others. The flimsy canvas-sided boat sank, leaving Graham Hayes to swim along the coast. With the help of several Frenchmen he eventually reached Spain, but this neutral country's police handed him back to the Gestapo. This incident proved the danger to Special Forces when they sought sanctuary in a neutral country, for Graham Hayes was shot in a Paris prison in the summer of 1943. Also in

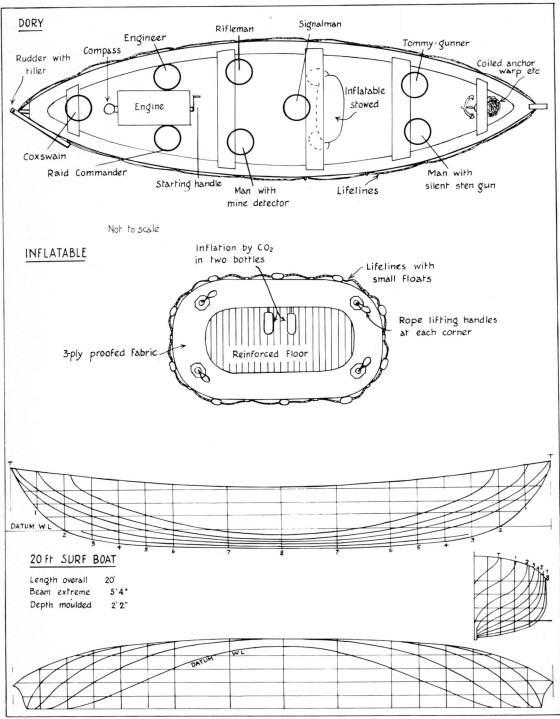

DORY

Rudder with tiller

Compass

Engineer

Rifleman

Signalman

Tommy-gunner

Coiled anchor warp etc

Engine

Inflatable stowed

Coxswain

Raid Commander

Starting handle

Man with mine detector

Lifelines

Man with silent sten gun

Not to scale

INFLATABLE

Inflation by $CO_2$ in two bottles

Lifelines with small floats

Rope lifting handles at each corner

3-ply proofed fabric

Reinforced Floor

DATUM W L

20 ft SURF BOAT

Length overall    20'
Beam extreme     5'4"
Depth moulded    2'2"

DATUM    WL

Raiding dory, inflatable and lines of SN6 Surf Boat.

1943, in July, Geoffrey Appleyard, who had gone on to help form the 2nd SAS Regiment in the Middle East, was reported missing presumed killed over Sicily where he was supervising an airdrop.

The second small raid of significance to the commando story came on 3-4 October 1942, when a few of the Small Scale Raiding Force and some men of 12 Commando landed on Sark in the Channel Islands. They took several prisoners, two of whom were killed in a later skirmish. There seems no doubt that the dead prisoners were handcuffed and this infuriated Hitler, who in October ordered that 'all enemy troops taking part in the so-called Commando operations . . . in uniform or not . . . whether in battle or whilst escaping . . . will be destroyed to the last man'.

The valour of these raiders was recognised after the destruction of the docks at St Nazaire by the award of the Victoria Cross to Lieutenant-Commander S.H. Beattie, Sergeant Tom Durrant, Lieutenant-Colonel Charles Newman, Commander R.E.D. Ryder, and Able Seaman William Savage. In the words of the citations for Sam Beattie's and 'Red' Ryder's awards, these recognised : not only the individual's valour but also that of a very gallant ship's company and the valour shown by many others of coastal forces. In all, 4 DSOs, 17 DSCs, 11 MCs, 4 Conspicuous Gallantry Medals, 24 DSMs, 14 MMs, 51 Mentions-in-Despatches, and 4 Croix de Guerre were awarded for this raid alone. One example may illustrate the nature of these awards: Michael Burn, who crossed the docks alone, had barely got ashore, being half-drowned by the weight of his equipment as he tried to swim to the dockside, and being rescued by Lance-Corporal Young. Yet the commando captain shook off the discomfort of this experience and went on to reach his objective. He was awarded the Military Cross. After the previous year's visits to Lofoten and Vaagsö, John Durnford-Slater and Peter Young had won decorations for their skill and bravery, and Gerald Montanaro and Trooper Preece were decorated. Men of the Small Scale Raiding Force on one raid alone were led by five officers none of whom survived the war, who would all earn awards for gallantry, including a VC, a DSO, and six Military Crosses. The valour is unquestioned, and although only the decorations of those officers and men mentioned in the unit histories of Appendix 7 are shown in this book, commandos would be - I believe - the first to accept that those who received awards usually owed a good deal to the support of their fellows, in spirit if not by arms.

Planning these raids had moved a long way in a few months, as explained in Chapter 10. This was in large measure due to their senior commanders; men like Brigadier Charles Haydon, whose report of February 1941 had done much to shape the commandos from an unwieldy collection of Troops expected to act independently, to a cohesive force of raiders in units suited to their various roles - the SBS for recce, the complete Commando for raids in force. There were no longer the possibilities for ship-based guerillas to flit along enemy coastlines, but now small parties could be landed and withdrawn in a fast-moving or underwater approach. The traditional British verve for raiding had been restored after too many years under the shadow of the World War I failures at Gallipoli.

Not all early raids were successful and the plan to raid Bayonne failed through lack of information on beach conditions. This raid would have cut all railway and road bridges in this area between France and Spain, on the *same* night that St Nazaire was raided, in the original plans. But when the LSIs *Princess Beatrix* and *Queen Emma* with 1 and 6 Commandos had 'crept along the north coast of Spain undetected' in their disguise as Spanish merchantmen, the LCAs came in to find long and heavy Atlantic swells pounding a bar across the target beaches in the river Ardour estuary. Many of the craft would have been lost and commandos were not hazarded in foolish risks, although often taking calculated chances. They re-embarked and returned to the UK after more than a month at sea.

# SOME NAVAL ASPECTS OF AMPHIBIOUS WARFARE IN WORLD WAR II

Allied navies were equipped for hydrographic surveys by submarines and other ships measuring offshore currents and scouting the channels to a landfall. But new techniques were needed to find landing points for assault craft and ships, for not only minor craft and major craft (LCTs etc) would be put ashore but also Landing Ships Tank (LSTs) of over 300 feet (90+m) weighing 4,080 short tons would beach. Assault craft and ships on a beach too shallowly shelved might ground by the stern, leaving their bows in water too deep for vehicles or men to cross without risk of drowning, while vehicle-carrying craft on a steeply inclined beach might not ground firmly enough to offload their cargoes.

Once the landing points had been selected, the navies had to escort the assault troops' ships to their dropping zones, sweeping mine-free passages for both LSIs and assault craft. These were marshalled into their landing sequence before the run inshore while a bombardment by naval and air forces covered the approach. Pre-assault bombardments were made when surprise was unnecessary, as in most Pacific island assaults when the Japanese could not reinforce a garrison. The American army engineer Underwater Demolition Teams (UDTs) and US Marine Corps recce squads worked near beaches under the cover of such bombardments often begun several days before a landing. Naval tactics early in the war avoided such ship-to-fort confrontations; but by 1943 the accepted practice was to blast coast defences, stripping them of camouflage, if not destroying their guns in sea and air bombardments that were timed so navy shells did not cut the path of straffing planes. The majority of aircraft in both Europe and the Pacific amphibious assaults were land-based, but carrier aircraft played their part.

In support of the build-up of beachheads, naval ships, directed by observers ashore with assault forces, fired on shore targets. Refuelling and re-ammunitioning these vessels and those protecting an anchorage involved a complex fleet-train of ships in the Pacific, sometimes operating nearly 2,000 miles (3,700+km) from its nearest land-base.

# 3  ASSAULT PILOTAGE

The Allied raiding forces would include many units with special skills, landing not only on the Channel coast of France but across the world from northern Norway to the South Pacific. Belgians of 10 Commando would land in the Adriatic, US Marine Corps raiding battalions operated in the Pacific; and American Army Rangers landed alongside the commandos in Europe and spearheaded the Philippines landings. All depended on the navy and sometimes on the air force to land them at least somewhere near their target beaches.

Lieutenant-Commander Nigel Clogstoun-Willmot RN, navigating officer of the force intended to raid Rhodes in the summer of 1941, thought of his uncle with the Australians, while planning the beach reconnaissance. They had landed with the Anzacs at Gallipoli, when the battleships were deterred by fear of mines after HMS *Irresistible* and HMS *Ocean* were mined in the Dardanelles on 18 March 1915. Other ships had also been lost in World War I while navigating other narrows where there is the added risk of going aground. Indeed, more than half the Allied ships lost off Norway in 1940 foundered on shoals or rocks, as Nigel Clogstoun-Willmott knew from his service aboard a Q-ship in that campaign. With searoom a prerequisite of safe ship handling, naval training and other deep-water seamanship has always been more concerned, therefore, with keeping clear of land than with approaching beaches. There would be precious little searoom off the beaches in amphibious landings, and putting a 4,000-ton assault ship ashore was at one time thought so hazardous that none was expected to survive. Yet they did. However, such risks could be taken only with very exact knowledge of the shore - where changes of the undersea bed are highly variable in comparison with the unchanging contours ashore. In the Pacific, coral reefs were even less adequately charted than the beaches of North Africa or the fjords of Norway, but as the techniques of assault pilotage developed, more details of the natural hazards became clear.

A ship could nevertheless be navigated accurately, especially when up-to-date hydrographic data was available from offshore surveys by submarines. The problem, therefore, was not one of technique, as much as training, for there were relatively few fully trained navigators in the Allied navies of 1940-41 and many training facilities were needed for air force navigators. These constraints put out of the question any prospect of training fully fledged navigators for the thousands of landing craft crews. At best they had a few lectures in coastal pilotage before joining the minor craft - those carried aboard ships. Officers in the major craft - the LCTs and LCIs (see Appendix 4) - had a little more training but not very much: navigation is a science not learnt in a four-week course.

In European waters there were coastal pilot handbooks, but these cautioned the sailor away from rocky beaches, the forbidding shores on which commandos expected to land. Many charts gave details only to the low-water lines, while maps cut off their contours at the high-water mark.

Nigel Clogstoun-Willmott, caught up in something of the optimism in the British Imperial Headquarters at Cairo after General Wavell's sweeping desert victories of December 1940, was aware of these and many more problems as he completed a survey through the periscope of a mine-laying submarine off the island of Rhodes, which lies close to the Turkish coast (see map p. 116). As the submarine nosed around the island's waters for three days, often making one and a half knots or less, there were a number of unanswered questions. Was that apparently empty fisherman's hut an abandoned home or a gun emplacement? Were there any hidden sand-bars a dozen yards from the beach, for a man could drown easily in the eight feet of water beyond them as in eighty?

In time, beach reconnaissance would become a scientific study of landing areas and their immediate hinterland - the littoral across which Nigel Clogstoun-Willmott's men would lead raiders and the van of invasions, guiding the landing craft crews with marker canoes and other devices that in part at least made up for these flotillas' limited experience of coastal navigation. However, there was nothing over-scientific about the Commander's first beach reconnaissance. Nor were some of the earlier beach reconaissances the most encouraging of precedents, although Clogstoun-Willmott did not know this at the time. Another officer, Lieutenant-Commander Milner Gibson RN, who led in crash boats on the raid near Boulogne in 1940, had made nine reconnaissances in the three weeks before that raid, going ashore alone probably in a dinghy. An officer who had lived on Guernsey also made a reconnaissance of that island before Ronnie Tod and John Durnford-Slater visited it in their July raid the same year. But in both cases the pre-raid recces were not much help on *the* night, for Milner-Gibson's compass failed and the German dispositions on Guernsey were changed by the time of the raid.

In preparing for his reconnaissance of Rhodes, the Commander had set himself an exacting routine of training, with long-distance swimming and other exercises hardening his physical endurance: habits of training his men would later find exhausting almost to the point of mutiny. That January in 1941 the plans were entirely personal, however, because Nigel Clogstoun-Willmott had difficulty persuading the Force Commanders that there was anything to be gained from beach reconnaissance. All too easily they feared, a recce might leave traces of the visit which, even if the lone navigator was not captured, could give away the intended landing point for an assault force. Throughout these reconnaissances, therefore, the raiders went to extreme lengths - even possibly to self-destruction - to avoid being caught or their special gear falling into enemy hands, for its nature made clear the purpose of the visit. However, Nigel Clogstoun-Willmott, swimming into the beaches at Rhodes, with his army compass covered in periscope grease and his water-proofed torch in its rubber sheaths of issue contraceptives, was unlikely to reveal his purpose.

He made this reconnaissance with Captain Roger Courtney, of the SBS, who had been in the Mediterranean for some months after training around Arran in Scotland. They were introduced by the commanding officer of Layforce, Brigadier Laycock, other exploits of Roger Courtney are described later in Chapter 8. The army Captain taught the Commander the knack of hoisting himself aboard a canoe over its stern, and how to vault astride one steadied by a paddler already aboard. He learnt then and in later practice how to jump into a bobbing canoe, letting his feet give under him without capsizing the frail Folbot. He became adept at launching himself over the canoe's side; first leaning back with legs outstretched athwart the cockpit, a quick flip of the body brought him face down towards the water before lowering himself onto it. Although this may sound a simple piece of gymnastics it was no parlour trick at night with a sea running and the canoe's stability always in doubt.

The first action using any new technique is usually one of the most interesting, for the simple principles can be seen without any complications of secondary purposes or complicated gear, and this is true of the first beach reconnaissance at Rhodes. The army captain and the naval navigator practised swimming ashore at night, taking turns to act the part of a sentry while the other stalked around the acting guard until this could be done without the swimmer being detected. A stone hurled at a raised arm splashing casually in the approach, or the noise of stones crunched underfoot, was sufficient reminder of more deadly missiles that would come the way of a careless visitor on an enemy beach. In these practice runs the characters of the two canoeists contrasted: Nigel Clogstoun-Willmott, tall, good looking, and in his early thirties, meticulous over details with the mathematical approach of a navigator in facing the problems; Roger Courtney, as we have seen in training off Arran, a heavily built man, something of the adventurer with the flair for improvisation in a tight corner. For all their mutual confidence in each other and their shared patience - although one suspects from the records that the navigator had more of this essential quality than the adventurer - each brought his own special talents to this technique of beach reconnaissance. Nigel Clogstoun-Willmott has described it as an art 'needing the patience of an animal', and undoubtedly there would be times when physical strength and endurance were the key to survival, for survive they must to make any contribution from their efforts. For men on beach reconnaissance had further to go than the saboteur or the raider bent on mere disruption: the reconnaissance report had to reach the main force.

In March 1941 the drill was very simple, but in later years all manner of complexities were necessary. Nevertheless, landing in heavily greased jerseys and long-john underwear, with a revolver in a supposedly waterproof packet and carrying the waterproofed torch and compass, was difficult enough after several days in the confined quarters of submarine HMS *Triumph* while she made a periscope survey of Rhodes' beaches, often having to dive below 60 feet (18m), because in these clear waters a submarine at shallower depth is plainly seen from the air. On reconnaissance nights, the submarine had to use precious hours of moonless darkness while she charged her batteries before trimming down in the water with her saddle-tanks just awash, the slight swell breaking occasionally over the casing. Ratings now steadied the canoe as it was put over the side, lying on the hydroplanes. They took a soaking no doubt relieved in an attitude of 'rather you than me, mate' as they watched the canoeists jump and sit in one motion the way they had practised boarding. Already aboard were a tommy-gun, grenades, a thermos of coffee laced with brandy - they would need this - and the infra-red signalling gear. This 'RG' equipment (see Appendix 3) sent a beam of invisible infra-red light from an Aldis-type lamp, the signal being visible only when the beam was on the little black box camera-sized receiver with a screen which, when the beam was intercepted, showed a green spot against a speckle of green pin-pricks of infra-red light from the stars.

Once cast off from the submarine they began the steady rhythm of paddling that took them along their course with a mile and a half to the beach, their sweat-raising stroke giving 3 knots - equal to a steady walking pace. A hundred yards from the beach Nigel Clogstoun-Willmott followed the drill and went over the side. The sharp cold, after his warm exertions, took his breath away for a moment as he hung on the stern of the canoe, but as soon as he had recovered his breath, the Commander struck out for the shore in a strong breaststroke that did not disturb the phosphorescence more than he could help, and barely ruffled the water. As his feet touched the bottom he was thinking of the tanks the Allies had intended to land on the rocky promontory before him; clearly this was not possible, for now in the starlight he could see its rock face was impassable.

He swam back into the bay and along the coast some hundred yards before swimming in again. The sand felt firm here under his feet and he dog-paddled while checking the depth before easing on shore to lie with his chin on pebbles at the water's edge, hearing the talk of sentries and just able to make out two figures behind a wall beyond the beach. In the surge of each wave he slithered forward until, for a moment, he felt the sentries' eyes turned towards him; he froze clenching his teeth to stop their chattering. Several minutes rock still and the sentries no doubt mistook him for a part of the shore over which the seas were gently breaking. The Italians moved off, and the Commander crossed the beach to a road. Making four landings in this way at different points along the shore, Nigel Clogstoun-Willmott discovered a number of things. There was a false beach 15 yards (13m) from the shore, the water on the shore side deep enough to drown a tank. In the grounds of the hotel used as an Axis headquarters, he heard a sentry yawn but found no guns. Shingle samples were stuffed under the navigator's jersey. From these scientists could calculate whether a metal road was needed across the beach or if tanks could pass over it without help from engineers, and what size of wheeled vehicles could pass over the pebble bank. Next time he came on one of these recces he would bring a bag for these trophies, but the chinagraph pencil had worked well in noting on his slate the depths of water and the position of that false beach.

Checking his watch he saw it was time to swim back to the canoe and his rendezvous with Roger Courtney, who had been paddling offshore for the last few hours, keeping the canoe head or stern towards the beach so that it was less likely to be seen. The stimulus of the Commander's benzedrine tablets was wearing off as he swam out to sea after three hours' creeping and sliding around the beach, and now, his senses dulled by a chilling exhaustion, he felt the first pangs of doubt: would Roger Courtney see the flickering torch among the waves before an enemy patrol boat caught sight of it? He summoned all his will power, forcing numbed fingers in his upstretched arm to flash again the morse 'R'. Out of the darkness came Roger Courtney with firm, fast paddle strokes bringing the canoe alongside the Commander. The commando had been waiting with disciplined patience some 400 yards (365m) out. Every time he lifted the cap of his luminous watch the hands seemed to have barely moved, but now he hauled Nigel Clogstoun-Willmott into the canoe and passed him the flask of coffee. The swig merely prickled the swimmer's gums - beach reconnaissance teams usually spoke of 'the swimmer' as the man who went ashore and 'the paddler' as the man staying with the canoe. A gulp from the coffee thermos, however, brought the first faint warmth to his bones as they paddled into a thickening mist. This cleared and the submarine picked up their infra-red signals, taking them back aboard before continuing her patrol.

They made landings on each of the following four nights, the last when Roger Courtney was the swimmer, being a near disaster. Gripped with cramp at the water's edge he could not move, and the furious barking of a dog drew Nigel Clogstoun-Willmott inshore, his tommy-gun cocked. The swimmer's great frame was contorted in agony, yet he struggled out to the canoe and with a supreme effort of will got aboard in a tortuous heave. As they returned from these reconnaissances with a good deal of useful information, authority was pleased. However, the invasion of Rhodes was cancelled when German troops came into the fighting in Greece. Nigel Clogstoun-Willmott went back to his planning duties, although he did one more beach reconnaissance ahead of ships' detachments of Royal Marines landing on Kupho island (off Crete) in a modest raid that destroyed a radar station, and might have brought back code books had not their metal safe been lost as a ship's boat tilted in being hauled aboard a destroyer gathering speed. Roger Courtney went back to the raiding of the SBS which we will follow in later Chapters.

The Combined Operations' planners were in Richmond Terrace near Whitehall, yet conveniently distant from service ministries. Here in May 1942 - before the raid on Dieppe that August - plans were being made for the landings in North Africa that would put an American Task Force ashore on the Atlantic coast near Casablanca, a second force ashore at Oran in the Mediterranean, and a third further east at Algiers. Nigel Clogstoun-Willmott was ordered home to the United Kingdom that summer as beach reconnaissance was part of the Allied plans for these 'Torch' landings, but final approval for training the necessary teams was not cleared until 8 September, a mere eight weeks before the date for this invasion. This illustrated the urgency of many commando and other wartime activities when the time needed to set up a special operation was almost impossibly short, but the official records do not show the efforts behind the scenes in preparing the ground. The Commander, having decided the personnel he hoped might join him, contacted several, but needed official approval and Lord Mountbatten's support in recruiting Lieutenant Neville McHarg RN, a conscientious navigator and Lieut Norman Teacher RN to the teams. In October, an increase in the number of landing points for Torch led to Roger Courtney's brother coming to assist with the training of the beach reconnaissance canoeists.

The equipment they had at Rhodes hardly justified the risks in getting ashore to use it, but the Commander had improved the original ideas and over the next two years a comprehensive yet simple range of tools would be devised for this survey work. The training would also become increasingly complex, with landings from midget submarines late in 1943 and early in 1944, but in October 1942 the best that could be produced were canoes to get the swimmer inshore and a cumbersome rubberised canvas suit of the type used by charioteers riding human torpedos. The canoes were improved in a seamanlike fashion with a canvas canopy buttoned round the paddlers and air bladders around the cockpit and sides (see p. 25 and Appendix 4). But all their training that October was put to limited use, for after they had flown to Gibraltar, the Admiralty forbade any landings, the Flag Officer Gibraltar considering these would compromise security and warn the French of the invasion. The teams of paddlers (some of them from the SBS) and the navigators therefore spent two weeks making periscope reconnaissances, drawing the profiles of the hinterland to target beaches. Copies of these could be used by landing craft flotillas and at

least one survey showed an intended landing point for trucks was backed by impassable cliffs - shades of Rhodes. After these reconnaissances during October, a final reconnaissance was made a few days before the invasion, by the teams going inshore one night so that each navigator could show the paddlers their canoes' positions as navigational marks guiding in the assault waves on D-day. (For convenience planners referred to D-day, or Z-day early in the war, as the day of a landing and H-hour as the time of landing. The day after landing was then D+1, the minute after landing 'H+1 minute' and so on.)

Guiding in a main force became the second phase of assault pilotage, for having reconnoitred a beach some weeks or months before a landing, these teams had the most up-to-date knowledge of local conditions. At the Torch and some other landings they also supplied navigators on the leading assault waves in the Mediterranean; men of the US Engineer Special Service Brigades did a somewhat similar job in the Casablanca part of the operation. During the final canoe-position recces for Torch, a sudden storm caught those of the eastern reconnaissance, and Lieutenant L.G. (Geoff) Lyne RN with Commando Thomas as paddler were in its teeth. Fight as they did to keep the canoe on course they were driven westward of Castiglione (near Sidi Ferruch) when they should have been east of this port. They strove to keep the canoe's bows heading into steep seas while they baled with tin mugs whenever there was a moment's let-up in the fury. They had an hour to get back to the rendezvous with their submarine when the storm strengthened, tossing them high on one wave before they slithered off its back to meet the next great sea, all the time in danger of broaching-to across the waves that could then roll them over. One great comber filled the canoe before she shook free from the cascading crests; now they could not expect to make much headway and had to fight even harder to avoid broaching-to. They flashed signals more in hope than expectation of catching the submarine's attention before dawn broke and the wind abated, giving them their first chance to force free fingers locked around the paddle

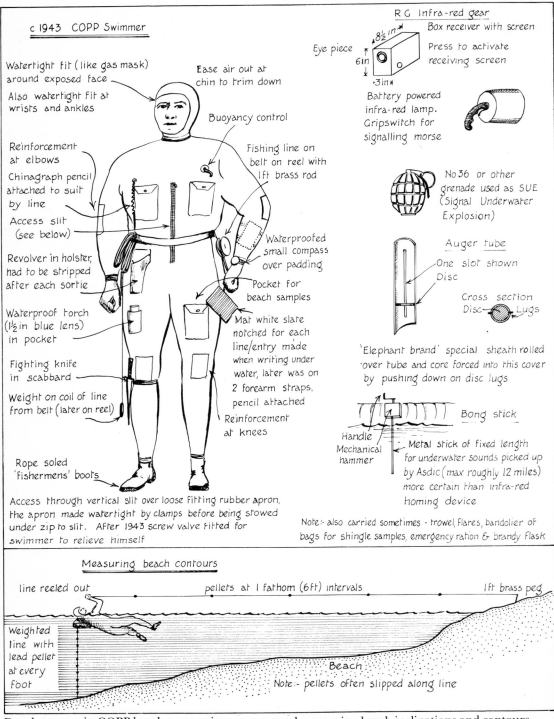

c 1943 COPP Swimmer

Watertight fit (like gas mask) around exposed face

Also watertight fit at wrists and ankles

Reinforcement at elbows

Chinagraph pencil attached to suit by line

Access slit (see below)

Revolver in holster, had to be stripped after each sortie

Waterproof torch (1½ in blue lens) in pocket

Fighting knife in scabbard

Weight on coil of line from belt (later on reel)

Rope soled 'fishermens' boots

Ease air out at chin to trim down

Buoyancy control

Fishing line on belt on reel with 1ft brass rod

Waterproofed small compass over padding

Pocket for beach samples

Mat white slate notched for each line/entry made when writing under water, later was on 2 forearm straps, pencil attached

Reinforcement at knees

Access through vertical slit over loose fitting rubber apron, the apron made watertight by clamps before being stowed under zip to slit. After 1943 screw valve fitted for swimmer to relieve himself

R G Infra-red gear

Box receiver with screen

Eye piece

8½ in

6 in

3 in

Press to activate receiving screen

Battery powered infra-red lamp. Gripswitch for signalling morse

No 36 or other grenade used as SUE (Signal Underwater Explosion)

Auger tube

One slot shown

Disc

Cross section
Disc — Lugs

'Elephant brand' special sheath rolled over tube and core forced into this cover by pushing down on disc lugs

Bong stick

Handle
Mechanical hammer

Metal stick of fixed length for underwater sounds picked up by Asdic (max roughly 12 miles) more certain than infra-red homing device

Note:- also carried sometimes - trowel, flares, bandolier of bags for shingle samples, emergency ration & brandy flask

Measuring beach contours

line reeled out

pellets at 1 fathom (6ft) intervals

1ft brass peg

Weighted line with lead pellet at every foot

Beach

Note:- pellets often slipped along line

Developments in COPP beach reconnaissance gear and measuring beach inclinations and contours.

handles in a muscle-spasm grip. Two miles offshore they were seen by a French trawler and taken aboard, not before Geoff Lyne had time to slit the airbags, sinking the canoe with its tell-tale gear.

Others were on the edge of the storm and Nigel Clogstoun-Willmott had a wild ride with young Sub-Lieutenant White, who was having his first introduction to canoe reconnaissance. The canoe of Edwards and Mangnall - 200 miles to the west of the Commander - found the only way to escape the playful attentions of porpoises was to stop paddling. For another team, more dangerous company appeared when the local fishing fleet came out, and the paddlers bent over, face down in the canoe, keeping her stern-on to the newcomers by deft tweaks of the paddles as they drifted less than 30 yards from two boats. These fishing fleets would continue to be a hazard for reconnaissance parties, and by the summer of 1943 there were often several German guards with each fleet to prevent the smuggling of people or information between the Allies and occupied territories.

On the night of 7 November the teams were again off the North African coast ready to flash their signal lights and RG infra-red beams along the limit lines on the flanks of target beaches. In deteriorating weather the force commander aboard the transport USS *Samuel Chase* was considering whether to carry his craft inshore before launching them, and Lieutenant-Commander Nigel Clogstoun-Willmott's advice was sought. He insisted the force keep to their plan, and aboard the leading assault craft he led the flotilla from confusion caused when the carriers, drifting on a current, launched the craft some way from the intended dropping zone. The landing craft's compass was not properly 'swung', and using the north star for a back-bearing the Commander brought this LC Vehicle (LCV) on to the correct beach. Among the five teams working that night was Stan Weatherall with Sub-Lieutenant Peter Harris RNVR, marking the limit of Arzew beach where the American Rangers would land. His canoe was launched at 1900 hours on Saturday night, 7 November, and paddled the six miles (10km)

inshore while their submarine, HMS *Ursula*, steamed further out to act 11 miles (18km) offshore as a beacon for the approaching troop convoys. There was a fresh breeze and the canoe shipped water in a choppy sea as it was launched, forcing the paddlers to ditch all their gear except a tommy-gun, a Colt 45, and their signalling equipment. The baler was washed forward into the bow so they baled with their berets, taking turns to paddle and resisting the temptation to lean forward and clout the porpoises darting at the bow. They dropped their kedge anchor 200 yards offshore and settled down to await the first wave of assault craft. In the next three hours they heard and saw nothing ashore before setting up the signal light and infra-red beam at 0015 that Sunday morning: an hour or so later the first craft - carrying the Rangers - came past, some 10 minutes late. As they had no receiver to check the RG gear, they also flashed a Z by red torch signalling the centre of Z beach. The final wave of the initial assault, LC Mechanised carrying jeeps and tanks, went by at 0415, making a bow wave that flirted the canoe aside, and a quarter of an hour later this canoe team followed the craft ashore. Anyone who has been alongside a ship when he or she is in a small boat knows the way she towers over you at a dockside. At sea the ship can appear enormous, and even minor landing craft travelling at a brisk trot were a hazard to canoes, for the minor LC's blunt bow pushed out a small wall of water. A tank landing ship (LST) bow's wave could be one or two feet high.

Ashore, Stan Weatherall and Peter Harris followed the general practice in a beachhead: lending a hand where they could. They paddled out carrying some kedges for craft that would then tow themselves off to these anchors, and with nothing more to be done on Z Red beach they paddled round to Z Green. Here they were 'captured' by Rangers who thought the canoeists were enemy torpedo riders - human torpedoes. The confusion cleared up, the paddlers left the beach at 0625, nearly 12 hours after they had been launched from their submarine. A tow to the SS *Reina Del Pacifico* was followed by a wash in the Chief Petty Officers' quarters, interrupted by two hits on the ship from a French battery, and when the canoeists came back on deck they found the canoe had been stripped by souvenier hunters, who now began asking for autographs. Other pilotage parties had seen mixed fortunes: Don Amer's help was spurned by one flotilla officer who managed later to put his cargo personnel ashore 1½ miles (over 2km) off their target. However, the value of assault pilotage was recognised at Combined Operations headquarters.

Many other lessons were learnt from the Torch landings, which would never have succeeded against serious opposition. The problems became clear in marshalling hundreds of landing craft as big as single-decker buses, but without any brakes, in a confined seaway. They would need all the help they could get from beach surveys and marker canoes, so 50 Combined Operations Assault Pilotage Parties (COPPs) were proposed. However, there were never the trained navigators nor Royal Engineer specialists available to recruit this number, and in all some 11 teams were trained. Their organisation (see Appendix 2) was flexible so that any man could do most of the jobs. All were trained canoeists and they were, in Commander Clogstoun-Willmott's words, to become 'Rolls Royce equipped commandos'. Before they reached this happy state, however, they were to carry through several operations and long hours of dangerous training from their base at the Hayling Island Sailing Club on an isolated spit of land called Sandy Point on Hayling Island (near Portsmouth, Hampshire). Near there one night their training officer, Geoff Gal-

COPP-type canoe set up as marker with masthead light (date not known but probably late 1944), when canoeists provided navigation guide lights for incoming assault craft.

wey, had one - probably of several - anxious moments while his swimmer, Major Scott-Bowden, was stuck fast in mud before an incoming tide, but the canoe floated the stuck swimmer and his paddler free when the tide rose. The base was run in the manner expected from Nigel Clogstoun-Willmott, with no concessions to careless habits or moments of inattention which could cost lives on a beach.

In February 1943 two parties went to reconnoitre the Sicily beaches, after some frustration in Algiers. Their senior officer, Lieutenant-Commander Norman Teacher RN, was only thirty years old and one of COPPs' greatest difficulties in the early days was persuading senior command staffs to listen to the young navigators. The sometimes lethargic HQ at Algiers needed a prod from Lord Mountbatten before COPPs 3 and 4 were sent on to Malta for the submarine approach to their recce. Here they met up with a team from the Combined Operations base in the Suez Canal Zone, with two canoe parties under Lieutenant Robert Smith RN. These seven officers and ten or so ratings had done rudimentary training with gear they bought mostly in the Cairo bazaar, and they were most interested in the COPPist's equipment, which included some new suits designed by Siebe Gorman but not tested fully by the wearers. The reconnaissance parties divided up their gear, to share out the better UK equipment, before COPP 3 sailed in HMS *Unbending* for a reconnaissance of the beaches between Sciaco and the river Belice, some 15 miles (24km) of coast on the south-west shores of Sicily.

A complete set of drills had been worked out by this time with, for example, five phases in recovering a swimmer after his recce. First he swam out shining his torch for the paddler to see. As there was always the chance that the swimmer's faint light might be missed and he might go beyond the canoe, in the next phase (two) he turned and shone his torch shorewards. Having collected his swimmer in phase one or two, the paddler now set course for the submarine rendezvous, beaming the infra-red light seawards in phase three and then, in phase

four shorewards when the submarine might have passed inshore of the canoe. Should they not be picked up, the paddlers made for a second rendezvous (phase five) further offshore or headed back to the beach to lie up for the following night, when the submarine would come to a different rendezvous. Each meeting-point was timed with as much leeway as moon and tide might allow - say an hour on occasions, although many submarine captains took bold risks in staying offshore beyond the agreed times when no recovery had been made, just in case the canoeists were late.

The tall and ever-cheerful Norman Teacher and his paddler Lieutenant Noel W. Cooper RNVR, were launched in a strong onshore wind but got away successfully from the submarine. Three hours later she was back at the rendezvous but there was no sign of the canoe, only the sound of surf breaking on the beach two miles away. The skipper was preparing to take her out to a second rendezvous arranged for that night when the lookouts saw the grey canoe with a lone paddler. Noel Cooper was lifted aboard: he had seen nothing of Norman Teacher since the Lieutenant swam off towards the shore. The next night, the burley George Burbridge, a captain in the Canadian Army, took a canoe into the beach to look for Norman Teacher but there was no sign of him. The team worked on several beaches that and the following two nights, recording the exact position of enemy strongpoints in places only 50 to 100 yards apart. They checked the beach incline and its contours, looking for points where minor craft could beach. They also checked possible 'berths' for major craft and LSTs, where more space was needed for a safe beaching and suitable ground on the beach for the LSTs' vehicles to deploy. These berths might also be improved for the build-up phase, by bulldozing earth ramparts to speed the off-loading of bulk stores carried by many LSTs. The team checked the incline for some 200 yards out from the beach at one point. On the fifth night they were dog-tired, having had little relaxing sleep in the cramped quarters of the submarine and spending several hours each day writing up their notes on the previous night's recce. Nevertheless George Burbridge and Noel Cooper went in once more: nothing was seen of them again.

No.4 COPP was to survey a beach on the north-west coast, and Neville McHarg with Lieutenant Sinclair paddled shorewards from HMS *Safari*. A confusion of fishing fleets, sardine nets, and the glare of flares silhouetting the submarine as Allied bombers attacked a nearby port forced them to withdraw. The next night, Captain Edward (Ted) Parsons RE and his paddler, Leading Seaman Irvine, prepared to land, Ted Parsons taking a ducking as he tried the first time to board the canoe in a nasty swell. They righted the boat, however, and got away at the second attempt. Ted Parsons had got ashore, but when lying rock-still he felt a gun behind his ear and was captured. Irvine was caught next day as he paddled along the coast.

Bob Smith and David Brand from HMS *United* got inshore on their first night's recce to find a long and unchartered sandbank off the south coast port of Gela, where the Rangers would land that summer. The next night Bob Smith took soundings over the stern of the canoe while David Brand held her steady as she bucked in a rising wind while they fixed the exact position of this bank. By midnight the weather was a deal worse and they caught the full force of the gale as they cleared the lee of the land, making their way towards the rendezvous. *United* was not there - or at least not where Bob Smith expected her - and an SUE charge (see diagram p. 62) tossed over the side failed to attract any attention. Going back inshore, a tough and, wet hour's paddling, they rechecked their bearing from the landmark of Casa Bittaleni, forcing their way back out into fierce seas. On this course David Brand's double paddle snapped. A second charge over the side brought no more response than the first, and a rising moon showed up the wild seascape. Three more hours of paddling and bailing, bailing and paddling, brought them to the second expected rendezvous, but in the great troughs and high seas the submarine lookouts could miss the torch signal or RG beam from a 16-foot (5m) canoe. By daylight it was

clear they had missed their rendezvous, and at about 0800 they set course for Malta, taking a back-bearing from Mount Etna. The overcast sky was merged with spume as the salt spray stifled easy breathing and they were losing their battle with fatigue after 20 hours' paddling. Consequently there was little they could do early that night when a mammoth sea caught them dangerously broached-to, but the buoyancy of Mae West lifejackets wedged in the bow and stern kept the waterlogged canoe afloat till the storm eased around midnight - some 24 hours after it blew up. David Brand's hip was weakening his strength as an old wound opened up after hours in the water, and now the canoe was little more than a tiny hulk. Nevertheless, Bob Smith kept edging her towards Malta and at first light they saw the island over the long swells following the storm. A patrolling MTB picked them up, and Bob Smith later launched the battered canoe to paddle her across the harbour to the submarine base.

HMS *United* was still at sea. Her second canoe, with Archie Hart and Eric Folder, had made a rough-and-tumble landing in heavy surf near Gela. Archie Hart's suit filled and perhaps incautiously he made a dash for the shelter of some dunes, where he hoped to drain it out. Unfortunately he ran into barbed wire that twanged a warning which brought a sentry along the beach, and Archie Hart was captured. Eric Folder was caught next day by two German guards in a fishing smack. The other Middle East commandos fared worse: Lieutenants de Kock and Crossley RNVR vanished after being launched from HMS *Unrivalled* on their first raid. Lieutenant Davis was caught ashore next night and his paddler, Able Seaman McGuire, was picked up by an armed fishing boat.

Despite these disasters all the submarines eventually returned to base, although HMS *Safari* had a lively homeward passage dodging searchlights, E-boats, and aircraft. Their attention may have been aroused by Ted Parson's cover story, every man going on beach reconnaissance having one carefully rehearsed - as Nigel Clogstoun-Willmott had rehearsed Roger Courtney off Rhodes: for the tenth time by one report! Ted Parsons's story involved a submarine's wrecking, but no doubt the Germans - if not the Italians - took this with some hefty pinches of salt. As for HMS *United* she had been on station at the rendezvous; but as it is barely possible to see a 10,000 tonner at 400 yards on a rough night there is little chance of seeing the recognition signals from a canoe when these torch or RG beams are a mere four feet (just over a metre) at arm's length above the waves.

A study of the failures at Sicily gave Nigel Clogstoun-Willmott three lines of thought: more training was essential - he had let Nos. 3 and 4 COPPs go out only with reluctance; more attention was needed in fitting the suits, for which these teams had not been adequately measured; and thirdly, the life-jackets they wore could not always be inflated in emergencies. The bravery of men swimming ashore in these pioneer beach reconnaissances is beyond question, and knowing Norman Teacher as a friend, as well as being his CO, the Commander feels there is a strong probability that the young Lieutenant made the supreme sacrifice in swimming to his death rather than risking his capture, as others, too, may have done. Having attended conferences with senior planning staff, they all had dangerous knowledge of the precise Allied intentions.

The development of COPPs forms part of the broader story told in later chapters, in which these teams' contribution to other major landings is shown. (For a summary of the COPP history see Appendix No.7). But in the late spring of 1943, Don Amer took No.6 COPP to the Med and was followed by Ralph Stanbury with No.5. Between them, these teams made a successful survey of the Allied landing beaches near Syracuse, and the work of No.3 off Gela was handed to the Americans. In the summer of 1943, the commander passed on his desk work at COHQ to Surgeon-Commander Murray Levick RN, an authority on endurance who was able to make major improvements in the COPPists' diet with more meat, fresh fruit, and other foods not readily available in the ration allowances for most units. Nigel Clogstoun-Willmott could now concentrate on the preparations for the Normandy landings, although he was still not fully fit after the months of hard training he did with his men.

The extent of Allied naval support for Special Forces is exampled by the navigational specialists provided for COPPs, in addition to Lieutenant-Commander (Navigation) Nigel Clogstoun-Willmott. Initially eight regular navy officers and one ex-merchant navy RN Reserve officer commanded COPPs: Lieutenants - Norman Teacher, (No. 3), A. Hughes (also No. 3), N. McHarg (No. 4), R. N. Stanbury (No. 5), Don Amer (RNR of No. 6), Geoff Hall (No. 7), Freddy Ponsonby (No. 8), Geoff Lynne, No. 9, and J. Townson (No. 10) who commanded this COPP throughout its time in the Adriatic.

Other aspects of naval support are briefly shown in the Beach Pilotage School on the Kyles of Bute (Scotland) that greatly improved landing craft crews navigation. While the cool courage of submarine crews in bringing canoe teams to beach areas cannot be over-emphasised. The skippers of the LSIs (described for brevity as LC carrier ships) were equally skilful, Commander T. B. Brunton, RN, bringing HMS *Princess Beatrix* on one engine from Bayonne to Falmouth, safely returning her commandos. The 'PB' was - in the Commander's words - 'the best seaboat . . . I ever had'. Other naval personnel became frogmen clearing obstacles including elements-C and diving to disarm Goliath beetle tanks off Normandy, later clearing river obstructions often under fire in north-west Europe.

Their senior officers believed in setting an example, Lord Mountbatten diving the one-man Welman submarine in a trial. 'At 28ft the front window cracked and I had a job getting up again' he writes, the Prime Minister did not approve of such risks by senior officers, but the CCO felt his men expected such leadership.

The interchange of amphibious ideas was common among the Allies, and Lord Mountbatten sketched the LCI(L) for General Marshall who had 300 built.

# THE FAR EAST, DECEMBER 1941 TO JULY 1942

Japanese forces, with four years' battle experience in China, were expected by the Imperial Command to destroy the American fleet in Pearl Harbour (Hawaii) in the early Sunday morning of 7 December 1941. This strike, which relied on diplomatic and military surprise, was to be followed by the occupation of the Philippines in 50 days, of Malaya in 100, and of the Dutch East Indies (Celebes, Borneo, and Java) by mid-summer.

Although the American fleet was destroyed, its aircraft carriers were at sea and unscathed. Nevertheless, the Japanese, with relatively few elements of their three-million strong army, achieved more rapid success than they had expected: by 11 January 1942 they had occupied the Celebes; on 4 February the Allies on Amboina surrendered; on 15 February Singapore fell; and on 19-20 February Timor was invaded, the main force of its defenders surrendering a few days later. All Allied regular forces had been withdrawn from Java and Sumatra, but guerrilla operations continued in Portuguese eastern Timor until early in 1943. Here the neutral Portuguese were prevented from reinforcing their garrison by Japanese command of the sea and air.

During March, the Japanese landed on the north coast of New Guinea, an island of high mountains and jungle twice the size of the British Isles. Over confident after their quick victories, the Japanese began an invasion of the Solomons and planned a landing at Port Moresby in south-east New Guinea. Occupying Guadalcanal among other Solomon Islands, they were checked when the invasion fleet had to be recalled before reaching Port Moresby, for an American naval task force, despite heavy losses, turned back the Japanese fleet on 5 May in the battle of the Coral Sea 300 miles (550km) south of Guadalcanal.

The Japanese were not going to win a short war for control of oil and other natural resources in south-east Asia. On Timor - for example - one of their 51 active divisions was deployed in 1942, only to be by-passed later in the Allied counterstrokes of 1942-43.

# 4 GUERRILLA WARFARE: AUSTRALIAN INDEPENDENT COMPANIES

Although getting to the right beach was the first logical step in amphibious raids - as the ISTD Centre had implied in their 1938 studies - the chronological development of these operations was less orderly. When Captain J. Michael Calvert RE arrived with Colonel Mawhood and the schoolmaster explorer, Captain F. Spenier Chapman, in Australia in November 1940, this small military mission was to teach methods of training 'a new variety of soldier': the commando. For the Australian army was among the first, if not *the* first, Allied service taking up the commando idea, even though they already had nearly four divisions overseas. The plan was to use Independent Companies for raids in the Middle East, and a sixth centre, a remote natonal park, a hundred miles south-east of Melbourne, was set up to train them. This at Mike Calvert's suggestion, was officially No.7 Centre so enemy agents might be confused in looking for No.6. Men from these Companies would be the first commando soldiers to fight a prolonged guerrilla war, not in the Middle East but in defence of the approaches to their homeland.

The officers were selected from established units, with colonels putting forward men like Lieutenant Bernard J. Callinan who were chosen for their independence of mind as well as soldiering ability. The Lieutenant had once leapt fully clothed into a river, demonstrating to a casual enquirer the purpose of a Royal Engineer's lifejacket as he continued building a bridge while swimming fully armed among the pontoons. Such incidents could influence the future not only of individuals but, in this case, of a whole series of skirmishes and mini-battles on the island of Timor. Officers and volunteer NCOs were trained at the centre for six weeks before joining the Independent Companies in which *volunteer* soldiers were trained for a further six weeks by their own officers. By the winter of 1941-42, four Companies had completed these and other courses, and a further four completed their training in 1942. Their brief histories are shown in Appendix 7. The campaign of the 2/2 Independent Company on Timor island would become a classic guerrilla campaign.

Nine out of ten of the 2/2 Independent Company were from the dry country districts of Western Australia, used to living in the bush, butchering their own meat, and improvising motor repairs - skills they found essential in living off the country in Timor and during their first year or so as an Independent Company stationed 250 miles (400km) south of Darwin in the little town of Katherine with its corrugated buildings, its one hotel and two stores. All these men were volunteers for world-wide service with the Second Australian Imperial Force, which provided the prefix 2 of the 2nd Company's number (the First AIF had served in World War I).

In December 1941, 2/2 Company sailed as part of Sparrow Force, 2,000 men in all mainly from the 2/40 Battalion going to reinforce the Dutch on western Timor, an

A patrol of the Australian 2/2 Independent Company on Timor - 'pigi, pigi' - as the native helpers lead the guerrilla's pony on a patrol forever going somewhere in 1942.

Captain R. R. Baldwin, Major B. J. Callinan (with magazine) and Captain E. Hennesey with Captain G. R. Dunkley and Major G. G. Laidlaw on Timor-Belulic, 17 November 1942. These officers of the 2/2 Independent Company had little relaxation in their 11 months on the island.

island seventeen times the area of England and Wales, about 300 miles (480+km) long and on average 40 miles (64km) wide. Only 13 to 35 degrees south of the equator, it is mostly arid hills covered with scrub and rises to 10,000 feet (3,040m) in the mountainous central regions. Around the coast and in river valleys there are stretches of tropical jungle with pythons and other snakes. Sparrow Force landed at the island's north-west port of Koebang to protect its airfield, but within a few days the Independent Company, with some Dutch troops, was sent east along the coast to occupy Dili in the Portuguese half of the island (see map p. 77) where they landed on 17 December 1941. The Company was 327 all ranks - for their war establishment, see Appendix 2 - with 60 tommy-guns between the three platoons. However, the effective force was soon down to 50 men: their issue shorts exposed men to malaria mosquitoes, and as the quinine powder had to be taken rolled in a cigarette paper - an anti-malaria dose many men dodged - illness spread quickly.

By the time the Japanese landed at Koebang on 19 February 1942, the main elements of Sparrow Force were also ravaged by malaria. They had only three or four NCOs who had seen action before, and 50 replacement troops had never fired a rifle before they reached Sparrow Force. As the Australians retreated eastwards, attempting to form a defence perimeter, 630 Japanese paratroops were dropped to snipe among them, slowing their retreat and allowing the battle-hardened elements of the Japanese 38 Division - some 5,000 men - to outflank the Australians' withdrawal. Although all but 78 paratroop snipers were killed, the Australians were forced to surrender within four days, leaving the 2/2 Independent Company and some Dutch troops to carry on the fight 160 miles (257km) to the east at Dili.

The Company's contacts with its parent force had been slight, and transmissions from their 109 wireless set (see Appendix 5) would not carry across the mountains and headlands to Koebang. However, their independence was no hardship as they exchanged stores for local honey, eggs, and other native produce. In January, one ship had visited Dili bringing four officers and some 50 reinforcements who apparently thought independence meant lack of discipline. Under an armed guard on their first night ashore they learnt the truth: as guerrillas, their discipline must be more ruthless than in regular forces for there are no guard-rooms or time for punishment details.

In the Dili area that winter, there were 300 Europeans and 5,000 native villagers working on their sweet potato, pineapple, and peanut plots or in the larger and more ordered government plantations on higher ground where crops of rice, maize, and coffee grew. Among the Europeans lived an elderly German whose papers were found with instructions to buy a plot of land on the south of the island 'overlooking the Timor Sea'. This was required, so the instructions read, for other than commercial reasons: a submarine refuelling point, perhaps. There had been a number of Japanese businessmen in the town whose interests appear also to have been 'other than commercial'. In this way, Axis governments anticipated a Pacific war that had been studied by only a few individuals in the Allies' interest.

The Dutch were discussing plans to evacuate their nationals when Bernard Callinan had a dinner one night at their headquarters. In the party was the British consul: the Australian David Ross. They had gone to bed after enjoying those mountains of rice and bowls of curried concoctions, no doubt, that were a feature of expatriates' meals in the east, when shouts and running feet stirred Bernard Callinan from his sleep. The thump of a shell hitting the far end of the barrack building brought him wide awake. It was 2310 hours on 19 February 1942. In minutes he was dressed and looking for his signallers at the Dutch HQ, for as second in command of the Company he must warn headquarters and the platoons in their hill positions above the town, as well as contacting Sparrow Force, whom he did not know were under attack the same night. Dodging the shell bursts' debris as branches fell from the large wahrazin trees above shallow trenches by the headquarters, Bernard Callinan could not make out what craft was shelling them, but through the mist he could hear the rumble of small boats' engines. Enemy searchlights probed in from the sea, going out before a renewed burst of shelling and heavy machine-gun fire added to civilian casualties in the town.

The Company's precautions in placing their platoons above the town now paid off. Lieutenant Gerry Mackenzie reported by telephone - the civilian network remained open long after the Japanese invasion - that he could see lights in the estuary of the Comoro river and a patrol went out for a quick recce. They confirmed there was a landing before the platoon moved down from the hill and astride the road west of Dili, where a Bren gun team caught a marching column of Japanese. These troops, clearly oblivious to danger, were at first thought to be a Dutch contingent, and had come so close that the Bren gunner could fire only two magazines before grenades knocked out his weapon. In the next four hours Gerry Mackenzie's men stood off Japanese attacks, sometimes using the bayonet to keep the enemy from the airfield, but the platoon had to withdraw before daylight, destroying the airstrip installations as they left.

Although wireless networks could not be linked in the mountains and that night fog obscured lamp signals, the platoons regrouped at pre-arranged rendezvous. This arrangement is typical of the forethought that would go into all the Company's future operations, and was a major factor in their survival. They had also spent the previous six weeks familiarising themselves with the country, getting to know especially the lie of the rivers, which would become torrents after the heavy rain that fell in the afternoon and at night during many months of the year, while the same river beds higher up the hills could be dry at times.

Bernard Callinan came out of Dili with the Dutch headquarters between two files of their native troops and reached the Company positions at Three Spurs above the port (see map p. 77). Cutting across country in the morning light he saw the Japanese transports moored peacefully in Dili harbour. Requisitioning the Portuguese gover-

nor's 1925 Chevrolet, he drove to the Company headquarters at Cailaco where it was safe from immediate attack in the event of this landing that the CO - Major A. Spence - had anticipated. Unaware of events at Koepang, the Major now decided to withdraw the Company to the south coast and maintain its role protecting Sparrow Force's eastern flank. All the stores that could not be moved by native porters or the gallant Timor ponies were destroyed on 22 February and the Company moved south into the mountains, from where they were able to watch an area of 300 square miles (over 770km²), patrolling for negative reports as often as they made enemy sightings. By knowing where the enemy was not established, the platoons could be better deployed watching where the Japanese had bases.

An attempt to contact Sparrow Force was made by Bernard Callinan, with a Dutch native soldier, whose experience as a schoolmaster and whose knowledge of Portuguese, English and Malay were invaluable in translating the polygot languages of the different people they met on the westward journey. After a couple of days on horseback they reached Memo on the Dutch/Portuguese border. Here rumours were rife. The Japanese were within eight miles (13km) of the border at this point on 3 March. Crossing into Dutch Timor next day, they moved over the dry coral rocks and through occasional dells of trees around clear springs before reaching a Roman Catholic mission church where the priests told them of Sparrow Force's defeat. They also collected some weapons recovered from parishioners and - more important in this mounted guerrilla warfare - they collected several saddles.

The first Japanese pincer movement against the Company was made later that week. Captain R.R. (Bill) Baldwin's platoon had a patrol out under Corporal Palmer when the Japanese launched their first attack (see map p. 77) and the platoons withdrew through enemy patrolled country, laying ambushes in the scrub. The first Japanese they killed was a 'richly dressed gent on horseback' who was followed to his Valhalla by two other officers shot by Bill

Baldwin, an ex-shooter of kangaroos. The right prong of this drive was met by Captain G.G. Laidlaw's platoon withdrawing in good order on Liquissia, but the left pincer made quicker progress towards Railaco and three of Lieutenant T.G. Nisbet's Section were killed above Bazartete the enemy moving skilfully around ambushes. These troops of the Japanese 38 Division, being specially trained for amphibious assault, were not to waste their talents in chasing guerrilla bands, and their sudden departure surprised - not to say, relieved - the Australians, who considered these were the best troops they had fought. In time, Bernard Callinan has recorded, the Australians also 'came to admire the soldierly qualities of other (Japanese) units'.

After the main Sparrow Force surrendered, the role of the Company was truly independent. Concentrated in the area of Hatu-Lia and Cailaco, the patrols could see from these hill positions across the wide Nanura Plains, covered in 6 feet to 8 feet (2-3m) high buffalo grass, to the Dutch border. Food was short; they had no sugar, and the large denominations of Dutch guilder coin in the Company's cash box were too valuable to exchange for a basket of minute potatoes or two bottles of milk. Nevertheless, three meals, often consisting of scraps or little more, were served each day. The guerrillas were helped, however, by an educated native who discovered that Bernard Callinan was a Roman Catholic and was persuaded that others in the Company were of the same faith. Throughout Portuguese Timor the church was still preaching the faith, and although priests were questioned there was little brutality in the early days of this occupation. Yet guerrillas fighting in ambush one moment could within the hour be kneeling in church, and the story of these operations, as with all guerrilla campaigns, evolved around the Independent Company's relationships with the indigenous population.

During that spring and summer the Australians enjoyed a good deal of help from the locals. Each man, NCO, and officer had his personal bearer, a *criado* who carried his pack, blankets, and other gear except his weapons. This enabled the patrols, usually led by a corporal, to move across considerable areas. But during late March when they were hemmed in, there were many rumours unsettling the less resolute, even though

Australian with his *criado* native servant who carried all the rations and gear, except for the Australians' weapons, on patrol.

their officers kept them occupied, leaving little time for worry. Maintaining an offensive spirit was a different matter, and the return of Corporal Palmer and his patrol was the boost in confidence the men needed. The Corporal had led his men westwards clear of the advancing Japanese, then south and back east from across the Dutch Timor border in a week's march back to Cailaco; proving that the Japanese could be outwitted. However, some natives at this time became unreliable guides and could give away a patrol's position.

The move south was now imperative in an attempt to contact Allied ships, and platoon areas for future operations were picked by the dubious but only available criteria: those towns in bold type on Bernard Callinan's map were chosen as platoon centres. Attempts to contact Australia 400 miles (over 640km) to the south were unsuccessful, but the 109-set picked up a Dutch broadcast which was translated for the Company by a passing Dutch soldier: it announced the surrender of all their forces in the East Indies. The native troops were shattered by this, but many Dutchmen and some natives fought on, others joined the increasing numbers of hostile bands roaming the country. Or - like a few men of Sparrow Force whom Corporal Palmer had found near the coast living off the Company's abandoned-in-transit Christmas parcels - they wandered aimlessly until captured, or killed by native factions. Some Portuguese gave the Company invaluable help, and Senhor de Sousa Santos, the Portuguese administrator of the southern province, would save the whole Company through his work in civil administration and respect among the local population. But early that spring, these adventures seemed unlikely if not impossible: the men had little quinine, their boots and clothes were worn thin, and when attack was unlikely they went around barefoot. Men with malaria now had to go on patrol. Yet in spite of these difficulties the Company turned down any chance of surrender 'and would be treated as brigands' according to the message Donald Ross brought to Hatu-Lia on 13 March - three weeks after the Japanese landed. The same week a Portuguese manager was taken into custody from a Japanese plantation where Bill Baldwin found a powerful multiband radio receiver. The manager had been held by the Portuguese, but when Bill Baldwin took charge of him the local population, including the Chinese, knew that the Australians intended to continue the war, preferring to be the hunters rather than the hunted.

With the platoons now established inland from the coast, some way to watch Dili and possibly raid the airstrip was planned. A Section was camped in a knoll at the end of a spur near Nasuta and they built an observation point which was approached by a crawl through thickets before climbing a tree to a branch chair - the comfort of its armrests had more to do with the watcher keeping absolutely still than with his ease. This post was used for several weeks before the men were recalled, despite their plans for a raid 'fixing charges to the noses of planes'. The Japanese almost certainly knew the Australians were in the area, for a young Chinaman had served food to officers passing through Railaco, and he was later to be 'shot at sight' after his Japanese contacts were discovered.

The Dili watchers came back to the Company headquarters to find the 2/2 was now linked to Brigadier Veale's 200 survivors of Sparrow Force with a base at Mape, in the hills (see map p. 77). They had also established contact with 40 men under Major Chisholm who were organising a base for patrols from Memo, but contact had not yet been made with Australia, the powerful radio stations on the mainland's north coast drowning out signals from Timor. However, Signalman Lovelace of Sparrow Force was to build a remarkably powerful transmitter, even though he had neither electrical testing nor other meters. This 'Winnie the War Winner' was made from two 109-sets, parts from the plantation manager's receiver collected by Bill Baldwin, and bits and bobs laid out in a contraption of wires and valves around a room 10 feet square (3m²). Batteries were charged by native power turning a four-foot wooden wheel geared to a car's generator, a minor miracle of improvisation designed by Sousa Santos. Through this contact with Australia the nature of the guerrilla operations changed to a role foreseen by Collin Gubbins and Major Holland in 1938: acting in concert with the plans for an army's main campaign.

The 2/2 Independent Company could now fulfil this role because they had remained a cohesive force, not just as a result of their training and leadership but in no small measure because these were men used to living in dry country and capable of fending for themselves in the basic departments of survival. Most of them would go for four or five months before any change of clothing reached them, not perhaps such a hardship as, without a change of clothes, Bernard Callinan found his irritating prickly-heat rash disappeared. But more enervating diseases took their toll, and a man with the malaria shakes every afternoon is not at his best when aiming a rifle. Now, however, some relief was at hand: contact with Australia would lead to new supplies, mail from home the greatest morale booster, and air support. The RAAF using delayed action and other bombs on occasions delayed and confused Japanese column coming into the hills.

The Australian patrols laid ambushes in the way Mike Calvert had taught them: pinprick harassment frustrated the Japanese until every misfortune was blamed on the guerrillas.

Such harrassment did not always need a fighting patrol's strength: Lieutenant J.A. Rose with three men ambushed a couple of trucks one evening, killing 12 men before melting back into the shadows of the scrub. Hit and run were the tactics, the Australians preferring to kill five or six Japanese than risk casualties to themselves by tarrying longer to kill more enemy in one skirmish.

The Japanese reaction to these ambushes often showed their high standard in the martial arts. Four Australians, for example, above a road to Three Spurs and halfway up a steep hillside, once knocked out most of the men in the first of two trucks passing below the patrol. But before the firing from the bren, the tommy-gun, and two rifles could be switched to the second troop transport, its men were in action. Without any

fuss they were setting up a machine-gun while a party came straight up the hill towards the ambush positions. The Australian bren gunner might have been caught as he moved smartly back up the steep hill had not 'two natives appeared from nowhere' and carried his gun at a quick trot over the hill.

These actions and the cycle of patrols, with the same Sections covering many miles of territory in repeated visits, led the Japanese to believe that there were several hundred Australians in the hills immediately above the Glano valley. Yet there were never more than 23. These had to be redeployed under Japanese pressure in late April because Mape HQ set a 60-mile (95+km) base line - from Memo, through Cailaco, Atsabe, and Maubisse to Remexio overlooking Dili - from which patrols could go' forward into occupied territory. This jumping-off line gave some order to the patrolling, and behind it the many administrative essentials could be organised. Stores were distributed in pony treks that carried not only ammunition and food but also mail and the force's own newspaper. There was a paymaster providing ready money to pay natives, and a signals officer controlling the flow of reports back to Australia and the incoming news of airdrops or bombing raids: essential organisation, for even the most independent force needed supplies, and these had to travel over hundreds of miles of mountain tracks before reaching some platoon areas.

When the Japanese base was established at Ermera during the early summer, its 20-mile supply route led through country familiar to the Australians, the road running south from Dili, and despite the Japanese posts guarding the convoys, Australian ambushes made it a hazardous supply run. As soon as a post's routine was established it would be attacked: Sergeant James and two sappers lay for two days watching a post before deciding that breakfast-time was the right moment for such an attack. Next day a sharp breakfast-burst of fire killed 12 Japanese before the patrol dispersed in the scrub. When the Japanese counter-attacked on other occasions they made a great hullabaloo, often shouting to each other as they came forward. Although the Australians thought this was purely a morale-boosting ploy, in thick cover over difficult terrain or at night, the commandos would use a similar tactic with good reason - as no doubt the Japanese did - in distinguishing friend from foe. When they wished, the Japanese could make silent attacks.

The Independent Company's constant patrolling - 'pigi, pigi' as the natives called it, for whenever asked, an Australian was always going (pigi) somewhere - was extended eastward and the first contacts made with the Portuguese on the east coast during May. Not all patrols escaped the attention of Japanese counter-measure, however, but the Australians' skilful use of field craft - the infantry phrase for individuals' movement in action - saved many losses. Using the numerous hollows and small rises unnoticed to untrained soldiers on a bare hillside, Turton and his men once lay hidden in this deadground while the Japanese moving to encircle them passed by, leaving the Australian patrol to come off the hill at nightfall. On other occasions a guerrilla could snake along such cover on his stomach, his legs pressed flat, knees to the ground as he wriggled closer to enemy positions, or - like one Corporal - he squirmed away from possible capture. The corporal lay that afternoon among hot stones on an exposed and open slope, his skin scorched by the stones; nevertheless, he stayed flat to the ground and escaped being captured or shot. Despite their expertise in such field craft, though, there was a limit to the area the Australians could control, and they had to send more men south to protect their supply line from the coast.

To distract the Japanese attention from the weakening hold of the Independent Company on the western side of the island, Laidlaw's platoon mounted a raid on Dili, reaching the hills near the town undetected. On the night of 15-16 May, the leading Section of this fighting patrol, their faces blackened from native cooking-pot soot, crept up to the wire around the port. They found no sentries before moving into the town along the storm drains, a convenient cover from rifle fire and running either side of the main road. Passing lamp-lit windows through which they could see sleeping Japanese soldiers and men talking in small groups, they had gone as far as a machine-gun post among the buildings - probably part of the anti-aircraft defences - when a Japanese soldier came up. He was within three yards of Laidlaw when the Lieutenant shot him. Pandemonium! Every Australian weapon was firing and their grenades, lobbed through open doors and windows, were bursting among the men struggling to find their weapons. Down on the beach a covering party under Lieutenant Nisbet added to the Japanese confusion, for they rushed reinforcements to the shore, no doubt expecting this raid was made from the sea. Certain they had bottled up the Australian patrol, the Japanese searched the town house by house next day, but Laidlaw and his men were long gone. A column of 400 Japanese followed them a few days later and reached Remexio, but there were no Australians in the town. Laidlaw's raid, however, had other repercussions, for the Japanese built more extensive defences around Dili and manned them day and night; a use of men and resources that in eight or so weeks would be desperately needed on Guadalcanal, or later that year in defences against other Allied landings.

The Australians by now renamed Lancer Force, had a hospital and training base at Ainaro in addition to the HQ at Mape. Through this facility, since 'base' might suggest the steady jobs associated with most camps behind a front line, men of 19 units were given some training in Independent Company's skills. Postal clerks and refrigeration engineers became passable guerrillas, giving them the added confidence they needed when men from this camp faced Japanese attack. Others joined the constant patrolling, giving rise through deliberate and other rumours to the Japanese belief in a steady flow of reinforcements from overseas. The successful training of these men suggests that no extraordinary qualities were needed for commando work in the field, only the right spirit and sound training. On Timor by late May, however,there was the

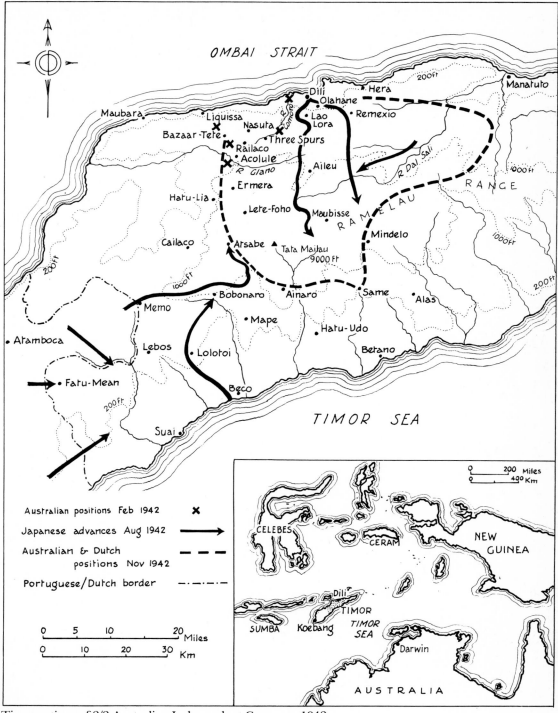

Timor actions of 2/2 Australian Independent Company 1942.

comforting knowledge that the most seriously wounded could be evacuated by seaplane through Suai and that others could be cared for in the Ainaro hospital - a different picture from the days of doubt and dismay some eight weeks earlier. Brigadier Veale was flown out on 23 May and Major A. Spence took command of Lancer Force, Bernard Callinan being promoted major in command of 2/2. With the 23 May air-flight went muster rolls giving relatives at home their first news of survivors in the Force.

Operations continued, with the many paradoxes of guerrilla warfare: both sides used the civilian telephone network; several Australians attended Sousa Santos's wedding anniversary celebrations. On the telephone, they used rhyming slang in case they were overheard; at the celebrations, the fine crystal glass and good company belied the hazards of patrolling a few dozen miles away. Going around the Sections posts could take a fortnight, for many of them were beyond the '60-mile line'. By June, new wireless sets had arrived, although the first consignment in one of the few supply errors, had no acid for their heavy 'wet' (distilled water) batteries. These radios and other stores were brought in by the small steamer *Kuru*, which was fitted with a device in her stack to prevent the tell-tale streamer of fumes; these she released in occasional puffs. She anchored off the south coast beach at Beco for a couple of hours while the stores - quinine, mepacrine (atabrin), boots, ammunition, and rations, were rafted ashore. But what the Allies could do, the Japanese could also achieve at that time; only in later months would American sea and airpower prevent the Japanese reinforcing their island garrisons. They had already sent in a force of specially trained jungle fighters to hunt the guerrillas. A hundred of these were ambushed by Corporal Aitken, unfortunately ahead of the platoon or his bag might have been greater. Nevertheless he shot the 'Singapore Tiger', an arrogant character who had been seen several times before and was strutting ahead of his large patrol when the Corporal's bullet killed him. By now, though, the Japanese were getting wary of ambush, and following their usual high standard of training they had sentries hidden in the bushes rather than marching to and fro as ready bait for a commando knife.

In the middle of the summer the Japanese had plans to develop the island with aircraft bases after the American counter-stroke of 7 August landed on Guadalcanal, more than 2,000 miles (3,000+km) to the east of Timor. There is reason to think they were also feeling the loss of their carriers that June at the battle of Midway, and were looking for more land bases for aircraft. But in Timor, much depended on the containment, if not defeat, of the guerrillas.

On 10 August the Japanese bombed most Portuguese towns on the island to discourage support for the Australians. The HQ at Mape was bombed, although this did not seriously disrupt the defence plan as four columns of Japanese, some 2,500 troops in all, drove inland (see map p. 77). The two columns from Dili, with 600 to 700 in each, would be met by Laidlaw and Bill Baldwin's platoon. At Ainaro, as many men as could be collected were put under Gerry Mackenzie's command - there was nothing 'base' about these wallahs. Their task was to watch and delay any drive from the south, where the Japanese had landed at Beco, the 'port' of entry in previous weeks for Australian supplies. Away to the west towards Memo, Lieutenant D. St. A. Dexter, supported by Turton, blocked the enemy's eastward push that had overrun Dutch positions, but with the difficult hill country between them and Mape, they were unlikely to link up with the other columns. In this fighting, the Australian plan was to be bold while steadily withdrawing eastward, even though once boxed into a small corner of the island they would lose their precious mobility. The tactics for keeping off the ropes, so to speak, had been explained to every platoon commander the previous June, and they knew 'every mile towards the east was a serious loss'. The most serious setback in their fortunes, however, was a marked change in the attitude of the natives, who rose against the Australians in two widely separated areas. Natives also stalked Australian patrols and then stood up, giving the Japanese mortars the range and location of ambushes.

While the Australians had been winning their mini-battles, including the fight above the Glano valley, the natives considered them supermen. But with the tide of war now running against the Allies, many of the natives decided to join the winning side, just as they had in Dutch Timor the previous winter. In a land where survival was so nakedly a prime instinct, food supplies were the key that opened local hearts if not minds. The Japanese, holding the Glano valley, had this authority, for most of the hill tribes' food was normally traded from its fertile plots. It was a handicap becoming increasingly clear to the Australians, and Bernard Callinan was later to put a surplus of food as the prerequisite for guerrillas' friendly relations with a local population. (Without it or without secure supply lines, guerrillas might last a fortnight or so before their own food resources ran out, for there are strict limits to the weight of rations they can expect to carry with them.)

Retreating over the Ramelau Range, the Australians were attacked on 14 August by natives. High on this ridge top, only 10 to 15 feet (2-3m) wide, the weary soldiers felt an earth tremor as the mountain shook. They drove off the hostile bands and shortened their lines of communication, now running back to Ainaro, to where the headquarters had moved. Five days later the platoons were preparing to strike at the nearest Japanese column when this swung clear of the counter-punch. The enemy's withdrawal was probably due to lack of supplies, for they also had to bring food into the mountains.

The Australians were recovering again from the brink of disaster, although a ruthless reprisal raid by Portuguese against the natives who had helped the Japanese was storing up trouble for the future. Reinforcements for the Australians arrived when 2/4 Independent Company landed, but their destroyer transport - HMAS *Voyager* - ran irretrievably aground and was strafed by Japanese planes, although without injury to the Australians. The stores brought ashore were then loaded on pack teams of 30 to 40 horses with native handlers and a couple of Australians as guards. Moving across coun-

try, they were attacked by Japanese planes and sometimes by infantry patrols, but although several horses and their loads were lost in these skirmishes, the native grooms and their Australian escorts usually escaped into the scrub.

Communication is a two-edged weapon, however, and Lancer Force began to receive some ill-conceived directions for section attacks and platoon operations that were dreamt up by mainland staff with no comprehension that a force without artillery, and facing an enemy superiority of ten-to-one, is likely to be obliterated in conventional infantry attacks. Realising that the Australians were not so foolish as to engage in pitched battles, whatever their masters decreed, the Japanese sent a picked force of guerrilla fighters to take up the chase where the major columns left off. One of their companies reached Ainaro, questioned the local priests and some natives, but did them no harm. This unit had been caught in several skirmishes, losing their CO and second-in-command along with a third of their strength, yet they were seen doing physical training after a short rest in the town - a measure of their quality. A major force of 5,000 Japanese were moved into Aileu and a second visit to Ainaro by men of another Japanese unit (which, is not clear) was full of brutality: the priests were killed; some houses were burnt down. Although the officers of these contrasting units might be held responsible for both the good and the bad behaviour, there is a touch of the 'kind' and the 'nasty' treatment often meted out to prisoners in the hope of gaining information. On the second visit, a few days after the first, the Japanese used natives in their ravages of the town, much to the disgust of local tribes. On 1 October there were further signs of Japanese influence over native affiars when eight Portuguese men and women were killed by tribesmen in Aileu. From there, the enemy could patrol against the Australians while developments took place along the east coast with an airstrip at Fuiloro, where in 1934 (!) some so-called agricultural specialists had taken soil samples for a Japanese company.

The guerrilla role changed once again, for

there was little they could do against well-defended airstrips when the natives gave away patrols before they were within striking distance of Japanese posts. Moreover, the Japanese themselves were more wary, allowing no one - native, Portuguese, or disguised guerrilla - to approach their positions. The Independent Companies were therefore forced into a more passive role which nevertheless made a contribution to the main forces' campaigns. Information not seen in aerial photographs of jungle fringes was fed back to Australia and enabled the United States and RAAF planes from the Northern Territory of Australia to bomb with a greater chance of finding targets. And knowledge of the naval routines of Japanese occupied ports enabled US submarines from Fremantle to attack shipping again with greater chance of success.

In watching the Japanese build-up, a typical platoon deployment was made by a platoon of 2/4, with their forward posts having a wide view of Lete-Foho. The platoon headquarters were in a deserted village surrounded by a native rock and rubble wall 8 to 10 feet (3m) high with only two narrow entrances that led into the village with its three large circular huts, each 30 feet (10m) in diameter with conical roofs about 20 feet (7m) high. Between the huts were stone platforms holding *Lulic* poles carrying sacrificial buffaloes' horns. A native singing ceremony had been performed to clear bad spirits away before the Australians took up the positions. As this village was inaccessible, the enemy patrols were unlikely to reach it undetected, but if they did the platoon headquarters was sufficiently mobile for the captain, sergeant, and their two runners/signalmen to withdraw quickly over the hill, taking their radio with them - a different proposition to moving a 109-set, for now the guerrillas had dry battery radios (see Appendix No. 5) designed by Lieutenant Barcham, a New Zealander, for use by the Independent Companies. However, the platoon cook no doubt would have left his clobber behind, while the batman who acted as bodyguard (striker) and the two snipers would have protected the withdrawal of the vital radio.

The three 16-man Sections (see Appendix 2) were deployed further down the hill each sending out patrols of four or so men to scout the surrounding countryside. Information they gathered was sent back to platoon headquarters by runner and radioed from the village to Company headquarters. Not all positions were as healthy as others, for 4,700 feet (1,400m) up Tata-Mailau mountain a Section post was established that needed a fresh 16 men every week, the cold - Tata-Mailau is 9,000 feet (nearly 3,000 metres) high - bringing on the malaria latent in almost every man of the Companies. At most observation posts, though, the Sections could work for several weeks without relief.

The platoons were losing much of their mobility in these static patrols, and the Japanese developments along the eastern seaboard reduced the opportunities to bring in supplies. Although the old post above Dili was still used from time to time, this port was no longer important as transports off-loaded Japanese air force and other supplies at Bancau stretching the areas to be watched by several hundred square miles. Supply lines were therefore extended across the hills and imperilled at sea, despite the Independent Companies' landward reconnaissance of likely landing points for the RAN supply ships. Some vital supplies were lost when natives attacked pack-horse trains. They were helped by one-time Allies of the Australians: long-term Portuguese prisoners who had escaped from custody during the summer and now wandered the island in groups of six or more. Such disruption led, by December, to the men of the Independent Companies spending as much if not more time securing their lines of supply, administering the areas of their platoon bases, and fighting hostile natives than were spent watching the Japanese. Some six men were, however, employed in training loyal natives whose chiefs wanted fighting men who could fire rifles, but these forces were of doubtful value. There was no doubt that maintaining several hundred Australians on Timor was now counter-productive; and in December the 2/2 Independent Company were taken off the island, after nearly 11 months of constant movement, if not always

Australians move through jungle country on the Timor coastal plain, November 1942.

in action. The Company made a 60-mile withdrawal to the beach at Betano and were picked up with Portuguese and Dutch civilians evacuated at the same time, the relief ships being bombed during their approach for this night landing.

Although 2/4 remained on the island for several more weeks, they were constantly embroiled in unsatisfactory skirmishes with natives supported by Japanese machine-gun teams. Food was short, and resupplying the Company put the ships at even greater risk than in the previous month: as a result the platoons were taken out on 9-10 January 1943, leaving only a small party under Lieutenant Henry Flood to gather information. This 'S' Party was scattered by a Japanese attack but regrouped before February, when they were taken off by an American submarine. There remained only 'Z' Special Force, an undercover operation on the island run by Captains Broadhurst and Wylie, former members of the Malay police force, who organised native lookouts and a radio reporting system which at one time had 25 radio stations on the island, demonstrating how a few guerrillas may succeed in adverse local conditions where a larger force cannot survive.

The Independent Companies had never taken a prisoner, although this was not from want of trying. They did kill an estimated 1,500 Japanese for the loss of only 40 of their own men; a sharp contrast to the 166,500 Allied losses (mostly prisoners) in Malaya, Hong Kong, and in the Dutch East Indies, where the Japanese lost only 15,000 men in the campaigns of the 1940-41 winter. The few hundred Australians on Timor had also contributed to the Japanese conviction that the island was to be re-occupied by the Allies, and the enemy reinforced his garrison with men of the 48 Division in the autumn of 1942 when these forces might have been employed to better effect against the Allies on New Guinea and elsewhere. Few commando guerrillas, therefore, can claim to have had as great an influence over their main forces' campaign as these Independent Companies, for in the Allied advances of 1943 many garrisons could be by-passed and the Japanese on Timor did not quit the island until a month after the armistice in 1945. The success of these Australian guerrilla companies, with their high standard of individual field craft, their sound leadership deploying platoons with forethought for their mobility, and above all the men's ability to live off the country while fighting a war of high mobility, had made their campaign in Timor one of the most important of small force operations in World War II.

# DIEPPE, AUGUST 1942

Dieppe, with its narrow streets and harbour set between chalk cliffs 150 feet (50m) high, was the intended target of a commando and RM Division raid, as soon as sufficient craft were available for the simultaneous landing of a division. This raid in force against a defended port was essential to test the Allies' amphibious techniques. COHQ's plan avoiding a frontal assault was changed when direction of the raid passed to the Army's UK Home Forces Command, after a political decision was made to replace the marines with Canadian forces. Later the planned intensive bombardment was foregone - against the advice of Lord Mountbatten and others. Bad weather led to the cancellation of the raid planned for 7 July. Despite security risks - even though no written minutes were kept - the raid was remounted in August, with commandos replacing paras for the flank forces when two LSIs became available and as weather conditions for air-drops differ from those for seaborne landings.

The experience at Dieppe, in the words of their official history, 'undoubtedly led Canadian soldiers to view the question of their employment more soberly'. Others, who unlike the Combined Operations staff, had expected a second front in Europe that summer, saw what forces would be needed to invade Europe. Many major lessons were learnt and Lord Mountbatten has written 'the successful landing in Normandy was won on the beaches of Dieppe'.

4 Commando approach Orange 1 beach west of Dieppe.

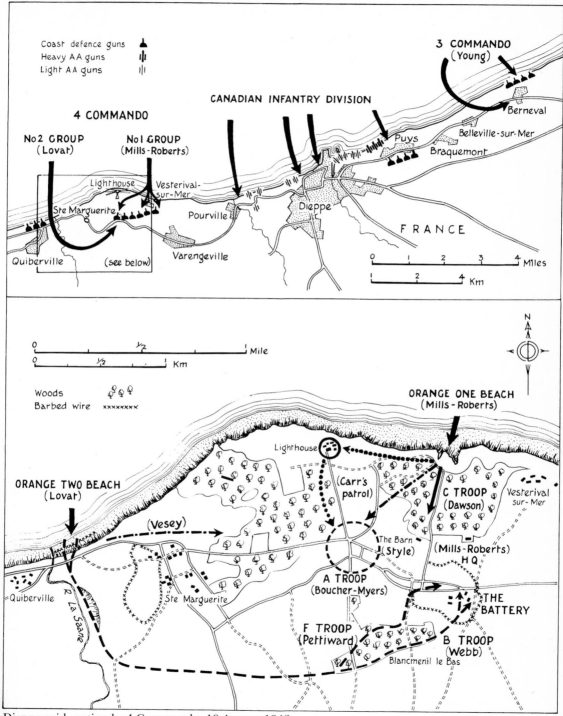

Dieppe raid - action by 4 Commando, 19 August 1942.

# 5 A PERFECT FLANK GUARD

In sabotage, beach reconnaissance, and guerrilla operations, the commandos showed their abilities in exploiting unconventional military tactics, but they were also fine exponents of such conventional military manoeuvres as fire-and-movement. This simple tactic engages the enemy with rapid fire from one unit while other attackers move closer to enemy positions: as the enemy's heads are kept down they can neither see nor fire on the assault group positioning themselves for a short charge the moment the covering fire lifts. The principle is easy, but its execution requires exact timing and the assault troops' complete confidence in the accuracy and sustained fire of those covering the movement forward - a matter of sound training as much as of resolute leadership. At Varengeville-sur-Mer, three and a half miles (5.6km) west of Dieppe, four Troops of 4 Commando in August 1942 carried out a perfect assault on enemy batteries by using fire-and-movement tactics.

For all the subsequent debate - mentioned earlier - over less bloody alternatives, the main landings at Dieppe were an essential preliminary to the invasion of Europe. In the late spring of 1942, COHQ planning staffs considered the capture of a major port or ports would be essential for the sustained supply of invading armies. The Canadians, whose 2 Division provided the main landing force, accepted the plan for a frontal assault on the town's beaches, holding it for the morning of Wednesday 19 August 1942,

while the port's defences, a radar station, and the aerodrome at St Aubin (south of Dieppe) were destroyed. There were about 60 German landing barges in the port and capturing these, along with information in the German divisional headquarters and from prisoners' interrogation, would assist the Allies in their invasion preparations. There were also plans for an air battle into which the German fighters might be drawn from their defensive attitudes inland. The port was not thought to be heavily defended.

Copies of the original operation orders have manuscript alterations changing the proposed bombing support for the laying of smoke-bomb cover. Several reasons have been put forward for the change, but fear of killing French civilians and of rubble-strewn streets becoming impassable to tanks are the most likely. Whatever the reasons, there is evidence suggesting that bombing would not have necessarily led to a successful landing, for the Germans had guns hidden in cliff positions that were unseen on aerial photographs. The beaches east and west of Dieppe are backed by cliffs, except for a narrow gap at Puys (also called Puits) (see map p. 83), a small beach further west at Pourville, and two beaches west of the town near and at the mouth of the Saane River.

Covering the sea approaches to Dieppe were two batteries, each with 150mm (5.9in) guns - thought to be four in the east, six in the west - that could traverse through 360 degrees, and with a range of nearly 12 miles (20km). These would have to be knocked out before the main force carrier ships were off the beaches, and so 3 Commando was chosen to land against the eastern Berneval battery and 4 Commando against the one at Vasterival. Their targets lay behind high cliffs and in each case would have to be approached over rocky beaches to gulleys, or up the Saane river estuary. Landing at high water (0455 hours) in the dark, the commandos would later have to make a difficult withdrawal as the tide fell and their craft moved further offshore where cliff-top defenders had a clear shot, which they would not be able to get at craft on high water under the cliffs. With the main force were 40(RM) Commando who, if they had not first been committed from their role as a floating reserve, would cut out the German landing craft.

The force sailed from Southern English ports on Tuesday 18 August on a fine summer's evening, with John Durnford-Slater's 3 Commando in 25 LCP(L)s (see Appendix 4) as the most easterly of the assault convoys. They moved in four columns with Steam Gunboat No.5 in the van and LC Flak No.1 and ML No.346 astern. The Flak craft had two twin 4-inch guns that could be used for beach bombardment or anti-aircraft fire. The voyage of nearly 70 miles (112km) was covered by two escort destroyers under the command of the Polish captain of *Slazak*. These escorts were four miles north-east of the convoy when it ran across five German ships, including armed German trawlers escorting a tanker. Several of the frail wooden LCP(L)s were damaged and all were scattered in the blaze of 20mm fire concentrated on the SGB as she reeled out of action with John Durnford-Slater aboard, her bridge a 'collapsed rugger scrum of wounded and dead'. From the craft scudding away into the night, only four made their target beaches Yellow 1 and 2 (see diagram).

Major Peter Young - 2 i/c 3 Commando - with 18 men was in the solitary craft to reach Yellow 2, west of the Berneval battery, at 0450 five minutes before their H-hour. Off the beach he briefly debated the point of making a landing, for the intended Troops had not reached the beach, but the orders were clear: 'The battery guns should be engaged by fire at the earliest possible moment and continually harassed by snipers if insufficient commandos get ashore for the planned attack.' Lieutenant-Commander Buckee RN took the craft ashore and promised to wait: he even offered to bring his four-man crew ashore, but at the Major's request they stayed with the craft off the beach.

Under covering fire from ML No.346, five other craft came near Yellow 1 beach, and three got their commandos ashore with at least one commando steering his craft, most of the crews being either dead or wounded. Some 50 men from Nos. 2,5, and 6 Troops then followed Captain R.L. Wills ashore. With them were four French marines of 10 Commando. They fought their way through the beach defences of wire and several machine-gun posts, one being taken in a lone bayonet charge by Corporal 'Banger' Halls. The craft had landed half an hour late, and in the strengthening daylight were seen on their run-in, giving the Germans time to deploy their reserve platoon and to eventually hem in Richard Wills's assault in a small perimeter as the commandos tried to fan out from the road topping the gulley. Richard Wills was wounded in the neck and Lieutenant Loustalot of the US Army Rangers was killed, the first American serviceman of World War II to die in land warfare on the European mainland. Sergeant-Major Montailler of 10 Commando, wearing his red pompom French marine cap, was in the van of this spirited attack. When the enemy counter-attacked in strength, the commandos were forced back to the beach, only to find that under heavy fire, the tide had ebbed from the rocky shore and that the craft were caught on rocks or holed. The only commando to be brought off was a signalman with the naval beach party. The French Sergeant-Major, gravely wounded, was taken prisoner along with Richard Wills, and others.

The action by Dick Wills's men drew off some of the battery's defenders, an estimated 350 men although apparently without mortars in this area. At first they were seemingly unaware of Peter Young's landing and he and his men hauled themselves up the steep cliff gulley, using the anchor pegs of German wire as footholds. After 20 minutes they were at the top in daylight, reading a convenient signpost *Achtung Minen*. They moved cautiously around this minefield and forward towards the battery which, as it opened fire, they ran 'to engage it at the earliest possible moment'. They had gone down the village street of Berneval and reached the church when a burst of machine-gun fire, and not the expected support of Dick Wills's men, greeted them. Casting around for sniping points, Peter Young found there were no steps up the church tower, so they moved towards a wheat field. The men - 18 of them - were so well spaced that the rear rank could fire through gaps in the front, but their view was limited because the battery was on the same level as the corn field in which the riflemen and one bren gunner had to kneel to aim shots, shifting their positions after every two or three rounds. They remained a couple of hundred yards or less from the gun positions which had fired about 20 rounds, and the commandos - firing steadily to conserve ammunition - were irritating the gunners sufficiently for one gun to traverse 180 degrees. A great orange flash followed by clouds of black smoke and a 40kg (90lb) shot winged its way into France. Three more followed it but the gun could not be depressed for a 150-yard (140m) range, and the rumble of blast on each firing was just far enough away not to hurt the commandos, even though it deafened them. A few small arms in the right place at the right moment had defeated the battery, for when Peter Young looked towards Dieppe there was a great bank of smoke hiding the ships.

With their ammunition getting low and German reinforcements likely to arrive any minute, Peter Young's men shot up a German observation post on the cliff-top before withdrawing to the beach, to where Lieutenant-Commander Buckee brought the LCP(L) back as three or four men under Lieutenant John Selwyn formed a rearguard through which the others withdrew down a gulley in the classic tactic for disengaging from an enemy. This manoeuvre is simple

enough when practised in a field as the rearguard's fire draws the advancing enemy's attention. At the top of a gulley in the likely confusion of even a well-rehearsed withdrawal, the rearguard can come unstuck. Their fire should at least unsteady the advancing enemy's aim, but where are their own commandos out front? Have they all gone through? When should the covering (rearguard) party pack up and move? At the gulley top, all went to plan, the other dozen or so men moved past John Selwyn's bren team and riflemen before they picked up the bren and in turn withdrew.

This gulley was mined, unlike the one they had climbed some three hours earlier, and L/Cpl H.A.R. White was wounded in the foot when one exploded. Nevertheless, he got back to his 3-inch (76mm) mortar down on the beach, firing four rounds as the advance party of Major Blücher's assault engineers from 181 Division reached the cliff-top. ML No.346 also gave covering fire as the commandos including the mortar team waded out to the landing craft and a safe evacuation, although some men were carried 300 yards (270m) out to sea on the craft's life-lines before being hauled aboard.

Peter Young has described his own trait of 'inborn stubbornness or bloody-mindedness' as one aspect of his determined leadership, but the Major (later Brigadier) had shown a masterly touch for his military good sense is one of the golden threads of this story. Few commanders, however, had Peter Young's acumen. Many as brave as him would have rushed the battery and experienced certain failure, but the Major's cool calculation in action engaging 200 Germans with a tenth of their number achieved certain victory, for as far as is known no hits were scored by the battery that morning.

The westerly battery near Varengeville-sur-Mer (see map p. 83) had six 150mm (5.9in) guns set 1,100 yards (1,000m) inland behind high cliffs, the battery being some 400 feet (120m) above sea level. Three sides of its defences were wired with a double-apron fence protecting heavy machine-gun posts facing the sea, and behind it was a flak-tower. The cliffs appeared too steep to scale quickly and the only direct approach from the beach was up two gulleys (Orange 1 beach, see map). A mile and a half (2.4km) further west, the cliff line was broken where the river Saane runs into the sea (Orange 2 beach) by the village of Quiberville. This beach was covered by machine-guns in two pill-boxes and some wire.

Lieutenant-Colonel the Lord Lovat, at 31, was commanding 'No.4' and prepared his plan for this assault, with rehearsals during late July and early August in eight practice runs over measured ground at Lulworth Cove on the Dorset coast. He used only four Troops, preferring 250 men for a quick action rather than all six Troops in his Commando, who would require a larger force of craft or possibly two flights (or lifts) in their carrier's craft. Group 1, with 88 men, under Major Derek Mills-Roberts, a fine soldier (a Liverpool solicitor before the war), would land on Orange 1 beach, move up one of the gulleys, and engage the battery with small arms and mortar fire from a wood about 300 yards in front of the battery. This provided the covering fire in a tactic of fire-and-movement. Group 2, with 164 men led by Lord Lovat, would land on Orange 2 and sweep behind the battery to positions where they could launch a charge - the movement element of this tactic, and a plan they executed to perfection.

Sailing on the HMS *Prince Albert* (cf. Appendix 4), this western flank force was called for breakfast at 0130 hours on 19 August. The craft were launched in a calm sea and ran towards the beach with the lighthouse at Pointe d'Ailly, halfway between the two Orange beaches, flashing its correct signal at least until the craft were a mile offshore, when it went out and star shells were fired from its observation post. The light had provided an accurate navigation beacon and dispels any notion that the raid was expected. Lieutenant David Style spotted the cleft of the eastward gulley and landed. dry-shod on the full tide in the dawn's half-light. Although the LCAs were overloaded, mainly because each man carried two mortar bombs, they landed at 0453 within minutes of their H-hour. To save weight the men did not wear tin hats and carried neither water bottles nor rations.

Running quickly under the lee of the cliffs where an enemy would have difficulty firing on them, they cleared the craft in less than a minute, proving their expertise in this amphibious technique. The left-hand gulley proved impassable without an hour's work clearing chalk rubble and possibly mines, so the Major ordered a gap blown in the right-hand gulley's wire with bangalore torpedoes (see Appendix 3). The first blew a smallish gap which the men could widen through the concertina coils. At the second wire barrier another bangalore torpedo was set. After a longish pause - moments of frustration: was the fuse dud? - the charge went off with a relieving explosion that created a gap through which David Style led his Section in single file.

Behind this leading Section came the C Troop commander, Captain R.W.P. Dawson, and the Major (who was second-in-command of 'No.4'). By now it was full daylight, and although the Major thought they may have been discovered 'like thieves in an alley when the policeman's torch shines', the noise of 3 Commando's action seven miles away had drowned the explosions of the bangalore torpedoes: equally fortuitously, four Allied light bombers flew overhead as the commandos climbed the gulley. The battery defences were manned by men of 110 Division, Germans who had seen action in Russia but not all of whom appeared to realise the urgency of their plight; one cook, in his white cap, stood watching developments, and no enemy - the Major learnt later - occupied the shuttered houses of Vesterival-sur-Mer. As the commandos moved through these, Derek Mills-Roberts saw the carrier ships arrive ahead of time; and as the battery fired he pressed forward taking a calculated risk on the Germans (if any) in these houses not interfering with the action. Meanwhile Lieutenant Knyvet Carr led a fighting patrol from A Troop to cut the lighthouse OP's telephone cable, before joining the rest of this Troop, under Captain B.W.S. Boucher-Myers, astride the double cross-roads (see map p. 83). There, as well as firing into the battery, they prevented a possible counter-attack by the German company believed to be in Sainte Marguerite. C

Troop and Derek Mills-Roberts had meanwhile crashed through the waist-high undergrowth in a wood until they saw the battery across a clearing. The Major and his mortar officer, Lieutenant J.F. Ennis, worked their way further forward some 50 yards to a patch of scrub beyond the wood, where the commando mortar's fire could be directed into the battery. However, radio contact was not established with the mortar at this time. They could, however, clearly hear the orders given to the guns, which fired six salvos over their heads, before the Major moved back to a barn, where he had a 'splendid view'. C Troop's three snipers, their faces and hands painted green, were in the area of the barn, 'taking their time with the first pressure on their triggers' before the final squeeze, took a rising toll of Germans. The bren gun teams were silencing several machine-gun posts. However, the Germans, with their professional soldier's tenacity, replaced the machine-gun crews three times on the flak tower, although this could no longer rotate after some 60 hits from the commandos' Boys anti-tank rifle (see Appendix 3). Six Rangers were among those firing into the battery from near the barn, and Corporal Koons was sniping through a slit over a manger in a small stable. He was probably the first American soldier to kill a German in a land action during World War II, although this 'first' might go to one of the Rangers with 3 Commando that Wednesday morning - Corporal Koons was awarded the MM.

Shots fell among the commandos from at least one of seven German machine-guns. Some 20mm shells and mortar bombs fired from farm buildings on C Troop's extreme left also fell among them. The snipers, by shifting their positions, remained elusive targets, fortunately for them, as a shell from the battery later blew a hole in the barn you could drive a cart through. Sergeant Garthwaite RAMC was killed by the mortar fire as he attended to a casualty on the edge of the wood, and Derek Mills-Roberts had most of a tree brought down on him by another mortar bomb. The 3-inch mortar was still not in contact with the forward OP; C Troop's 2-inch (51mm) mortar was firing from the edge of the wood, and although

the first shot fell short, the second set off a stack of cordite charges by the battery's No.1 gun. The shouts of men caught in this great burst of flame could be heard above the noise of battle, and the fire spread. No more rounds were shot by the battery after this fire.

There were few civilians about, but one middle-aged Frenchman watched with Gallic indignation as his cabbages were trampled underfoot by several commandos. He went off to change from his nightshirt and returned as the Major was passing, offering him a glass of wine. The Frenchman's pretty daughter, watching Derek Mills-Roberts refuse the hospitality, asked 'Are you going to shoot Papa?' But the Major had no such thought; the need to press on with sustained fire that would keep the enemy occupied precluded even a momentary pause for a drink. At about 0600, he sent a situation report by runner to the beach, where it was passed to an officer of the Phantom Group. These observers were in touch with Combined Operations Headquarters' through RAF Uxbridge, near London, and - like Wellington's roving staff officers at Waterloo - kept their respective headquarters informed on all major British operations. The Phantom message was passed over the carrier ship's radio to Lord Mountbatten's staff, but Derek Mills-Roberts had no news of Group 2, and his own Group's casualties were mounting. With the German fire getting more accurate as the minutes went by, Group 2 came on the air at 0615: they were forming up for the assault. At the same moment the mortar OP established contact with the team in the wood and the accurate 3-inch mortar fire, directed from this post a hundred yards from the battery wire, continued throughout the rest of the action until Group 2's assault went in. Already the supporting fire from positions of both C and A Troops were having the right effect, as any movement in the battery area brought an instant response.

Lord Lovat's Group 2 landed on the Orange 2 beach on time at 0430 hours, their five landing craft putting them ashore in battle formation as their small support craft's machine-guns engaged the German pill-boxes. This converted landing craft carried one or two 5-inch (13mm) and two other machine-guns and was able to give some covering fire while the commandos moved ashore: nevertheless, four men were wounded as the leading Section slithered over rabbit wire they had flung across the barbed wire defences. Lieutenant A.F.S. Vesey's section from A Troop poked their tubular ladders (see Appendix 3) up the steep bank west of the landing point and rushed the two pill-boxes, killing their machine-gunners with hand-grenades, before setting off to join the rest of A troop (see map p. 83). The German mortar fire - no doubt shooting along pre-set lines - was hitting the beach, and eight more men were wounded before the mortar crews extended their range and fired at the landing craft moving offshore to join the boat pool. The Allied aircraft that had passed over Group 1 also distracted the defenders, drawing their fire as the planes flew over.

Again an obliging *Achtung Minen* sign enabled B and F Troops to skirt trouble, and they kept off the footpath (in case of other mines) to form a column for the march along the left bank of the river Saane. With the boats gone, however, there was no way to evacuate casualties, but three who could walk were led by a medical orderly along the cliff-top towards Orange 1 beach where the whole Commando would be evacuated. Two of these walking wounded were killed when caught in German fire, but those left with the second medic - brother of the first - were taken prisoner.

The speed march along the river bank was led by Captain Gordon G.H. Webb's B Troop followed by Lord Lovat's HQ and the F Troop (Captain R. Pettiward). Doubling over the ground made heavy by the river's recent flooding, Group 2 could hear the fire-fight around the battery, and were encouraged by the whump of the cordite charges going up just before these Troops came to the river bend, 1,000 yards from the beach and a feature easily found in the bright morning light. They turned east (left) crossing more open country in extended formation, one sub-Section ready for enemy action while it covered the movement of the

other half-Section, thus moving forward in a series of bounds to the Blancmenil le Bas wood. Following the planned routes (see map p. 83) B Troop moved inside the eastern fringe of trees, from where they could see the flak tower. A German toppled from its gun platform 'shot like an Indian falling from the cliff in a western film'. Coming quickly through the trees they crossed the perimeter wire into an orchard, where they moved more cautiously with bren teams giving covering fire while riflemen moved forward under smoke from the 2-inch (51mm) mortar. By this fire-and-movement they knocked out a machine-gun post. In a little more than an hour and a half since landing, they were formed up for the assault just short of the battery buildings.

F Troop came through the west side of the wood and under cover of smoke struck north for about 400 yards down a road. Among some farm buildings here, at the edge of the battery complex, were some 35 *Stosstruppen* unloading a truck in preparation for a counter-attack against Mills-Robert's Group 1. In a brisk exchange of fire most of the Germans in the farmyard were killed or wounded by commandos firing brens and tommy-guns from the hip, but other Germans inside the buildings took a heavy toll of their attackers. Captain R. G. Pettiward was killed by a stick-grenade as he led the men towards the building. Lieutenant Macdonald was mortally wounded, and the sergeant, who took the lead, was killed almost immediately. Captain P. (Pat) A. Porteous, the liaison officer between the two Groups, was moving forward with Lord Lovat's headquarters, taking a position between B and F Troops, and he came across to lead F Troop. Shot in the wrist as he charged a German, he killed him with his good hand. Other commandos of the Troop were in hand-to-hand fighting around the farm, battling their way to the cover of a ditch along the road, that was the start line for their final assault against the battery's west side where there was little or no wire.

While this *mêlée* had been going on, Derek Mills-Roberts was preparing for the intensive fire that C and A Troops would lay down just before Group 2 put in their final assault.

The brens firing in such a barrage would lay a narrow cone of fire (see Appendix 3), in many respects a drawback on these occasions, when what was wanted was shots scattered over an area. However, tapping the butt of a gun as it fired helped to spread out the cone. In the field, these finer points of weapon handling were instinctive rather than calculated moves, and in a similar way the range of mortars was less important on occasions than the terrain in which the bombs burst. In soft ground their lethal area was small, but on rocky hillsides a 3-inch (76mm) bomb's lethal area could have a radius of many yards. The bombs could be fired at five a minute, and there were several types (see Appendix No.3), but using the smoke-bomb needed more than a sense of the wind's direction for trees or other natural features might break up a screen. If this was not close enough to the enemy they could also get an advantage when attackers broke out into clear view unsupported by their fellows still in the smoke.

A heavy barrage of smoke from Group 1's mortars at 0625 hours marked the target and obscured anti-aircraft gunners' aim as Spitfires of 129 Squadron came in to strafe the battery. There had been some debate about the dangers to commandos from this attack, but as it was along an east-west line risks were felt to be small, and so they proved: only a few cannon shells struck the buildings from which some commandos and three rangers were firing. None was hurt and the strafe was over in a couple of minutes before 0630. By this time the Colonel's headquarters were in position, the four tommy-gunners of the Commando orderly room forming a protection squad for the two runners, the three signalmen with their 38-sets (see Appendix 5), the adjutant, and Lord Lovat. They were joined as they reached the edge of the wood by a signaller from the beach; he had been laid out for 15 minutes, but on coming to he realised he was the only signaller in his Section and so made his own way across the open country from the river side.

Lord Lovat fired a series of white Very lights to signal the start of the assault. C and A Troops stopped firing into the battery, as Captain Gordon Webb and Pat Porteous led the charges into the battery area. Gordon Webb, his right wrist broken by a mortar fragment more than an hour and a half earlier, fired his revolver with his left hand as he led a yelling B Troop in a bayonet charge towards the battery buildings. Pat Porteous, the first man to reach the guns, was shot again. Hit in the thigh, he fell against the breach of one gun but pulled himself up to lead F Troop on. A third wound then knocked him over, but the gun emplacements were cleared of Germans.

'Screams, smoke, the smell of burning cordite - mad moments soon over' is Lieutenant Donald Gilchrist's description of B Troop's charge. He remembers one ugly scene when a German stamped on a wounded commando before this enemy was shot in the stomach. However, in such passions the ugliness is seldom one-sided: a wounded German was bayoneted a few moments later beside a wounded commando receiving a pain-killing shot of morphine.

F Troop's demolition squad could have blown the guns in the dark after their hours of practice in Lulworth, Dorset, and in minutes the demolition charges were set on the breech blocks and underground magazines. B Troop cleared odd groups of Germans from tunnels around the battery, catching two officers - one the battery commander, probably - in a deadly chase through the buildings, but many Germans continued to fight from mutually supporting strongpoints and only four prisoners were taken - including the cook in the white hat. The commando dead were brought to lie at the foot of the flagstaff when Messerschmitts flew over low enough to see some cheerful waves from commandos, deceiving the fliers into believing their troops still held the guns. A Union Jack was hoisted above the British dead in the warm sunshine of this summer's morning. Dead Germans lay behind the sandbag breastworks around the guns, many of the bodies badly burnt from the cordite fire; others lay where they had fallen to the snipers' bullets - outside buildings, bunkers, and in slit-trenches.

The withdrawal of 4 Commando was swift, although the Germans were not expected to bring major reinforcements to the area for a couple of hours, and at one point in the planning 'No.4' was going to stay ashore for some hours; in the event German reinforcements did not move from Amiens until 1600 hours that afternoon. Now, following the final plan, the commandos prepared to come out over Orange 1 beach, the difficult withdrawal they had foreseen. Lord Lovat, sporting corduroy slacks with a grey sweater under his khaki denim and carrying a Winchester rifle, ordered the battery buildings set on fire: 'Burn the lot' - the cry of a Highland chieftan, for the Lord Lovat is head of Clan Fraser.

C Troop covered the withdrawal with smoke generators along the track to the beach - one prisoner, pressed into carrying a generator, complained that he was excused such heavy work because of frostbite scars after service in Russia. Bren gun teams in pairs covered each other as they withdrew alternately behind the smoke while their rifle squads and the other Troops moved down to the beach. A Section from A Troop had accounted for a German patrol moving out of Sainte Marguerite, an action for which an old French lady rewarded each of them with a fresh egg, which they proceeded to carry back safely to England. Meanwhile a heavy mortar had ranged on the beach as the commandos were ferrying their wounded out in Goatley boats, and judging its position by the flight of these bombs, the Commando's 3-inch (76mm) mortar crew silenced it with counter-fire. Other enemy fire slackened, with only desultory fire from near the lighthouse, as the commandos crossed the beach through a lane of 18-type smoke generators and out into a path of naval smoke-floats that shrouded their re-embarking on the landing craft: a neat solution to the problem of withdrawing across an exposed beach. Two miles off the coast the casualties were transferred to a destroyer as the landing craft headed for home.

While the flank forces were experiencing mixed fortunes, the main assault by some 5,000 Canadians met fierce opposition. The German commander - according to one report - made a weekly practice of closing-up

his defence force to their guns just to remind them there was a war on, and on this Wednesday morning they had more than a rehearsal: they had a field day. The southerly breeze drifted the Allied smoke screen clear of the beach by 200 yards in places, exposing the incoming craft. The 24 LCTs carrying the new Churchill tanks included three craft intended to put their armour ashore with the first assault wave at 0520 hours, but these nine tanks were late in landing. The resulting 10 to 15 minutes delay enabled the German gunners to recover, after bombardment from four destroyers and a low-level attack by five squadrons of Hurricanes covering the craft nearing the beach. The infantry and assault engineers, without covering fire for these vital minutes, were cut down before they could dislodge the German gunners and obstacles, with several guns appearing from emplacements hidden from aerial view under the cliffs overlooking the flanks of the beaches. The second wave of LCTs piled in on the first under heavy fire and only 13 or possibly 15 tanks got over the promenade. None broke into the town although one made some limited progress beyond the sea wall. Not all the German guns could knock out these tanks, but their tracks were knocked off by 37mm (1.4in) guns' fire, and heavy fire from the Casino jutting out over the shingle enfiladed the beaches. A few groups of Canadian infantry got into the town but only confused and misleading reports reached Major-General J.H. Roberts MC, the Force Commander, aboard his headquarters ship: consequently the true position was not realised when the floating reserve, 40 (RM) Commando, was committed at 0830 hours.

Trained for their role as a cutting-out force, 'No.40 (RM)' was clearly not going to be able to perform this task, for even the gunboat HMS *Locust* had not been able to enter the harbour. The Commando was therefore transferred from the French *chasseur* fast patrol boats intended to follow in the gunboat, and was taken on assault craft towards the Casino where the Royal Hamilton Light Infantry were thought to have a toehold on the west of the main beach. The

Commando's commanding officer, Lieutenant-Colonel J.P. Phillipps RM, was following in the leading flights of craft as they came out of the smokescreen into bright sunshine. He found that the few craft already ashore were under heavy fire as the marines landed 'with courage terrible to see' (official report). Strewn over the beach were dead and wounded Canadians under concentrated fire. There was not even a slim chance of the Commando getting ashore and 'pushing farther west to capture the headland' as General Roberts had hoped. The Colonel's craft was close inshore as he pulled on a pair of white signal gauntlets and jumped on the foredeck, standing where his men in the following craft could clearly see him wave them back. Their craft put about just before the Colonel was shot through the head, giving his life in saving 200 men from certain disaster. Several of their craft were sunk and Major (later Lieutenant-Colonel) J.C. Manners RM was one of many commandos pulled from the water by crews of rescue craft.

The few Royal Marines already on the beach, among them Lieutenant K.W. Smale RM, took cover behind a stranded LCT. They kept up a steady fire for a time but all were killed, probably within the hour. After the withdrawal - which could be made only according to a strict timetable for the RAF to drop smoke cover - a Royal Marine was picked up swimming a mile from the beach. His rifle lay across the Mae West he was pushing towards England.

Dieppe was not altogether the disaster some historians suggest, for the 3,369 Canadian casualties (including 907 killed or who died while prisoners-of-war) made a sacrifice that would save many thousands of lives two summers later in Normandy. Their defeat showed the price of taking a defended port was too high, and the Allies would tow their Mulberry Harbours to the Seine Bay beaches in June 1944. Although this was the most important lesson of the raid, there were others - the landing timetable must be flexible, heavier supporting fire from ships was essential, and training was necessary for a permanent naval assault force. On the other hand, the Germans learnt nothing, for their continued concentration of defence around the main Channel ports proved a wasted effort in 1944, when these defended harbours were by-passed in establishing a beachhead.

For the commandos, Colonel Phillipps had saved 'No.40 (RM)' for other battles. Under Peter Young's cool leadership, fewer than 20 men, a tenth of those who should have landed, had disrupted a heavy battery's fire. Lord Lovat had proved that a well-trained Commando could succeed against an alert defence even though the ratio of attackers to defenders was less than one-to-one. Bearing in mind the advantages defenders have *if* they can catch incoming boats on open water, the amphibious invader would probably never get ashore unless the enemy strongpoints were neutralised by ships' and air bombardment as described in Chapter 11. However, one lesson from the action of 'No.4' showed the dangers for casualties in landing at one beach and coming off at another some miles away. Colonel Durnford-Slater revisited Dieppe after it was captured in the summer of 1944 and has

Coastal batteries on the cliffs near Dieppe bombarded by warships on 19 August 1942.

A US airman being rescued by landing craft off
Dieppe, 19 August 1942.

written : 'Without a doubt had our 3 Commando landed .... (they) would have succeeded if a proper number of men had been safely delivered to the beach.' He doubted, however, whether the Canadians had any chance at all in a frontal attack against skilfully sited concrete emplacements, especially as there was no heavy bombardment before the assault. Among the gallantry awards were several to commandos, including a Victoria Cross awarded to Pat Porteous. The US Ranger party under the small and cheerful Captain Roy Murray - six officers and 45 men - proved the quality of Rangers soldiers. One captured ranger answered the question of how many rangers were in England with the reply: 'Three million, all as tall as I am'. His interrogator had a sense of humour, fortunately.

For all the 15 French marines of 10 Commando, men of the 1re Bataillon Fusilier Marin, this first major raid gave their Troop a reputation that attracted more volunteers for their future raids. And the seven marines who had landed with the Canadians at the Casino managed to re-embark, when other units were less orderly in their withdrawal.

One outcome of Dieppe was a successful Allied air battle which provided an effective defence of ships, under an air umbrella that included 69 RAF squadrons, twenty-three Flying Fortresses making a raid on a nearby German airfield. Although the Allies lost 165 planes for the destruction of only 48 German aircraft, only one naval ship, a destroyer, was sunk by enemy aircraft.

This first major raid in Europe illustrated the growing complexity of commando objectives while still employing simple tactics with light weapons. A great deal of thought had gone into these questions of weapons when the US Marine Corps Raider Battalions were preparing for their Pacific landings earlier that August in 1942.

# THE FAR EAST AUGUST 1942 TO OCTOBER 1944

The Japanese failed to isolate Australia from the Americas, and notwithstanding Allied agreement to defeat Germany before Japan, sufficient forces were found for American counterstrokes in the Pacific. Admiral Nimitz controlled one theatre that was shaped to include the eastern Solomons - a small part in a vast area that covered oceans and islands from the Asian coast north and east of the Philippines, down to the equator and further south in its eastern sectors. General MacArthur commanded the second theatre, covering New Guinea and the Indonesian islands to Sumatra, Malaya and Thailand that were in the British South-East Asian Theatre (SEAC).

In the south-west Pacific, MacArthur's armies fought a campaign in New Guinea and northwards to the Philippines. Nimitz led the drive across the central Pacific after the initial landings in August 1942 on Guadalcanal, were followed in 1943 by the recapture of the Gilberts and Marshall island groups, and in 1944 recaptured Guam and other islands in the Marianas. That autumn 70,000 Americans landed unopposed on Morotai Island, north-west of New Guinea, and captured the Palau Island air bases to protect the flanks of an October 1944 landing in the Philippines. The distances of these advances were equivalent to several journeys from London to Moscow: from Darwin (Australia) to Luzon in the Philippines being over 2,000 miles on a convoy route.

United States marines of the 3rd Raider Battalion leaving their APD in inflatable rubber boats to land in the Russell Islands, February 1944. These APD carrier ships were the primary transport of the Raiders.

# 6   RAIDERS IN THE PACIFIC

Amphibious raiding has been a role of marines since they were first raised as sea soldiers towards the end of the 17th century. More than two hundred years later, the United States Marine Corps (USMC) practised their raiding with three Provisional Rubber Boat Companies, a development of 1930s' raiding innovations and tried out on the Atlantic coast in the Fleet Landing Exercise Flex-7 10 months before Pearl Harbour. This showed some of the problems in special service units, but their success in the exercise was encouraging enough for the Marine Corps to follow through with further companies formed on the West Coast.

When war came, President Roosevelt wanted commando-like formations. He was influenced in this by Prime Minister Churchill and, no doubt, by Captain James Roosevelt USMC (the President's son), who, in January 1942, wrote to his Commandant proposing marine units of commandos, stressing in his letter the value of guerrillas in China as well as British experience. The Corps, however, had already made a study of the British commandos when Captains Samuel B. Griffith II and W. M. Greene Jr visited Scotland. Largely on the basis of their report the 1st and 2nd Separate Battalions - later renamed Raider Battalions - were formed on 6 January and 4 February 1942 (see Appendix 7 for these units' histories). The 1st Raiders were formerly boat companies of the 1st Battalion 5th Marine Regiment on the East Coast and now became part of the Amphibious Force, Atlantic Fleet.

Boat Companies on the West Coast, reinforced by a company from the 1st Raiders, formed the 2nd Raiders. Their roles included 'landing on beaches generally thought inaccessible, raids requiring . . . surprise and high speed, and . . . guerrilla operations for protracted periods behind enemy lines'. The commando parallels are clear. However, the Commandant, Major-General Thomas Halcomb, directed that 'Marine' in these battalions' title covered these roles 'and the injection of . . . Commando . . . is superfluous'.

There was also some confusion of aims not uncommon in the politics of Special Forces, although the Marine Corps saw the amphibious limitations for raiders. Captain James Roosevelt suggested, however, among other raids the possibility of landings 'on Japan proper from Mito north to Aomari (as these) would certainly demoralise the enemy'. The Commandant was also under pressure from a 'very high authority' - presumably the President - to accept Colonel William Donovan of the American army as a brigadier-general commanding the raiding project. These intentions seem to imply a force with aspirations closer to the Chinese guerrillas' style of warfare than the British uniformed commando raids. But General Halcomb resisted the political pressure, although the Marine Corps were to some extent forced into forming raider units even if 'all amphibious force marines were considered as commandos'. Colonel Donovan subsequently became head of the Office of

Strategic Services (OSS), the forerunner of the Central Intelligence Agency (CIA).

The American marines were prepared for the campaigns across the countless islands and atolls in the Pacific, where amphibious landings would need exceptional logistics in carrying supplies thousands of miles, and careful reasoning in the selection of stepping-stones around the stronger enemy bases to set up a chain of airfields flighted towards Japan. The Americans' landing exercise Flex-7 had shown the six Rubber Boat Companies of the 5th Marines, with 100 men to a company, were neither 'fish nor fowl', their special weapons (see Appendix 2) making their use difficult in other roles for regular marine battalions. This was one reason contributing to their eventual formation as a separate battalion. In the longer term, preparations for a Pacific war had been made in the personal reconnaissances of the 1920s by Major Earl H. Ellis USMC, whose detailed notes on Japanese-occupied islands became the basis of Marine Corps strategy in the Pacific. Many of his ideas and practical suggestions proved invaluable in the 1940s, including his idea of beach obstacle demolition by swimmers placing charges. This became a reality in 1943-44, but the Major had died in mysterious circumstances 20 years earlier while on the Japanese-held island of Palau.

The colonels appointed to command the Raiders were both men of exceptional experience. Lieutenant-Colonel Merritt A. Edson commanding the 1st Raiders was a quietly aggressive World War I veteran, a pilot, and captain of the Corps' Rifle and Pistol team. He had seen the Japanese in action around Chapei, China, in the late 1930s. Lieutenant-Colonel Evans F. Carlson commanding the 2nd Raiders also had first-hand knowledge of the Japanese, having travelled widely with the communist Chinese Eighth Route Army studying guerrilla tactics. The colonels handpicked their officers, supplementing those of volunteers formed into Raiders, and annoying the devil out of the general commanding the USMC 1 Division, for this levy - as he described Merritt Edson's recruiting - came at a critical time six weeks after Pearl Harbour.

A great deal of thought was given to the way the Raiders should be armed; problems already seen briefly in the overloading of 4 Commando's LCAs approaching the Varengeville beach near Dieppe being one example of the many logistical problems of amphibious raids (see Appendix 3, weight details). An analysis of one American assault team showed seven men carried loads in excess of 100lb (45kg), five carried 75lb (34kg), and the other seven had at least 50lb (22kg) on their backs. Such weights limited the numbers that could be landed in one assault craft and the weapons that might be taken aboard their carrier, for with larger mortars the weight of ammunition was a major factor in loading even an Auxiliary Personnel Destroyer (APD) carrying raiders' craft to a beach area - points sometimes overlooked by war-gamers in the 1970s. There were also more obvious restrictions ashore where the heavier mortar's ammunition could not be moved quickly without motor transport during a sustained advance. Merritt Edson, in a letter of 7 April 1942, explained these considerations and his preference therefore for the 60mm (2.4in) mortar and its 3lb bomb, despite the more effective fire of the 81mm (3.1in) mortar. A compromise might be made by carrying larger mortars without their specially trained crews, much in the way early Commandos used their 3-inch (76mm) mortars, allowing riflemen to fire these specialist weapons. Otherwise, elements of an 81mm Weapons Platoon could be carried only on an APD destroyer by seriously reducing the number of riflemen. The risk of losing heavy weapons if too many were in one transport had also to be taken into account. There were further compromises in balancing the weight of equipment landed against effective firepower, with Merritt Edson's 60mm mortar squads' leaders each carrying the mortar base-plate, a pistol or M-1 carbine with its ammunition, the cleaning brush, and field glasses, loads which prevented them carrying the more powerful Browning Automatic Rifle (BAR) of their counterparts in regular marine platoons.

Although the organisation of Raider battalions was flexible, their operations were based on a company of fewer than 143 all ranks - the cargo-personnel capacity of an APD. Whether these companies might include all mortar teams (see Appendix 2), or whether this fire-power might in part be under battalion control with the 81mm Weapon Company together on one carrier, was one of several problems resolved in different ways by the 1st and 2nd Raiders during their training in February 1942. Six months later the ideas were put to the test in battle.

The 1st Raiders made the initial landings on Tulagi, while the main marine assault was made 20 miles (32km) to the south across Iron Bottom Sound, where the 1st and 5th Marines landed at Lunga Point on Guadalcanal (see map p. 98) in the first counter-stroke ashore against the Japanese. The landings were planned for 7 August, despite the lack of landbased air cover, although three carriers deployed 250 navy planes in support of the assaults. These were unable to isolate the Japanese from their reinforcements, and for some time the outcome on Guadalcanal was in the balance, swinging against the Americans in the early stages because a cardinal principle of amphibious warfare had been neglected in the planning: the sea passages for forces building up the bridgehead were not entirely secure. Tulagi - the planners at first had difficulty finding the island on their maps - lies in the Gavutu Harbour of Florida Island, a small island on a north-west/south-east axis which is only two miles (3km) long and about half a mile wide.

The leading two companies of the 1st Raiders landed over heavy coral outcrops on the western tip of the island at 0800 hours on 7 August. This beach was undefended, probably because it seemed an impossible landing point, and boats from the four APD - USS *Calhoun*, USS *Gregory*, USS *Little*, and USS *McKean* - hung on reefs 30 to 100 yards off the beach, forcing the marines to wade chest deep to the shore. The three follow-up companies - five companies landed from four carriers, overloaded despite the theoretical limitations - came ashore and little resistance was met until the marines reached the saddle between the island's hills. Merritt

Edson had his men dig in for the first of many nights that American marines would stand-to in the Pacific. Four separate attacks on the Raiders failed to exploit minor penetrations through the companies' defences, and by daybreak the 2nd Battalion of the 5th Marines had come ashore. Their 81mm mortars with the Raiders 60mm teams put down a concentrated barrage on the enemy's main defence position in a ravine, before this was cleared by the Raiders early that afternoon, and the whole island was secured by nightfall (8 August). At the end of the month the 1st Raiders were taken across to Guadalcanal.

Meanwhile, on 17-18 August, elements of the 2nd Raiders had carried out a diversion raid on Makin Atoll in the Gilberts 1,000 miles (1,600+km) northeast of Guadalcanal. This battalion was organised in a slightly different way (see Appendix 2) to the 1st Raiders, for Evans Carlson based their formations on a fire group of three men: a scout with a Garand rifle and two tommy-gunners. Three of these groups usually made a corporal's squad of nine men with one BAR man replacing a tommy-gunner. 'A squad so armed', the Colonel wrote, 'can cover a front from 100 to 300 yards long against the 50 yards covered by an orthodox infantry (rifle) squad'. On Makin they were to prove the value of their fire-power, although the ammunition needed to sustain it might prove a logistical headache without strict fire discipline. A later report by Colonel Carlson states 'very, very seldom were automatic weapons placed on full automatic ... one machine gunner fired only single shots getting a Japanese with each'. In these later patrols raiders set out carrying 224 rounds per rifle, 1,000 rounds for the .30-calibre machine guns and 24 bombs for the 60mm (2.4in) mortars. These rounds for the machine guns were a four-man load and two men could carry the mortar bombs.

The intention of the Makin raid was to divert Japanese reinforcements from Guadalcanal, and as the approaches to Makin were patrolled by enemy sea and air forces, the Raiders were taken in two 2,700 ton submarine cruisers, USS *Nautilus* and USS *Argonaut* for the eight-day passage from

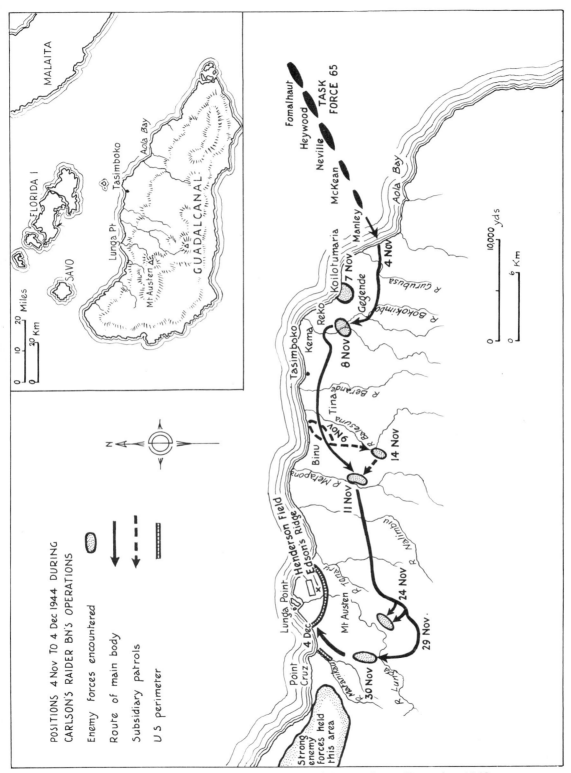

**Map labels (inset, top left):**

MALAITA

FLORIDA I

SAVO

Aola Bay
Tasimboko
Lunga Pt
Mt Austen
GUADALCANAL

20 Miles
10
20 Km

**Main map labels:**

Fomalhaut
Heywood
Neville
McKean
Manley

TASK FORCE 65

Aola Bay

4 Nov

7 Nov
Koilotumaria
Reko
Kema
Gegende
R Bokokimbo
R Gurabusa

8 Nov

Tasimboko

R Berande
Tina

9 Nov
R Balesuna
14 Nov

Binu

R Metapona
11 Nov

24 Nov
R Nalimbiu

29 Nov.

Henderson Field
Edson's Ridge
Mt Austen

Lunga Point
Point Cruz
4 Dec
R Matanikau
R Lunga
30 Nov

10,000 yds
6 Km

**Legend:**

POSITIONS 4 NOV TO 4 DEC 1944 DURING
CARLSON'S RAIDER BN'S OPERATIONS

Enemy forces encountered

Route of main body

Subsidiary patrols

U S perimeter

Strong enemy forces held this area

N

USMC Raider Battalions' principal actions on Guadalcanal, September to December 1942.

## DIARY OF KEY EVENTS:
### 1st Raider Bn (Edson)

**8 Sept** Three coys landed at Tasimboka and were joined by paramarines in an attack on the rear of Japanese positions, the enemy withdrew leaving a bivouac area the Raiders destroyed.

**12 Sept** Raiders with para-companies took positions on 'Edson's ridge' south of airfield.

**13 Sept** Dug in on ridge before heavy attacks after nightfall, Raiders hold out during 10 hours close combat.

**14 Sept** Remnants of Japanese assault force withdrew.

**15 Sept** Raiders relieved from ridge positions they had held with support of artillery and divisional troops.

### 2nd Raider Bn (Carlson)

**4 Nov** Landed Aolo with elements of 147th Inf Regmt and 5th Defence Bn.

**6 Nov** Detachments of 2nd Raiders moved out carrying 5 units of fire at start of a month behind enemy lines.

**7 Nov** By-passed Koilotumaria where enemy concentrations reported.

**8 Nov** Fought off ambush by small enemy force at Reko.

**9 Nov** Binu base established and supplied by LCP(L), men usually cooked individually their rations of dehydrated foods, tea and rice.

**11 Nov** Raiders engaged by bn of Japanese near Asamana and succeeded in forcing this enemy away from their intended concentration area.

**12 Nov** Occupied Japanese defence positions etc. killing many messengers and others coming into Asamana area.

**13 Nov** Raiders directed artillery fire in breaking up five attacks by Japanese columns, before returning to Binu.

**14 Nov** F Coy patrol destroyed 15-man outpost in narrow valley near Binu. During the next two days small groups of enemy stragglers mopped up, ammo and food captured.

**15 Nov** Moved base to Asamana at end of first phase of operation.

**17 Nov** Ordered to take artillery position shelling Henderson Field and find any enemy bases south and west of upper Tenaru river.

**18 Nov** Bn moved in two stages camping on the upper Malimbiu river (not shown on map) before reaching base on Tenaru. Col Carlson made a personal recon each day to select camp sites etc. during these moves.

**23 Nov** Joined by A Company landed from transport.

**24 Nov** Base for patrolling established on upper Tenaru.

**29 Nov** Moved base to position nearer Japanese trail from Lunga lines concentrating patrols higher up Tenaru valley.

**30 Nov** Entire bn crossed ridge using ropes to scale cliff before surprising Japanese killing 75 and destroying 75mm mountain gun that had been shelling airfield, enemy camp sites were destroyed, one 9-man Raider squad catching some 100 enemy unprepared.

**4 Dec** Raiders entered 1 Marine Div lines—approx 175 enemy had been killed for the loss of 6 marines in a month of patrolling.

Pearl Harbour. *Nautilus* carried out a periscope reconnaissance of the target beaches on the afternoon of 16 August, and that night the two submarines made their rendezvous in a heavy rain squall. By 0300 hours early next morning they were 500 yards (450m) off the southern beach of Butaritari Island which forms the base of the atoll's triangle of islands around its lagoon. Here a one to one and a half knots (2.7kph) current pushed them westward towards a reef, making station-keeping difficult because the submarines had constantly to keep going astern. The pounding of heavy surf drowned any shouted commands, but all 13 officers and 208 men - two rifle companies each less one Section - followed Evans Carlson towards the beach. Some outboards on their inflatable assault boats broke down, and these rubber boats then had to be paddled or towed; in the resulting confusion all boats were ordered to one landing beach, not the two as planned.

Butaritari is three miles (4.8km) long and less than half a mile (800m) wide, covered from shore to shore by a thick growth of coconut palms. Despite the surf on the exposed southern shore, 15 of the boats reached the target beach; two landed a mile north-east of this point but the men joined up with the others, while a third boat drifted westward, coming ashore behind a line of Japanese defences protecting the rear of the island's Government House and wharves on the north shore facing the lagoon. Some 70 to 80 infantry, with at least four machine-guns, a flame-thrower, two hand-grenade launchers, and automatic weapons defended these installations, and were bumped by A Company going across the island at first light - 0600 hours. They captured the Government House without opposition and moved south-west down the lagoon road. Reinforced by B Company which broke through the defences about 1130, Sergeant Clyde Thomason's gallantry in this action being recognised by a posthumous award of the Medal of Honour. The enemy continued to snipe at the marines by firing from coconut trees, where their positions were only exposed by sawing off the palm fronds with machine gun fire. Some support from the submarines' single 6-inch (152mm) guns was given early in the battle but the raiders lost radio contact with the submarines about 0716 hours. A little later 'false plane contacts' caused them to dive and they did not resurface until 1000 hours. Enemy activity around the atoll was increasing, however, and the American submarines sank a small transport (3,500 tons) and a patrol craft (1,500 tons) by gunfire. These actions brought Japanese reconnaissance planes, and early in the afternoon 12 aircraft spent an hour dropping occasional bombs and strafing the likely American positions. The last air attack fell where the Raiders had held positions before Evans Carlson withdrew his right flank. By this move he hoped he would draw out some of the Japanese, which he did, some being caught by bombs; but as night would fall quickly on this tropical island, the Colonel now pivoted his flank platoons, moving the men back to the boats, which were launched at 1930 hours.

Despite their extensive training in surf, the Raiders were caught in a rapid succession of great waves that swamped outboards and drove many boats back against the beach. A few got beyond the breakers, with flailing paddles and props screaming as they were thrown clear of the water during the boats' short trip to the submarines. For others the struggle was 'so intense and so futile . . . it will forever remain a ghastly nightmare', with four or so boats unable to get off the beach. They had lost most of their gear and some weapons in the hour's struggle to get beyond the breakers, and those boats that were not swamped in sea water were filled by heavy rain. By dawn the surf was still high, great walls of water crashing against the exposed beach, and after repeated air alerts the submarines were forced to withdraw, having arranged a rendezvous for that night.

The day ashore was spent in patrolling for Japanese weapons to replace the Raiders' losses and for food. Few enemy were found alive on the island; 1,000 barrels of aviation petrol (avgas) were destroyed, and some documents were taken from the Japanese headquarters before the Americans withdrew. That night the rubber boats were car-

ried across the island and launched on the smoother waters of the lagoon, where they were lashed to a native outrigger. In eight minutes the outboards brought this makeshift raft alongside the *Nautilus* off the entrance to the lagoon at 2308 hours.

The Raiders had lost 30 men, 14 killed in action, seven drowned, and nine whose fate was unknown until after the war. The nine were possibly in a boat that drifted westward trying to come off the beach on 17 August and after a brief captivity they were executed by the reinforcements the Japanese sent to the island. Reference has already been made to one authoritative view of the raid's adverse effect in stiffening Japanese defences. However, these were early days in the Americans' war, and the Japanese certainly diverted forces to Makin Atoll and the defence of other islands, tying up men, materials, and shipping when - as happened on Timor - these resources might have been diverted to militarily more profitable ventures. However, there was no way the Japanese could control all or many of the Pacific islands unless they retained air and sea superiority, a lesson they would first learn in the Solomons.

Guadalcanal, with 'its mountains cutting the island lengthwise in an even wall of blue and green, with peaks tapering into the cloud masses of a brilliant tropical sky', looks pleasant enough from a distance. But from these mountains coral ridges reach towards the beach. Some are covered in knife-edged kunae grass high enough to catch a man's throat, and on other spurs lush jungle blacks out the sun from steep ravine sides cut by torrential streams that carry water northward from the rugged interior. Incessantly damp from one of the highest rainfalls in the world, with debilitating humidity, malaria mosquitoes, stinging ants, and disease-carrying black fly, this is an unhealthy - even hellish - island. There were hopes of using the independent battlions to mop up Japanese units on islands by-passed in the later sweeps towards Japan, but the Marine Corps Commandant and other senior officers saw the dangers in diluting regular battalions through further drafts of their best men to the Raiders, and formation in the field of a second '2nd Raiders' was abandoned. However, a 3rd Battalion was formed in Samoa, and a 4th raised in California during October that year, 1942.

Two companies of Raiders had made one uneventful patrol in an APD in the first few days of September on coming over to Guadalcanal, and they were to make a landing the next week from three destroyers at Tasimboko, 20 miles (32km) east along the coast from Lunga Point. Coming ashore before dawn on Tuesday, 8 September, three companies of the 1st Raiders swung west, supported by 23 planes flown by USMC pilots and by two warships. Moving against the rear of the Japanese positions facing Henderson Field, the Raiders were heavily engaged by mid-morning. The paramarine companies now under Merrit Edson's command were also landed by boats as the battle developed against the flank of some 4,000 men of the Kawaguchi force preparing to retake the airfield. This morning the Japanese withdrew, but they would fight within the week.

After destroying the abandoned Japanese camp, the Raiders and paramarines were brought back to the main beachhead around Henderson Field. Anticipating the renewed Japanese counter-attacks against this perimeter, the 1st Raiders and three paramarine companies were sent forward on Saturday night (12 September) to take up positions across a ridge rising southward from the airfield over open ground to the edge of the jungle. When they had dug in across the ridge, their line of defended positions ran from the east bank of the Lunga River to the paramarines' positions of the east side of the ridge - a line some 500 yards forward of the main perimeter. The whole beachhead was overlooked by Japanese observers on the lower slopes of Mount Austen 1,000 yards further south-west, so these dispositions, which formed a breakwater against mass attacks rolling against the southern perimeter, were clearly seen by them.

Throughout Sunday the marines dug in, improving their fox holes and network of mutually defended positions under sporadic sniper fire from units they had bumped against several times the previous night. Shortly after nightfall the first attack came in against the right and centre of the marines' line, and during the next few hours the Japanese made more than a dozen frontal attacks - screaming waves of assault troops from three battalions of Major-General Kiyotake Kawaguchi's brigade. By 2200 hours that night, two under-strength parachute companies and B Company (less one platoon) of the 1st Raiders faced two enemy battalions on the left of the ridge; the enemy along the battle line outnumbered the marines by 2 to 1. The shouts of the Japanese, and their methodical use of flares announcing each renewed attack, gave the marines some points of aim, but for 10 hours they were locked in hand-to-hand fighting. Insults were shouted at the marines in the hope of making them lose their tempers and then rashly expose their positions. There were shouts of 'Gas . . . gas' in the hope that this might put the marines in

A Raider Company's patrol with native guides on Guadalcanal, November 1942.

some panic. But there were more than words, more than sticks and stones, for the Japanese made their usually expert use of mortars, cutting off the forward marine positions from immediate support with a wall of mortar bombs around the fox holes. Taking every advantage of dead ground and other cover, the Japanese came forward. The 105mm (4.1in) American howitzers in the perimeter were elevated dangerously high, lobbing shells almost back on the gun crews as they fired at below the howitzer's minimum safety range. Blind in the dark and smoke, these crews ranged their guns, by ear on occasions, at the uproar from the enemy assembly areas. At other times the guns were ranged by map reference, even though the 'cartographic data' was poor: the maps were inadequate because details familiar to gunners in Europe were not shown. Despite these handicaps, the gunners' superb performance saved the Raiders as frenzied assault waves drove them back in a tight perimeter around the centre of the ridge. Here they held on, preventing any Japanese who got through the barrage from reaching in any strength the borders of Henderson Field. Only two small groups got as far as the rear areas, here four enemy killed a sergeant with a sword blow before they were shot near the 1 Marine Division's command tent. Feints against other sectors east and west of the Raiders' positions caused some sensible delay before marine reserves were committed, but at the height of the Kawaguchi attacks the 2nd Battalion of the 5th Marines was sent forward. Despite the Japanese ruses to unnerve them with shouts of 'Gas - gas' and insults tempting marines from their cover, the Raiders and the 2nd Marine Battalion kept their heads and the defence positions.

At dawn on Monday the remnants of the Kawaguchi force could be seen withdrawing towards the lower slopes of Mount Austen. The Kawaguchi force was broken. They had fought, as the Japanese would do throughout the war, with fanatical bravery, and although they had no artillery support in their assault on Edson's ridge they were able to press forward despite the losses from American shell fire. The raiders came off the

ridge on Tuesday 15 September having lost 20 per cent of their strength in this battle of Bloody Ridge.

The 2nd Raiders, rested after Makin, came to Guadalcanal on 4 November, landing at Aola ahead of a defence battalion and a construction battalion to build a new airstrip, 25 miles (40km) east of Henderson Field. For the Americans, the crucial battles would be fought at sea in the next few weeks, when Japanese attempts to neutralise Henderson Field by sea bombardment failed and many of their transports were sunk bringing the 38 Division to Guadalcanal, despite the superior naval strength of the Japanese west of the island. While these battles were fought, and while American army troops reinforced the marines in the main perimeter, Evans Carlson led a 30-day patrol by the 2nd Raiders inland, parallel to the coast and westward to beyond the main perimeter (see map p. 98). Their first base was established at Binu on 9 November 'because it was located about 3 miles (5km) south-east of the enemy and placed my forces to cover the enemy's rear (south side) . . . also Binu was the last place between the Balesuma river and the division's positions . . . where natives still resided, making easy the task of securing information and carriers' - to quote Evans Carlson's report. The enemy were boxed in by the main marine force. The Colonel planned to fan out strong patrols each with a TBX radio coming on the air every two hours to report to the battalion's command post. When contact was made the plan was to concentrate the battalion and destroy any enemy force slipping south into the mountains.

On 11 November C Company on one of these patrols ran into a Japanese force about 1010 hours, they were three miles (5km) west of Binu. The Japanese took advantage of the marines' difficulties in concentrating the battalion, and moved their major force through woods running south between grassy fields, a smaller party turning west possibly to attack the airfield at Cactus. Evans Carlson decided to attack the main force and leave those moving westward for later mopping up.

F Company made a forced march that

morning to return to Binu about 1300 hours, and the Colonel decided they should rest and be fed before he took them up to C Company's positions where they arrived - after an hour's march - about 1630. C Company were bogged down, their initial success that morning had been thwarted by the Japanese troops' quick recovery, for after the marines' scouts caught the enemy camped in a wood, heavy Japanese fire came down on the platoons in open country running up to the wood. Most of the afternoon had passed before the marines extracted themselves back the 700 yards (630m) to cover. Evans Carlson sent F Company down a finger of wood where many of the enemy mortars and machine guns had been hidden, and two fighter-bombers were called in 'dropping their bombs on target' further into the woods during the attack that went in at 1745. F Company's advance enabled B Company to cross the open ground, but the Japanese had withdrawn all but a few snipers and the wood was cleared by 1830.

Night fell and the battalion withdrew 'as we were unfamiliar with the terrain'. F Company was left to hold the wood until morning. Although they had failed to concentrate as quickly as the Colonel planned - even in the last stages of the battle E Company had failed to disengage from their action by the river and block the enemy's late afternoon retreat - the Raiders had pre-vented the enemy concentrating his much stronger force, and the Colonel's next move was to Asamana where there were positions the Japanese had prepared for a battalion or more. In the three days from the 12 to 14 November many Japanese messengers were killed coming into these positions and on the 13 November five attacks by 'companies . . . in massed columns, each individual being covered from head to hips in a curtain of foliage' were broken up as mortar and artillery fire fell on what appeared as 'a patch of brush'. These and later actions are summarised in the diagram.

A typical Raider company patrol made use of the flexible organisation and might - on Guadalcanal or elsewhere - include three rifle platoons, a weapons platoon, and company headquarters. Each platoon's three squads were divided into three fire-teams, giving squad corporals better control than when working with nine individuals. The weapon platoon in each company might have three Sections - two with a pair of the quick firing Browning light machine guns (see Appendix 3) and the third Section with 60mm (2.4in) mortars. (But the organisation was changed to suit specific operations and only representative examples are shown in Appendix 2). This organisation placed the weapons for immediate supporting fire under the command of each company. The company commander also had 15 men in the headquarters who might act as a reserve of

The well camouflaged Japanese guns were difficult targets for planes and warships to find, this gun at Enogai (New Georgia) was captured by the USMC 1st Raiders in an overland approach after coming ashore at Rice Anchorage, July 1943.

riflemen, but who were also each trained as a sniper or a demolition man. The arguments for putting a major part of the machine-gun and mortar support in a *weapons* company under battalion control may be suited for routine infantry deployment, but in the opinion of Evans Carlson, supported by Major-General Alexander A. Vandegrift who commanded the 1 Marine Division on Guadalcanal, the organisation of support weapons within companies was superior for the Raiders' operations. This helped the six companies of the 2nd Raiders with their headquarters company - seven in all - fighting as large company patrols more often than as a battalion. The arrangement also spread the risk among several APDs rather than risking the majority of its heavy weapons in one ship that might be sunk or delayed. The 1st Raiders did have some support weapons with each rifle company - two 60mm mortars and two Browning machine-guns in a small platoon of support weapons, besides a Weapons Company.

After their actions on Guadalcanal, both the 1st and 2nd Raiders were regrouped under the command of the 1st Raider Regiment in March 1943, along with the 3rd and 4th Raider Battalions. From their bases in American Samoa and French New Caledonia, over 1,000 miles (1,600+km) east of the Solomons, they were used to spearhead a number of landings described in their brief histories in Appendix 7.

Late in June two companies of the 4th Raiders and half the HQ company, a force of some 150 men, landed under Lieutenant-Colonel Currin on the east coast of New Georgia, where they joined the coast watchers at Segi Point. This patrol reported Japanese movement to reinforce the defences of the key Munda airstrip, cleverly sited behind swamps in the west of the island. Six days later, Currin, in a war canoe, led his men from Segi Point along the coast to land from inflatables near Viru harbour on 27 June: their intention was to destroy the coast guns before the main force landed to take the harbour. Trekking waist-deep at times in mangrove swamps under heavy rain, the Raiders had some setbacks (see Appendix 7) but by the evening of 1 July

they had moved inland around the harbour and taken from the rear its main defences on the western shore of the narrow entrance. Other Raiders were active on the north-west coast of the island, and on 5 July the New Zealand-led 1 Commando Fiji Guerrillas - known to the Americans as Fiji Scouts - landed from canoes east of Munda to establish an observation post on high ground behind the Japanese positions. After moving a mile inland, they were in contact with the enemy. However, the Fijians moved silently, only firing when they had a target, in contrast to the heavy fire laid down by US Army formations before an advance. Although on this occasion the commandos did not reach the high ground, they later carried out a number of long patrols (see Appendix 7) behind enemy lines.

Casualties and sickness through this and other campaigns that summer severely reduced the Raider battalions' fighting strength, with only some 260 fit men in the 2nd Raiders that August, and the 1st Raiders down to 676 men against an established strength of 1,106 all ranks by 1943. Nevertheless, in the autumn of 1943, the 2nd Raider Regiment (Provisional) was formed to co-ordinate the Raiders operations against Bougainville, one of the largest of the Solomon Islands.

There were to be many more amphibious operations in the Far East, but for the marines advancing across the Central Pacific these would not be the soldier's battles of small units in thick jungle. Their first, 43/4 landings were on the atolls and tiny islands of the Gilberts and Marshalls, each with their small land area and difficult approaches across reefs and surf as at Makin; then through the islands of the Japanese inner defence ring at Guam and Okinawa among other heavily defended bases captured after artillery, naval, and air bombardment: a series of slogging matches on the atolls that left little room for outflanking or other raids, and then against sophisticated beach defences and hostile islands. No doubt with these prospects in mind the Raider battalions were reassigned to a newly formed 4th Marine Regiment. The men of the original 4th Marines had stood against the Japanese for five months in the siege of Corregidor, when guns on the mainland of the Philippines pulverised their defences and air bombardment was practically continuous.

The War Plans Division of the Chief of Naval Operations brought the Raiders into the 4th Marines because 'a separate regiment ... in lieu of abolishing raiders ... will be specially trained for raider operations but will be organised and equipped so it can be effectively employed as a standard infantry regiment ... such a separate regiment will find frequent employment ... primarily as shock troops or to augment divisional troops'. This begs a number of questions on encumbering Special Forces with gear for a defensive role - discussed in Chapter 14 - but as the 4th Marines the old Raiders were to land at Guam in July 1944, and on Okinawa in April 1945. Long before these actions, they took part in the last Solomon Islands landing, unopposed in taking Emirau in the Matthias group 200 miles north-west of Rabaul, thus slamming the door on this Japanese stronghold which was being by-passed in New Britain.

The lessons of Guadalcanal and other Solomon Islands landings were mainly to benefit General MacArthur's army command in matters of jungle fighting and malaria control as they continued jungle campaigns through New Guinea and the Philippines. But the wider implications of mounting amphibious assaults on a grand scale would benefit all Allied planning of future invasions, as the annotations on the British copies of reports on these Pacific actions suggest. As far as weapons were concerned, the marines on Guadalcanal had .300 calibre Springfields, which compared unfavourably with the US army's Garand rifle. This robust weapon of the same calibre had better fire-power, although its 8-round clip could be wasteful of ammunition for it was usual to put in a fresh one before the next Banzai charge as topping up a clip was a difficult job. The mechanical reloading (see Appendix 3) made the weapon easy to use in rapid fire, and its hitting power was much greater than the carbine's, the Garand having nearly 50 per cent greater muzzle velocity at over 2,700 feet per second, which

approached that of the BAR. This velocity, like the range, varied with the type of bullet, but after August 1944, when ball ammunition was in general issue, the Garand could be used effectively at 2,000 yards (1800m) to 'search' the reverse slopes of a hill. Despite its weight at 9½lb (4kg) to the carbine's 5½lb (2.5kg) and the smaller magazine with eight rounds to the carbine's 15 or 30, the marines preferred it. Dowsed in salt water, covered in sand, tangled by jungle vines, it still fired eight fast rounds, and the large aperture back-sight gave a reasonable aim in even the poor pre-dawn light; with telescopic sights, the Garand made a sniper's shot deadly at 700 yards (630m).

The Thompson sub-machine gun, of which a Raiding battalion had about 200, was a delightful weapon to fire, and an experienced shot could get off single rounds although his weapon was on automatic fire. The mechanism, however, was complicated and easily fouled by grit, sand, or salt corrosion. Nor, for other reasons, was this weapon the answer to every raider's or commando's prayer. The effective and accurate range was limited to tens rather than hundreds of yards, and even though it could be fired at a rate of 600 to 725 rounds a minute, the actual rate was always limited by the time needed to change magazines. More comparisons are shown in Appendix 3 dealing with weapons, but in the same way that the weight of ammunition for mortars was a factor in the logistics of amphibious raiding, so also was the weight of .45 inch (11mm) ammunition needed if tommy-guns were fired too frequently in long and literally heavy bursts.

The overwhelming superiority by 1945 in American heavy weapons - guns, planes, and ships - took three years to build up from the relatively slight superiority the US forces achieved in the Guadalcanal campaign. This ended in February 1943 after six months of fighting in which the American marines and army had 6,111 casualties including 1,752 killed. The Japanese, skilful to the last, evacuated more than 13,000 men but lost many men killed in the campaign.

# FRENCH NORTH AFRICA, MOROCCO, AND ALGERIA, 1942

These French colonies were controlled in 1942 by Vichy France under German influence. The Free French General de Gaulle expected to win over these colonists to the Allied cause, but he was a difficult ally, not least because he mistrusted the Americans, who had tenuous relationships with the Vichy government before Pearl harbour. Many senior American and some British commanders had misgivings over the proposed North African landings, code-named 'Torch', for if the French fought with German support the Allies would be caught up in a conflict that could give little help to Russia. Yet Stalin wanted proof of the western Allies' intention to fight the Germans on more than the Eighth Army's desert front in Egypt.

Success in North Africa would open the way to landings in southern Europe and offer the prize of French fleets in the North African ports. These ships fought, but the French army put up only a token resistance, largely because American diplomats had paved the way for a swift armistice.

Two weeks before these landings, at 2130 hours on 23 October, the British Eighth Army opened their offensive at El Alamein, and by early November Rommel was in retreat from Egypt. His Afrika Korps skilfully withdrew to Tunis, fighting their last major battle against the US 1 Armoured Division and the British 6 Armoured during mid-February 1943. But brief victories at Kasserine and elsewhere could not withstand the Allied squeeze, between the First and Eighth Armies, that drove the Germans and Italians from Africa by mid-May 1943. The Mediterranean could now be used for convoys sailing through Suez to India and the Far East war, even though the Germans occupied southern France in response to 'Torch'.

The proposed Ranger force was discussed in April 1942 by General Marshall and Lord Mountbatten who suggested the name Ranger - a link through the Royal Americans to the British 60th Rifles (KRRC). At that time General Truscott was the senior American staff officer in COHQ, and later commanded 3 Division with an experienced staff drawn largely from COHQ.

# 7  RANGERS IN AFRICA

The World War II use of special forces as shock troops owes something to the German *Stosstrüppen* shock troops of World War I. Their élitism, their discipline, and their fighting qualities were well-known to the senior British officers who created the commandos. However, the idea blended into the commando concepts of guerrilla troops which were as old probably as war itself. Their use with regular formations has included some striking victories such as that won by French-Canadians and Indians, 900 strong, who defeated a hand-picked expedition of 1,400 British and American colonists in 1755. The experienced Scots General, Edward Braddock, expected the enemy's light forces to be helpless when faced by a line of battle and the first French attacks were repulsed by Colonel Cage as his leading troops in the expedition formed line. But the woodsmen and Indians moved around the flanks of the forest road, pouring steady fire at the disciplined ranks of Redcoats whose volleys and controlled bayonet charges could find no targets. Edward Braddock was mortally wounded and defeat became a rout, although George Washington extracted the provincial troops he commanded in a controlled withdrawal. This defeat led to a re-thinking of military tactics that would later have influences in Europe, and in the Americas the Rangers were formed under Major Robert Rogers, John Stark, and others who took on the woodsmen and Indians at their own game in the wars of 1755-63. Nearly two centuries later,

the Rangers gave their name to the American army's commando-type formations of World War II.

These 20th century Rangers were raised after General Lucien K. Truscott had reported to the Chiefs of Staff on 26 May 1942 that there should be an immediate formation of an American force along Commando lines. As mentioned earlier, the President had already given his support to such American formations, and a battalion of Rangers was recruited from American troops stationed in Northern Ireland. The appeal for 'volunteers not averse to dangerous action' was answered by some 2,000 men and after vigorous selection this was whittled down to 500 on the initiation course at Carrickfergus on the coast north of Belfast. General Eisenhower expressly asked for a different name to commando, since 'the glamour of that name will always remain - and properly so - British'. The historic origins of the name must have escaped the General, for the Boers have a prior claim to commando, but associations are probably more important than nationality for the 18th century Rangers were fighting for the British. This certainly was no bar to the naming of the 1st Ranger Battalion, formed on 19 June 1942.

The few Rangers in action with 3 and 4 Commando at Dieppe have been described, and these had parallels to the parts played by a handful of Rangers in General Wolfe's assault on Quebec. Of the men at Dieppe one British commanding officer wrote:

'Everyone liked them and enjoyed their company'. In the next few years Commandos and Rangers would be in each other's company on several occasions.

After the 1st Rangers had completed their training at the Commando depot at Achnacarry they moved to a bleak island in the Hebrides for the 'most miserable part of the training' in driving rain and cold nights. Living on Royal Navy rations, they found, was plain fare by comparison with the GIs' normal chow. Other comparisons between British and American service life were quite marked in the two Allies' differing approach to military discipline in World War II. The Americans had fewer restrictions but tougher penalties: for supplementing their meagre rations with a deer he had stalked, one ranger was fined £40. His commando counterpart would no doubt have had two weeks confined to camp, but if he had taken 10 shots to kill the beast - as the ranger reportedly required - the commando would probably have been ordered back to his unit for basic training in small arms. So, I suspect, would the ranger had his Colonel heard of it, for there was little to choose between the standards of weapon training expected from rangers or commandos. Comparisons of pay - a typical ranger private earned about twice as much as a commando - led to some friction, just as the British Tommy's pay of a shilling in World War I had angered the French Poilu on a few sous a day. Fighting between the Allies in British pubs, occurred although not with Commandos and maybe the ranger's 48-hour thrash during a leave in Oban was the

origin of a widely held but unfounded British view that all rangers were ex-convicts. Certainly the return of Captain Roy Murray's men from Dieppe had a sobering effect on the battalion, for these raiders 'looked older, weary and deadly serious'.

Not long after this action the 1st Rangers moved into civvy billets in Dundee, Scotland, for the only time during their service, and in October 1942 they completed their training with rehearsals for a major landing. They then sailed from Glasgow, joining a convoy from the States, for the invasion of North Africa. Their carrier ship, the LSI(H) *Royal Ulsterman*, which landed the Independent Companies in Norway, cleared the danger zone of U-boat operations before the men were briefed for their part in the landings - code-name Torch - spearheading nearly 14,000 Americans in 35 transports headed for the eastern landing of a series that would envelop Oran in the Vichy French colony of Algeria. The Rangers were to land at Arzew some 30 miles west of Oran; their task: to clear the two forts dominating the approaches to the harbour.

The night of 7-8 November 1942 was so dark 'you could not see 10 feet in front of you' as the rangers mustered to climb aboard the landing craft, a platoon in each boat. (These were hand-hoisted on *Royal Ulsterman*, as a Landing Ship Infantry (Hand Hoist), LSI(H)). The mortar team boarded first, going aft, with the two Sections (see Appendix 2) one each side on the LCA's low seats either side of the well and under the side decking. The platoon commander, his top-sergeant, and their runners boarded last

Typical terrain near Arzew, North Africa, where the Rangers made a night landing spearheading invasion troops on 8 November 1942.

to be first out on the beach. The *Ulsterman's* hand-davits were strong enough to lower loaded boats, and they were successfully launched although 12 rangers had a swim when catapulted from their craft as one of the falls broke. A more serious loss in this mishap was the only radio that would net the rangers into the fleet frequencies and the support of the 20 British warships protecting the transports.

Despite this hitch the Rangers were only a few minutes late - as you may remember - when they passed Stan Weatherall in the canoe marking the left limit of their beach. Landing below the bluff, Lieutenant-Colonel William Darby led his four companies up a steep cliff path, D Company pushing their trolleys carrying 81mm mortars, a ranger device for moving these forward quickly. One platoon commander had been unfortunate enough to be stranded as the LCA hit a false beach and its coxswain refused to hazard his craft by going back against this rock ledge, but the rest of the companies followed Bill Darby clear of the low cliffs and up two and a half miles (4km) of rocky and winding hill paths to the ravine at the rear of the Legion's fort and battery. Scouts out ahead found four machine-gun positions and two double aprons of barbed-wire, the well-prepared defensive positions expected from French troops.

The sound of sporadic bursts of fire came from the town: A and B companies were in action. Up on the bluff, Bill Darby's scouts went forward again to cut the wire, the companies forming a skirmish line, each man two yards from his neighbour, when machine-gun tracer flicked the ground around them. F company was withdrawn slightly from its exposed positions as the 81mm mortars and the light machine-guns of the Rangers opened fire. Any hold-up at this time could court disaster: out of touch with the fleet, the Ranger companies would be caught in their own naval gunfire which was planned to a timetable should the fort not be taken. After two minutes of covering fire the skirmish line moved forward to the wire where they found the three scouts had cut gaping holes before lying within 20 or 30 yards of their own mortar burst. Across this

Ranger team with improvised cart carrying 81mm mortar and 32(?) bombs, North Africa February 1943.

open space beyond the wire the Rangers stormed with those yells that well-trained assault troops keep for the final charge. The French machine-gun crews had left their guns and were found with the battery teams in dugouts. At 0400 Bill Darby fired the green Very light signalling success.

The two companies in the port had shot two sentries on the jetty and caught most of the garrison asleep, but later that morning the Rangers faced a brief display of resistance with some fire from the Legion's fort and from the battery near the harbour. However, the French surrendered the port after this token resistance and a little shelling by their batteries further inland.

American Combat Teams - the 16th and 18th - with an American armoured force had been landing since dawn, but during the morning they ran against stiff opposition some seven miles (11km) down the road south-west of Arzew in the hills behind Oran. Here, at St Cloud, the French had fortified a village and held its stone and concrete houses with the support of a 75mm (2.9in) and a 155mm (6in) gun. C company of the Rangers moved forward that evening (8 November) and next day took part in the assault on this village. Charging across open ground led by Lieutenant Chuck Shund-strom, they breached the French defences but Lieutenant Gordon Kleftman was killed.

The apparent ease with which the Rangers had taken the forts led the Allied Force commander to send HMS *Walney* and HMS *Hartland* - two ex-US coastguard cutters - into the naval base of Oran. Aboard were 400 men, mainly from the US 6th Armoured Infantry Regiment and some canoeists hoping to prevent the scuttling of ships, but the French were not caught unawares and the cutters were savaged by fire at close range from destroyers, the landing parties being all killed or captured.

From the armour ashore in the initial assault, a task force swung east but was stopped by a battery of French 75s some nine miles (14km) along the coast road at La Macta. E company of the Rangers was sent to help clear this block, and Lieutenant Schneider, with rangers who had served in the 1 Armoured Division, took over a few half-tracks, attacking the battery from the flank while HMS *Farndale* gave them supporting fire. The guns were captured. The main battle - more of politics than weapons - was settled after two and a half days when Oran surrendered.

The Rangers, if not their senior army commanders, felt they had established a fighting reputation at St Cloud and La Macta, but Bill Darby knew the necessity for more training before they met serious opposition. For the next few weeks, therefore, he had the battalion practising landings from LCVR (LC Vehicle Ramped) and LCVP (Vehicle Personnel).

Night fighting had been a speciality of Roger's Rangers, when in silent movement without voiced commands these woodsmen in their buckskin jackets stole through an enemy's forest, their surefooted silence in moccasins bringing them under a fort's timbered walls: they had climbed it with hatchet holds taking them into his camp before anyone realised they were there with their fighting knives. For the 20th century rangers and commandos, similar night movement became almost more familiar than daylight attacks, and so the 180 men of the 1st Rangers were trained night fighters

when they set out under Bill Darby for an overland raid in February 1943.

The Italians, with German support, held three strongpoints guarding the Sened Pass where the road to the coast (at Sfax) goes between the Majoura and Biada mountains. These positions had to be carefully recced by Colonel Darby before he brought his raiders by truck to the French outpost 20 miles (32km) west of the pass. The men were prepared for a silent night march, having left behind such jangling equipment as the GI's issue concertina cup; besides their weapons, they carried a shelter-half (groundsheet), a small ration pack, and a single canteen of water. Their boots were saddle-soaped to prevent any night-shattering squeaks; the dogs of their equipment were taped down; they wore cap-comforters which enabled them to hear the slighter sounds a tin-hat might muffle.

They crossed the pebble plain of enemy-patrolled country before snaking in a long file led by A Company across the ridges and boulder-strewn slopes of the central Tunisian mountains. For the men in the rear platoons, as in every speed march, the pace increased until they were jogging if not running to keep up, and in a little more than two hours they had crossed 14 miles (22km). In 'a bluish dawn' they reached a bowl-shaped saddle between two towering peaks, the bivouac area Bill Darby had selected two nights before on his reconnaissance. Scouts were set on the rim of the hills; the men spread their shelter-halves for camouflage and shade between the boulders and over rock crevices where they would sit out the day. There was no movement except for essential relief, and the valley must have appeared deserted to the German reconnaissance plane that flew over. The day was brilliantly clear when junior commanders edged cautiously between rocks at the saddle's rim for Captain Roy Murray - the veteran of Dieppe - to brief Section leaders. He showed them the Sened Pass, a cleft in the mountains behind three hills six miles (10km) away to the east across a plateau. Bill Darby had seen four enemy armoured patrols cross this plain in the first three hours of daylight, but none came near the rangers' bivouac as they sweated and catnapped through the day.

After dusk they came down from the saddle towards lower ground bathed in eerie bright moonlight, but when the moon set they were ready for a compass march on a bearing across the plain. Beyond the enemy positions they could hear the rumble of tanks (or other heavy vehicles?) which lent urgency to their march, now only a few paces apart. (If the man ahead is lost in the dark, those behind become detached : all lost in the night.) In an hour they were across the plain, the scouts guiding the night march having silently killed several men in an enemy patrol. By 0200 hours the companies were forming line by companies, a notoriously difficult manoeuvre in the dark as each company swings forward on the flanks of the centre one. Swing too far wide and a company can lose contact, but this night the Ranger companies came in line moving forward up a slope, with A Company on the left, E Company having paused in the centre allowing the others to move up, with F company on the right. The drill so often rehearsed went smoothly and the battalion moved forward half a mile (800m), each platoon in files kept abreast of the company headquarters by watching the brief pinprick of red light from the company commander's torch, while the squads could see the occasional light of their platoon commander's small green torch. Bill Darby kept control by radio on each company's progress.

Marching forward, the men felt the tingle of apprehension when no fire met them at a comfortable distance. They were a mere 50 yards from the enemy wire when A company on the left was fired on, and as they and the centre company moved forward they could hear the sentries 'Qui va la? . . . Qui va la?' as the machine-guns were manned, opening fire across the whole Ranger front. A 47mm (1.8in) cannon was also raking the advancing line as the rangers went to ground. Their only chance lay in going forward, for there was no cover, not even the occasional boulder, on this bare hillside. They wriggled on their stomachs in the way they had been taught to crawl, snaking forward for 40 yards (35m) pressed to the ground, driven by that element of urgency which enemy fire gives to battle action and distinguishes it from even the most arduous training. On damper ground just below the last rise before the enemy guns, the rangers were below his line of fire: the squads moved into skirmish lines. A grenade tossed, a shouted yell, each man has moments - testing his courage - and these rangers all passed theirs, for they bounded up the slope, firing from the hip although still facing stabs of tracer from out of the darkness behind the enemy's front positions. The defenders were not to be dislodged in one rush. Two rangers crawled within feet of an Italian machine-gunner firing aimlessly over the attackers' heads: he and his crew probably never felt the point-blank tommy-gun burst that killed them. One ranger - James Altierei - fell into a nearby slit-trench, landing face to face with an Italian. He 'nearly panicked, then I remembered my commando knife snugly sheathed around my right leg'. A lightning thrust killed the Italian and as the warm blood spurted over his hand James Altieri was sick.

The rangers stormed on in anger, and no doubt in fear as men fell wounded. 'It was sickening, it was brutal . . . but that was our job', Altieri wrote later. They cleared the hill and took several prisoners. These, along with the 18 wounded rangers on improvised stretchers slung between rifles, were taken with the force as they moved out two and a half hours before dawn. What little water they had was passed to the wounded.

Bill Darby led them, his long steps hurrying them back across ridges and ravines, then stretching their stride to cover the last six of 20 desert miles. Ignoring their thirst and the ache of hunger after two nights and a day in the enemy's hills, they pushed on fearing his tanks might encircle them. The wounded suffered the pain of this rough journey without complaint, and as the sun rose the Rangers carried them clear of the mountains. Bill Darby stood at the foot of the path, his blackened face glistening with sweat, his uniform torn and tattered. 'Keep pushing', he urged the stragglers as they covered that last six miles to the comparative safety of the French outpost which was now

Lieutenant-Colonel William O. Darby leads his rangers in a speed march in North Africa. Later in the War while still under 35, he was killed in Italy in April 1945.

guarded by some British armoured cars that moved out to cover the last stages of the rangers' withdrawal.

The direct military gains from the raid were some 100 Italians killed, six quick-firing cannon and 12 machine-guns destroyed, and useful intelligence gained from the prisoners on German and Italian dispositions in Tunisia. A further and far-reaching outcome was the proof of the 1st Rangers' ability to hit hard in a complex operation, in which their skill and daring had kept their own casualties to one killed and 18 wounded. German radio paid its own peculiar respects to their prowess, referring to them as 'the Black Death'.

Two days after the raid in the foothills of the Sened Pass, on 14 February 1943, Ger-

man tanks broke through the American lines and Rangers covered the withdrawal of II Corps, marching out under the fortunate cover of a heavy mist. For several weeks the Rangers - as did 1 Commando and ·6 Commando - fought as infantry, taking more than 30 prisoners in active patrolling.

On 21 March, the Colonel led the battalion 12 miles (19km) along a mountainside track - it almost goes perhaps without saying: through the night - along a route reconnoitred the previous two nights by ranger scouts. The path crossed low cliffs, along fissures, and wound through high valleys to a plateau overlooking Italian positions blasted out of the Djebel El Ank gorge in the mountains east of El Guettar. This gorge was on Patton's line of advance and the nests of strongpoints would be difficult to take in frontal assault. High on the plateau behind them, however, the rangers formed a skirmish line and in the half-light before dawn rose on a bugle call, they were leaping down the slope with shrill Red Indian warcries, jumping from rock to rock. They were on the Italians before this enemy could redirect his machine-guns to defend the rear of these positions, and in 20 minutes the Italians were overrun. The battalion then worked their way across the gorge, reaching the foot of the opposite slope by midday. Here their Italian-speaking padre, Father Basil of the Commandos was able to persuade the enemy officer to surrender his unit, saving many lives which would have been lost had both sides of the gorge had to have been fought for.

Although this pass was cleared, there would be many battles fought before Patton's army joined Montgomery's Eighth Army coming from the east. The Rangers themselves fought in a dozen soldiers' battles in the fluid situation around their army's main thrust. D company once being cut off, some time was needed for other rangers to relieve them. Although this war in Tunis would not be over until early May the Rangers were pulled out of the fighting on 27 March 1943. Their history is followed in later chapters and summarised in Appendix 7, but the 1st Rangers' companies were the nuclei of other battalions.

# THE EASTERN MEDITERRANEAN, 1940 TO 1943

In the last months of 1940, the British desert army took only 10 weeks to advance 700 miles (1,100+km) into the Italian colony of Libya, crossing its province of Cyrenaica and penetrating the province of Tripolitania. In mid-February 1941, General Rommel and his Afrika Korps landed at Tripoli, driving the British back into Egypt during April, although their garrison at Tobruk held out.

The British and Commonwealth army in Africa had been depleted when an expeditionary force was sent to Greece. The Germans entered Greece and the Greeks capitulated on 6 April 1941. The British extracted most of their forces from the mainland, but lost 29,000 men fighting the German airborne invasion of Crete late in May.

Against this background of changing fortunes in the desert, and the Axis occupation of many Mediterranean islands - although not Malta and Cyprus - the commandos mounted a couple of major raids and several small ones.

The consequences of the victory at El Alamein and the November 1942 landings in North Africa have been described earlier. But the Americans continued to consider the Mediterranean a less important theatre than north-west Europe, where a 'second front' would require almost all the available shipping. Nevertheless, an invasion of Sicily was agreed at the 'Trident' conference in Washington (May 1943). This operation 'Husky' was carried out in July 1943: three American divisions landed, spearheaded by Rangers, on the south coast, to drive north across the western part of the island to Palermo; and, four British divisions with Commandos landed on the south-east tip of the island to advance north along the east coast to Messina.

General Alexander held the US Seventh Army in the west of the island, protecting General Montgomery's flank, but once these Americans turned east along the north coast road, there was a race to Messina as the British made their way around the slopes of Mount Etna. Despite attempts to cut their escape route, the Germans skilfully evacuated 60,000 of their men and 75,000 Italians during the five days to 17 August, when Sicily was finally secured by the Allies.

# 8   MEDITERRANEAN SHOCK TROOPS

By 1943 the roles of the Commandos had multiplied since the winter of 1940-41 when Roger Courtney took his SBS canoeists from Arran to the Med, and raiding from the United Kingdom was made by small units with the only raid by a full Commando - Lofoten in March 1941 - attacking a soft or undefended target. Nigel Clogstoun-Willmott had pioneered a specialist role in beach reconnaissance, the United States Marine Corps were landing Raider companies, and the US Rangers were expanding with five battalions and eventually six. Other commando and raider units, large and small, were in various stages of development, as will be seen in later chapters dealing with theatres outside the Mediterranean. But in the Mediterranean and Middle East, there were, in the changes that took place in commando roles between 1941 and 1943, many parallels to other theatres. Similarly there were parallels to the changes in personal relationships between individual services and between Allies in the developments of amphibious raiding.

In March 1941 a force of 7, 8, and 11 Commandos arrived in Egypt at a time when General Rommel's Afrika Korps were gaining the initiative in the desert and German troops were moving through Yugoslavia to support the Italians in Greece. Known as Layforce, after their commander, the resolute and professional Lieutenant-Colonel R. (Bob) E Laycock, these commandos were joined by 50 and 52 (Middle East) Commandos raised in Egypt. Although the force was initially used as a reserve brigade of the British Eighth Army, Bob Laycock was asked to mount a raid on Bardia. This port lay on a forbidding coast some 250 miles (400km) west of Alexandria and, because the Germans were within 50 miles (80km) of the British Imperial Headquarters in Cairo, was beyond British fighter aircraft cover. The Colonel was keen his men should do well in this first major raid likely to meet opposition - Vaagsö was nine months away - but things went wrong from the start.

HMS *Glengyle* (see Appendix 4), carrying 7 Commando designated A battalion in a brigade of 6 Division, arrived with her escorting anti-aircraft cruiser and three Australian destroyers off Bardia on the night of 19-20 April 1941. Roger Courtney, his submarine already late after being attacked by British (!) planes, damaged his canoe on launching and was unable to fix the intended navigation marker light on an

Landing craft used in Sicily and other invasion landings: top left - LC Infantry (Large) for shore to shore operations; LC Support carried by landing ships with LCAs etc; LC Mechanised for landing a single tank or vehicle; LC Tank Mk III carried 5 Churchill tanks but the Mk III was too deep draughted for flat Normandy beaches; LC Personnel (Large) an American designed raiding craft built for RN with weather protection hood etc; top right - LCT Mk V used to ferry vehicles from assault transports to beach; LC Assault the principal British minor landing craft of which nearly 2,000 were built; LC Vehicle later replaced by LC Vehicle Personnel as wooden minor craft in general service with American forces and used by other Allies.

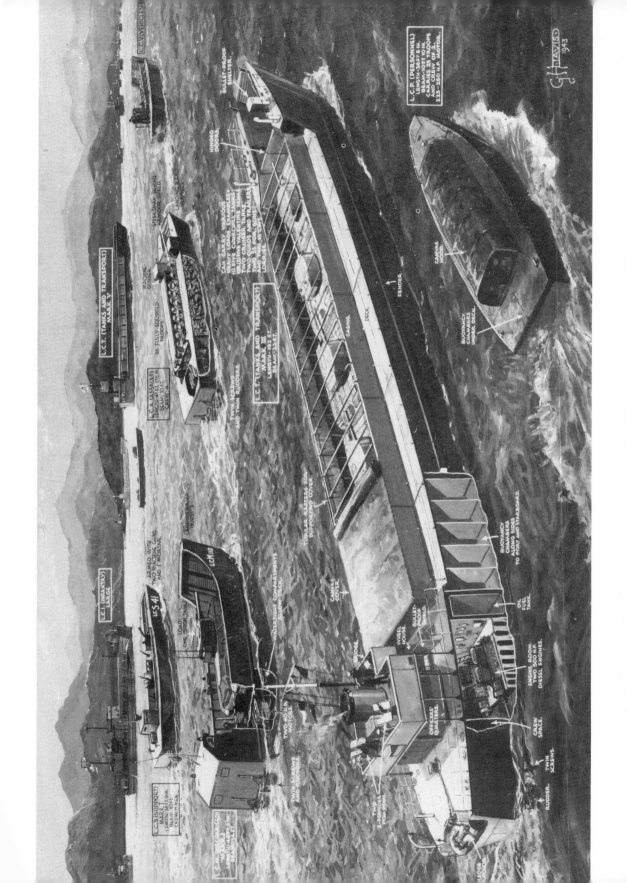

L.C.V. (VEHICLES)

BULLET-PROOF SHELTER.

L.C.P. (PERSONNEL)
LENGTH-36 FT 8 IN.
BEAM-10 FT 8 IN.
CAN CARRY 30 TROOPS
AND CREW OF TROOPS
225-250 H.P. MOTOR.

HINGED DOORS.

STEERSMAN BEHIND
ARMOUR SHIELD.

L.C.T. (TANKS AND TRANSPORT)
MARK V

LANDING RAMP
RAISED.

MACHINE
GUNNER.

CANVAS
HOOD.

CAN CARRY VARIOUS
HEAVY LOADS, EXAMPLES:
6 FIVE CHURCHILL TANKS,
OR NINE MEDIUM TANKS,
TWO CRUISER TANKS
AND TWO QUADS AND TRAILERS,
OR 350 TONS OF
LORRIES.

L.C.A. (ASSAULT)
LENGTH-41 FT 1½ IN.
BEAM-10 FT
CARRY 4-C

35 FULLY EQUIPPED
TROOPS.

FENDER.

BUOYANCY
CHAMBERS
UNDER DECK.

TWIN SCREWS
AND TWIN RUDDERS

DECK.

CASING.

LANDING RAMP
RAISED.

L.C.T. (TANKS AND TRANSPORT)
MARK III
LENGTH-192 FT.
BEAM-31 FT.

L.C.I. (INFANTRY)
LARGE

ARMED WITH
TWO 4 IN. GUNS
AND 1 MORTAR.

LANDING ROUND
TRUSSON.

TUBULAR RAFTERS FOR
SUPPORTING COVER.

WATER-TIGHT COMPARTMENTS
BUOYANCY CHAMBERS.

CANVAS
COVER.

BUOYANCY
CHAMBERS
ALONG SIDES
TO PORT AND STARBOARD.

OIL
FUEL
TANK.

LCS 41

LOAD,
ONE DESTROYER.

BRIDGE.

WHEEL
HOUSE.

BULLET-
PROOF
SHIELD.

OFFICERS'
QUARTERS.

ENGINE
ROOM
TWO 500 H.P.
DIESEL ENGINES.

L.C.S. (SUPPORT)
ASSAULT
LENGTH-38 FT 9 IN.
BEAM-10 FT
CREW-11 MEN.

TWO 40 H.P.
MOTORS.

TWO
CHAMFERED
CHAMBERS.

TWIN SCREWS
AND RUDDERS

CREW
SPACE.

TWIN
SCREWS.

TWO
RUDDERS

G.H. DAVIS.
1943

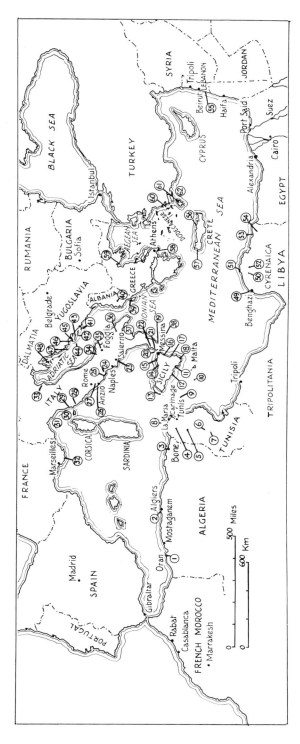

Location of Special Forces' Mediterranean, Italian and related operations showing large forces' actions in capitals (date and *code name*) in alphabetical order by year. Numbered locations broadly follow coast lines: 1-10 in French North Africa; 11-18 in Sicily; 19-32 western Italy and southern France; 33-38 in eastern Italy; 39-48 in Adriatic; and 49-62 in eastern Mediterranean.

**1941**

| | |
|---|---|
| Appollonia (18 Nov, *Cooper-Flipper*) | 51 |
| Apulian aqueduct (by paras, 10 Feb, *Colossus*) | 36 |
| BARDIA (19/20 Apr) | 54 |
| Beda Littoria (18 Nov, *Cooper-Flipper*) | 52 |
| Benghazi (May) | 49 |
| Berbera* (16 Mar, 1/2 & 3/5 Punjabis, *Appearance*) | |
| Cap d'Ali (28/30 July, SBS) | 16 |
| Cirene (18 Nov, *Cooper-Flipper*) | 50 |
| CRETE (May) - not numbered | |
| Gulf of S. Euphemia (27 July, SBS) | 20 |
| LITANI RIVER (9 June, *Export*) | 55 |
| Rhodes (Mar, beach recces) | 61 |
| Senigallia (27 Oct, SBS) | 29 |
| Seracino River (27/8 Aug, SBS) | 27 |
| Tobruk 'Twin Pimples' | 53 |
| Torre Fili (28 May, SBS) | 38 |

**1942**

| | |
|---|---|
| Algiers (60 miles east of, 21 Oct, SBS) | 2 |
| ALGIERS (8 Nov, *Torch*) | 2 |
| Antsirane (by RMs, 6 May) not located | |
| ARZEW (8 Nov, Torch) near Oran | 1 |
| BIZERTE (30 Nov to 3 Dec) | 8 |
| BONE (11 Nov) | 3 |
| Calato, Rhodes (Aug/Sept, SBS *et. al.*, *Anglo*) | 62 |
| Gibralter as a Cdo base - not numbered | |
| Gulf of Genoa (29 Nov, SBS) | 31 |
| Herakleion (13/4 June, Free French) | 56 |
| Kastelli (9/10 June, SBS) | 57 |
| Kupho Nisis (15/6 Apr, *Lighter*) not located | |
| MATEUR VALLEY (Dec) | 4 |
| Maritza, Rhodes (Aug/Sept, SBS *et. al.*, Anglo) | 62 |
| ORAN (8 Nov, *Torch*) | 1 |
| Rhodes (Aug/Sept, *Anglo*) | 62 |
| Tabaka (30 Nov) see Bizerte | 8 |
| TOBRUK (14 Sept, *Agreement*) | 53 |

**1943**

| | |
|---|---|
| Aegean raids began† | |
| AGONE (13/4 July) | 17 |
| BAGNARA (3 Sept, *Hooker*) | 21 |
| Bova Marina (27/8 Aug) | 19 |
| BROLO (11 Aug, US infantry) | 14 |
| CAP D'ALI (15 Aug) | 16 |
| CAP MILAZZO (15 Aug) | 15 |
| DJEBEL EL ANK (21/2 Mar) | 7 |
| GARIGLIANO (29 Dec) | 25 |
| GELA (9/10 July, *Husky*) | 11 |
| GOUBELLAT PLAIN (winter/flspring 1943) | 5 |
| LAMPEDUSA (June, by infantry) | 10 |
| LICATA (9/10 July, *Husky*) | 12 |
| NAPLES-FOGGIA (Dec, 'North Americans') | 35 |

*not on this map

†Raiding Forces Middle East landed on some 70 islands in the Aegean and eastern Mediterranean (for examples see 'Greek islands' map and Appendix 7), these raiders concluded their 381 separate operations with a landing on Rhodes, 2 May 1945.

††COPP No. 10 operated in the Med from 1 June 1943 to 30 Nov 1944 and with other COPPs surveyed beaches of southern France, not all the locations of these and other COPP recces are shown in this diagram.

islet. The LCAs were not launched until 2235, some two hours after *Glengyle* reached the dropping zone. One craft stuck in the davits and others were late beaching after the 40-minute run to the shore, but there were no enemy troops on the beach as the men - in 'ankle putties, oldest battledress and gym shoes' - came ashore, wading chest-deep through a nasty swell. One party crossed a *wadi*, the dry bed of a desert's flash-flood river, crossed over a flooded tank trap, and then 'at a beast of a clip' marched on a compass course of 101 degrees to the Italian barracks, taking these in a rush after pausing to assemble the Sections before the attack went in at 0030 to a timed plan, apparently. The attackers killed or wounded some 45 Italians according to an eye-witness and fired 25 vehicles, but the stone barracks could not be burnt down. They came back on a reciprocal compass course to the boats guarded by several Sections. Other parties failed to find the local pumping-station or were too late to set charges on installations before having to withdraw - again apparently to a timetable - because the boats had to leave the beach in time to allow the carrier to clear the coast before daylight. However, some Italian naval guns' breaches were blown before the commandos left the beach. The LCAs returned to their carrier although many had trouble with their compasses, not an uncommon event before crews realised how easily a tin hat or box of ammunition placed too near the binnacle might upset the magnetic needle.

The raid did draw some German units from their lines further east, and several early lessons came from this raid. The difficulty of moving quietly *and* quickly over rough ground was clear, although a man moving quickly at night is a much harder target for defenders to hit. The carrier ships - HMS *Glengyle*, *Glenroy*, and *Glenearn* - were specially equipped Landing Ships Infantry (Large), LSI(L)s, able to carry more than 1,000 troops but able to land only about 400 with the full complement of their LCAs in one flight. This proved a handicap and smaller LSIs came to be used for raids; there was little point in hazarding a 10,000 tonner when a ship half this size could land 400 men and do so with easier ship-handling. The Glen carriers were taken from the commandos, however, and transported troops for the campaign in Greece.

11 Commando was moved to Cyprus and the rest of Layforce ordered to Crete in late May. They could not get ashore on 25 May because of heavy weather but were landed from a fast mine-layer on 26-27 May at Suda Bay on the island's north-west coast. Here, near the German's most westerly of three airborne landings six days earlier, the commandos held positions astride the road going south to the evacuation port of Sphakia. They experienced their first dive-bombing attack, less physically dangerous than nerve-shattering to troops in slit-trenches. The men's nerve stood this test, and in the next few days they fought a rearguard action. Bob Laycock sent small fighting patrols, seven or eight men, to counter-attack the Germans just before dark each night, discouraging the enemy from too-aggressive night actions. A bayonet attack by G Troop of 7 Commando showed this enemy - no less than many other troops - had a distaste for cold steel. In the flurry of such skirmishes the Commando headquarters was overrun on 28 May. Bob Laycock and the Brigade Major jumped into a nearby tank and drove off these Germans, the tank rumbling forward still in its swath of camouflage netting. A foretaste of Bob Laycock's positive leadership.

By the time the Commando reached Sphakia, most if not all the evacuation craft had left and only a quarter of the unit survived. Many were prisoners but a few sailed a landing craft for six days, reaching North Africa under a sail made of blankets held together by boot laces. 11 Commando was now the only effective amphibious force in the Med, and was called on to outflank the 22nd Algerian *Tirailleurs'* positions north of the Litani river, which the Australians were to cross in driving north from Palestine into French Syria.

Captain C.H. Petrie RN commanding HMS *Glengyle* knew that the river-mouth would be hard to find at night and the frequently heavy surf on this coast made any landing difficult. He therefore searched for someone with local knowledge and found Sub-Lieutenant F.N. Colenut RNVR, an ex-Palestine Policeman, who with great courage swam ashore on the night of 6-7 June to reconnoitre the beaches. The next night Captain Petrie was ready to put the Commando ashore at first light *north* of the river. They were commanded by the fiery and some say 'hated' Lieutenant-Colonel P.R. (Dick) H. Pedder, whose second-in-command was Major Geoffrey Keyes, son of Admiral Keyes, at that time Director of Combined Operations.

Dick Pedder divided his Commando into three groups. Captain George R.M.H. Moore's men landed on the left (most northerly) beach and struck at the French artillery lines some way back from the river. The other two groups - under the CO and second-in-command, intended to circle the redoubt covering the bridge at Kafr Bada, capturing this crossing before its demolition charges were blown. George Moore and the Colonel got ashore to plan, although a near-full moon was setting behind them and they faced a sunrise giving too much light for comfort on the run-in. Geoffrey Keyes's cavaliers, as he called his Troop which was recruited from several famous cavalry regiments, moved inland some way before discovering they were south of the river. They had to borrow a boat and under intermittent but sometimes heavy fire, the cavaliers ferried themselves to the north bank.

Meanwhile Dick Pedder's men pushed toward the rear of the redoubt against stiffening resistance. He was killed, his junior officers all wounded, and RSM Fraser - this was the Scottish Commando - led the men forward, capturing the local barracks and some French troops moving forward to reinforce the redoubt. George Moore, by this time, had taken several field guns and howitzers, his men at one point becoming embarrassed by having more prisoners than commandos. However, the French Algerians were not yet finished, for an increasingly heavy mortar barrage was falling on the Commando's positions when Geoffrey Keyes arrived to reorganise the attack, taking the redoubt by lunchtime (1300 hours). 'No.11' returned to Cyprus having lost a quarter of their strength with 123 casualties, but Layforce was not brought up to strength. Although the Greek islands, among other obvious targets, offered scope for raiding, the shortage of escort ships and the senior commanders' preference for formal battles as the best way to destroy large enemy forces prevented any further major amphibious raiding during that summer and the winter of 1941-42 in the Med.

A night raid was made, however, by 40 men from 8 Commando going outside the perimeter of the besieged Tobruk. On the night of 17-18 July 1941, they slipped through the Italian lines and 'walked briskly, it was like an English summer night' to the rear of two Italian strongpoints known as Twin Pimples. Their rubber boots helped them move silently and quickly while the 18th Indian Cavalry Regiment put in a frontal assault on the hills. The commandos got within 30 yards of the Italians before being challenged. Forming line - a skirmish line as the Rangers would say - they charged,

and in three or four minutes controlled the two hillocks. Australian sappers blew up the ammunition bunkers and the commandos left the hilltops within 15 minutes of their attack, a timing judged to a nicety for Italian artillery began a bombardment of the positions when the commandos had barely left them.

One of Bob Laycock's aides, Captain Evelyn Waugh, a Royal Marine at that time, has left some revealing diaries and notes of the brigade's service aboard the Glen ships. Describing the clash of service personalities seen through this novelist's eyes, 8 Commando was 'boisterous, xenophobic, extravagant, imaginative, witty, with a proportion of noblemen which the (Royal) Navy found disconcerting'. For, he goes on to explain in his diaries, the Royal Navy Volunteer Reserve (RNVR) officers aboard included many callow youths self-conscious of their position. Captain Philip Dunne

General Sir Bernard L. Montgomery listens to Lieutenant-Colonel John Durnford-Slater (on left), 19 October 1943.

likened this to the guard on a train in which the army were first-class passengers. Philip Dunne had been in the raid on the Twin Pimples and was a former member of parliament; like many other officers in 8 Commando he was well-connected, for this Commando included many Guards Brigade officers and men, their CO, Bob Laycock, having served with the Royal Horse Guards. To many of the bank clerks, insurance salesmen, and other juniors from industry and commerce, the young RNVR officers in charge of landing craft flotillas, such pedigrees meant more than they would to most men in the 1970s. But as the war years passed, these youths became men and experience in action counted in their favour. Relationships improved by late 1943, although Evelyn Waugh has suggested that they might have done so in 1941 had 'both (services) been inefficient in the same way (as, indeed, the navy liked 3 Commando)'. The comparison may not be the whole story, for John Durnford-Slater commanding 3 Commando was by no means inefficient, even if he gave all the appearance of a casual approach to his soldiering. There was also a carefree attitude among the many peacetime yachtsmen who set the tone of RNVR crews in Combined Operations: the soldiers going ashore into hostile fire had to take a more serious view or they would not have survived.

Layforce was disbanded in the late summer of 1941, most of the men returning to their regiments. Others went back to the United Kingdom and six officers with 53 men under Bob Laycock remained in the Middle East as a raiding force attached to the Eighth Army. There were already a number of other special service units operating in the desert, and Nigel Clogstoun-Willmott was serving for a time with one of them: the Long Range Desert Group. Jock Lewis and Paddy Mayne from Layforce joined David Stirling's 62 Commando (see Appendix 7) that became the Special Air Service (SAS), but theirs is another story.

Bob Laycock's small force were given the job of capturing or killing General Rommel in what was thought to be his headquarters at Beda Littoria some 125 miles (200km) from the coast (see map p. 116) and over 500 miles (800km) from Alexandria. Sailing in the submarines HMS *Torbay* and HMS *Talisman*, they were off Hanna on the night of Thursday 13 November 1942. Captain J.E. Haselden, a British Intelligence officer disguised as an Arab, signalled the beach was clear and the commandos paddled ashore. With a heavy sea running, several men had been washed off HMS *Torbay*'s casing and only half the party were able to land. They spent Friday drying out their gear until rain added to their discomfort as they lay up till nightfall. At 2000 hours Geoffrey Keyes, recently promoted Lieutenant-Colonel, led inland 32 men who would attack Rommel's house. With them was Lieutenant Roy Cook and six men who would cut the headquarters communications with Cyrene/Tobruk. Bob Laycock with a sergeant and two men stayed near the beach in the hope that the remainder of the party could land, and they protected the assault parties' escape route.

After travelling for a couple of days they were brought by their guides to a cave, and on Monday morning (17 November) during several thunderstorms Geoffrey Keyes reconnoitred the enemy buildings. With the help of an Arab boy he was able to draw a map of the headquarters' layout, Corporal Drori - a Palestinian - acting as interpreter. The raiders moved towards the German headquarters at 1800, although the storms made the going ankle deep in mud. They had six hours to midnight when their attack would coincide with the opening of the Eighth Army's November 1941 offensive against Rommel.

After four and a half hours of slipping and sloshing through the mud, the commandos were at the bottom of a 250-foot (over 75m) escarpment, its slope treacherously slippy in the wet. Halfway up a dog barked as the raiders froze still while a door opened, its light streaming out less than 100 yards away. A man shouted. The dog stopped barking and the door slammed shut. At the top of the slope they followed a track towards the headquarters. Geoffrey Keyes and Sergeant Jack Terry, who had been with Keyes at Litani, went 50 yards ahead after the Arab guides left them and Roy Cook set out for the telephone pylon he was to demolish. Then the main party was approached by an Italian and an Arab but Captain Robin Campbell and Corporal Drori persuaded them the patrol was German and they reached the positions for their assault.

Keyes, Terry, and Campbell pushed through a hedge and ran up some steps, opening the front door. A German coming through the vestibule beyond, grabbed Geoffrey Keyes's tommy-gun and in the confined space the four men jostled for a split second before Robin Campbell shot the German - a .38 pistol making less noise than a tommy-gun. Inside the large hallway the raiders found an empty room leading from the hall and a man coming down stairs fled at the thump of a tommy-gun burst. A second door opened on to a room with 10 Germans standing about. Geoffrey Keyes fired a few rounds (from his Colt .45) before closing the door, while Campbell drew the pin from a grenade. On reopening the door to lob this in, Geoffrey Keyes was shot before the grenade exploded.

They moved Geoffrey Keyes outside the building, a natural reaction among even the most highly trained soldiers, but their commander was dead. Going back into the hall, Robin Campbell found all was silent and he went out towards the back of the building where he was mistaken for a German and badly wounded by one of his own men. Hit in the leg, he would not allow the men to carry him back to the beach and Jack Terry led them there, a difficult journey over bare hills and skirting sand seas they reached the coast on Thursday, two days after the raid. That night HMS *Torbay* signalled that conditions were too rough to take off the commandos and she would be back the next night, but during Friday the commandos were attacked first by Arab levies of the Italians and finally by Germans.

By breaking the party into small groups, Bob Laycock with Jack Terry got through the line of enemy riflemen and into the hills. Others were not so skilled or lucky - escaping in these situations needed a fair measure of good fortune, however skilfully the commando made use of his field craft. Five or more of them were murdered by Arabs; others were captured.

The Colonel and Sergeant, however, made an incredible trek covering many hundred desert miles in 41 days, often living on berries, and once eating the stomach of a goat whose remains they went back to dig up after burying them two days earlier. Despite their starvation they reached the Eighth Army lines, with the help of friendly Arabs, and were in time for Christmas dinner. Within the week Bob Laycock flew back to England where he took command of the Special Service Brigade (see Appendix 7) on Charles Haydon's promotion as military adviser to Lord Mountbatten.

For his leadership in the raid on what was thought to be Rommel's headquarters Geoffrey Keyes was awarded the Victoria Cross, but the raiders' bravery was misdirected through no fault of theirs. This headquarters was a supply troops' centre, and Rommel as far as is known, had never visited it. Such errors of intelligence would be avoided during 1942 and later by an extremely efficient intelligence organisation attached to Combined Operations Headquarters. A brilliant RAF Officer of World War I, Wing-Commander the Marquis of Casa Maury, organised this hand-picked team of intelligence officers from all three British services who were later joined by a number of Americans. From this department came a completely detailed file for the St Nazaire raid, the flow of reconnaissance studies on Normandy beaches, and the many cross-links between commando, SOE and partisan reports building up a picture of enemy dispositions on the beaches to be invaded.

In operations, however, the full benefit of this knowledge could not always reach the small parties of raiders who were involved in what might be termed support for local armies. M-section of the SBS, for example, were landed from the submarine HMS *Una* with little time for proper rehearsal on the afternoon of 11 August 1942. Their purpose was to disrupt a German bomber base in range of a relief convoy sailing to Malta. The available information was meagre - sketchy might be more apt - before the three officers, two NCOs, a guardsman, and a marine, under Captain George Duncan prepared to launch their canoes when the submarine surfaced about 2100 hours. 'After 36 hours in artificial light, the night seemed terribly black', Eric Newby has written, but once the canoeists were accustomed to it 'it seemed very bright indeed'. One canoe was holed in launching and had to be left behind: the other three got away in arrowhead formation with a strong wind at their backs raising a nasty swell. Bombers thundered a few hundred feet over their heads.

Corporal H. H. Butler and Eric Newby - whose book *Love and War in the Apennines* opens with a full account of this raid - felt very lonely when they reached the beach, for 50 feet (15m) away was a wire entanglement some 20 feet (6m) wide. They carried the canoe to the wire, set the fuses in their thermite bombs - 'big black conkers' on white cordtex lines of fuse - concocted with plastic explosive. They buried the canoe and retraced their steps to the water's edge, so they could remove all their own footmarks, before cutting a path through the wire midway between two blockhouses 150 yards (over 130m) apart. Avoiding the more obvious anti-personnel mines, they were through the wire an hour after leaving the submarine, but they were behind schedule. This was a quick in-and-out job, and the submarine would lie off the coast until an hour after midnight. They hurried on, down a deserted track, hearing the appalling sound of marching men which turned out to be only the champ of a horse's teeth as it chewed grass; they crossed a high wall and blundered into a farm, but its barking dogs roused no one. Half a mile further on they were in the workshop area of the aerodrome among buildings frighteningly bright with lights. Here they left some bombs on crates of new engines - 'it seemed a terrible waste of explosives' when they intended to prevent bombers taking off the next day.

They were just about to split up and place their charges when a squad of Italians came up. George Duncan's *'Camerati Tedeschi'* did not sound very convincing: an Italian took a shot at these 'German comrades'. Yet all might have been well had not one of the raiders fired back. Immediately floodlights lit the airstrip, lorries started up, Very lights were fired. In the confusion Eric Newby was about to shoot a German shouting loudly when the figure growled in lowland Scots: 'Don't shoot you stupid bastard. It's me.' The raiders dodged into the shadows of the workshop buidings, thankful there were no guard dogs as reported from Cretan airfields.

'What we ought to do', said George Duncan, 'is . . .'

'Eff off' answered an NCO. 'Eff off while there's still time.'

This experienced raider's advice was taken, and the parked JU 88s were left in their many ranks as the men headed back for the beach. They dropped their bombs at the base of a pylon which could be repaired in a couple of days or less, and were moving south-east when a lone RAF Wellington bomber came in, a planned diversion that put out all the airfield lights - by its presence, not its bombs. By now it was 2230 and they were among the coastal batteries and apparently empty trenches when Sergeant Dunbar, bringing up the rear, stepped on what he took to be ordinary ground. He fell through the groundsheet cover of an Italian defence post and was wounded before being captured. Fortunately for M-section, though, this outpost apparently had no telephone contact with its company headquarters.

Coming through some wire they were equally lucky when 12 Italians saw them, but instead of starting a fuss, they pushed off, and the commandos continued their scurry towards the canoes. But which way were these? North or south of where they now came through the wire? Rather than follow the Italian patrol, they turned left and came to the gap they had cut in the wire some two hours previously. One canoe was unusable and they launched the other two with three men up, in a rising wind. Offshore they flashed their hooded torch but no submarine appeared and they had no infra-red RG. By 0300 both canoes were waterlogged, and when Eric Newby's sank they clustered round their last canoe, pushing it towards the shore opposite the rendezvous for the next night. They never reached it. The sun was rising on a beautiful morning, Mount Etna's smoke-plume 'like a quill of a pen' away to the north above the haze, when some friendly fisherman pulled them out of the water about breakfast time.

HMS *Una* came in three nights running, but M-section were all prisoners. Despite the German bombers, however, five of the 14-ship convoy reached Malta, including the oil tanker *Ohio*.

A month later the Middle East Commando, temporarily reinforced by Royal Marines and other troops, carried out the last North African raid to take place before the commandos took over their new roles spearheading invasions. In a series of disruptive forays aimed at diverting the Axis' attention from the build-up of forces for the El Alamein battle, the commandos were to land at Tobruk, reoccupied by the Axis that summer. This port lay some 300 miles west behind the Axis front and on their main supply route from Tripoli a further 300 miles (480km) to the west. Although supplies could be landed at Tobruk, it could handle only a tenth of the 600 tons a day needed by the German and Italian armies, but it was nonetheless a forward supply area with vital storage tanks holding petrol essential to the Afrika Korps if they were to maintain their positions before Alamein. Around the time of this raid SBS canoe parties would land on Rhodes, the SAS (Special Air Service) would go overland to raid Benghazi, others would attack the airfield at Barce; while a fighting patrol from the Sudan Defence Force raided the Giallo Oasis.

In the Tobruk raid, Lieutenant-Colonel J.E. Haselden - whom we left as a junior captain signalling in Bob Laycock's men for the raid on Rommel's headquarters - was in overall command and led a party going overland to set up beach marking lights. John Haselden, Egyptian-born son of an Englishman and his Greek wife, was a cotton mill owner whose service with the intelligence units was more often clandestine than regular soldiering. His Troop included men of the Special Indentification Group (SIG), among them former German nationals resi-

dent in Palestine in the 1940s and two British officers: Captain Herbert Bray, an Oxford scholar fluent in German, and Lieutenant David Lanark, who is reputed to have spoken six German dialects. John Haselden's men would filter through the Italian perimeter of Tobruk, passing themselves off as a German patrol, a role played with such attention to detail that four men not only wore German uniforms but also each carried a couple of love letters from their girls supposedly in Germany, and they marched in the German style, swinging their hands across the body. Once inside the perimeter they would hold a small bay near the harbour and signal in the main forces. Known as Force B, John Haselden's men had a long and difficult approach march - if travelling with Long Range Desert Group vehicles can be described as a march, for it was closer to a voyage across the Great Sand and other so-called seas, over hills, and the scrub of the desert.

The landing of the Royal Marine Force A was delayed when no radio signals were received from John Haselden, and after the decision to land was made at 0210 for launching the boats at 0300, there were further delays caused by trouble with the assault craft. The first flight eventually began their run-in and the destroyers moved back out of range of the coastal batteries. On returning half an hour later, expecting the craft to be coming offshore for the second flight of marines, they found only broken-down craft, including the Colonel's which carried the only ship-to-shore radio. Coming within a mile of the shore about 0415 they could see fighting on the beach, but after standing off this headland for threequarters of an hour HMS *Sikh* was caught in a searchlight beam as she engaged shore batteries. In 20 minutes she was on fire with only X-turret and her 20mm firing. Despite *Zulu's* efforts to tow her, she had to be abandoned about 0800 when X-turret was out of ammunition and an hour later she sank.

John Haselden's men, having realised around 0530 that the raid had failed, set out to fight their way clear of the Italian lines, the SIG men burning their German uniforms. Pinned in by a large force supported by tanks and trapped in a *wadi*, they made a final stand during which John Haselden was killed; others attempted to refloat an MTB and were fired on by an E-boat searching the coast. The few machine-gunners who had landed held off some attacks but they ran out of ammunition, and of the few small parties that finally got clear only Lieutenant Tom Langton of the SBS, Sergeant Steiner of SIG, and Sergeant Evans from Haselden's Troop reached British lines. Others were murdered by Arabs or killed in a brush with Italians during the trek across the desert.

The navy lost a number of ships on their run back to Alexandria, including the anti-aircraft cruiser HMS *Coventry*, and only 90 marines of Force A reached Egypt as many were killed or drowned when the destroyers' boats were caught by shore fire. John Haselden's original plan to go in with 12 men and set fire to the storage tanks seems more likely to have paid dividends than the complex operation attempted.

SBS sections made a number of raids during this period (for brief details see Appendix 7) and several undercover operations. These included a landing in North Africa on the night of 22-23 October 1942 when some senior 'brass', including Major-General Mark Clark, second-in-command of the Allied forces for Torch, were landed by canoe for discussions with the French General, Mast, on the likely reactions of Vichy French forces to the proposed invasion.

In the North African, Torch, landings the primary role of all the special forces - commandos and rangers alike - was the capture of batteries flanking the main landing beaches: for example, as the 1st Rangers captured the forts at Arzew. Other Americans landed after a 4,500 miles (7,200km) voyage from the States and achieved their primary objectives within a day or so.

In the Mediterranean the first integrated Allied force sailed 2,300 miles (3,700km) north around Ireland, a week's voyage for the troop transports and longer for the slower convoys carrying tanks. Nevertheless, they reached their dropping-zones in the right sequence at the right time, even if some ships muffed the launching of craft because their merchant navy and reservist crews did not all have the experience of those Royal Navy personnel on the longer-serving LSIs like HMS *Royal Ulsterman,* HMS *Glengyle*, and HMS *Prince Albert*. The integrated Allied command, with American, British, and Commonwealth officers, worked in close harmony on these plans, with only those differences one might expect in family squabbles - for all the journalistic mileage made in post-war memoirs.

This integration ran from top to bottom, the commando force landing in the Algiers area being a composite force from 1 and 6 Commando with elements of the 168th US Infantry Regimental Combat Team. These RCTs were typically an infantry regiment with attached troops - three battalions of infantry, a field artillery battalion, a company of combat engineers, medical, ordnance, and other attached specialists. Several rifle companies as Troops from the 168th were joined with 1 Commando and four with 6 Commando, for convenience referred to as 'No.1' and 'No.6' and all equipped with the American Garand rifle that 1 and 6 Commandos retained until the end of the War. Group A from 'No.1' and Group B - 'No.6' - landed west of the port while Group C (another party from 'No.1') landed east of Algiers. Group A under Lieutenant Colonel T.H. Trevor (CO of 1 Commando) were put ashore late, but by 0300 they were being welcomed in Fort Sidi Feruch by General Mast, who, true to his word to Mark Clark, had ordered his French division not to fight. The men of 6 Commando, Group B, had a rougher passage because the merchant navy crews of HMT *Awatae* had trouble launching the LCVPs and these crafts' crews made a hash of the landing: only one in five finding the motor launch that was to lead them in the dark to the canoe markers off their beach. The others tossed about in rough water, their newly built landing craft springing leaks and suffering many engine breakdowns. All commandos wore American uniforms in this landing as these were thought less provocative to the Vichy French, and the basin-shaped tin hats came in useful as balers. Nevertheless, the Colonel's craft was sinking fast as she reached the beach, two hours late. French searchlights played over the water but it was broad daylight when the last boat beached at 0630.

Three boats had attempted to land east of their target and came on the rocky Ilot de la Marine, a fortified strongpoint inside the harbour entrance: here Major A.S. Ronald was killed with several of his men, and the remainder of the Troop were captured. There may be some explanation for the tangle of landing craft coming ashore at Algiers, for the town was not blacked out until 0100 hours, and anyone used to a darkened shore where the pin-pricks of COPP or SBS marker canoes' lights were possible, if difficult, to find stood no hope of seeing them against the myriad lights of a port.

The delays in landing nearly caused the few pro-Allied Free Frenchmen in the town to lose their hold on vital installations when attacked by Vichy forces, and the Fort Duperre's batteries fired at the ships even though 'No.6' had crossed the rocky beaches of Poine Pescado and had surrounded it about 0830. Their light weapons' fire made no impression on the garrison, who ignored appeals from a French-Canadian commando's loud hailer (bull horn). They also ignored an attack by RN Fleet Air Arm Albacores, who dropped 36 bombs for one hit, but when threatened with naval bombardment the garrison gave in, no doubt feeling that as they had held out until 1330, honour was satisfied.

Instructions given to men of the SBS on passing out from the Ardrossan (Ayrshire) depot, signed, by Major R. J. Courtney and stressing the world-wide nature of the Section's activities.

---

## SPECIAL BOAT SECTION                                    SECRET
### PASSING OUT INSTRUCTIONS

1.  You are now considered fit to operate on your own, and should be proficient in Navigation, Demolition, and Scoutcraft.

2.  You have to be selected on your character qualifications as much as anything else and as far as we can judge, you can be trusted to take responsibility and can be trusted on your own.

3.  Try and be "world minded", remember you belong to an organization which stretches round the globe, your S.B.S. badge should be a passport into any Naval Mess. We are jealous of our good name, and our reputation is in your hands.

4.  If you go abroad you will very largely have to administer yourselves. People are usually helpful, but remember if you have to deal with military establishments ashore, that the personal touch will get you more than a mass of paper work would.

5.  Give of your best at all times, first for the War Effort, secondly for the S.B.S., and lastly for yourself.

6.  If you find any way that our system can be improved, put it into practice and let us know the results, and we will do the same for you.

7.  The S.B.S. Depot is your servant, let us know what you want and we will let you have it by the quickest possible means.

8.  Keep in touch, and let us have regular progress reports.

9.  Good luck and good hunting.

**KEEP THIS AND LOOK AT IT OCCASIONALLY**

ARDROSSAN                                              R. J. Courtney (Major)
23 JUN 42.                                    Commanding Special Boat Section
RJAC/HA.

The bulk of the American force - the main body of the 168th RCT - were spread around the coast on either side of 'No.1's' west landing, although they should have landed just north-east of Cape Sidi Feruch. They were, however, rallied by some vigorous leadership and advanced elements had reached the suburbs of Algiers by 0830. By then, Colonel Trevor had already taken some of his commandos in a 20-mile (32km) dash to the airfield at Blida, where, arriving about 0800, he was negotiating its surrender when a detachment of the British 11th Brigade drove up at 0930 and a Martlet of the Fleet Air Arm landed on seeing the French surrender. The men landing east of Algiers - also from 'No.1' - were in craft delayed by a bank of fog and they did not invest Fort D'Elrees until some two hours after the planned time for its assault. This fort did not surrender, despite bombardment, until late in the afternoon, and by then the main Allied force in the eastern area were well-established. Unlike the commandos, this 39th RCT had got ashore more or less on time and by 0130 were moving inland. In Algiers, as at Oran, an attempt was made to land troops directly into the harbour. The 3rd Battalion of the US 135th Regiment were taken in by two destroyers, HMS *Broke* and HMS *Malcolm*, but 250 of the landing parties were captured.

While the invasion was coming to a successful conclusion in North Africa, Stan Weatherall and Captain R. (Dicky) Livingstone were embarked on HMS *Ursula* for a sabotage raid in North Italy that could not be carried out by bombers. Aboard *Ursula* there was room only for a canoe slung above the forward messdeck table, and a second canoe in place of a torpedo. *Ursula* was on a 21-day patrol, although CSM Stan Weatherall had found a three-day patrol the previous week was long enough. Going north up the Spanish coast into the Gulf of Lyons the weather was 'very *very* rough' and the sea's movement could be felt even at 125 feet according to the Sergeant-Major. There were two feet (60cm) of water in the control room; the asdic, the giro-compass, and one motor packed up, but Lieutenant Laykin RN

continued the patrol that was not being specially mounted for the SBS operation. The SBS men took their watch as lookouts before the sixth night of the voyage when the submarine was in the Gulf of Genoa, north of Ligurian sea. On Sunday, 29 November, they landed in a canoe about 2000 hours by the coast road near a village not far from Ventimiglia. They hid the canoe, cut their way through some wire into the grounds of a big house, and crossed a road to find a sheer drop to the railway line - their target. They therefore had to move into the village outskirts where there were large houses each side of the road and backing on to the railway track. Cutting through the back gardens they came to a small bungalow with a verandah overlooking the track. From this perch above the railway they could make out one sentry above the tunnel entrance and another on the track. There would be no chance of catching a train inside the tunnel for they had strict orders not to interfere with any Italians, as this raid must go undetected. One long train rumbled by as they watched.

They were standing on the verandah when a soldier suddenly came through the door and relieved himself into the darkness beyond the verandah. He chatted over his shoulder, unaware death was an arm's length away as the commandos, deadly still, each held a knife for the silent kill. They slipped back to the road parallel to the track, and found a curve where the pressure fuse (see Appendix 3) could be laid with charges to blow out six feet (2m) of track on the outside bend; the train's own weight would then topple it off the lines. This was an electrified railway with overhead cables and pylons that also carried power supplies along the coast. Taking extreme care for the slightest clink of metal to metal might arouse the sentries 100 yards down the line, they linked charges with instantaneous fuse to two pylons and the track. Once in place these charges would blow when the pressure of a passing train lowered the rail a few millimetres releasing the striker on the coiled spring which in turn would fire the percussion cap.

They had 20 minutes to get back aboard

or they must wait till next night, for after the moon rose at 2330 the submarine could not risk surfacing. They returned to the village road and were boldly walking along it, Dicky Livingstone whistling an Italian classic. No one took any notice, although when one of some drunks passing the SBS men came up to them Dick Livingstone's Italian - he was a university don - passed muster and they reached the canoe, getting back aboard before 2330. The submarine was moving out to sea when an explosion lit the sky and the lights along the coast went out. They may not have been able to derail a train in the tunnel but they blocked the line for four days, for the damaged track was on a 20-foot embankment. Their voyage continued with the submarine sinking an Italian schooner: after she was boarded the canoeists had placed a charge on one of her depth charges - less costly than using gunfire. This was kept for a train attacked a couple of days later, and to stop a ship in ballast - again sunk by SBS charges, 25lb (11kg) set in the forward hold. They rejoined the submarine's depot ship in Algiers at the end of the patrol.

By now this port was safely in Allied hands, although the two composite Commandos, after joining together south of the town on the airfield, had taken part in a couple of outflanking landings and many patrols. They landed at Bone, two days after the first Torch assault, reaching the airport 250 miles (400km) east of Algiers as Dakotas of the US Army Air Force landed some British paras. The commandos' name alone was sufficient to sway one French commander's decision to fight. When he was told of the Allied support, he replied: 'It isn't much.' Then, after a pause, he added: 'All the same they have got Commandos with them, that's worth something. Gentlemen, we fight.'

'No.6' was moved a week later by train, but going east into Tunis they were shot up when their lone Spitfire escort had flown off to refuel and many men were caught in the moving wheels of the train. The Allies were not to establish complete mastery in the air for some weeks, and the Commandos paid the penalties of units without their own supporting anti-aircraft guns. Nor did they have much transport - officially. They had to win what they could; a Christmas present here of a staff car and three trucks; there, several vehicles swiped from the roadside before the official recovery units could get to them for repairs.

'No.1' sailed in landing craft from Bone to Tabarka and were sent further east along the coast at dusk on 30 November for the first of many raids commandos and rangers would make in outflanking enemy positions. The composite force - six British and four American Troops - dominated the coast for some 125 miles (200km) and up to five miles (8km) inland, holding sections of the Bizerte to Mateur road where it skirts the north shore of Lake Garaet (see map p. 116). From positions under the tall Mediterranean heather, higher than a man in places, they were able to hold a major crossroads for 72 hours and a minor one for another 24, although the Germans put patrols in Arab dress and one was wearing a green beret. After more than three days on short rations two tins of stew, half a tin of bully beef, three bars of chocolate per man - they were withdrawn. The raid may have been only a modest success, yet they reached within four miles (6km) of the major German base at Bizerte, and prevented the free use of the supply road to the enemy's forward positions for the loss of 60 British and 74 American raiders.

While 'No.1' had been raiding, 'No.6' was also in action, losing 80 men on 30 November in trying to take the 900-foot (275m) high strongpoint known as Green Hill on the railway running east from Tabarka. This natural redoubt defeated the commandos, with only five of No.5 Troop surviving an ambush by Germans dressed as Arabs. Indeed, the redoubt never fell to direct assault, even by larger forces with adequate artillery support when ammunition had become more plentiful.

After these losses the commandos were reorganised, and 65 American volunteers stayed with them in the six Troops of each Commando, all the Americans rejoining their units, however, by 31 January 1943. A small headquarters staff came out from the Special Service Brigade and Lieutenant-

Colonel William Glendinning coordinated their deployment in working with the 'First' Army - a British Corps holding a 30-mile (nearly 50km) front through the mountains west of Tunis. Their base was an old iron mine belonging to the Bey of Tunis, situated off a lonely road running west from Beja and within reach of the green Mateur valley. The Canadian journalist Ross Munro has described a typical raid from here, 'led by the Colonel, a big rugged man with a great moustache, riding a mule' - Lieutenant-Colonel Tom Trevor commanding 1 Commando. They went down the road from the mine and slogged 15 or so miles through mud and darkness to reach their positions in some wet bushes, where they lay up all day, eating bully beef and hard tack washed down with steaming sweet tea. That night half the party went further north to Cap Serrat where they were to join two landing craft; however, these had mishaps so the move eastward was dropped. The force, still in bivouac, sent out patrols that discovered little more than the inaccuracies in their maps, and set light to some hostile Arabs' villages. The men who had been to the beach made a 50-mile march in 30 hours back to the mine across enemy patrolled country. This raid shows a little of the frustrations and patient drudgery of patrolling, often in dangerous places, when the physical effort is more wearing than the adrenalin-racing actions of close contact with the enemy.

'Nos.1 and 6' had their heart-racing moments in Tunisia, for when 'No.6' took over 75 square miles (200km) of the fertile Goubellat plain, patrolling in front of the British lines, Derek Mills-Roberts, their new CO, decided they must use 30-man patrols in active probes of enemy positions. One of these Section patrols was surprised by a strong force of Germans at dawn on 26 February. Derek Mills-Roberts counter-attacked at once, leading his Headquarters Troop and organising his other Troops for a drive to push the attackers back eastwards. But the ambush turned out to be stronger than the Colonel expected, for the Germans were about to launch an attack on a fifty-mile (80km) front. Against the commandos were Koch III and IV parachute battalions

of the Herman Goering Jäger Division, a unit that had seen extensive action. They succeeded in breaking up the Commando into pockets of resistance among steep-sided hills and isolated farmhouses, yet the commandos held them off with the help of some armoured cars and carriers from the Reconnaissance Corps, long enough for a regiment of British Churchill tanks and a battalion of Grenadier Guards to move forward and redress the balance of forces, although 'No.6' had lost more than 40 per cent of their strength - 100 men of the 250 who started the action.

Their numbers were now far below strength, and after making further patrols in March they were withdrawn from Africa along with 1 Commando late in April 1943. They were replaced in the Med by 3 Commando, brought up to strength after Dieppe. Bill Darby's Rangers were training their new battalions, and in Scotland men of 40 and 41 Royal Marine Commandos were being trained for spearhead landings. All these Special Forces would be deployed in Sicily, where their roles not only included the capture of flank batteries but also the establishment of links between various landing points within a beachhead.

The Sicily landings were to put the American Seventh Army on the west of the island's southern promontory and the British Eighth Army to the east and around this point. The 30-mile (48km) gap between the British left and the American right was to be closed - according to the plan - by the evening of D-day 10 July 1943. From this southern point, Sicily may be seen as a triangle stood on its apex; the size of Wales or Vermont, its rugged mountains rising to 3,000 feet (1,000m) with the volcano Mount Etna (3,279ft, 1,000m) in the north-east. In 1943 the Sicilians were mostly barefoot peasants, providing the bulk of the defence forces, the soldiers being stationed near their families. These lived in homes with few modern services; a hole outside, often near the door, might sometimes have to serve as a privy.

3 Commando held rehearsals in Sfax, where they were welcomed, for in their Colonel's words, 'the Eighth Army took its

tone from its commander, and Monty's influence spread right down to the lorry drivers who would always stop and give you a lift'. He might have said the same for any military unit - or business organisation - and his own Commando always had a dedicated professionalism, more efficient for their kind of warfare than the paperwork of regular battalions. The army commandos were volunteers, however, and they resented - and some still do - the Royal Marines' redesignation of battalions as Commando. Perhaps the army were not aware of the RM volunteer's usual welcome in 1942-43 at a recruiting office: 'It won't be big ships for you, y'know - it'll be wading ashore.' (Not until 1944 were any conscripts directed to the Royal Marines.)

Other services' commando units had been formed by November 1942, including the RAF Servicing Commando units. Their first deployment was in the Torch landings where they took over forward airfields, bringing in stores and equipment to service Allied planes. Details of these RAF units and Naval Beach Party commandos are shown in Appendices 2 and 7, but in later years attempts were made to limit any further use of the name 'commando' to units of the Special Service Brigade.

The Special Forces' orders for Sicily have a familiar ring. Furthest west were the 3rd Rangers under Major Herman W. Dammer who landed on the flank of the American 3 Division; Bill Darby led the 1st and 4th Rangers, whose initial target was the pier at Gela; the 40 and 41 RM Commandos were to land on the left flank of the Canadians, with 3 Commando landing on the north-east extremity of the invasion to take the machine-guns overlooking the 5 Division's beaches in the Gulf of Noto. Each special force had a second objective, 3 Commando having to move inland three miles (5km) to take a battery north-west of Cassibik.

Late in June the COPP reconnaissance parties of Don Amer and Ralph Stanbury made a detailed reconnaissance of the British target beaches south of Syracuse, and on the night of 9-10 July they were on station as canoe markers for the landings, or at least all the canoeists believed they were in the correct positions despite the dangers, and Sub-Lieutenant Saice was lost, probably run down by a landing craft. The day before there had been rough seas and most of the rangers were wretchedly seasick aboard the LSI(S)s HMS *Prince Charles* and HMS *Prince Leopold* heading for Gela. These two, small 3,650-ton carriers had eight LCAs each and accommodation for an assault force of 270 men. They, ships and men, reeled and tossed on a sea described in the log of Gunboat 658 as 'Harry roughers', although the armies might have expressed the conditions in stronger terms. Yet despite the storm, the Rangers' ships reached their dropping zone, two of many fine pieces of seamanship that night.

Herman Dammer's 3rd Rangers came ashore three miles (4.8km) west of Licata and formed the spearhead force in the 7th Regimental Combat Team of the US 3 Division. They were landed from British ships in LCAs, as was Lieutenant-Colonel Brookner W. Brody commanding the 7th RCT, taking all their beach objectives on the morning of Saturday, 10 July. In the next few days they were in the van of the 3 Division's sweep along the coast - Compobello di Licata, Naro, Favare, Monteparte fell to the Rangers, some after little resistance, others in company and several in battalion assaults. By the time they reached the outskirts of Porto Empedocle they had taken more than 600 prisoners and 10 armoured cars, and other vehicles were overrun with a dozen artillery batteries along the coast road. The senior army commander - the British General Alexander - ordered General Patton to hold the Seventh Army as Alexander did not want the left (west) flank of the invasion exposed in heavy fighting. However, he did allow General Patton to make a reconnaissance in force. The 3 Division's commander, General Truscott, who 14 months before had recommended the formation of Rangers, now sent their 3rd Battalion forward as his reconnaissance in force. The port of Empedocle was held by several hundred Germans and Italians, of whom the German artillery was experienced and working with an Italian railway battery. The ship-to-shore fire of the cruiser USS

*Philadelphia* and two destroyers did not shift these gunners, and any prolonged bombardment might destroy the harbour installations Patton would need in landing supplies for his army's drive north to Palermo.

Although they had no artillery support, the 3rd Rangers attacked the town, relying on their own 60mm (2.4in) mortars. These opened the attack which moved forward at about 1420 on a hot July afternoon - Friday, 16 July. Herman Dammer - with one company protecting his left flank and rear - led two companies into the east of the town, where snipers and several strongpoints had to be cleared before they reached the port area: moreover, they were handicapped by some 200 prisoners. The other three companies of the battalion, under the Executive Officer (2 i/c), Major Miller, had circled the port and came in from the west down the opposite side of the draw running north-south out of the town. Meeting tough opposition from Germans holding a walled cemetery and in coastal defences, these companies used fire-and-movement tactics with determined probes exploited when enemy strongpoints were isolated in turn. Miller's men eventually broke the resistance, and the port was taken. At about 1900 hours, a US Navy spotter plane was 'induced to land in the harbour', being surprised to find it in Ranger hands. The Navy willingly supplied medical stores and food urgently needed by the battalion whose CO was flown over to the cruiser USS *Philadelphia* which was in touch with 3 Division's HQ.

The British crews carrying the 1st and 4th on D-Day were to land the 1st on the left and the 4th on the right of the Gela pier. Coming inshore - they were launched at about 0130 hours - the craft alternately 'sank into a deep trough, then shot skyward into the piercing gleam of a searchlight'. Several large beams swept across the wave tops as Bill Darby, aboard a support landing craft, chivvied the assault boats towards the beach. Five miles (8km) from their carriers they reached their forming-up line at 0245, coming line abreast for the final half-hour's run-in. Mortar fire began to fall among the craft, lifting some bodily and hurling men, helmets, and rifles to one side and back to

the other as the LCA slammed back on to the water, buckling the craft's armoured shields around the raiders. A British support craft forged ahead of the line and fired into the searchlight beams. The water was calmer now in the lee of the land and when some craft sank, others - against orders, no doubt - slowed to pick up the drowning men. Near the right side (east) of the pier several machine-guns and other quick-firing weapons caught F Company (4th Rangers) as their landing craft approached these pillboxes. D Company, however, landed without casualties in a dash to the shelter for some low cliffs; they were five minutes ahead of H-hour (0315). Lieutenant Walter Wojak - who had made the night reconnaissances finding the hill route behind the El Ank Pass. positions - led his platoon across the soft sand and half of them were tripping the wires of a minefield before they realised they were in it. Walter Wojak was killed along with four others, men were blinded, and many wounded before a platoon sergeant found a route and led the rest of the company safely over the dunes. One young officer went to pieces and was quietly sent to the rear of his company. Then, in one of many - if not the inevitable - changes of plan vital for success in assault landings against strong resistance, D Company abandoned their planned objectives in Gela. First they must clear the machine-guns firing on F Company's boats. All seven of these strongpoints were knocked out, but the troops of the 429th Italian Coastal Battery fought hard, losing half their men. Their commander in this sector - Captain Della Minola - refused to surrender before he was killed by rangers' grenades. D Company then moved into Gela.

F Company, coming ashore late after picking up survivors, were shaken by an explosion as the Italians blew a gap in the pier. But the company took no further casualties on the beach as they moved off, and by 0344 they were warily making their way towards the cathedral square in Gela.

The 1st Rangers landed on time, although two LCAs had been hit with consequently heavy losses. The destroyer USS *Shubrick* shot out two searchlights as the first waves of assault troops landed to smash through the line of mines, wire and pill-boxes into the cobbled streets of the town. In the pitch-dark streets one soldier looked like another: a mere darker patch of shadow which flitted momentarily into vision. One BAR-man was joined by another soldier as he fired from a window, but when the American suggested they move forward to another building he found his companion was an Italian. Knocking him to the ground with the butt of his automatic rifle, the ranger dodged clear of this Italian-occupied building.

Another American called out in the language of his grandparents: 'Veni qua supits!' Four Italians came running into captivity. Confounded, one kept repeating: 'But we're Italians, too.' Dawn was breaking by the time the skirmishes in the square died down, and several rangers got the last defenders out of the cathedral about 0600. The rangers were then formed up in files and marched to their defensive positions 'a few blocks north of the square'. Artillery fire from the open plain beyond these positions was beginning to hit the town, and three German planes made a low-level attack on the beaches where the American 1 Division were - and had been - landing. For the Rangers at Gela the battle was just beginning, further east along the coast the RM Commandos were landing in their first spearhead roles of World War II.

The Royal Marine 40 and 41 Commando came ashore on rocky shelving beaches west of Punta Castellazzo, the direction of the enemy coast lit by flares and bombs from an RAF raid inland. Both Commandos were lifted in the 22-assault craft of the transports *Derbyshire* and *Durban Castle*. Lost in the dark and with some lack of resolution by the crews in forming a line for the last stage of the run-in, the craft carried 'No.40 RM' eastward to land among the Canadians on the Commando's right. 41(RM) Commando was ashore first, although half an hour late at 0300, drenched by spray and water slopping into the craft from the strong swell. Wirelesses and 3-inch mortar bombs were damaged by the soaking. Although put ashore at the wrong point, Lieutenant-Colonel J.C. (Pops) Manners - who had been at Dieppe - quickly had them assembled in a

hollow surrounded by dunes. From here they moved off to capture machine-gun posts in a sharp dawn action. Bob Laycock had come out with a small headquarters staff, leaving Lord Lovat as his deputy in England. The wealth of experience now ran through all commando ranks, and this Mediterranean Brigade staff landed with 40 RM Commando. They were scattered over a wide number of landing points but their CO, Lieutenant-Colonel B. (Bertie) J.D. Lumsden, got them to their objectives where in the full light of day 'No.41(RM)' were seen to have taken both Commandos' objectives - including some 'heavy guns' which turned out to be machine-gun posts.

Away to the north-east on D-day, 3 Commando landed from HM Transport *Dunera* and HMS *Prince Albert*, an infantry landing ship of proven ability. John Durnford-Slater led the Commando - his craft, with the left group moving shorewards, was nearly run down by the transport *Sobieski*, illustrating that the hazards at sea were mounting in proportion to the size of amphibious operations. The landing craft flotilla commander, Lieutenant Holt RN, made an accurate marking another beach - and then the two miles out of position! - and then the silhouette of the high Scoglio rock which confirmed they were on course for the right beach. Two hundred yards (over 180m) from the water's edge some machine-gun fire was answered by the leading flight of landing craft's bow gunners. The Italians promptly stopped shooting and the Colonel stepped ashore to find 'masses of wire and many pill-boxes, all useless unless manned by determined troops'. The men were formed up for their march inland. Meanwhile, for Peter Young with the right-hand group of 'No.3', practically everything went wrong. One craft never joined up with the flotilla for the run-in. Craft came south-west of their course and never picked up their intended direction from a sonic buoy (Appendix 3). They were fired on, but the LCAs' armour prevented casualties before they eventually landed in daylight.

The Colonel's three Troops of the left group were out of their landing area, moving in two-column files across flat, open country with steep, stone-walled banks five feet high (nearly 2m) and four feet wide dividing the fields every hundred yards or so. Bright moonlight, the smell of wild sage, the occasional olive grove, and lemon trees made this a pleasant enough approach march. Although the commando who caught his gear on the prickly pear hedges common throughout Sicily, if not on this march, had a different view of the local flora. There were also patches of low brush that remained unseen until your face was cut by it, and invariably some ankle-twisting stones lay underfoot, unnoticed on the brightest of nights.

Following two scouts 50 yards ahead, John Durnford-Slater became anxious they were not moving fast enough - he had promised to knock out the battery they were heading for within 90 minutes of landing - although each man carried the usual load of a 10lb (4.5kg) 3-inch mortar bomb in addition to his own weapons; the mortarmen had heavier loads. Padding along in rubber shoes, the column made little noise as they followed the Colonel's hooded torch 'showing everyone the direction of advance'. They might have been on a night exercise until a spirited Italian farmer took a shot at them; he was killed with regret, for they admired his pluck. The battery was also firing as they left the mortar Section 400 yards (365m) from these guns, each man dropping his contribution to the mortar ammunition as he passed. Ten men went down a dry river bed to open harassing fire at the front of the battery while the remainder swung in behind the guns. The attack was made using a technique devised by Derek Mills-Roberts, CO of 6 Commando. Parachute flares illuminated the site while heavy fire was concentrated on it with small arms and mortars. Then there was a pause, followed by silence and darkness. The defenders' eyes were not re-accustomed to the dark as assault troops crawled nearer to them; a second burst of illuminated covering-fire and then - when the flares died down - the final assault. The moves went to plan: radioed orders brought down fire under the light of flares; a five-minute interval during which two Troops advanced with one in reserve; they cut the wire with bangalore torpedos; another burst of light and fire; when the bright light died, the bugler sounded the charge and the Troops dashed through the gap in the wire. The Italians 'stuck it fairly well', their automatics' fire ceasing only on the final bayonet charge - five minutes before the Colonel's deadline for taking the battery. The commandos met some stouter resistance from a house nearby but overcame this when the roof was set alight from a flower-pot bomb (see Appendix 3). They exploded 1,000 shells from the battery before joining the other group and returning to HMS *Prince Albert* next day.

For the Rangers at Gela, D+1 was a rough day although the weather remained hot and sunny throughout Saturday and Sunday (10-11 July). Having gained all their initial objectives on D-day morning, the Americans were held up when there was a delay - partly through the pier being breached by the Italian demolitions - in building up the force in the beachhead. As a result the Rangers were without support when the Italian *Gruppo Mobile 'E'* counter-attacked with 32 French 10-ton tanks and some other armour. The Rangers saw the tanks speeding across the flat wheatfields between bursts of naval shell-fire, and none too soon the rangers took fresh positions in the tops of buildings as the first tank came into the town. They knew their rifle fire, including armour-piercing bullets, would have no effect, but as the tanks shrugged off this fire and grenade bursts, Bill Darby found a 37mm (1.5in) anti-tank gun. Bare-headed, his sleeves rolled up, he and Captain Charles Shundstrom fired two rounds into the teeth of the leading tank. The first hit the turret, the second knocked the tank back several feet and set it on fire. Bazooka shots knocked out the second tank and a pole-charge caught the third (see Appendix 3). This charge was dropped from a building, and as other tanks were hit the Italians withdrew. That night the rangers stood-to prepared for further attack, wondering why no Allied aircraft had caught the tanks in the open and what had happened to the American paratroops dropped north-east of the town the previous night.

The first American tanks came ashore late on D-day (Saturday) evening at Gela, but heavy surf prevented more than a few being landed, and many anti-tank guns were lost when an LST (Landing Ship, Tank) was sunk by fighter-bombers; early on Sunday morning, D+1, General Patton came ashore. Always a man for seeing for himself, he realised why the division had failed, through lack of Allied tanks and guns ashore, to get forward, and take the airfield as planned for D-day afternoon. He spoke to Bill Darby, among other commanders, and was ashore when the first Panzer attack was repulsed about 0830. The German tactics became clear as the morning battle developed with 40 tanks making a frontal attack while 20 others tried to break through to the coast, so splitting the American bridgehead. The first of this renewed series of tank attacks came in, an awesome sight, with the Panzers moving forward and some Tigers' 88mm (3.5in) guns firing; Italian infantry of the Livorno Division moved in the shelter of this armour. Shells fell among the rangers, the 88s demolishing the houses around the defenders' ears. Stone chips and shell splinters flew everywhere from the dust clouds. Holding their fire, the rangers watched the tanks come through the naval barrage and were preparing to take on the infantry when once again Bill Darby found some anti-tank guns: several Italian 77mm (3in). With these and scratch ranger gun crews, seven tanks were engaged only 1,000 yards from the beach. About 1030 hours, more American tanks were landed to close the widening gap between the Rangers and the American 1 Division. The division's artillery came forward on amphibious trucks (DUKWs) to fire over open sights at the Panzers, and by noon the main tank attacks had been repulsed, the accurate Ranger fire having broken the back of the infantry attacks. The Axis forces then began an orderly withdrawal by 1400 hours, heading for the hills that dominated the Gela plain.

The deployment of paras in combined operations with amphibious forces was always a problem, for the seaborne force preferred darkness whereas parachutists needed moonlight. The compromise for Sicily landings was to choose a night in the period of a waxing moon. Nevertheless, the US 505th Parachute Infantry Regiment was scattered and isolated on landing during the early hours of D-day, and an attempt to drop 2,000 men into the beachhead on the Sunday (D+1) night was one of the greatest disasters of any Allied invasion - whether or not their 145 Dakotas were on course. Certainly, they flew over the fleet not long after an air raid, and many of the 504th Regiment of paras were killed when the planes were hit by the Allied fleet's guns. In the east near Syracuse the previous night, early on D-day, 60 per cent of the towing planes - American-crewed Dakotas - let slip their gliders short of their targets and 252 men of the British 1st Air Landing Brigade were drowned. But on Tuesday, 13 July the British 1st Parachute Brigade dropped near Primasole bridge with the intention of securing the Eighth Army's advance to Catania.

This last drop was part of two right hooks planned by General Montgomery, who told John Durnford-Slater that morning, 13 July, that 'the enemy is nicely on the move and we want to keep him that way'. They stood, the General and the Colonel, among bomb-damaged buildings on the quay at Syracuse in fierce summer sunshine. The paras' drop would be some 20 miles (32km) north of the British 50 Division's positions, and 3 Commando would land 10 miles (16km) ahead of this Division at Agnone to go inland and take the Ponte dei Malati bridge. Both bridges lay on the road running north to Catania and, if taken intact, they could ensure a rapid advance. Such landings of amphibious or airborne forces ahead of a main advance are a tempting military stratagem to cut off the enemy, but - as General Mongomery knew - they needed nice judgement: if too small or lightly armed, the outflanking force is easily destroyed. Yet mounting too large a right or left hook may necessitate weakening the advancing main army, depriving them of naval and other support diverted to help the outflanking troops. Getting ashore may be the least of the outflankers' worries for seldom are there sufficient assault craft, suitable beaches, or adequate lines of retreat should the ploy go wrong.

Commander Peate RN, the captain of HMS *Prince Albert*, dodged her round two torpedos from an E-boat as they sailed up the coast with their escorting destroyer. By 2130 they were five miles (8km) off Agnone The ship's galley provided each commando with a packet of sandwiches, adding a touch of the routine exercise; low-flying Dakotas thundered overhead, taking the paras to Primasole bridge. To the south, the commandos could see heavy anti-aircraft fire driving Axis planes away from Syracuse. The Commando headquarters and Nos. 1, 2, 3, and 4 Troops set off in Lieutenant Holt's flotilla - the one that had made a perfect landing four days before - the plan being to push Nos. 1 and 3 Troops quickly inland to the bridge, while No.2 Troop and the headquarters held the beach. No.4 Troop was to send patrols north to contact the paras and south to join 50 Division. Moving steadily line-abreast in the moonlight, the assault craft were nosing inshore on an unsurveyed beach when bursts of enfilade fire came from above a steep cliff that dominated the landing area. The Colonel was not entirely surprised, for he expected the Germans to defend their main supply and escape route to Messina. But when Lieutenant Holt excelled himself and put the Colonel ashore two boats' length ahead of the flotilla, even he was momentarily taken aback. The officer following him got a bangalore torpedo jammed across the LCA's bow and for some seconds John Durnford-Slater stood alone. 'Sand boiled up around me', he has written, 'as bullets struck. Somebody also started throwing grenades down the cliff at me. I thought the bullets were enough without the extras.' Peter Young landed moments later on the extreme right as the Commando swept towards the wire. Despite the bright moon, the Italians fire was not very accurate, in part perhaps because of the commandos' counter-fire from the boats and because distances are deceptive in moonlight. The destroyer - HMS *Tetcott* - also came right inshore to take on the pill-boxes. The inaccuracy was not, it seems, from lack of resolution, for, as a prisoner later confirmed, German troops were in the area.

The commandos were jostling to find a gap in the wire as a shower of red-devil Italian grenades fell among them, and the shrill whistles of Troop commanders as well as No.1 Troop's hunting horn could be heard above the din. Peter Young, cursing loudly, restored order and got a ragged column of commandos moving inland. Charlie Head, in this confused fighting, came upon an Italian machine-gun in action and without time to draw his revolver kicked the gun over.

The Troops moved off along a railway track, one file each side of the line, while the landing craft returned for the second flight - Nos. 5 and 6 Troops. The craft were just moving out of range of the anti-boat fire when Lieutenant Holt was fatally wounded in the neck. By the time the craft returned, the Italians had anti-tank guns on the shore, and despite the destroyer's smoke-shells several craft were hit. Meanwhile, Peter Young and his men had reached Angone station and were exchanging the password 'desert rats' for 'kill Italians' with a party of airborne dropped short of their bridge but now making north to reach it overland. There were some three miles (5km) of cactus patches, occasional orange groves, and those steep-sided ravines on which a knee may be twisted as easily as an ankle in marching 'at a desperate pace' as the commandos crossed towards the bridge. A mile short of it, Bill Lloyd - recovered from his wound at Vaagsö - plunged in over his head trying to find a way across the river and was pulled out, the river being waded finally. At about 0300 hours the defences on the bridge's north side were taken, grenades being dropped through the pill-box gun-slits.

The Troops from the second beaching by the landing craft came up about dawn and some 300 commandos consolidated their positions around the north end of the bridge and for 15 minutes all was quiet. The arrival of a German half-track ammunition carrier gave a Section officer the chance to ambush it with a PIAT (see Appendix 3), but he was mortally wounded in the resulting explosion, for this anti-tank weapon had to fire at less than 100 yards (40m) range to give a reasonable chance of a hit. A German tank came up but, after some shelling, pushed off, leaving the next counter-attack to the Italians. Almost all the commandos removing charges from under the bridge, and those from the Troop sent to take its south-west defences were dead or wounded, and more German tanks were arriving with men and ammunition going south to reinforce their line holding off 50 Division. Although some trucks were set on fire, it was clear by 0530 that the Germans had held the Division; however, these few German reinforcements would have little effect on that battle - 12 hours later the leading elements of 50 Division reached the bridge. By then the Commando was long gone. Should they have attempted to seize both ends of the bridge? Probably such a division of their small force might have led to neither end being taken and the pill-box defences were at the north end of the bridge. There was also a limited field of fire to the south, where orange groves came within 30 yards of the bridge.

The Commando broke up into small parties that hoped to lie up during the day, but some were caught, although not easily - a Troop Sergeant-Major held out in the Italians' fortified beach headquarters until a forward patrol of the Eighth Army arrived. Others were freed from capture when the advance swept forward, but they had 153 casualties, including Bill Lloyd who was killed. This sacrifice was not in vain for when 50 Division reached the Leonardo the bridge was intact and unguarded. The paras and airborne had even greater losses but held their bridge with 250 men for two days before being overrun, despite bringing their anti-tank guns into action.

The right hooks would probably not have been thrown had the General known the enemy's strength in that area: three battalions of Panzer Grenadiers; the 101st (German) Tank Battalion, some self-propelled guns of the Herman Goering Division; the 904 Fortress Battalion; and many Italians with no thoughts of surrender. These forces would have influenced General Montgomery's decision, for he was a commander with careful consideration for casualties, having seen the slaughter of World War I, and he did not hazard men unnecessarily, although he was always prepared to take a calculated risk.

Command of Special Forces - from the corporal's squad to the general's use of spearhead forces - is fraught with such chances of error or, more correctly, misinformation in calculating the odds for success. In Sicily, as the British pushed north and the Americans swung east along the road from Palermo, such decisions led to several ranger battles in Sicily, as shown in the unit histories in Appendix 7. Bill Darby, however, helped the odds with six self-propelled 105mm (4.1in) guns, and later formed the Ranger Cannon Company with 18 self-propelled howitzers. There were also further outflanking attempts in landings, as at a point two miles east of Agata where a battalion of the US II Corps got ashore easily, ahead of the advance along the north coast. Here, on 8 August, the battalion's position was for a time in doubt: were they cutting off the Germans or vice versa?

On 11 August another landing ahead of the American II Corps was made further along the coast near Brolo, but after an initial success it was again caught in heavy German pressure. Down to 650 men after taking 160 casualties before being relieved, this force had advanced 10 miles from their landing beaches. On 15 August a landing, at Patton's insistence, went through, although the 3 Division already held the target beaches on Cape Milazzo. On the east coast there were also landings, with 2 Commando as part of a Canadian force attempting to cut off the Germans at Scaletta (see history Appendix 7). They were landed on the wrong beach, the white house landmark selected as a navigation point being hidden by a grove of cypresses, and although landed with a squadron of Sherman tanks and a troop of Priests (105mm (4.1in) self-propelled guns) they were too late to cut off the Germans retreating to Messina.

In Sicily the commandos' and rangers' reputation was firmly established. In conversation with Bob Laycock, General Dempsey described 3 Commando as 'the finest body of soldiers I have ever seen anywhere'. The Brigadier was pleased, for his commandos were being used - as were the rangers - in roles for which they had special talents.

# THE ITALIAN AND BALKAN CAMPAIGNS, 1943 TO 1945

Although many senior Allied commanders considered the Mediterranean a secondary theatre, Prime Minister Churchill wanted to carry through a campaign into Italy. This was brought about despite the shortage of equipment and men, on which other theatres had a priority,

Italy signed an armistice early in September when Allied forces were moving into Calabria in the Toe of Italy and were preparing to land at Salerno further north. After initial difficulties the Allied armies established a line across Italy, but they were held by the Germans. In this mountain war, an advance of 10 miles (15+km) could take two months.

In January 1944, an attempt to outflank the Gustav line with a landing at Anzio, not far from Rome, failed; and throughout the rest of that summer the Allies made slow progress.

The Yugoslav partisans had been fighting in the Balkans since 1941, and by late 1942 they had seven shock-troop divisions plus men and women living among local communities. Despite German offensives - Marshal Tito's partisans lost 10,000 men in the fifth of these during May 1943 - the partisans maintained a fighting army with little outside help until late in 1943, when 14 German and five other Axis divisions drove a major part of the partisan army from the mainland on to the island of Viz. From here they fought back in 1944 with 200,000 men and women, disrupting German withdrawals that might otherwise have reinforced their armies in north Italy or those fighting the Russians in Bulgaria. One in ten of the Yugoslav population were killed in this guerrilla war and nearly two-thirds of their national wealth was destroyed. For their Allies, cooperation often raised political as much as military problems, but in their support of these partisans and of Greeks and Albanians, the British soldiers' ability to exercise tact (if not always patience) prevented serious disharmony.

Having crossed the Arno in September 1944, the month of landings by Allied troops in southern France, the armies in Italy moved north from Florence but were checked again at the Gothic line. With insufficient men to break these defences, the Allies in Italy did not move forward until April 1945, when this line was broken by bombing, and the German east flank was turned in crossings of the Po estuary.

Men of 9 Commando after their raid on the Garigliano river estuary defences, December 1943.

# 9   THROUGH ITALY TO THE BALKANS

Before the Fifth American Army - the American X Corps and British VI - went ashore at Salerno, a reconnaissance was made on the mainland nearer to Sicily across the Messina Straits. A Section of No.5 Troop from 3 Commando visited Bova Marina (see map p. 116) and found no troops in the area on the night of 25-26 August. The following night Peter Young landed five parties with 21-sets, which were used in artillery fire control and were manned by signallers without commando training. However, the bulky 47lb (20kg) sets failed to operate, despite having a range of 15 miles (24km), and about a third of this on voice (R/T) transmissions when not on the move. Peter Young returned the next night and was obliged to stay ashore when the LC Infantry - a shore-to-shore craft that could beach after a passage from her sally port - landed so firmly she could not be got off. The parties of commandos, signallers, and sailors, without any radios, then made what reconnaissance they could in the jagged hills behind the beach. Some were attacked by Italian soldiers, others were received with hospitality - a mixture of feelings that epitomised the Allied forces' reception throughout the Italian campaign. The inadequacy of commando signals' gear was no greater than for other troops, although coming ashore exposed their sets to water damage and some improvements were made as explained in Appendix 5. Yet even the following year, the commandos coming ashore at Normandy were still bedevilled by sets damaged in

landing, so perhaps taking artillery signallers was a gamble in 1943, although no lessons seem to have been learnt from the Timor experience of 1941.

Although the reconnaissances had failed, the lack of their reports may in part have influenced John Durnford-Slater and other senior officers in choosing Bagnara Calabria, as a landing point for the Special Raiding Squadron crossing from Sicily. This Squadron, commanded by the enormous Irishman and rugby international, Major Paddy Mayne, was one of several special service units in the campaigns through Italy, on the Yugoslav Dalmatian coast, and in the Aegean. After a sharp engagement when they had landed near Bagnara Calabria, the Squadron held the town for 24 hours until relieved by the British 15 Infantry Brigade of XIII Corps, which landed on 3 September at Reggio. These southern operations' final details were planned and mounted in 10 days, a feat of organisation that required collecting the craft at sally ports, repairing some craft, and loading them as well as issuing the relevant battle orders, which included a fire plan in which the Eighth Army's artillery fired 29,000 rounds (400 tons) of shells in the opening barrage across the straits in the early hours of 3 September. For the commandos, after their experience in Sicily, the planning and mounting of raids was becoming almost routine.

They sailed on 7 September at 1630 hours from Messina, 'No.40(RM)' with two reinforced Troops from 3 Commando spearheading the British 231st Infantry Brigade's landing at Port San Venere. Despite a hiatus going into the harbour, where the breakwater could not be seen against the looming background of hills behind the town, they landed in the early hours of 9 September with little opposition. As General Montgomery invested the Toe of Italy the speed of advance was slowed by the nature of the terrain rather than strong German forces, for these intended to make their stand further north.

The Bay of Salerno (see map p. 140) is the shore of the Lower Sele basin with a base of some 15 to 20 miles of beaches funnelling into an apex 12 miles (19km) to the east.

The landing area was just within Allied fighters' range from their airfields in Sicily, but bringing reinforcements by sea was a 12-hour voyage from the island's northern ports and a two-day passage from North Africa. To the west of Salerno, tucked in the hills, is the village of Vietri by a small cove named Marina. The Salerno - Naples Route 18 road runs north-west, winding through the defile of La Molina and passing near to three villages - Pigoletti, La Molina, and Dragone - perched on the hillside, as were most houses in this area that was once a pirate haunt. The COPP canoeists visited these beaches on several nights 'at very great risk'.

The 1st, 3rd, and 4th Rangers, the 1st and 4th under Bill Darby, would land at the fishing village of Maiori and move six miles (10km) into the hills to hold the Nocera defile in positions overlooking the plain beyond and the road to Naples. Maiori is seven miles (11km) up the coast from Marina cove, where 2 and 41(RM) Commandos would land, taking the coast battery before moving inland to hold the defile at La Molina. Mark Clark's army could then pass through the mountains that cut off Salerno from Naples and take this city by D+4. At least that was the plan. The 16th Panzer Division, in four battle groups roughly six miles (10km) apart and three to six miles inland, lay in an arc from Salerno to southeast of Ogliastro to thwart this intention.

The Rangers landed at dawn on 9 September and overran a loosely organised Panzer reconnaissance company, even though the German divisions were all on maximum alert, and the 16th Panzer's observation post overlooking the bay had reported 'six ships offshore' at 0158 hours. This was followed at 0735 by 'major landing operation in plain of Salerno. Battles in progress. Otherwise quiet.'(!). Moving rapidly inland, the Rangers covered six steep hill-miles to be above the Nocera defile before Bill Darby radioed their successful landing.

2 Commando under Jack Churchill - Mad Jack of Vaagsö and of a brief outflanking raid in Sicily - had been rebuilt since St Nazaire. With 210 men in the first two waves of assault craft, they landed at 0330 hours (9 September) unopposed on the Marina Cove beaches. One Troop formed a beachhead and Jack Churchill led the rest up to the battery on high ground behind the beach, finding it undefended and taking six prisoners. The third and fourth assault waves - the same craft having to make the first and fourth trips - brought in the rest of 2 Commando, another 170 men, and 41(RM) Commando. With the 400 marines were a troop of 6-pounder anti-tank guns, six guns, and an American Engineer Chemical Warfare Company with their 4.2in (107mm) heavy mortars with explosive - not gas - bombs. On the run-in, artillery fired from their LCTs and the Commando were also in radio contact with the destroyer HMS *Blackmore* and an LC Gun (Large) which could provide covering fire from her 4.7 inch (119mm) guns; a truly combined operation tactic that would prove invaluable in the coming week.

For simplicity, in this book two or more Commandos are often referred to as a brigade, although not officially designated as one; see organisation details in Appendix 2. Bob Laycock and Brigade headquarters came in with 'No.41(RM)'; moving up towards Vietri village they ran across a German patrol. The signalman, batmen, and orderlies quickly routed this small force, the Brigadier having a chance to fire his revolver. Reaching Vietri they set up the Brigade headquarters among the village's

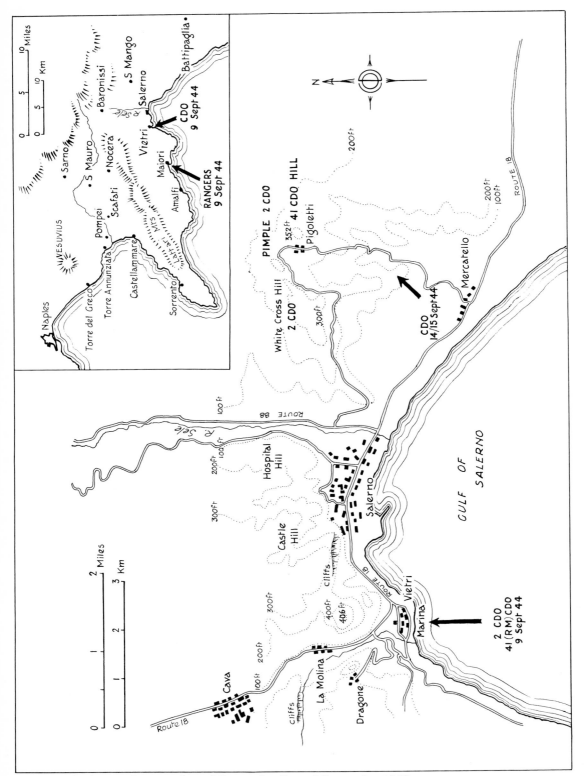

The Bay of Salerno – Commando and Ranger landings, 9 September 1943.

pink and white houses as 'No.41(RM)' passed through in making for the defile at La Molina. According to plan, two Troops (from 2 Commando) under Captain the Duke of Wellington patrolled to the outskirts of Salerno, reporting enemy tanks - disabling one with a couple of Piat shots from a house window. The 138th Brigade landed south of Salerno but were held on the town's eastern outskirts. Bob Laycock now learnt that all was not well on the beaches. The commandos' heavy gear - packs, rations, and reserve ammunition - had not been put ashore at Marina, and if the main beach parties had not brought it through their supply route, the Commando Brigade would have been in difficulty.

Rounding a bend in the road as 41(RM) Commando had hurried to reach the planned positions before first light, the leading men of B Troop came face to face with a large stationary tank, possibly a Tiger. Too close to safely fire the Piat, the leading Section 'jumped into a ditch and opened fire on the crew'; surprised as they slept by the road. Captain John Parsons writes: 'We clambered on to the tank and threw a 36-grenade through the open hatch'. Racing on, they were clear of the blast as the tank's ammunition exploded, and a few minutes later they were digging in on the high ground to the right (east) of the road and railway in a well-wooded steep hillside just short of a bend where the road turned sharply right. The commandos carried 'a Mark V anti-tank mine slung around our necks like a cow pat'. These they laid in a necklace across the road and in the ground beyond it, setting up their Piat and rifle positions to cover what proved an effective obstacle. As the day grew brighter and pleasantly sunny, several German tanks nosing round this corner from La Molina were stopped by the mines and in trying to reverse were caught in the commandos' fire. No tank got through.

The confusions of such battles are made up of a thousand personal stories: of tired men making errors in map reading, of patrols mistaking one hill for the next, of lorries bogged down in quagmires despite the hot sun, of river crossings just too deep

and fast for a tired man to keep his feet. Rumours were rife as the marines fought in the defile. Before nightfall on the Thursday they were joined by units of the Reconnaissance Corps and were under mortar fire, as were the commando headquarters in Vietri. At one time they knew on the defile they had been outflanked, but a second report might or might not be true. John Parsons was not sure whether the Piat should be resited to face attacks from the rear or kept in its position covering the roadblock. He made each decision in the light of what facts he could sift from rumours and his military good sense, advised by his fellow officers. For commandos in their slit-trenches, this was a lonely time: although usually in pairs there is not the comforting brotherhood of a crew cocooned in a tank, nor the familiar surroundings of a sailor's action station. The infantry soldier is in strange, dark woods or gone to earth where he knows nothing of events a few hundred yards away; at best he has the reassuring stutter of his Section bren firing from its crew's slit-trench 20 yards to his left, perhaps, while the other rifle squad is to his right. But are they still firing or did that last mortar bomb cave in their fox-hole? These situations, without the cohesion of well-established defences, require steady nerves and men who will stay put in the confidence that those on their left and right are doing the same. The commandos stood their ground throughout Friday, as did the rangers.

A few Allied tanks had gone forward during Thursday but were withdrawn from the commandos' area, and the reconnaissance troops - a squadron of the 44th Reconnaissance Regiment - were forced to withdraw on Friday after reporting heavy concentrations of enemy across the valley from the marines' positions. The best that Mark Clark's Fifth Army could expect to do was hold key hill positions, although they were not able to drive back enemy artillery beyond their range of the beaches. As the morning of Friday passed, a number of heavy machine-gun teams were seen high on the hill overlooking Vietri; the commando and American mortars caught some of these and the rest were captured as two Troops from 2 Commando scaled the 1,300 feet (390m) of its near sheer face. Supplying them was difficult and a foretaste of supply problems in the mountains in Italy. The Brigade now had pickets spread a hundred yards or so apart trying to prevent infiltration. On the left the Commando were in contact with the Rangers and the morning was relatively quiet, although A Troop of 'No.41(RM)' were in action. That afternoon, however, the first heavy shelling hit the marines - Bertie Lumsden was wounded as were others when the Commando headquarters was hit about 1430 - and Major J.R. Edwards RM took command. A Troop was again heavily attacked in the bright hot sunshine just before 1700 hours.

Sergeant D.C. Bullock was killed bringing forward a machine-gun with Q Troop and his four-man team all wounded, but they saved A Company, although the left flank was still exposed and was not secured until later that night when No.3 Troop of 2 Commando captured the ridge overlooking the marines' leftward positions. Supported by a troop of tanks giving covering fire, this attack was successful and the commandos were reinforced by three infantry companies as 2 Commando moved to the south slope, joining the marines. Saturday passed without incident and at midnight the Commandos

In invasion landings Allied naval support became an integral part of the fire plan, HMS *Ledbury*, with her 4in gun, supported the Rangers on the flank of the Salerno landings.

were relieved, moving into Salerno.

The Fifth Army had also reached the Montecorvino airfield and late on D-day (Thursday) No.3202 RAF Servicing Commando made a reconnaissance. These units with ten officers and some 189 airmen included engineers, airframe fitters and armourers. They worked in parties of about ten providing round the clock servicing on forward airstrips, their unit's specially equipped Bedford truck being landed early in an operation. On landing at Salerno their ten or so support trucks and two motorcycles were collected from the beach area on the Thursday night (D-day). Next day they brought in fuel and dispersed ammunition, although the field was under fire and not secured until Saturday. For the first week or so it could be used for emergency landings only as it was within range of German guns until 20 September. (The organisation and history of these servicing commando are shown in Appendices 2 and 7). An airstrip was in use, however, in VI Corps's sector at Paestrum and by Saturday (11 September) work had started on two other fields.

During these few days Rangers had directed fire from HMS *Ledbury* among other warships, and were helped by one of the Air Observation Post No. 654's flights whose advance party landed on the afternoon of D-day (9 September) and found a suitable field 150 yards (135m) from the beach. The spotter aircraft were assembled and flew off next day - 'the Squadron shot all varieties of targets with naval, medium, and field artillery'. Two other flights arrived some days later and used two other fields. These observation flights by Royal Artillery Officers and the Rangers' OPs (observation posts) directed the bombardments to such good effect that the Germans were forced to move their vehicles only at night; enough reason for the repeated counter-attacks that elements of the German 2 Parachute Division and SS Troops put in to shift these OPs. However, with slight readjustments the Rangers' line held. At night the rangers also sent patrols harrying German artillery positions, forcing a commitment of reinforcements the Germans urgently needed against the main beachhead. The Rangers were joined by

companies from the US 82 Parachute Division hurriedly shipped from Sicily, and by a 4.2 inch (107mm) mortar battalion. At times all these units were cut off from the Fifth Army or nearly so, withstanding seven major attacks - outnumbered at times by 9 to 1 according to one report - before being relieved on 18 September (D+9).

The German build-up was achieved more quickly than the Allies could reinforce their beachhead, although General Eisenhower juggled the convoy plans and American parachutists dropped into the beachhead on the night of Monday-Tuesday 13-14 September. Ammunition was scarce. For the Commando Brigade, after an eight-hour rest, German pressure early on Sunday meant they were called back to their old positions. Such 'mucking about' gives rise to many a moan to the corporals in any unit, and that fine Sunday morning was probably no exception. Commando corporals, like any others, lived with the men all the time and had to handle friends as well as those less pleased with discipline, orders, and doing what they were told. In the special service units, this was a less difficult junior command than for a corporal in a regular outfit, for almost all commandos and rangers would probably have held some rank in ordinary regiments.

As the Brigade took up their old positions, 'No.41(RM)' moved into the hills south and south-east of La Molina and 'No. 2' climbed to positions on the hills north of Vietri. The Brigade was down to 619 all ranks after taking casualties on the previous three days, but no reinforcements were available despite Bob Laycock's request for them: every cook, clerk, and reserve of X Corps was committed. The naval support ships were no longer offshore, having moved away for re-fuelling and re-ammunitioning; fire support from the 138th Brigade's artillery and mortars was available, but they had nothing to spare, having held the early morning German thrust towards Salerno and then Vietri.

The other early attacks were held, Troop sergeants making that contribution to steadiness in battle for which British NCOs are renowned. In commando and American ranger units, the senior NCOs had an experience of the technicalities of infantry warfare - overcoming the problems of ammunition supply to forward positions, spotting the lie of the ground suited to a bren gun position or route for its advance - that enabled their young Troop officers to bring off bold moves or outwit attackers. That morning, in steep and broken hill country beyond the Salerno beaches, the commandos had too few men for a continuous chain of defence posts and their nerves were stretched 'even when nothing particular was happening on their patch'.

These attacks died away by mid-morning and the rest of Sunday (12 September) was quiet. Next morning at dawn a heavy barrage of artillery and mortar fire fell on 2 Commando's positions. This Monday, 13 September, was to see the Germans' supreme effort. They had skilfully shifted their mobile and other artillery positions throughout the battle, making them difficult to find, as were their OPs in wooded hills. A Royal Marine officer, stumbling into one on a reconnaissance, was captured early in the landing but later escaped, as he was being taken out of the woods, leaping from rock to rock to make his way back to his Troop, despite being shot in the leg. The German artillery's success, the rumours of Allied evacuation German reports say were heard over radio networks, and the 16 Panzer Division's confidence led the German Generals von Vietinghoff and Block to believe they could retake Salerno. At a breakfast-time conference (0800) they planned to attack with the division's four original battle groups and a fifth one that had come up, the line of attack falling on the American IV Corps either side of the Sele river. Why the move should not start until 1330 that afternoon has been explained by some commentators as the result of less enthusiasm among the lower ranks than the generals felt for an attack. But when they came forward the attack fell as planned on the American IV Corps either side of the Sele river.

The preliminaries to the main attack had forced the commandos to give ground when two Troops were overrun. No doubt in part this gave cause for optimism in the German headquarters that breakfast-time, for the Germans were over the steep hill above Dragone and through this village, firing on the rear of the British defences. The Commando Brigade headquarters was hastily withdrawn, leaving their medical teams working in a small stone hut. The German thrust was broken up by fire from 25-pounders and 3.45-inch (87mm) gun-howitzers, of the British 71st Field Regiment RA, ably directed by their forward observation officer with the commandos. Jack Churchill saw the moment for a counterstroke on Dragone hill and sent off a Troop from 'No.41(RM)' and a Troop from 'No.2'. Major Dick Lawrie at their head was killed and his place taken by Captain the Duke of Wellington, who led the charge with Major Edwards RM. The Germans withdrew behind a smokescreen and the commandos rejoined their medical teams four hours after they had left them. Although the medical officer, Captain Brian Lees RAMC, knew the Germans were around him he kept his staff working quietly and they were not disturbed.

The Commandos were withdrawn to billets a bare mile from the front but late on Wednesday afternoon the Brigade was once again on the move. 'No.41(RM)' had received reinforcements of 48 men and a patrol of an officer and 15 men got back through enemy lines to rejoin 'No.2'.

They marched to the village of Mercatello, 2½ miles (4km) south-east of their old positions, and 'on the other side of Salerno'. Here three hills overlooked the British 167th Brigade's positions from across flat meadows. At 1730 hours the marines launched an attack on the crags of the hill on the right of the road where it passes over a ridge to the small Pigoletti village valley. Here, as elsewhere, the Troop officers, like the Ranger Platoon commanders, had to lead with 'plain bloody aggression', for although their many automatic weapons - tommies, brens, or BARs - gave them plenty of fire-power they were small units often fighting on their own. Success came in leading from the front; the Troop officer up with his scouts rather than behind the leading section where normally a unit's officer advanced. One Troop commander has written: 'We had to get the opposition cowering and saying "Ker...ist" then we had the initiative', vanishing the moment the enemy opened fire before the lead Troop returned this at a high rate so he felt it was coming from all over the place. Such tactics enabled the hill near Pigoletti to be taken with the loss of only one marine killed and two wounded.

While 'No.41(RM)' took their hill, 2 Commando moved in six columns up the heavily wooded valley with a few steeply terraced vineyards clinging to its sides. Each Troop shouted 'Commando, Commando', every five minutes, firing occasional tommy-gun bursts and following Jack Churchill. He was with No.6 Troop on the road and they got ahead of the line across the valley, surprising several Germans in the village, one of whom was persuaded at sword point - the Colonel thought an officer not properly dressed for battle without a sword - to give the password on a round of the sentries who each surrendered in turn. With 70 prisoners the Commando were back at the start line by midnight. Then they were sent back up the valley, and with the moon rising they stormed the first hill and were in touch with the marines on their right when the Duke of Wellington led two Troops against the third hill. He and many of his men were killed in fierce machine-gun fire and a barage of grenades, that forced the Troops to fall back on the village. Throughout Wednesday, 15 September the Brigade held the village and two hills but were under fire from 88mm (3.5in) guns and supply was difficult, for lubricating oil for automatic weapons, ammunition, and medical supplies had to be brought forward as well as rations.

The Germans were also having supply problems in the Salerno area. The XIV Panzer Corps had started the battle with seven 'units of fuel', a unit probably being enough for 50 or fewer miles in their worn vehicles over hilly country. Of the Corps' 4,074 vehicles, including 455 armoured tanks and self-propelled guns, over 10 per cent had been lost by 15 September. In battling up and across these Salerno hills, in attacking the Ranger stronghold that was never held by more than a few thousand men, although the Germans thought there was a division with two or three times this strength apparently, the German Panzer strength was weakened. They never dislodged the Rangers who, 13 days after they landed, moved on 22 September through the Sals-Chinnzi pass towards Naples.

Waiting for 'chow' outside a dugout kitchen, men of the North Americans, 20 April 1944, in the Anzio line.

The British Eighth Army, with their share of supply difficulties, reached the Salerno beachhead a week after the landings (16 September), having come over 200 miles (300+km) from Reggio with only minor losses - 635 out of 63,663.

The Fifth Army was to fight up the west coast and the Eighth Army in the east. With them went the Commandos and Rangers - 'No.41(RM)' lost Major Edwards and many men trying to take the hill where the Duke of Wellington was killed: this made a difficult start to the drive north, for although a Troop reached the hilltop, only six of them survived to come off it next morning. (The notes on other actions by Tom Churchill's Brigade (2, 9, 41(RM) Commandos), by John Durnford-Slater's Brigade (3 and 40(RM) Commando and the Special Raiding Squadron), and Bill Darby's Rangers are shown in the unit histories in Appendix 7). A good part of that winter of 1943-44, however, was spent by special forces in infantry work. They made a number of landings, from which the following paragraphs give some indication of how a Commando Group, an individual Commando, and other special forces were handled.

The first of these landings was at the small Adriatic port of Termoli (see map p. 116), two miles north-west of the mouth of the Bifurno river. The landing there would turn the natural defence line of the river and the German's left flank. The Eighth Army was in contact with the enemy eight miles south of the river when the 22nd Landing Craft Flotilla - four LCI(L)s towing seven LCAs - sailed from Manfredonia at midday on 2 October 1943. Their departure was something of a triumph for John Durnford-Slater, as he had signed the sailing orders earlier, getting the craft up to this little port before it was cluttered by Royal Navy authority. Indeed, it had been occupied by the adjutant of 'No.40(RM)' and an advanced party from the brigade, and the Colonel's informality has about it that special forces' touch which got things done. However, a navy or army would be a rabble if the discipline of movement orders and so on were not strictly maintained. In this conflict

lay much of some senior officers' dislike of special forces, for whereas the seniors needed order and method, commandos expected prompt action, and achieving all three took the genius of men like Lord Mountbatten and Bob Laycock.

Four Troops from 3 Commando commanded - as Peter Young was ill - by Arthur Komrower, recently recovered from his wounds received more than two years before at Vaagsö, Pops Manners's 40(RM) Commando, and Paddy Mayne's Special Raiding Squadron landed on 3 October. By 0800 they had taken their objectives, plus 500 prisoners, many found sleeping in a train about to go north, and the commander of a German battle group. By 0930 the Squadron were in contact with a battalion that had crossed the Bifurno River. The smoothness of these landings and their rapid development was due to the commandos' experience and their close understanding with the landing craft crews. The entire orders for the operation, involving 1,000 men, had been set down on half a sheet of paper, and because everyone knew what was expected of him, this brief instruction from John Durnford-Slater sufficed. Such administrative brevity, had not been achieved without much practice.

German supply trucks kept rolling into the town, and 12 or so were ambushed by the marines, who were joined before midday by the 56th Reconnaissance Regiment with armoured cars and carriers, followed that night by other advanced units of the British 78 Division. Next morning the commandos were withdrawn into the town, but by 1200 hours 3 Commando's Troops and a Troop from the Special Raiding Squadron were sent back to positions they had occupied in an olive grove on a hill overlooking some crossroads held by the Raiding Squadron. On their left were the 8th Argyll and Sutherland Highlanders with elements of the Reconnaissance Regiment holding a church and a factory. With 'No.3' were four six-pounders and a 17-pounder anti-tank gun, and three machine-gun teams from the Kensingtons (London). Lieutenant-Colonel Chavasse took command of this sector and John Durnford-Slater was in the town. There the townsfolk were making a nuisance of themselves, as explained in a moment, but the Commando Colonel decided he would give the marines and most of the Raiding Squadron an opportunity to catch up on their sleep - the men had only one night's proper sleep in the previous seven days, for the weather had been rough when they were brought up the coast before reaching their sally port. This morning he wanted them 'in tiptop shape', taking a calculated risk with 'No.3' who were now dug-in under driving rain.

A major enemy attack began at dawn next day, D+2, and the marines and Raiding Squadron Troops in the town were moved to form a perimeter on its west side. About this time, John Durnford-Slater called the male population together and threatened mass executions in retaliation for commando patrols being sniped on and grenades being thrown: he later wrote that this 'sent them home in a more cooperative frame of mind'. His own mind, although seldom troubled, must have been concerned that morning, for the heavy rains had washed away the engineers' bridge over the Bifurno. The town was cut off from the Eighth Army and the Recce Corps had brought in a prisoner from 26 Panzer Division.

About 1000 hours the Argylls lost the church, and tanks were rolling towards the commando's olive grove. The anti-tank gunners, their officer wounded, fired at too great a range and, having given away their position, took flight when the tanks knocked out a gun. More than 10 years would pass before the Commandos had their own guns but that would be in a different context when all Infantry Commandos were Royal Marine units. The Reconnaissance Corps had been driven back and the Argylls retired, leaving a sergeant and three men who preferred to stay, although now there was only 3 Commando, a Troop of the Raiding Squadron, the Kensington machine-gunners, Lieutenant-Colonel Chavasse, and his second-in-command two miles from the town in the olive grove. The Colonel called in an artillery barrage from across the river, and the officers spotting for this shoot crawled forward down the slope from the olive trees to pass the orders 'up

500, down 200' along a chain of commandos, lying on the forward slope, back to the radio. At 1530 hours this fire was supplemented by Kittihawks strafing the Germans and bombing their tanks, again called in by radio - the Commando prized their set so highly that John Durnford-Slater had it carefully brought in on a stretcher for landing.

From the town the Commando Colonel had warned Arthur Komrower that he would have to stick it out. Although there is no direct evidence of his reasoning, there seems every possibility that he knew any attempt to move the marines and other Troops forward was courting disaster, for the Argylls were already moving back and probably blocking the roads. German artillery fire had been falling with unpleasant accuracy, and the Brigade headquarters was hit, killing several staff in the room next to John Durnford-Slater - an enemy observer no doubt saw the aerials. A careful search was made and the German was found in the top of the church tower: he refused to come down and was killed by bren fire, 'a tough brave man, a great threat to the Commandos while he lived'. At night the fires in the town, with several haystacks afire, made it as bright almost as by day, and the crews of the landing craft that lay off the port throughout the action must have wondered how they might fare had they been called in.

The men in the olive groves had seen the bombers come in, but 90 minutes later 11 German tanks appeared 2,000 yards (1.8km) from the commando positions, followed by infantry that the Vickers machine-guns kept at bay. About 1830 hours, contact was lost with the Special Raiding Squadron Troop, and the tanks were within 100 yards of Arthur Komrower's headquarters: he could hear the crews talking from their open turrets as darkness prevented any further tank movement. The Germans lit a fire to brew coffee and Troop Sergeant-Major King, desperate for a cup of tea, left the headquarters to boil a mess tin of water on the far side of the German's fire. With men of such nerve the Commando Colonel need perhaps have had few worries, although he later said that 'this was the only time I thought we might be defeated'. He considered that had 16 Panzer Division been up to its old form it would have broken into the town.

At 0330 hours, 3 Commando and the machine-gunners were ordered back into the town as John Durnford-Slater and Colonel Chavasse considered them 'too exposed'. The next day, 6 October, 40(RM) Commando held off the last German attack, but the river bridge was rebuilt by then and the 38 Irish Brigade were in the town. Among the prisoners were men of the German 4 Parachute Brigade who had held the commandos and then pushed them from the Ponte dei Malati 10 weeks before. Some of these German élite were recognised as men who had captured commandos, and now the tables were turned the British could repay the good treatment they had received as prisoners in Sicily. Perhaps the professional respect the élite fighters had for each other contributed to their friendship, and as many of the 4th Paras spoke English there was an opportunity to exchange news.

The Bifurno line was turned and before sending them back to Bari, 'where there is plenty of everything', General Montgomery told the commandos they had saved the situation.

Handling a Commando - briefly described on page 13 - differed perhaps more in the independent nature of the command than in the actual military tactics of handling six Troops. Lieutenant-Colonel R.J.F. Tod's 9 Commando, for example, was sent across from the east coast to carry out a diversion on the lower reaches of the Garigliano river where it runs into the Mediterranean (see map p. 116), 35 miles (56km) north of Naples. He was an experienced officer, having landed in 1940 near Boulogne, but his Commando had not been under fire. Several schemes were put forward for this operation which was intended to draw the enemy's attention among the marshes and waterlogged estuary meadows, while the Guards' brigade holding the front a mile south of this marsh were moved up river for the major crossing. Overlooking the river mouth, the Germans held strongpoints on Monte Argento, which jutted into the sea

one and a half miles (2.4km) further north of strongpoints on the northern riverbank near the sea, (see '25' map p. 116).Inland they had fortified an old Roman amphitheatre by the broken bridge where the Appian Way from Naples had crossed the river.

Ronnie Tod divided his Commando into three Groups: X would hold the landing area, Y would attack the headland, and Z would attack the amphitheatre. They went into training once again, holding a signals exercise on Christams Eve, and while one day is much like the next in the field, special holidays are seldom forgotten, even in the midst of a campaign.

The Colonel wanted them back across the river before daylight, so time was an essential element of the raid. However, going into the beach in landing craft, despite being led by a radar-aided American scout boat, the Commando were landed 90 minutes late at 0025 hours on 29 December, and although correctly north of the river, they were 800 yards (720m) south of the intended landing point. This added twice that distance to the ground Group Y must go to and from their assault. By now readers will be expecting changes in an amphibious plan, and Ronnie Tod was ready to make one. Group Z had earlier put out a patrol and moving over the waterlogged ground were now more than 90 minutes behind the timetable. Captain Cameron radioed Ronnie Tod: should the attack go ahead? The Colonel made the decision: they would attack and come out over the broken bridge. Artillery fire came down 50 yards ahead of the Group, breaking up an enemy counter-attack, and the amphitheatre was taken without further resistance. Meanwhile the Guards' brigade had been mounting a series of attacks against the south bank of the river and had men at the bridge. As Group Z turned south towards them, the commandos had to overcome strong defensive positions, prepared no doubt for all-round defence by the Germans.

Groups X and Y came across the 100 yards or so of river-mouth in a couple of lifts from nine amphibious trucks (DUKWs) of the RASC and three RE reconnaissance (inflatable) boats. The light was improving rapidly as Ronnie Tod called to the drivers to be sure to come back for a second trip. 'If I say I'll come back, I bloody well come back', was a tired reply. The two Groups were just clear of the river as a German artillery barrage fell on the crossing. Higher up the river Captain M. Long swam and waded the 15 yards of ice-cold rushing water, a rope around his waist, and once he was on the bridge's south side this line helped haul the Group over in a collapsible boat, their crossing covered by a well-laid smokescreen. One man was drowned, but this was the only casualty here despite mortar fire, although the Commando had several other casualties. The bodies of only five of the nine dead had been brought back, so four nights later Ronnie Tod and several men went back to try to find them. Tom Churchill considered it the height of folly: a man lost a leg on a mine during this search and no bodies were found. Yet in many ways this demonstrates the Colonel's devotion to his Commando, for, at the risk of generalisation, a colonel's command still involves thought for men as individuals, but for more senior commanders the military equations have to exclude personal feelings. That is not to say these gentlemen are heartless or even unsympathetic of their men's position, but in the chess moves of war some pieces must inevitably be sacrificed for eventual victory. The senior officers of Special Forces often had to make their equations of death right in the middle of those who might pay the price of victory, a situation Bill Darby faced on 1 February 1944 in the Anzio beachhead.

On 22 January 1944, the 1st, 3rd and 4th Rangers with 9 and 43(RM) Commandos spearheaded virtually unopposed landings at Anzio. This immediate success was not exploited, although there are reasons to believe the proposed 30-mile (45+km) advance on Rome - eventually an open city - would not have been as simple as it may appear in retrospect, for when the German Gustav line was outflanked their reserves had only to turn west in the hills above Anzio to block this left hook, which they did. A battle of World War I style in trench warfare fol-

Commando bren gunner in Anzio beach-head.

lowed, the special forces suffering a major defeat in its early stages.

The featureless beachhead of Anzio was in part reclaimed land from the Pontine Marshes, and that winter standing water in places prevented the men from digging in. A few villages and stone farmhouses were spread across this plain that was traversed by gullies, with the Mussolini canal, a useful tank trap, forming the right (south-east) perimeter. General Truscott brought the Rangers from Carrocetta-Aprilla, the factory area where they had been in heavy fighting for several days, and with Bill Darby planned a night infiltration. Two Ranger battalions would pass through the German ring of defences, which would eventually be held by 71,500 Germans to the Allied VI Corps's 61,332 but which, on the night 30-31 January 1944, was not thought by the Allies to be too firmly closed. Therefore the Rangers planned to take by infiltration Cisterna di Littoria, blocking two routes to Cassino on the Gustav line. The move would also relieve pressure on the beachhead. Both battalions, the 1st and 3rd, were to avoid enemy strongpoints, but if caught in a fight then the 3rd Rangers would hold off the enemy while the 1st Rangers put in the planned dawn assault on the town. The 4th

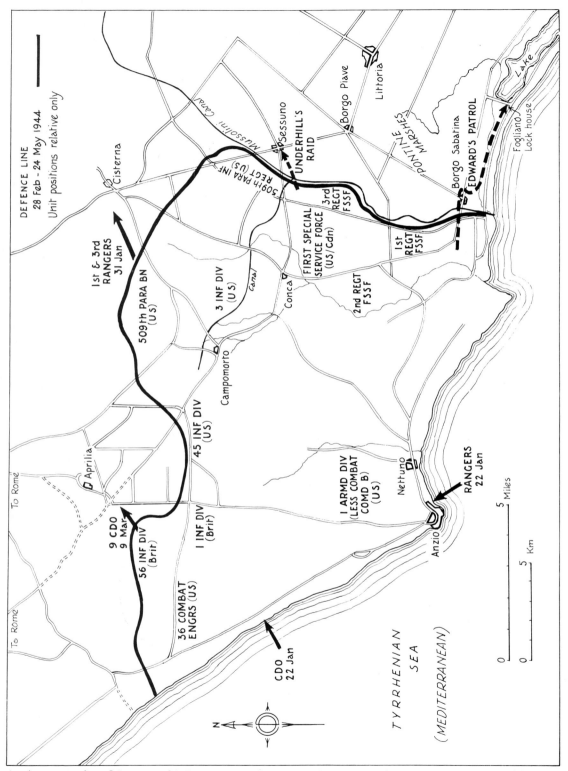

Anzio - examples of Commando, Ranger and North Americans' operations, January to May 1944.

Rangers were to follow an hour behind the others and clear the Anzio-Cisterna road.

The 1st and 3rd Battalions were through the enemy lines as planned in a long crocodile of men whose scouts, at about 0100 hours, killed enemy sentries beyond the Mussolini canal. Moving in this formation, as they had done several times in Africa, is one of the more risky manoeuvres for even highly trained troops: enemy enfilade fire can obliterate such a column before they get to ground, and at best the companies are not in a handy formation for all-round defence. For the 700 or so rangers crossing frozen ground that night, edging their way through German artillery positions, the odds were against success. At around 0200 hours the 4th Battalion set off, but half a mile (800m) up the road they were fired on by a single machine gun. Within minutes they were stopped against a wall of mutually defended positions that they could not breach in repeated company attacks. Meanwhile, the battalions infiltrating the enemy rear positions were moving forward towards their start line for the attack on the town.

While the 4th Battalion were losing several company commanders and many men in the enemy cross-fire, the leading Platoon of the 1st Battalion found themselves just before dawn in the middle of several German positions. They shot their way through these troops and were within 800 yards (700+m) of Cisterna, but around them were elements of the German's 4 Para Division who, apparently, had moved into the Cisterna area the previous night. The Para Division with its nine battalions including Italian Facist units had been fighting around the beachhead since the first landings.

General Truscott's forces - the 504 Parachute Regiment on the 4th Ranger's right, the 7 Infantry Regiment on the left - put in their planned dawn attacks but were unable to break through. As the daylight became brighter these assaults, like those of the 4th Rangers, became costly in casualties. Bill Darby's headquarters, forward with the 4th Battalion, was straddled by mortars and several men including Major Bill Martin, the executive or senior staff officer, were killed. An American tank attack down the road came to nothing when two tanks were lost on mines and others became bogged down in fields on either side of the road. The 4.2 inch (107mm) mortars could not fire accurately as their base-plates slewed in soft ground, whereas the German tanks and mortars moving against the isolated Rangers in the hills, were on firmer ground. In the morning mist, one of their tank columns coming from the direction of the beachhead was mistaken for an American force and had overrun several ranger positions before the 1st and 3rd repulsed it. The CO - Major Alvah Miller - of the 3rd Rangers was killed and Major Jack Dobson was seriously wounded leading the 1st Rangers.

About midday German tanks overran these Rangers and Bill Darby received their last radio messages. Some fought on into the evening, but only two in five survived and were marched through Rome as prisoners. Bill Darby, his grief apparent, asked his staff for a few moments on his own, but in minutes he was re-forming what units were left, the 4th Battalion having taken 50 per cent casualties. Subsequent interrogation of German prisoners showed 'our attack on Cisterna was expected . . . and a parachute regiment . . . moved to defensive positions south of the town'. Despite attacks from all sides, rangers had reached the railway station as early as 0800 hours before being captured.

Although battalions could still be defeated by well-sited defences, the war by this winter of 1943-44 had become one of technology as much as of military tactics. The Kittyhawks called in at Termoli had weaponry that could stop a tank or at least some types of tank, although the mists around Cisterna had probably prevented any similar success aiding the Rangers. Control of Troops by radio had enabled 9 Commando's colonel to smoothly change the battle plan on the Garigliano river, and the special forces were exploiting more unusual methods of warfare. Some of these are described in the Normandy landings of Chapter 11, and another is of particular interest for its attempts to combine the scientist's analysis of a potential target for special forces and technology for the equipment they would need. Geoffrey Pyke, a scientist whose long face and pointed black beard appeared at many Combined Operations conferences, analysed European weather patterns and found a fourth element: snow. This covers 70 per cent of the continent's land mass for more than four months of the year, and raiders with adequate vehicles could exploit this, destroying much of Norway's and Italy's hydro-electric power and the oilwells in Romania, forcing the Germans to defend normally inaccessible areas when these became potential raiding bases. The idea has much to commend it, but when the special snow vehicle, the Weasel, was developed it could be lifted only by the new Lancaster bombers and these had a priority for bomb loads; as yet the US C-54 was not in production. However, this carrier was built

Amphibious Weasel, the T15 prototype was modified as the M26 (M29 below). As the M28 several hundred were built with a better power-to-weight ratio and no propeller, relying on tracks for propulsion across water. The final design was a field-kit modification of the M29 carrier with bow and stern cells, a hinged rudder, and hinged side panels over the tracks controlling the flow of water to track blades of the M29C amphibian.

and used later not on snow, but despite its limited speed over water, in several amphibious landings and over swamps.

The men for this special raiding outfit were not therefore dropped with their carriers but were the unique First Special Service Force, known as the North Americans. Recruited from Canadian and American woodsmen, lumberjacks, and explorers, they took many of their styles and titles from the North American Indian (see organisation and history Appendices 2 and 7). A highly mobile force with great fire-power, the North Americans although trained with carriers, were landed without their original complement of carriers in the Anzio beachhead on 1 February 1944. Their losses in previous actions had been heavy, but they had some of the most highly developed techniques for raiding in mixed forces of infantry and armour. The 68 officers and 1,165 men took up their positions on the right of the beachhead with a ratio of one man per 12 yards (11m) of their front along the Mussolini canal. The German plan, split into three phases, was to pinch out the British salient up the Albano road during the week 3-10 February, to drive back down this road to the sea between 16-20 February,

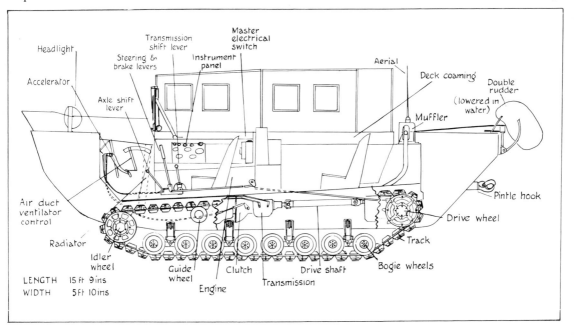

LENGTH   15 ft 9 ins
WIDTH    5 ft 10 ins

Men of the 1st Special Service Force, The North Americans, in Italy, 1944.

and to attack on the Cisterna front, turning the canal defences by 2 March. The British on the left and the Americans in the centre took the brunt of these attacks and, although the British salient was punched back, the second and third German attacks were contained.

For nearly four months, until 23 May, the North Americans were on the right-hand sector, and although they faced fewer sustained attacks than the British and Americans they were able to ease the pressure on other sectors by their active patrolling. They also showed great ingenuity in building up camouflaged breastwork defences where trenches could not be dug in wet ground. During the first two months, all major patrols were made at night from these defences, and even the small three-man daylight recces were a doubtful venture on the exposed ground in front of the North Americans. A considerable number of raids were made: 'many officers and men making forty distinct patrols, with a few hardy souls, engaging in 75 patrols during the Force's 100 days in the line. However, the casualty rate was high, and according to one report the Force's 'old bite had gone', despite reinforcements from remnants of the 4th Rangers, among others, before the North Americans were relieved (see map p. 150).

A night patrol illustrates the technique and the fire-power of the North Americans and shows a little of the stress they were under in Anzio. Staff Sergeant Edwards, 4 Company 2 Regiment, with 12 men, was briefed by the battalion commander before 1400 hours, thus giving the Sergeant and the selected men time to have a look in daylight at the ground they would cover that night. On occasions patrol leaders were flown over their raiding areas, but usually they had to make what visual reconnaissance they could from the forward positions. The battalion made all the arrangements to pass them out and back through the lines, and the Sergeant would make a last check with headquarters before moving off, their faces so completely blackened with an oil pigment that the Germans reported 'coloured troops ... in close combat at the Mussolini canal'. For this particular raid, against a stone lock house, the patrol carried: a rucksack (RS) load of 21lb (9.5kg) blocks of explosive in handy packs; bazookas (2.37in) (see Appendix 3) designed for anti-tank fire but used by raiders for other purposes; two Johnston USMC light machine-guns; rifle grenades fired from a cup-discharger; the usual tommy-gun, rifles, and grenades. Sergeant Edwards, an American, had a runner with a walkie-talkie in contact with the outposts during the seven or more hours the fighting patrol was out. His six Americans and six Canadians went through the forward posts at 2200 hours, and moved in bright moon-

North American's mortar team with 60mm (2.4in) mortar and Johnson light machine-gun in the Anzio beach-head April 1944

light on a cloudless night along the track near the coast. When they were 100 yards from the stone lock house they were forced to ground under heavy machine-gun fire which they returned. Having hit the wall with their first shot, the Sergeant and the bazooka man worked close enough, under covering fire of the light machine-gun to get a rocket into the house through a window. As the patrol moved forward again they came into an uncharted minefield - not one in the intelligence reports - and a man was killed and two were wounded by anti-personnel mines. Unable to find a way through this minefield the Sergeant withdrew; the dead man was lashed to a plank and the wounded men were carried on a door over the four miles (6km) back to their own outposts. They had not, its seems, been close enough to place the RS charge, had nearly a 25 per cent casualty rate, and little more than an additional minefield to report. But they had wounded, if not killed several Germans and those left in the lock house would need reinforcements by the next night.

Larger raids were mounted in platoon, company, and battalion strength, the force on average sending out three major raids a week. When the weather improved in April, raids were made with tanks brought forward before dawn, the noise of their movement

drowned out by heavy shelling and aircraft flying overhead. Then, at first light, this armour - from the US 81st Reconnaissance Battalion and other American units - would go forward two to four miles (3-6km) with a Special Force foot patrol to capture prisoners, observe the enemy's dispositions, and be back before his forces could take full counter-measures.

In an offensive night patrol that February to ease the pressure on the British and the American sectors, Captain Adna H. Underhill led a raid in company strength. He took two platoons across 1,200 yards (1+km) of flat terrain, moving forward behind an artillery barrage that allowed them to get into the outskirts of Sessuno (see diagram p. 150). No more than 50 or 60 Germans defended this village, and as the braves - the original name for the North Americans' soldiers - crossed the open ground they easily found the enemy's machine-gun posts; they then moved inside the zone of enemy defensive fire, which did not come down until they were on the outskirts of the village. The reserve platoon followed the assault platoons and, with the company headquarters, stayed on the Allies' side of the zone of Germans' defensive fire which was coming down on a pre-ranged area between the village and the main Allied positions. They were in contact with their own artillery and mortars by a telephone landline which had been reeled out as the reserve platoon moved forward, this line providing a more certain and unmonitored link - despite breaks by shell-fire - than the radios they carried as a secondary communication network. It also helped the stretcher-bearers find their way back to the outpost on their own front, from which the raid was mounted, and although German troops might have tracked a patrol by following the wire, they never appear to have done so.

Once in the village, Adna Underhill's men cleared the houses, a job the special forces would do frequently now they were on the mainland of Europe. At Sessuno, the drill was not unlike the Vaagsö action more than two years earlier, but the bazooka was used rather than a mortar. A few rounds into a house, or more if it was stubbornly defended, and then fragmentation grenades (see Appendix 3) were tossed into the building by two men getting close to it as they were covered by fire from automatic weapons. The house-clearing party then dived through a door or window to clear a room at a time, sometimes mouseholing their way with explosives through the inside walls from one building to the next in the terrace of houses. Heavier support was also used at Sessuno, the artillery blasting each house before the clearing party attacked it, a difficult shoot in the dark when the gunners were probably firing initially on map-referenced targets of previously registered ranges, to the direction of the forward observation officer with the assault platoons. With this artillery help, the company's 100 men held the village for four hours, fought off three counter-attacks, and retired under cover of another artillery barrage, having lost four men killed and eight wounded.

After the Italian capitulation, an Allied occupation of Kos, Leros, and Samos was reversed in a few days when Germans recaptured these islands. Consequently, when operations began in the more northerly Adriatic during January 1944, the Allies knew they could not expect any easy victories. The broad pattern of events after 2 Commando reached Viz in January 1944 was the crea-

Men of 30 Commando, an intelligence unit, search a cellar in a German HQ looking for information from plans, maps and other documents (Italy, August 1944).

tion of a mixed force including regular army units and some anti-aircraft guns and 4-pounders in the 1,000-strong Force 133. Their job was to help the Yugoslav partisans hold the island, mostly bare stony hills and 18 miles (28km) long and eight miles (13km) wide. Only 18 miles across the water were German positions on Hvar island, and they were also on the coastal islands of Brac and Solta. The Germans there and on the mainland included the 118 Jäger Division of mountain troops, but Jack Churchill began raiding without delay. On 27 January he led three Troops of 'No.2', with 30 Americans of the Operations Group in an attack on the airport of Hvar, taking four prisoners whose interrogation, along with other intelligence, revealed the strength of the German positions. Jack Churchill then decided that bluff would have to fill gaps in his relatively small forces' coverage of the many possible raiding targets supporting the partisans. Tom Churchill brought the Brigade HQ, along with 'No.43(RM)', to Viz late in February 1944, and 'No.40(RM)' joined them towards the end of May. The commandos had the help of destroyers, MTBs, and MGBs commanded by Lieutenant-Commander Morgan Giles RN, and a COPP for reconnaissance. A supernumerary extraordinary was also with them: the 72-year-old Admiral Sir Walter Cowan, who had contrived to be on the 1941 Bardia raid, and was later captured at Tobruk. Now, in 1944, his small but inexhaustible figure climbed with the commandos among the crags of this coast.

The raiding policy succeeded for five months, but late in May German paras nearly captured Marshal Tito when they dropped near his Drvar headquarters in Central Bosnia and disrupted the partisan organisation. Tito asked his partisans on Viz to create a diversion, and a major raid was mounted by 6,000 men, including the Commando Brigade. The Germans had withdrawn their smaller garrisons from outlying islands, but had 1,200 men on Brac.

Three separate raiding forces were to attack the island's defences, and a fourth would take the observation post. The North Force and OP Force, named after their targets, landed on D-1 to lie up near their

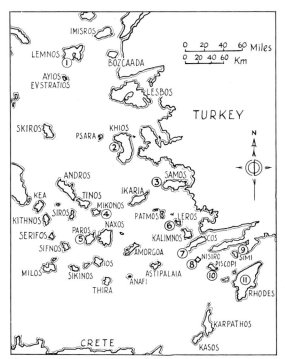

Commando operations in the Dodecanese and Greek islands, 1943/5.

Examples of Raiding Forces Middle East operations by highly trained personnel - parachute canoeists and demolition experts - who were not regarded as expendable. Location numbers from 1 in north run to 11 in south:

### 1943

11. Rhodes - early Sept - Majors Lord Jellicoe and Dalby parachuted on to island despite anti-aircraft fire, but could not persuade Italians to resist German occupation although some Italians attempted an initial resistance.

9. Simi - early Sept - Lt-Col (later Brig) Turnbull landed from captured Italian seaplane to negotiate surrender of nearby Rhodes, but Italians there handed over defences to the Germans.

* Castelorizo - 9 Sept - 50 men of SBS occupied this small island as a base, after slight opposition from 300 Italians.

7. Cos - mid-Sept - SBS prepared landing points for infantry but German counter thrust with paras and seaborne assaults on Sunday 3 Oct retook the island by 9 Oct.

6. Leros - mid-Sept - LRDG prepared landing points for infantry, but a German counter thrust on 12 Nov recaptured the island in 4 days.

3. Samos - mid-Sept - the Greek Sacred Squadron parachuted into the island but were

driven off by larger German force. (The Sacred Squadron of Royalist officers was a revival of the Squadron killed to a man at Thebes resisting Spartans in 370 BC.)

* Calymos - late Sept - base set up for island and anti-shipping raids, and for observation.

### 1944
10. Piscopi - 9/13 Apr - 10-man patrol landed by dory from ML, included Folbot team. The two canoeists were unable to get into Scala harbour, but the main force gathered intelligence after contacting the local Greeks and killed four Germans in an ambush.

4. Mikonos (Lazaretto Bay) - 22 Apr - recce patrol landed at night and next day attacked 8 Germans in fortified house in which the Germans made a stout resistance, until threats to fire the house led to their surrender and the capture of code books, documents and 6,000 gals of petrol. The fuel was distributed with food stocks to the islanders.

3. Samos - May - 40 Greeks of Sacred Regmt were probably betrayed, as they were ambushed but only 5 failed to escape eventually, most being picked up by RN at rendezvous during the three weeks after the raid.

* Anti-shipping raids during this summer were made by raiders boarding caiques and when possible taking their prizes to Allied ports.

5. Paros - 13/5 May - Capt Andy Lassen with 18 men made five co-ordinated attacks; a German officer was captured in his billet; a wireless post destroyed; but the three other targets could not be reached and the raiders were forced to withdraw.

2. Khios - June - a landing by 40 British and Greek raiders reached Khios harbour overland after crossing the hills, the cable installations were destroyed paralysing the inter-island telephone system, 13 caiques were sunk and a boat building yard destroyed. The raiders had no casualties although 184 Germans garrisoned the harbour.

6. Leros - 17 June - successful anti-shipping raid by RMBPD damaged two destroyers and two other ships. The repairs to the destroyers took three months, enabling raiders to move more freely around the islands and in greater numbers for any one landing.

8. Nisiro - July - Caique No. 6, 'a small blue tub', landed a party who gathered intelligence on 90 Axis troops' dispositions, food supplies, morale, shipping and reprisals after earlier raids. They evaded the German counter-espionage patrols and were helped by a local town mayor.

9. Simi - 13/4 July - 224 raiders captured the local garrison and stripped defences in the first of a series of major raids, evacuating the island after distributing food.

2. Khios (or Chios) - 28 Sept - a permanent raiding HQ established.

3. Samos - 4 Oct - 24 Greeks landed and were followed by Brig Turnbull with only 25 more raiders, but in a typical bluff he had used before on the islands: the local garrison were persuaded that a large force had landed. Some 1,200 prisoners were taken without the raiders suffering any casualties.

1. Lemnos - 16 Oct - an advance party of 75 raiders landed and with the help of bribes (gold sovereigns being a quieter persuader than force on occasions) reached the garrison port. Here they caused many casualties to Germans trying to escape by boat.

### 1945
11. Rhodes - 1/2 May - 180 raiders destroyed German camps and defences in a 6-hour raid. The next week the 10,000-strong garrison surrendered along with other Germans in the area.

*Note: locations not shown on map.

---

objectives. A few hours before the main landing on 2 June 1944, they were to cut off Supetar from Neresisce and eliminate the OP, hampering the battery's fire on the assault ships. Both these groups - 500 partisans in North Force and a company of the Highland Light Infantry with 20 partisans in the OP Force - got ashore and in position without being discovered. West Force consisting of 43(RM) Commando with the Heavy Weapons Troop, a rifle Troop of 'No.40(RM)', and 1,300 partisans, would come ashore over three beaches in the south-west of the island. Five miles to their east at Bol, the East Force of partisans would land with artillery to support the commandos - 25-pounders of the 111th Regiment Royal Artillery and 75mm (3in) guns manned by partisans. Some of the 25-pounders would also support the East Force advance. Air support included rocket-firing Hurricanes over the island plus three US Air Force bomber raids on mainland targets.

The North Force successfully cut the road south, but the Highlanders were unable to break through the OP's minefield although they did prevent these German observers from directing the battery. This was attacked by RAF fighter-bombers at 0600 hours, on a bright clear morning, before 'No.43(RM)' and the partisans attacked it. The assault over open ground beyond the crags was repulsed because minefields prevented the raiders getting close to the enemy's positions.

The Special Raiding Squadron and SBS were sometimes carried in local craft camouflaged with nets while lying in creeks and inlets; here, men of the SBS unload stores on the German-occupied Santorin Island 70 miles (110+km) north of Crete.

East Force was more successful in taking Selca, and several guns, along with 100 prisoners, were captured; 130 Germans were killed. A joint attack from north and south planned for later that Friday, was not carried out as partisan casualties, probably, prevented them from providing the necessary men. However, they continued to engage the posts throughout the night.

Early on Saturday (D+1), reinforcements were brought in with three Troops of Pops Manners' 40(RM) Commando, 300 partisans, and two more 25-pounders. Jack Churchill, known throughout the islands as Colonel Jack, had made a long reconnaissance before deciding that both Royal Marine Commandos should assault Hill 622, which was in part separated by the hill formations from the other positions. Points 542 and 648 north and south of the commando attack would be harassed by partisans, the attack going in at dusk. Artillery fire just before the assault would switch from 622 to the points being harassed by partisans. Once 622 was taken, the way into the whole defence system would be open but for Commando colonels, as for many other senior officers in the field, the best laid plans could founder on a chance mistake in a wireless message - one reason for the North Americans' use of telephone lines.

The orders for the commando attack went out by radio that Saturday on Brac, but for some unexplained reason they were received by the commando signallers as though 'No.43(RM)' alone would make the attack from the start line at 1930 hours. They got two Troops on the top of Point 622 by 2150 but were driven off, losing six officers and 60 men. The radio message of this failure, although probably sent, was never received by Colonel Jack. Earlier, Captain E.R. Wakefield, the Brigade GIII staff officer, whose responsibilities included distributing orders, was misled by his guide, and did not reach 40(RM) Commando with Colonel Jack until 15 minutes after the attack should have started. With their objective's sharp features visible in the moonlight, Colonel Manners and Jack Churchill advanced in a different direction from 'No.43(RM)' across a wide shallow valley. Here they found B Troop of 43(RM) Commando, who reported a mine field. Pressing forward, a fresh 10 rounds in each magazine, Y Troop of 40(RM) Commando came up the hill, bayonets fixed in a charge 'as if they were at Achnacarry' - the training depot; Jack Churchill was in the van playing his bagpipes. B Troop (from '43') attacked on the right. The Troops reached the summit and waited for the rest of 'No.43(RM)'. The enemy's fire was heavy,

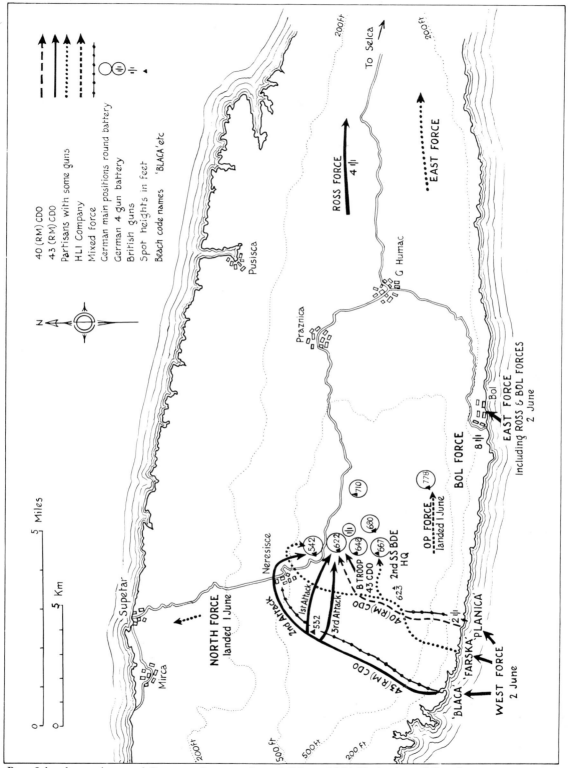

Brac Island - partisan and Commando operations, 1-3 June 1944 (D-day here 2 June).

provoked no doubt by Jack Churchill's two green Very lights signalling success, he did not know 43(RM) Commando were back in the valley. In this barrage of fire, Pops Manners was wounded, the signaller failed to raise the other Commando on his set even though he shifted his position for better reception, and soon there were only six men alive on the hill, including the wounded. A mortar bomb killed Captain Wakefield and two marines, and added to Pops Manners's wounds. Almost immediately 20 Germans appeared, following in behind this fire, but were driven off by Colonel Jack's revolver shots. In the waning moonlight he played 'Will ye no come back again?' but 43(RM) Commando were too far away to hear this piped call over the German bombardment echoing round the crags. The tune was not repeated as a flurry of grenades knocked out Jack Churchill. Two further attacks by 'No. 43 (RM)' failed to restore the position.

No. 43(RM) were regrouped but could not dislodge the Germans. Pops Manners died next morning while a prisoner of the Germans; Jack Churchill was flown to Germany, and despite a gallant watch by Royal Navy MGBs inside Supetar harbour all that night, the commando prisoners were taken off the island. Next day, 50 men of 2 Commando formed a fighting rearguard as the rest of the Brigade having lost 143 men,

re-embarked, leaving 15 commandos on the island to look for survivors.

Although the raid had been a tactical failure it achieved its strategic aim: the Germans reinforced Brac. After Major Edward Fynn succeeded Jack Churchill, Tito visited Viz and addressed 2 Commando, thanking them for their help to his people. Nevertheless, relationships between the allies were difficult, for the partisans resented the commandos' view of themselves as better-trained soldiers, and there were misunderstandings over the need for the meticulous planning that the Brigade put into any raid. For the rest of the summer, commando standing patrols of about 30 men were put on various islands, and some further raids were made. In July, Edward Fynn landed in Albania near Himara with 700 men - 2 Commando, plus elements of the Special Raiding Squadron, medical teams and a few other specialists. The Raider Support Regiment with batteries of mountain and other guns supported the commandos (see also Appendix 2). Brief details of their actions over the next few months are shown in the unit histories in Appendix 7.

Although there are arguments for saying that any well-trained regiments might have performed these raiding roles on land, there is little doubt that the special nature of

Lieutenant-Colonel R. W. Sankey 40 (RM) Commando, and Lieutenant-Colonel R. J. F. Tod with SS cap badge, on passage to Corfu, October 1944.

amphibious raiding needed more specialised training than could be given to every regular unit, a point considered in the final chapter. However, in many senses the Special Forces were the epitome of good regiments, for many of these units were represented in the ranks of the Commandos and Ranger Battalions. They had also developed, by 1945, an ability to discipline their independent actions in a way that made them invaluable elements in division and sometimes in army set-piece battles. Moving ahead of the chronological development of their story, the attack by 2 (Commando) Brigade on the right flank of the British Eighth Army in the complex of lagoons and canals where the river Reno and Lake Comacchio run by the sea at the east end of the Po valley, illustrates this.

Ronnie Tod had taken over the Brigade, and for six weeks in the early spring of 1945 they were in the line to gain experience of the Germans' fighting techniques. These men of Field-Marshal Kesselring's armies had put up a year's stubborn resistance before falling back to a line along the Po valley. At the extreme left of this line they held a spit of land separating Lake Comacchio, a shallow lagoon, from the Adriatic. Along this spit were a series of strongpoints manned mostly by Turkomans, Russians

Commandos unloading a storm boat on lake Comacchio.

from Soviet Asia Minor, stiffened with a fusilier battalion of the 42 Jäger Division - 1,200 men in all.

The 2 Commando Brigade - renamed as were all brigades from Special Service because its abbreviated SS had infamous German associations - were to attack these positions with four enveloping drives.

Their boats had to be heaved even further out than their 1,000 yards (.9km) start line before there was sufficient water to use the outboard, and others ran into shallows, the commandos slipping and sweating to get them over a mile (1.6km) of glutinous mud. 2 and 9 Commandos became intermingled in these hours of unpleasant exertion - stronger words were used at the time - before the boats were back in deeper water, by which time there were not many hours of darkness left. But Ronnie Tod decided there was no point in deferring the attack, for the conditions would not change and the guns were neutralising the enemy strongpoints. Shouted orders passed this decision across the water from one boat to the next. 2 Commando then lashed their storm boats in groups of four, with four lines of 9-man assault boats behind each group as the LVTs were bogged down. All four outboards had to be started together in each group for there were no clutch controls and once going each raft of storm boats surged forward.

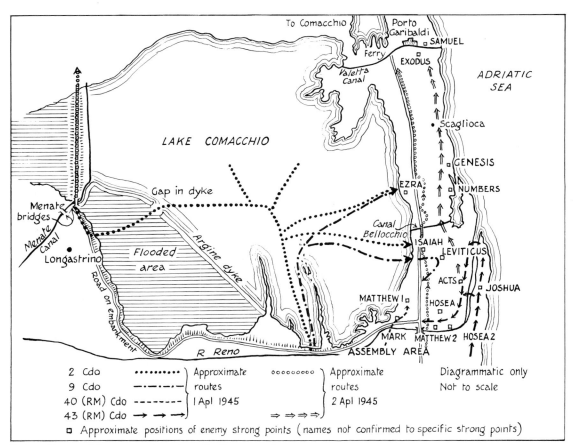

Lake Comacchio operation by 2 Commando Brigade, 1 April 1945.

Crossing the expanse of lake, some rafts reached the COPPists' markers, although other boats spread across the waters unable to get many shore bearings because the surroundings were featurelessly flat.

Some rafts reached the Argine dyke as 'No.40(RM)''s attack went in. This feint worked. No enemy countered 2 Commando, probably because they were at his back door and all the defences pointed seaward or to the south. Getting over the dyke at 0447 hours, No.1 Troop, the Heavy Weapons Troop, and HQ sections dragged the heavy storm boats through a gap and transhipped their stores and ammunition to some assault boats, before paddling them 600 yards (540m) to the start line for the final assault on the bridges. They had 200 yards more of slime to struggle through, but this most difficult of approaches caught the enemy unawares. Using their lifebuoy portable flame-throwers (see Appendix 3) to flame a strongpoint, the Troops established a bridgehead where a third Troop joined them.

Artillery fire against the southern base of the spit was so heavy that the smoke mingled with the mist, giving 9 Commando some cover as they came ashore to find a mixture of 'soft yielding fluid which could engulf a man completely, and a glutinous mud'. Struggling through this they reached Isaiah strongpoint (the biblical names of key points are shown on the above diagram). 43(RM) Commando captured Joshua on the strip of land between the sea and the river, and crossed the river against some opposition as they launched their assault boats before establishing a bridgehead on the north bank. 2 Commando advanced down the narrow enbankment above the inundated fields to take Peter bridge, but Amos was blown. Some of the 'lost' Troops from 2 Commando joined those of 'No.9' to take Ezra and Leviticus on the western side of the spit.

Next afternoon - 2 April - the Brigade advanced north, supported by tanks brought across the repaired Amos bridge. 2 Commando was on the left, and on the right 'No.43(RM)' moved steadily forward, skirting a large minefield before driving some enemy rearguards from houses in Scaglioca. Beyond this small town was bare ground stretching to the enemy defences of the Valetta canal. C Troop was pinned down as they led the advance across these open spaces, but Corporal Tom Hunter managed to reach a dyke from where he took on three Spandaus. Firing his bren from the hip, he ran 200 yards, driving these gunners from their positions in some houses. They took up new positions while he continued to fire at them, and now they were supported by six Spandaus in positions on the canal bank. However, although he was lying on an exposed mound of rubble, Tom Hunter's fire enabled C Troop to extricate themselves before he was killed outright, his self-sacrifice in saving the Troop being recognised by the award of the VC. The Brigade consolidated their positions that night 400 yards (360m) south of the Valetta canal and were relieved on the night of 4 April.

Four islands on lake Comacchio were captured by Special Boat Section patrols during the following week, and about midnight on 8 April Major Anders (Andy) Lassen led three patrols on a diversion raid from one of these islands - Caldirolo. The aim was to create an impression of large forces moving against Comacchio through a landing on the embankment road some 3,000 yards (2.7km) from the town, and after rowing across the lake - the gentle breeze rustling the reeds to cover the approach - two patrols landed. They were challenged when they had gone 500 yards (.5km) and answering in Italian that they were fishermen, Fred Green was called forward by two men in an outpost. He stepped into the middle of the 15-foot (3m) ribbon of road and shots were fired, the

commandos taking cover over the edge of the embankment a few feet above the flood waters. Andy Lassen worked his way to a strongpoint behind the listening post where they were challenged, throwing a couple of grenades they cleared the four machine gunners from this pillbox but were under fire from further along the road. Little was known of the layout of these defences as there had been no time for adequate reconnaissance, but the raiders could make out at least two more strong points and a firing position away to the left of the road. These kept up a steady fire while Andy Lassen led the men to clear a second machine gun position and on towards a third. They had taken a couple of Russians prisoner and when someone shouted 'Kamerad' Andy Lassen moved to the entrance of the third post. He was fatally wounded in a burst of fire. His last words to Sergeant-Major Leslie Stephenson were 'Steve ... try and get the others out'.

Andy Lassen had raided across the Channel in 1942, in the Mediterranean in 1944 and the range of SBS experiences could be encapsulated in his war service. This brave Dane was awarded the Victoria Cross for his actions near Comacchio as he had thrown three grenades despite his wounds, enabling his men to get clear of the road. His body was found there next day by Italian partisans. Three other raiders were killed and one seriously wounded, but after they got back to Caldirolo the survivors were later told that the Germans had reinforced the town's defences after the raid. This redeployment contributed to the Allied breakthrough further west on the Italian front in the following week.

These operations in Italy and the Balkans give some measure of the Special Forces' military skills and high standards of leadership, achieved initially through the enthusiasm of volunteers and honed to a fighting efficiency by rigorous training; training that taught them not only the fundamentals of light infantry tactics, but also - for some - the use of highly specialised equipment like the midget submarines the COPPists used in north-west Europe.

# THE UNITED KINGDOM HOME FRONT, 1943 TO 1944

The year 1942 had been a watershed of Allied fortunes: the Americans landed on Guadalcanal; the desert army won the battle of El Alamein and the Allies landed in North Africa; the Russians had encircled the German Sixth Army at Stalingrad where they would surrender the following February. These victories and a lessening of the German air raids - 52,000 civilians had been killed and 63,000 severely injured in these bombings - gave the British a glimpse of final triumph, and spurred on their total effort that had mobilised civilian and service forces alike, with rationing of food and clothing, direction of labour for men and women sent to essential jobs, and factory production controlled by the Government.

The British had survived the first three years of the war through their Royal Air Force's victories in 1940, because the waters of the English Channel were an historic moat against invasion, through the support of the Commonwealth and supplies from America, and as a result of the British determination not to be beaten - the spirit of the people. They made welcome any Allies, providing, for example, nearly a third of all the supplies required by American forces in Europe, except those in Italy, and by May 1944 some one and a half million Americans had crossed the Atlantic to the United Kingdom. The British also supplied and maintained Australians, Canadians, New Zealanders, Frenchmen, Norwegians, Poles, Czechs, Dutch, and Belgians as well as smaller numbers of Danes, Free Hungarians, and other allies.

In this great camp that was Britain of 1943 and 1944, commandos and rangers lived and loved as others did in the uncertainties of wartime - some married their wartime sweethearts, some found reason not to mention they would be gone by tomorrow's tide; only very few traded on their glory, despite the hero-worship of most civilians and some jealousy from regular formations.

Knife fighting practice.

# 10 REORGANISATION AND STRATEGY

The corner-stones of the Special Forces' success were a high standard of selection and meticulous training. Some indication of the qualities sought in volunteers were given in a circular sent by MO9 to British regiments in June 1940:

'. . . able to swim, immune from sea and air sickness, able to drive motor vehicles . . . with courage, physical endurance, initiative and resource, activity (being active), marksmanship, self-reliance, and an aggressive spirit towards the war . . . and must become expert in military use of scouting . . . to stalk . . . to report everything taking place . . . to move across any type of country by day or night, silently and unseen . . . and to live off the country for considerable periods.'

There are many stories, several no doubt apocryphal, about the selection of commandos and rangers who volunteered. Some were interviewed naked to satisfy an interviewer that they had the right physique and 'moral and mental attitudes for a commando'. One 1940s rumour - true or false the story enhanced the commando legend - put a bowl of eggs on the interviewer's table and describes his displeasure if the volunteer had snitched not more than one by the end of the 10 minutes of questions. Typically these were about the volunteer's interests in sports, in playing musical instruments (with beach survey instruments in mind), and his sex life. Was he a Boy Scout? This last was not a question of comparative morals, but Scouts had many qualities as practised

observers with a knowledge of field craft that was more important than muscle in Special Forces' work. Some Ranger volunteers were asked 'Have you ever killed a man?' which gave at least one of them some moments thought about the role of the new outfit. Did he think he could 'stick a knife in a man . . . and twist it?' Although the mere thought of using a knife repelled him, he answered that he thought he could do so in battle. Within a year he had done so. For him, like many Americans of German, Italian, or Japanese descent, there were added personal doubts - could he kill one of his father's people? The answer was in the comradeship of a Ranger unit that proved stronger than more distant blood relationships.

The volunteers were accepted only if they were proficient shots with experience of at least one automatic weapon and had completed a basic course in field craft. They were trained soldiers in the military sense, with a knowledge of fire-and-movement and similar elementary tactics. Their physical fitness was also tested, 25 per cent failing this medical. In 1940, though, the selection was informal: each Troop officer interviewed volunteers during visits to units, whose commanding officers were reluctant and sometimes understandably downright obstructive before parting with their best men. The Troop officers, themselves selected by each Commando's Colonel in 1940, included men like Peter Young and Mike Calvert who, in the next few years, would greatly influence the development of the commandos and other Special Forces.

Under their first senior officers each Commando took on an individuality suited to their independent role, with the trust between officers and men as the foundation of Special Forces' discipline. Their supreme punishment was a return to their regular units - RTUed.

Once the days of Admiral Keyes's private armies were over, the War Office reasserted its control over the Commandos; and under Charles Haydon's guidance the unwieldy 10-Troop Commandos were reformed, the Brigadier (later Major-General) revising their organisation into Commandos, each of six Troops, based on an organisation he set out in a report of February 1941 (see Appendix 2 for examples). At this date the Commandos officially had neither heavy weapons - heavy for them that is: 3 inch (75mm) mortars and medium machine-guns - nor adequate transport, for they were still essentially shipborne raiders.

The intention in 1940 was to raise 6,000 commandos and 1,750 men for the Independent Companies, but by the early summer of 1943 there were only 3,700 men in the Special Service Brigade, which had absorbed the Independent Companies; 2,000 rangers: and a few smaller units - about 150 men in the COPPs, for example - to cover a wide range of special operations, particularly those that would be essential to a successful invasion in north-west Europe. General Bourne, Adjutant-General of HM Royal Marines (analogous to Commandant in the USMC), was persuaded to offer his RM Division to General Eisenhower, who consulted Lord Mountbatten. At this time the British were getting the measure of the forces they would need for an invasion of Europe and the Admiralty wanted the RM Division to man landing craft. A logical step was to re-group the Division and some other RM forces, 10,000 Royal Marines remustering as landing craft crews and 6,000 forming two Special Service brigades with a 20 per cent reserve.

In his excellent history of the Commandos, *The Green Beret*, Hilary Saunders explains the commando soldier having 'to regard himself as expendable . . . [he bore] the same relationship to the general army as a monk or friar does to the ordinary Roman Catholic'. But whatever the type of operation, large or small, raiders were highly trained, for where they ventured there were plenty of dangers, without adding the risks of inexperience and needless casualties. This training not only included tactics and developing great physical endurance, but also gave men the motivation to become the 'expendable friar' of military orders. Although there were a number of colourful characters like Colonel 'Mad Jack' Churchill, most commandos and rangers were not supermen but Tommies and Joes superbly trained.

The aim of the training was to produce those individual soldiers capable of carrying through a mission on their own when others in their group or other groups were killed or put out of action. An obvious trait, perhaps, for SBS and COPP canoeists, but not as widely understood in relation to Commando and Ranger Battalion actions. In the early 1940s, much of this motivation and training was encouraged by the Commando's privilege of a civilian billet, which also saved the cost and trouble of organising camps, meals, and other barrack services. A daily allowance - initially 6s.8d., later 7s.6d. (37½p, or about $1.50 in the 1940s) - for billets was paid and the men were left to find their own quarters. In later years these were often found by the billeting corporal, but throughout the war commandos, in theory at least, could do what they wished with this allowance provided they appeared properly dressed on parade, Keyes having successfully fought off a War Office move to bring them to heel in barracks. A few commandos lived rough for a time: one officer in dispute with his hotel, saved 13s.6d. a day - his billeting allowance - by camping on the local golf course.

Most landladies made second homes for the men, running them hot baths after an exercise, cleaning their equipment, and treating them as the heroes they were in the early 1940s.

The reorganisation in 1941 enabled commanding officers to strengthen their units by reducing the number of junior officers, a few of whom had not proved satisfactory Troop or Section commanders.

By 1942, the typical Troop programme had settled into weapon training during mornings, map and compass exercises in the afternoons, with a weekly 20-mile route march or a cross-country run; every third week there was a Commando exercise in which all Troops took part. There was nothing routine about these programmes, for officers in the Special Forces excelled in creating initiative tests.

These fun and games had a serious purpose, for raiders trapped ashore after a raid had to make their way hundreds of miles across hostile territory to reach safety. Bob Laycock's and Sergeant Jack Terry's journey has been described. Graham Hayes reached Spain with the tragic consequences mentioned earlier. After the St Nazaire raid, Troop Sergeant-Major George Haines and Sergeant Challington, despite their wounds, got away from the port, but were captured in the nearby country, Lance-Corporal Howarth reached Vichy France and after eight months in jail finally escaped back to England. Corporal Wright and Private Harding reached Marseilles and home with the help of individual French men and women and an expatriate American woman. Corporals Wheeler and Sims, finding not all French people friendly and most of them frightened, made a 250-mile (400km) journey on foot and bicycles to Azay-le-Ferron in Vichy France, where they were befriended by several families, and escaped to Gibraltar after many close shaves. But not every escaper made a direct line for home. Sergeant-Major Tom Winter, captured when the SSRF's dory was sunk at St Honorine, found a way out and back into his Polish prison camp for a series of nightly visits to teach the Polish Resistance how to use explosives. Sentenced to 10 years' solitary confinement, he finally escaped when the Russian advance reached the prison camp. Captain Charles Shudstrom and other rangers were equally successful in continuing their fight after escaping from prison camps, leading Italian partisans in raids on German supply columns and lines of communication.

Commando training was put on a more formal footing in February 1942 when the Depot (later the Commando Basic Training Centre) was set up by Charles Haydon at Achnacarry. Set in a lonely glen some 14 miles from Fort William, the Inverness-shire Achnacarry castle home of the Chief of the Camerons became the finest infantry training centre in the world and perhaps of all time, for its motivation of men for battle, under the 'Laird of Achnacarry' or 'Rommel of the North', to give two affectionate nicknames for Lieutenant-Colonel Charles E. Vaughan, founder and Commandant of the Centre. The men even grew to ignore the weather, although the live ammunition and explosive charges placed along each battle course were a different matter. All trainees treated these with increased respect but less fear. On their arrival they were halted in the castle drive to read the tombstones among the trees - 'he showed himself on the skyline', 'he failed to take cover in an assault landing', and 'he did not know the difference between cover from view and cover from fire' were among epitaphs for imaginary recruits that all who survived never forgot. The assault course was part of the legend. Bill Darby's 1st Ranger Battalion had a stiff course, no effort being spared in exploding charges in the river and firing live rounds as the men came over the 'death slide' and other courses. But after an unimpressive first 10 days, in the view of one instructor, they 'got with it'. Later, Colonel Darby was to say after a Ranger action in Italy that 'the achievements were due entirely to the training at Achnacarry'. Many rangers also carried with them the repeated chant of their British instructor: 'It's all in the mind and the heart.'

Charles Vaughan was sure of this and believed that any man properly trained could march seven miles in an hour if he had the will. If this sounds fast by infantry standards of four miles an hour, the speed march should be explained as a march and run in which most men after Special Forces' training, could cover 14 miles (22km) in some five to ten minutes over two hours.

A landing exercise, renowned for the closeness of instructors' fire, a 36-hour

Crossing a cat rope.

scheme in the Scottish hills with a night attack, and some off-beat lectures were all part of the course. If the landing craft were on the wrong beach, the trainees just had to run to make up time. If they had climbed the wrong hill for that night attack, they had to run to the right one. They learnt to cook rats and eat them, to climb cliffs and enjoy it some practised on the cliffs in their spare time, a dedication perhaps, although there was nothing much else to do in your spare time. They learnt to kill silently; they fired enemy weapons; they practised unarmed combat. Above all, they learnt the determination to keep going or they failed the course.

Men of the smaller specialised units like the Special Boat Section (SBS) and Combined Operations Pilotage Parties (COPPs) did most of their training with their units, which evolved around their equipment. Each Troop in a Commando also specialised in particular skills with a Boating Troop, a Parachute Troop from which came men of liaison parties dropped with the Airborne Regiments, and a Cliff Climbing Troop. But on the exercise *Brandyball*, as in the Ranger

landings at Pointe du Hoc, every man climbed. The exercise was intended to put the whole of 4 Commando through a stiff climb up the 300 foot (100m) Brandy cliffs near St Ives, Cornwall, in one of the most startling examples of Special Forces' training: it was almost as dangerous as an operation against the enemy.

One fundamental difference between the commandos of 1940 and those of 1943 was the changed attitudes of many senior commanders to Special Forces. After watching *Brandyball*, General Montgomery considered 4 Commando 'real proper chaps', a quaint expression that became a catch-phrase in 'No.4'. It was a far cry from the early summer of 1941 when the detractors of the Commando idea ungraciously refused them the right to an individual cap badge: 'The Army Council feels men would rather carry the badge . . . of their own regiments', going on to compare the proposed special badge with those of Hitler's Blackshirts. The men of Commando units continued to wear their regimental badges but on a green beret. This was introduced in late 1942 after the senior officers of 1 Commando, stationed in Irvine

(Ayrshire) at the time, decided on a beret, probably at the suggestion of their Adjutant, Captain B.G. Pugh. There were men from 79 different units in the Commando and the beret would give them a uniform headdress that stowed away easily in a pocket. The Adjutant asked a firm of local tamoshanter makers for a sample, using the now familiar green cloth, this firm stocked at that time for a striped Scots hat with a red bobble atop. The beret was worn in battle by commandos, symbolising a spirit not dependent on military hierarchy but on a sterner self-discipline to win.

Special Forces training was closely linked to the various ploys devised by Combined Operations headquarters to further political stratagems that could not always be carried out by regular forces. Nowhere was this more clearly shown than in the training and organisation of the two Commandos - 12 and 14 - that operated in a series of raids on the Norwegian coasts the stark facts of which are summarised in the diagram on p. 171.

The hydro-electric power station at Glomfjord was a target for one raid which illustrates the way 20 well-trained and superbly led troops can achieve a strategic impact far beyond the likely military strength of so tiny a force. The power station supplied the principal aluminium plant in Norway, and its destruction could reduce the German supply of aluminium for aircraft and other military uses. Captain Gordon D. Black probably knew this when he led his men ashore from a Free French submarine and they set out to cross the 'black glacier' that Captain J.B.J. (Joe) Houghton had recced a few hours before in a four-hour climb with a companion. These men of 2 Commando, with several Free Norwegians, marched all next day (Saturday, 19 September) after crossing the glacier, and towards evening came in sight of the feed pipes carrying water down the steep mountainside to the power-house turbines. As the raiders moved along a narrow track across the sheer face of a mountain falling steeply into a lake, they trod carefully, for a dislodged boulder could send a small landslide crashing noisily into the lake. They successfully crossed this hazard, and by dawn on Sunday they were able to look down on the power station as they lay up despite the cold - snow lay deep

Men of the French Troops of 10 Commando storm ashore in an exercise at Achnacarry, August 1943.

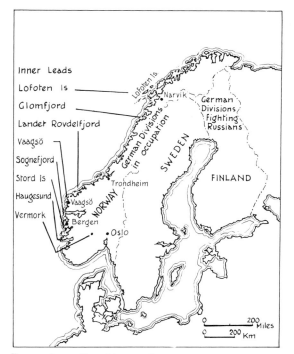

Inner Leads
Lofoten Is
Glomfjord
Landet Rovdelfjord
Vaagsö
Sognefjord
Stord Is
Haugesund
Vermork

Examples of raids against German occupied Norway, 1941 to 1944.

Inner Leads (ice-free channels between coast and islands)—No. 30 (Royal Norwegian) MTB Flotilla with 30 commandos some using Welman midget subs and Limpets, with naval personnel in chariot human torpedoes, attacked shipping in several raids during 1942–3, Norwegian-manned fishing vessels collected intelligence and set up dumps of fuel for the MTBs.

Lofoten Isl—3 Cdo 4 Mar 1941, 12 Cdo 26 Dec 1941, see text.

Glomford—12 men from 2 Cdo landed from submarine destroyed 2 of 3 turbines and piping of hydro-electric plant 20/1 Dec 1942, see text.

Landet Rovdelfjord—6 men from North Force were to keep swing bridge open for torpedo attacks but bridge guarded and raid abandoned 22/3 Mar 1943.

Haugesund—6 men from 14 Cdo in canoes from an MTB with coble were all lost no record of landing 27 Apr 1943.

Vaagsö—3 Cdo 27 Dec 1941, see text.

Sognefjord—16 men from North Force in 2 MTBs ashore 8 days despite bad weather in this 120 by 3 mile fjord, made recces and laid mines 22 Feb to 3 Mar 1943.

Stord Isl (Lillebö)—50 men from 10 and 12 Cdos in 4 MTBs, destroyed iron pyrites' mine and ore-handling installations, one nco killed, 23/4 Jan 1943.

Vermok—32 airborne troops in 2 gliders lost in trying to destroy plant making heavy water 19 Nov 1942.

on the mountain slopes. At 2300 hours that night they made their attack. Joe Houghton and a Norwegian(?) came from the cover and crawled close to the guardroom where they were able to overpower the sentries, killing one. Meanwhile two other commandos, Sergeant Smith and Guardsman Fairclough, set their charges on the power-house machinery, while Lance-Sergeant O'Brien, with a companion, blew a section from the large water-feed pipes. All six raiders returned to the main party, enjoying the flame of two successful explosions before they moved away over the mountains. However, they did not get far before they ran into a German patrol; both Gordon Black and Joe Houghton were wounded and captured with six other raiders. One of the party was killed. After being taken to Germany, the two officers were shot in accordance with Hitler's order to slaughter all who took part in commando raids.

In addition to the raids on Norway, the policy of cross-Channel raids continued through the winter of 1942. The Royal Marine Boom Patrol Detachment (see Appendix 7), following a policy of destroying economic targets, and ships taking the latest radar and radio equipment, etc. to Japan. Landing in five Rob Roy canoes they set out to paddle 70 miles (112km) to Bordeaux up the Gironde (see map p. 28). Two canoes were lost as they came through a tide rip after leaving the submarine HMS *Tuna* on 7 October 1942; a third disappeared after going inshore among moored ships. The remaining pair, under the detachment commander Major E.G. (Blondie) Hasler RM, reached a promontory by daybreak and spent the day under their camouflage nets, where some fishermen found them but did not give them away. Two more days and nights, hiding by day and paddling by night, brought them to Bordeaux docks, where they set about systematically fixing limpets with nine-hour delay fuses to several blockade runners. Blondie Hasler, with Marine W.E. Sparks in the canoe *Catfish* paddled up the west bank; *Crayfish* with Corporal H.E. Laver and Marine W.H. Mills, took the east bank. *Catfish's* crew successfully mined a 7,000-tonner and a *Sperrbrecher*, going unnoticed as they drifted on the tide while a sentry's torch flickered over them. They mined two more ships: another 7,000-tonner and a small tanker. In all they had placed 10 limpets, and *Crayfish* had used eight in mining a large and a small vessel, before the canoes met in mid-stream. Next morning, the tide running against them, these cockleshell heroes became separated. *Catfish's* crew were captured but later escaped to England, Corporal Laver and Marine Mills were shot while prisoners of the Germans.

Raids were also carried out by units from the Inter-Allied 10 Commando (see Appendix 7), whose two French Troops had done extensive training since the Commando's formation in January 1942. The Commando included Czechs, Hungarians, and the famous X Troop (formerly No.3 Troop) of Germans and Austrians with cover identities and false military records in British regiments. From among them were drawn men who joined British commandos on several raids, including those of Forfar Force who began raiding for general military intelligence when most of the French civilians were removed from a 15-mile (24km) belt along the coast. Under Major R.W. Fynn, who later that summer took command of 2 Commando, the Force made a number of raids. These in 1943 involved a veritable Chinese puzzle box of dories in MTBs, and inflatables in dories. In one of the raids a party, dressed in special camouflage suits, stayed ashore early in September for two days. Their only passports were the chocolate bars they exchanged with the fishermen near Eletot (see map p. 28) for picture postcards: no ordinary scenic views, but pictures marked to show German defences along the coast. The raiders might have stayed longer but peregrine falcons caught their carrier pigeons on the wing with messages to delay the commandos' pick-up.

The training and planning for such raids entailed close cooperation with the Royal Navy's coastal forces and some of their difficulties are made clear in a report of February 1943. The smaller MTBs could get within half a mile (800m) of enemy coasts but MTB 344 after almost six months raiding service began a four-week refit in January. The larger Class C MGBs could be seen on enemy radar scans and their slower speed meant they must be used in pairs for mutual protection off well defended coasts, precluding them altogether from the western side of the Cherbourg peninsula. When motorised dories were introduced the problems of bringing coastal forces craft inshore, the report suggests, 'is not so important' but the oared dories were not satisfactory in strong tides unless near the shore when launched.

Other means of landing reconnaissance parties were being developed and by the autumn of 1943 COPPs were training at Rothesay in Scotland on X-craft, the 52-foot (16m) midget submarines. Three COPPists, the submarine's skipper and his First Lieutenant made up a crew which was one more than the designed complement, even further overcrowding the cramped working-spaces. The craft had been modified, with extra navigation equipment replacing the control gear for the explosive devices normally dropped from these tiny submarines while under an enemy vessel.

In their confined quarters among the mass of wires, navigation and buoyancy controls, COPPists were always conscious of their breathing when the craft submerged, and they suffered from lack of oxygen on a long dive, despite the air purifiers extracting carbon-dioxide. This lack of oxygen led to hallucinations - a man might try to open a hatch before the craft had surfaced - and too much carbon-dioxide produced headaches, intensifying the difficulty in writing up recce notes or calculating a beach incline from the chinagraphed figures on a slate. All round 'everything was moist in an X-craft', for the

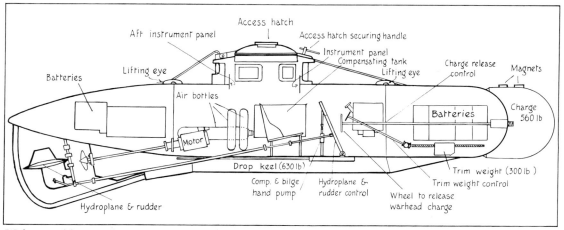

Welman midget craft.

Note: launched by derrick from transport or floated off Welman submarine-freighter, the operator could set by eye the direction of his target ship on the gyro direction indicator. After diving below this enemy, he adjusted the trim and allowed high pressure air into buoyancy tanks, forcing the charge up and against the enemy hull where it was held by magnets. The charge was later exploded by time fuse, or if the ship moved, or should divers attempt to remove the charge. The heavy drop keep was detached in an emergency allowing the Welman to surface even if partially filled with water. (For brief specifications see Appendix 4.)

condensation in such small, unventilated spaces made blankets dank and clammy, as were the change of clothes pulled on after a fitful sleep. Biscuits went soggy and bread became a damp sponge. What cooking was done came from the glue-pot-like little boiler with its electrically heated walls and an electric kettle.

Another craft, the Welman one-man submersible cylinder, was used like the navy's mini-subs and charioteer human torpedoes to place charges under enemy ships. All three types of craft had been in one flotilla, the 12th Submarine Flotilla, since 23 February 1943 with their headquarters at Rothesay, where, in 1944, a number of men from the Special Boat Section and several Norwegians trained in the use of Welman craft. These craft, launched from transports or their small freighter submarines, were used at Bergen, where two were lost. (See Appendix 4).

The difficulties in changing into rubberised suits in the claustrophobic atmosphere of a small sub, a job that could take more than an hour, and the fear of going underwater for long periods made some COPPists prefer the LC, Navigation (LCN)

X-craft midget submarine designed to place charges under moored ships and adapted for reconnaissance by COPPs.

LC Navigation equipped for accurate pilotage and used by COPP swimmers as transport to enemy beaches.

for their reconnaissances. These crafts' engines might be heard ashore, but as many boats were patrolling the French coasts by this stage of the war and as there were some fishing boats out on many nights, Don Amer for one did not consider the LCN's noise much handicap when he came back to the United Kingdom with No.6 COPP. No.5 COPP had also returned from the Mediterranean, and they joined No.1 COPP in the reconnaissance of the beaches for the Normandy invasion.

Brigadier Williams, chief intelligence officer of the Twenty-First Army Group, showed Nigel Clogstoun-Willmott a map of the Bay of Seine, and among the questions needing urgent answers was whether the original Roman peat workings on these shores were now impassable mud. Urgent or not, there were more stringent restraints than ever before on visits to potential invasion areas, for there were a vast series of deceptions - bombings *all* along the French coasts; General Patton's mythical 12-division army comprised of only a radio signals network broadcasting messages of implied plans for landings in the Pas de Calais - that would mislead the Germans over Allied intentions. As part

of these deceptions, and to gain additional intelligence after Forfar Force was disbanded in November 1943, seven raids were mounted by Layforce II commanded by Major Peter Laycock, Bob Laycock's brother. The force included Frenchmen of Nos.1 and 8 Troops from 10 Commando, who provided dory parties that also had British coxswains and signallers.

The Layforce II raids were made on Christmas Day 1943 and the following festive nights at the turn of the year. Mâitre (Warrant-Officer) Wallerand, with three French and two British commandos, landed near Gravelines on the French coast (see map p. 28), their dory capsizing as they landed. The two Britons baled it out and paddled back to the MTB, but the engine would not start and the MTB had to move inshore to help the dory's return to the beach. Mâitre Wallerand, a good swimmer as well as an intellectual, swam out towards the dory, which was again filling with water, but he was drowned. The others ashore made their escape but the two Britons in the dory were captured.

Lance-Corporal Felix Crispin acted as guide for a small commando party landing without incident that same Christmas night near St Valery. Lieutenant J. Pinelli and his party spent four hours trying to find a way up the cliffs at Etretat. On 26 December, Boxing Night, Lieutenant F. Vourch landed at Quineville near what would be the American beaches, returning with samples of wire, soil, and notes on a hitherto unknown obstacle: element-C. Two Anglo-French raids were made to the Channel Islands, adding to the intelligence on their defences. Three Frenchmen were killed in these island raids, one in a burst of fire as the dory left Jersey and two by Schu mines while reconnoitring Sark in a hurry to complete their survey before daylight.

The key surveys, however, were left to the COPPists, and as the intelligence on the peat workings, among other items, was urgent they landed in the first dark period in January (1944) when the tides were not suitable for X-craft as the Calvados reef would be exposed. Two LCNs from No.2 COPP were towed by MGBs to the edge of the enemy's radar screen on the night of 31 December - 1 January. The weather was so bad that both the swimmers - Major L. (Scottie) Scott-Bowden and Sergeant Bruce Ogden-Smith - and the LCN crews had a rough passage not helped by one or two unseamanlike mishaps. They saw in the New Year buffetted by wind and rain that nonetheless helped cover their landing when the LCN of Nigel Clogstoun-Willmott came within 200 yards (about 180m) of the beach of La Rivière and the swimmers went ashore. Their new style suits protected them from the worst of the buffeting, nevertheless they had a rough time but managed to swim back to the LCN with their load of rock samples. The lighthouse beam swept over the LCNs as they lay 500 yards (450m) out waiting for the rendezvous time, their G-set worked intermittently, and the echo-sounder on the swimmer's LCN had packed up. Nevertheless, they retrieved an anchor and the swimmers who had been ashore. They brought back sand and other samples and found the peat workings had turned to hard rock. However, the LCNs' troubles were not

over, and in rough weather and inky blackness they became separated before eventually finding their MGBs. Where they had landed, X-20 would lie the following summer as a marker for the invasion on 6 June - at the centre of the British landings.

On the night of 17-18 January a party from No.1 COPP returned to the Bay of Seine. This recce, made from X-20, began near Les Moulins and lasted three days with nightly landings and periscope recces from near the shore, often in a flat, calm sea. Behind Les Moulins on a hill was the village of St Laurent-sur-Mer, near which the American Mulberry harbour - built in the United Kingdom to British designs - would be towed and positioned a few days after the June landings.

Further raids were made by Layforce II late in January and early in February (see Appendix 7). On 24-25 February, four Frenchmen, led by Charles Trepel, went ashore at Schweningen in Holland. The watching dory crew saw flames and heard shouting after some time, but later there was no one on the beach, and in 1945 the raiders' bodies were found buried near the landing-point - four had died of exposure and one had drowned. The German defences were alert and Major-General F.W. de Guingand, Chief of Staff to the Twenty-first Army Group wrote in January 1944 that the more he thought about the problem, the more he came to the conclusion that a policy of raiding *anywhere* on the Belgian-French coast was wrong. He went on to explain that the raids were unnecessary because Allied information was very complete and they had the COPPs' reconnaissances. If raids were not made on the Bay of Seine beaches, the Germans would draw the correct conclusions should raids continue elsewhere.

Some raids had to continue, however, for the French raid in February had shown there were elements-C, and a series of underwater explosions were seen when Allied bombs fell near the shore in one bombing raid. Therefore, in succession to Layforce II, a new group of Tarbrush parties was formed from X Troop of 10

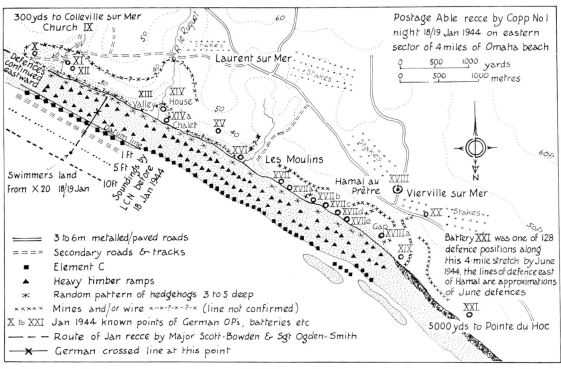

300 yds to Colleville sur Mer
Church IX

Laurent sur Mer

Postage Able recce by Copp No 1
night 18/19 Jan 1944 on eastern
sector of 4 miles of Omaha beach

0    500    1000    yards
0    500    1000    metres

Defences continued eastward

X
XI
XII

XIII Valley
XIV House
XIVa Chalet
XV

Datum line

1 Ft
5 Ft
10 Ft

Swimmers land
from X 20 18/19 Jan

Soundings by LCN before 18 Jan 1944

XVI

Les Moulins

XVII

Hamal au XVIII
Prêtre    Vierville sur Mer

XVIIa
XVIIb
XVIIc
XVIId
XVIIe    Gap
XVIIf         XVIIIa
XIX

N

XX    Stakes

Battery XXI was one of 128
defence positions along
this 4-mile stretch by June
1944, the lines of defence east
of Hamal are approximations
of June defences

3 to 6 m metalled/paved roads
Secondary roads & tracks
Element C
Heavy timber ramps
Random pattern of hedgehogs 3 to 5 deep
Mines and/or wire x-x-?-x-?-x (line not confirmed)
X to XXI Jan 1944 known points of German OP's, batteries etc
Route of Jan recce by Major Scott-Bowden & Sgt Ogden-Smith
German crossed line at this point

XXI

5000 yds to Pointe du Hoc

Beach survey for Normandy landings in COPP reconnaissance January 1944. Major Scott-Bowden and Sgt Ogden-Smith, swimmers from COPP No. 1 crawled up beach taking sand samples every 50yds at least. A German crossed the line at X but did not see it as meat-skewers held it to the sand at regular intervals. The US Army analysed these samples to check if beach suitable for tanks, etc.

Commando with some sappers. They made four landings - Bray Dunes, Les Hemmes, Quend Plage, and Onival - north of the planned invasion beaches (see map p. 28). Each party of eight went inshore by dory and then landed from inflatables, the MTB making a hydrophone search of the sea before launching the dory to check no other craft were in the area. At Bray Dunes, while the dinghy was within 100 yards of a man who had flashed a torch and lit a cigarette, Lieutenant Groom, Sergeant Moffat, and a signalman made a search for the element-C and took pictures with an infra-red camera of the beach obstacles. Here, and elsewhere, they found nine-foot (3m) beach stakes of rough poles some 14 inches (35cm) in diameter with waterproofed Teller mines

attached to some posts. They came offshore by following their tracer tape along the beach to the inflatable, and towing this off to the dory by a codline linking the two boats. Despite the MTBs' QF and echo-sounder being defunct, they were met at the rendezvous.

The Tarbrush party landing the same night at Les Hemmes brought back information on similar obstacles, and after a difficult rendezvous were picked up at 0410 hours. Their return was eventful, with one MTB firing on their own craft, which highlights the difficulty of night identification when running at 35 knots (65kmph). The party at Quend Plage had a smoother run, and after the dory went inshore at 2358 hours she was back at 0241, the MTBs hydrophone picking up the underwater noise of the dory's prop five minutes *after* she was sighted.

The men of X Troop's false identities cannot be unravelled even 35 years after they were originally devised, and the names - such as Lane, Brown, and Hamilton - used in these pages are those appearing in official reports of the time. The landing of Lieuten-

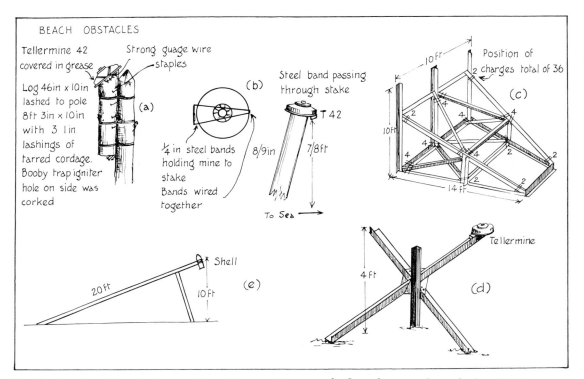

BEACH OBSTACLES

Tellermine 42 covered in grease

Strong guage wire staples

Log 46in x 10in lashed to pole 8ft 3in x 10in with 3 1in lashings of tarred cordage. Booby trap igniter hole on side was corked

(a)

(b)

¼in steel bands holding mine to stake
Bands wired together

8/9in

Steel band passing through stake

T 42

7/8ft

To Sea ⟶

10ft

Position of 2 charges total of 36

(c)

10ft

2   4   4   4
4       4
4       4   2
2       2
14 ft

Shell

20ft

10ft

(e)

4 ft

Tellermine

(d)

Beach obstacles: (a) mined post, Bray Dunes; (b) mined, Quend Plage – both (a) and (b) had a strong spring to prevent the sea exploding mines; (c) element-C – figures show number of charges required at each point to demolish this 10ft×10ft×14ft structure of 6in steel girders and weighing 2½ tons; (d) one form of hedgehog; (e) angled heavy timber set with old shell to impale LC. The Germans also used Goliath 'Beetle' 5-foot tanks with two electric motors remotely controlled: the Mk 1 by cable, the Mk 2 by radio each carrying 150lb (68kg) of explosive. The Mk 2s were used at Anzio with little or no effect and the Mk 1s found at Normandy were disarmed by LCOCUs before the Goliaths could be exploded alongside incoming craft.

ant G. Lane (The Buffs) on 15-16 May - six weeks before D-day in Normandy - was off target because the MTB's radar pulses 'all disappeared' when she reached her dropping zone on a land(!) surveyor's taut wire 'streamed from the East Bullock buoy'. They returned two nights later and went ashore in the correct spot near Onival, Staff-Sergeant E. Bluff and Corporal King staying near the dinghy after their initial search and noting the obstacles stretching in lines along the shore. Lieutenant Lane and Lieutenant Woodridge went off between these lanes to

search for element-C and the NCOs saw a red flash about 300 yards away. As it died away they heard a German challenge shouted, followed by a scream 'as if somebody was being knifed'. Then came the sound of three single shots. The signaller's message radioed from the dory reporting the activity was possibly heard by the German intercepters for star shells began falling around the boat. The NCOs had moved some 40 yards inland, but staying opposite their dinghy, when a patrol appeared and laid four canister-flares between the grounded dinghy and the dory. They appear to have missed the inflatable, for these flares made more smoke than light. Were they trying to cut off the men ashore from the sight of the dory? Whatever the intention a second patrol - 8 to 10 men - then approached the two raiders, fired a couple of Very lights and let off two shots. The sergeant was about to fire back with his pistol, but at the corporal's suggestion they withdrew quietly for it was past 0300 hours which was when the officers were due back. The flares had died down as they swam out, leaving the dinghy for their officers. The Sergeant had to drop his mine-detector but he was beyond the low-tide level so it would not be seen next day.

On the MTB, Captain Bryan Hilton-Jones, the commander of X Troop, decided to make a search of the beach, but as dawn was coming up there were only a few minutes for this. No one was seen on the beach. Lane, a Hungarian, and Woodridge had found the dinghy, after seeing two German patrols fire on each other - no doubt the reason for the Germans' later reluctance to fire on the raiding NCOs. They dropped the tell-tale camera and reconnaissance gear over the side and were searching for the dory when a German patrol boat captured them. Lane was taken from prison for an interview with General Rommel and other senior commanders before going back to the PoW camp, where he met Lieutenant-Colonel Charles Newman, a prisoner since the St Nazaire raid.

There is no reason to think the Germans expected the Allies to land in Normandy, and for several days after 6 June they believed the invasion might only be a feint with the main assault coming through the Pas de Calais, The COPPists' X-craft arrived off the beaches on Sunday 4 June. After a day submerged because bad weather delayed the invasion, each crew set up their shaded top-mast light above the box radar beacon. The landing craft appeared out of the greyness of sea and sky, the wind drowning their engine noise but not the shriek of rockets from an LCT(R) winging shorewards to clear a path on the beach. The pre-landing bombardment had begun shortly before 0530 on the British beaches and 0600 on the American. The skipper of X-20 was washed over the side in these manoeuvres, having unlashed himself from the air vent, and was rescued by the outstretched hand of Lieutenant-Commander Clerk, the COPPs' commander. He had taken over in May when Nigel Clogstoun-Willmott was invalided out of assault pilotage. (See history Appendix 7 for other COPP activities on D-day.) The Americans had turned down the offer of COPPist markers but their ships were led in by the Engineer Special Brigades' scout boats.

Beach-clearance parties had trained with Landing Craft Obstruction Clearance Units of navy frogmen and the crews of Assault Vehicles Royal Engineers to provide a way ashore for assault waves crossing the beach defences. In 1943 there had been some confusion as to the responsibilities for clearing obstacles between the high and low water lines, leaving a strip of beach that might be in a few feet (1m) of water with no one having direct responsibility for clearing mines and obstacles. However, by May 1944, a coordinated scheme was worked out, with Royal Engineer Companies and clearance parties trained to work alongside each other: the navy swimmers clearing underwater obstacles, the sappers clearing obstacles not covered by water. The last practice-landing of one army engineer company showed that the sappers were trying to carry more weight than each man could possibly have around him when setting demolition charges. Therefore the personal kit, blankets, hand trailer loaded with spare explosives, slings to tow obstacles, gap markers, and rum ration of each 12-man Section were put in a folding canvas boat. This was towed ashore by the assault vehicle carrying the Section as it swam to the beach for its own crew's task of flailing a path through mines or whatever. (See Appendix 2 for organisation of beach parties and LCOCUs.) The sappers of the clearing party each carried a webbing haversack with eight 3lb (1.4kg) packets of explosive, a haversack of igniter sets, their personal weapons, and ammunition. The 12 Sections of one Beach Clearing Company were to land in Normandy from the six LCTs carrying the assault vehicles, with two Sections on each craft.

The days of rehearsal, recces, planning, and training were over. Each man - commando and soldiers alike - had been shown a model of his part of the beach; every assault soldier knew exactly where he was to land and his individual part in the invasion's opening hours.

# NORMANDY TO VICTORY IN EUROPE, JUNE 1944 TO MAY 1945

A 50-mile (80km) stretch of coast along the Bay of Seine was chosen for the 6 June 1944 Normandy landings. These beaches were sheltered, the defences only 18 per cent complete compared with 80 per cent in the Pas de Calais, there were sites for air-strips and existing airfields near Caen. The whole area was within fighter range of UK airbases. Yet there were no German concentrations near enough to mount a major counter-attack.

The Allies needed only one large port, because they brought in two floating harbours ('Mulberries') and Cherbourg was less than 25 miles (40km) from the landings. The US First Army landed on the right to take this port, the British Second Army on the left (east) landing to secure airfields and protect the American flank.

East to west the beaches were code-named 'Sword', 'Juno', and 'Gold' for British sectors, 'Omaha' and 'Utah' for American. The British landed initially at five points, each about a mile (1.6km) wide and spaced across a 24-mile (38km) front, its westerly edge 10 miles (16km) from the American 'Omaha' beach. Most of the points open to counter-attack on the flanks or between landing-points were allocated to the Special Forces. Airborne landings were made on the night of 5-6 June outside the beachhead, and German communications and key coast batteries were disrupted if not neutralised. German resistance, especially by their 352 Infantry Division defending Omaha, delayed consolidation of the 50-mile beachhead until D+2. Bayeaux, some six miles (10km) from the beaches was taken on D+1, but Caen - eight miles from the landings - was not taken for more than a month. Here the British held German forces, while the Americans invested Cherbourg, captured on D+19, before they swept eastward in a rapid advance that brought them to Orleans by 16 August. That week, two German armies were caught in the Falaise pocket by Canadian, British and American armies, and by 1 September the Allies had crossed the Seine, liberated Paris, and were 85 miles (136km) from Antwerp.

Early in September the British and Canadians reached this major Belgian port, but an attempt later that month to set an airborne bridgehead across the Rhine failed at Arnhem. The same month the Americans reached the central sectors of the Siegfried line along the German border and were in the Vosges mountains further south.

# 11  D-DAY IN NORMANDY AND NORTH WEST EUROPE

The coast of France seemed strangely quiet from a distance as the sappers had their rum tot, but the thunder of gunfire increased as the LCTs carrying in the beach-clearance parties approached Jig Green West, the right-hand sector of the western landing-point on Gold beach. The onshore wind had given a higher tide than expected, for it was flooding some 30 minutes ahead of the almanac time, but after their rough crossing many soldiers were so seasick they were glad to land anywhere. Coming into Jig beach ahead of the sappers and AVREs should have been the DD swimming tanks, but the rough seas had forced their LCTs to carry them inshore and they were late. When the AVREs' craft came in at 0725 hours they were under fire, although the leading platoons of the 1st Hampshires had crossed the beach with few casualties. However, the enemy strongpoint at Le Hamel had been little affected by bombing or bombardment, and raked the beach with fire that knocked out most of the Royal Marine tanks landing to cover the beach clearance.

One AVRE craft, grounded in 6ft (2m) or more of water, got her first tank drowned on the ramp. Unable to clear her tank, this LCT broached to and took several hits as the mines on beach obstacles blew holes in her hull. This craft partially blocked the second LCT's landing but one sapper Section came ashore riding their AVRE. The third craft got the AVREs off but the sappers' canvas boat's tow broke - this landing in surf from six feet of water was rougher than any

rehearsal - and they then paddled their way ashore, others being ferried in by an LCA.

On the east side of the Jig landing-point, a fourth LCT got her sappers off but one canvas boat was holed on a obstacle and this Section swam to the beach. Those on the next LCT were towed so fast through the water that only five men managed to get in each boat, the rest swimming ashore. The sixth LCT beached in 7ft (2+m) of water and the armoured bulldozer towed off the canvas boats so ruthlessly they had their bottoms ripped out. After transferring to other craft, only one Section landed hours later. With so few men to cut the obstacles, not surprisingly something less than the 200-yard wide gaps were cut at both landing-points. The LCOCU swimmers when above the water 'wearing tin hats that seem somehow slightly ludicrous', cleared the seaward gap, but the hedgehogs here were of heavier metal than expected and the tetrahedra were of reinforced concrete, not metal as used in practice. In the hectic minutes after landing, demolition parties were firing their charges - double charges on the hedgehogs - within a few yards of each other as the assault infantry passed through. However, this enforced disregard of safety rules seems to have caused no casualties in the urgency to clear obstacles before the tide covered them, although observed fire from Le Hemel and behind the beach caused some losses among the clearance parties. Not all beach clearance followed the same sequence, for the Americans had only armoured bulldozers and not the so-called 'funnies' of the AVRE with their great, concrete-busting mortars, their mine-destroying flails, the fascines for filling smaller tank-traps and the scissor bridges placed by their tanks across larger gaps.

As the tide rose, however, there were still many uncleared lanes in the British sector, and on the American beach of Omaha - more exposed than their Utah beach - many amphibious vehicles were lost, including DUKWs bringing ashore the field artillery. As for the swimming tanks, at points all along the 50-mile stretch of coast many were lost or late ashore - as at the Jig landing-points - with the seas breaking over their canvas flotation jackets.

The Special Service Group, commanded by Major-General Robert G. Sturges with Brigadier John Durnford-Slater as his second-in-command, were to land in two Brigades with 47(RM) Commando in an independent role on the extreme west flank of the British sector. From there, they would swing further west, capturing Port en Bessin between the British and American sectors. Like all the Special Forces on this D-day, they had flank or linking roles as the Allies

Landings of 1944 were followed in 1945 by river crossings - marines cross Rhine.

came ashore at a series of separated landings within each beach area. The 3,4,6 and 45(RM) Commandos, with two French Troops from 10 Commando attached to 'No.4', would clear Ouistreham at the mouth of the Orne before pushing quickly inland. Reaching the bridges at Blouville and Ranville (see map p. 182) they would join the elements of the 6 Airborne Division dropped just after midnight. 1 Brigade, with the Airborne, would then form the eastern flank guard of the beachhead, along the line east of the Orne river, on higher ground among the orchards, woods, and small fields with their thick banked hedges (the *bocage*). 4 Brigade's Commandos formed two sides of the hinge between Sword and Juno, with 'No.41(RM)' landing west of Lion-sur-Mer on the right of Sword beach and five miles (8km) from 'No.48(RM)' landing at St Aubin-sur-Mer on the left of Juno beach. The Brigade, having cleared the fortified points allotted to them, were to move inland and invest the heavily fortified Douvres radar station; where intelligence engineers of 30 Commando hoped to gather codes and other documents, as they would in other German positions they raided on the heels of assault infantry.

The 2nd and 5th Rangers were to land at Pointe du Hoc - misspelt on many orders as

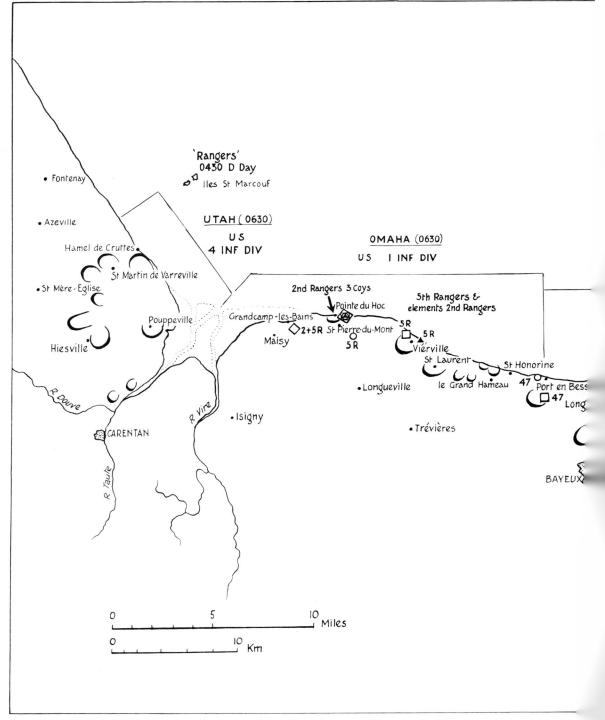

The Bay of Seine - Special Forces' landings and actions - D-day 6 June 1944.

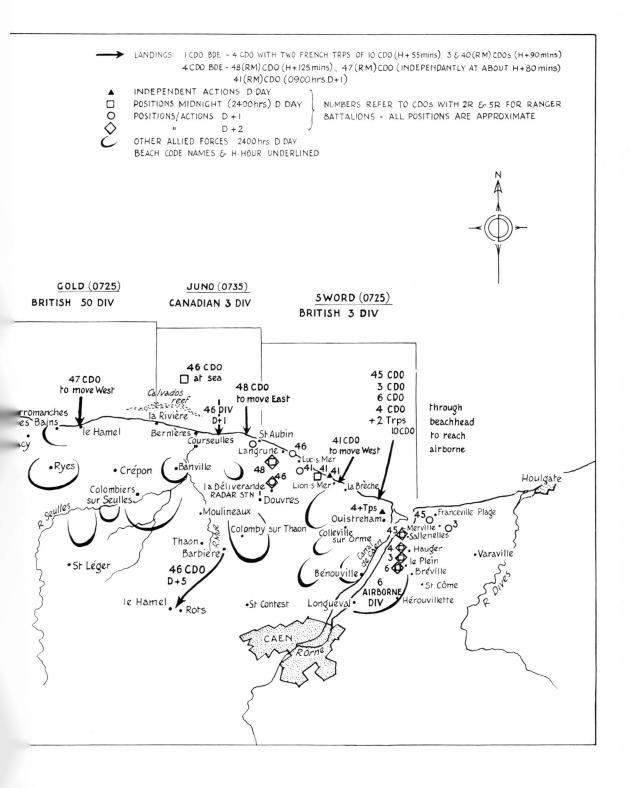

LCI(S) No. 502, one of 1 Commando Brigade's craft, in rough seas approaching Normandy, 6 June 1944.

'du Hoe' - destroying the battery above this chalk and clay cliff, which was between the initial landing-points on Omaha and Utah, being the most westerly landing-point on Omaha. Should the assault companies fail to take the cliff, then the remainder of the battalions would land to the east at Vierville-sur-Mer and fight their way to the battery. Its guns were thought to cover the approaches to both American beaches; and to the west were the inshore islands of St Marcouf, with casements for heavy naval guns and a system of defence strongpoints.

The first 'Rangers' ashore swam on to St Marcouf beaches at 0430 hours, two hours before H-hour for the American landings. Whether or not 'they came ashore with knives between their teeth', as one report suggests, these men - from a division's squad of 'Rangers' - found these islands undefended.

4 Commando's LCAs came ashore from HMS *Queen Astrid* at 0820 (H+55mins) to find the British 8th Infantry Brigade pinned to the shore line; mortar fire among the LCAs caused 40 casualties, the CO - Lieutenant-Colonel R.W.P. Dawson - being wounded in the leg. Passing through the lines of assault infantry, many wounded, some dead, and others firing from the water's edge, kneeling in two feet or more of surging waves, the leading commando Troop came up to a mound surrounded by

wire and with a machine-gun turret enfilading the beach. This armoured turret was set in a concrete strongpoint which the commandos worked their way around. Captain Knyvet Carr - known as 'Muscles' since the days of Dieppe - threw a grenade, but as he stood up after it burst, his heavy rucksack toppled him backwards down a bank. As he rolled over, a shower of stick-grenades fell around him, his own Troop's bren fire flew past his head, yet he remained unhurt. Two Germans dashing from the post were shot and the pill-box taken. It was one of a series about 100 yards apart, many with their 75mm or other guns facing diagonally across the beach so their slits were not exposed to incoming fire unless it was a difficult enfilade (diagonal) shot. Behind this post was an open machine-gun position that the commandos had overrun, just as others would do along the beach, often blowing in an emplacement's steel door, despite the larger defence complexes' better protection to the rear.

Once through the enemy's line of beach pill-boxes, the commandos reached their assembly area in the dunes, which baffled the noise of battle and made this a strangely quiet place. The two French Troops led off the column towards Ouistreham to take the Casino, a fortified point overlooking the left flank of the British landings: 4 Commando were to repeat their Dieppe success, taking a battery that flanked the landing. The men had taken the few minutes at the assembly area to clean sand from their weapons, reload magazines, and gather in their Sections, which then moved the mile or so along the coast road into the southern (inland) outskirts of this seaside town. Major R.P. Menday took charge of the attack, for the Colonel had been wounded a second time and would not catch up with his Commando until after they left the town. He would then stay with them until ordered to hospital by a senior medical officer.

The French Troops, who had taken casualties when their LCIs were repeatedly hit, met a M. Lefevre, from the town, who had gone out during the pre-landing barrage and cut the power-lines crossing the dunes to electrically fired flame-throwers protecting both the Casino and the battery. He went on to help the commandos that morning, showing them where the enemy positions were strongest, and guiding them to a successful assault on the Casino.

C Troop led the Commando up the road, dodging across the road junctions and passing a solitary rifleman, whose window firing-position was taken out when a tank of the RM Armoured Support Group blew off the house's gable end. The commandos dropped their rucksacks, each with two fins protruding from the pouch - 3-inch mortar reserve ammunition for the Heavy Weapons Troop - at the arranged point before crossing the main road, where two trams lay drunkenly together. A jubilant Frenchman in front of the café danced here in his pyjamas: 'C'est le jour! Le jour de la liberation.' Captain Murdoch C. McDougall, the 6 foot 5 inch Scot leading a Section of F Troop, has described this action in his book *Swiftly They Struck**. They were now nearing the battery, having turned towards the beach, and there was an open space to cross before reaching the start line for this attack. The leading Section of F Troop were across, but Murdoch McDougall's two leading riflemen dived for cover as flakes of whitewash, stone, and sand spattered around from bullets hitting a wall behind them. The Section officer dived to join them and got his bren gunner up, 'joined a second later in a

whirl of white dust and sand by the gunner's Number Two'. The men spotted the German machine-gun, and steady bursts of bren fire at this window 250 yards (225+m) away enabled the riflemen of the sub-Section to cross the 80 yards (70+m) of open ground. They in turn covered the bren gun team's crossing, and the second sub-Section followed this drill. The whole Section together - they were three or four minutes late at the start line - ran to follow the lead Section and F Troop HQ over the planks laid across an anti-tank ditch, passing through C Troop who had led to this point. Murdoch McDougall could see the blank wall of the white observation tower that D Troop were attacking. E Troop had swung right towards the easterly three emplacements, and F Troop made for the three on the left. A steady stream of German grenades was falling down the face of the tower, but over the commandos' heads the Vickers-K machine-guns of A Troop gave covering fire.

Ground churned up from the pre-landing bombardment and earlier air strikes gave the commandos some cover as they bobbed and weaved under enemy small-arms fire from houses overlooking the battery, and they arrived seaward of the tower to find a machine-gun firing down on them from a slit two-thirds of the way up its face. Murdoch McDougall's Glaswegian bren gunner silenced it with a stream of fire - tracer every fifth round showing him exactly where the bullets were striking. A few moments later the gunner, Commando McDermott, appeared at a crater's edge, wanting to swap his bren for a rifle because his shoulder was shattered by a bullet: blood was running down his side. No guns were mounted in the battery and as the leading Sections were coming back towards the town three heavy shells landed - possibly from Allied naval guns. The Commando formed column after leaving the town and headed for the bridges across the Orne and the canal.

6 Commando and advanced Brigade headquarters, 'every man washed and shaved' as were all commandos landing that day, took some casualties as they came ashore from LCIs at 0840 hours behind

*M. C. McDougall: *Swiftly They Struck*; the Story of 4 Commando - Odhams Press, London, 1954.

Commandos of 1(SS) Bde wade ashore D-Day, 6 June 1944.

'No.4'. In those few minutes the beach had cleared, but the dead remained, and for this commando, as for so many other troops that day, the landing appeared more like a nightmare on some lonely road than charging along in a football crowd. As they passed through the 2nd East Yorkshires mopping up resistance, they came across 'bodies sprawled all over the beach, some with heads, arms and legs missing, the blood clotting the wet sand'. A signaller picked up the Airborne's message confirming they held the bridges, and 'No.6' were urged on as they infiltrated through the enemy's second lines of defence. They crossed a swamp, attacking four strongpoints and a four-gun battery that was shelling the beach, and covered the 6.5 miles (10km) from the landing to the bridges in three and a half hours, arriving two minutes behind their schedule. They had relatively few casualties, but their second-in-command, Major Coade, was one.

'No. 3' and 'No. 45(RM)' followed them to the Orne where a cycle Troop of 'No.6' had crossed the bridges, and by this time, 1400 hours, their Commando had joined the 9th Parachute Battalion in taking the village of Le Plein. That evening, 1 SS Brigade dug-in on the high ground above a flat coastal plain eastward of the beachhead and were joined by the remainder of 6 Airborne Division flying in at dusk. The Brigade's landings had proved an old adage of combined operations: coming in in the third wave can be as dangerous as, if not more dangerous than, being in the first. 'No.3' had lost two craft through direct hits and all the Commandos had suffered casualties on the beach, even though they landed 50 minutes or more after H-hour.

The 4 SS Brigade in many respects had an even rougher landing. 41(RM) Commando, at the western limit of the initial landings on Sword, were put ashore 300 yards (270m) west of their intended beach near Lion-sur-Mer (see map p. 182). 'Everything appeared the same grey', a few houses and a litter of tanks with blobs of men taking cover behind them. Within the hour the Commando were across the beach and one Section reached Lion to find its strongpoint deserted. The rest of the Commando went further west to attack a chateau beyond the village but their Colonel and two Troop officers were killed, along with both FOOs (the artillery's forward observation officers). They lost contact with their RM tanks, and as the FOOs' signallers were wounded no covering fire could be coordinated for an attack. The commandos had to content themselves with neutralising the position, and it was captured next day by the 5th Lincolnshires.

48(RM) Commando - formed only 16 weeks before D-day from volunteers in the 7th RM Battalion - landed at St Aubin from shore-to-shore LCI(S), wooden landing craft built on the lines of coastal forces boats. These craft were caught because the tide covered much of 'Rommel's asparagus' of anti-boat obstacles, and H-hour had been delayed 45 minutes on this part of Sword beach. It seemed a confusion of activity to their CO, Lieutenant-Colonel James L. Moulton RM, as he scanned the shore with his glasses seeing a black line across it: his craft was checked by an obstacle and the adjutant, Captain Daniel J. Flunder, was flung into the sea 100 yards from the shore as he prepared to lead the men off the catwalk bow gangways. The Belgian skipper worked the craft clear and Dan Flunder only remembers the wall of her side towering over him.

The LCI beached with two others, but the craft further east were held off shore: Y Troop's being 150 yards (135+m) out and Z's a little closer to the shore. Enemy fire had caused casualties as they ran in, shell and mortar fragments ripping through the sides of the wooden craft. No voice commands could be heard over the din of the sailors' 20mm cannon answering the shore guns, and the Colonel had to go forward to get his 2-inch mortarmen firing smoke as they had dismounted their two mortars from

the bow on preparing to land. The other craft followed this lead as planned and a smokescreen soon forced the enemy gunners to fire blind. The craft ashore were not square on to the beach, their catwalks rising and plunging on the swell into waist-deep water, causing the marines to take longer getting ashore than they did in rehearsals. As they came up the beach the black line turned out to be 'the human debris of the assault: some dead, many wounded, some bewildered, some - like the stretcher bearers - with work to do'. The Colonel was joined by Dan Flunder, who has no recollection of how he reached the beach after being hit by the landing craft as she surged past him. They crossed the beach, the Colonel was hit but went on, and gradually collected as many men as they could. A line of LCTs followed the Commando in and disgorged their tanks, one running over wounded men until Dan Flunder knocked off its track with a grenade; the other tanks bogged down in the shingle.

Z and Y Troops with the stand-by HQ - every command had a stand-by, from the headquarters' ships to battalion commands - were too far out for wading and were taking further hits until an LCA ran a ferry service to put Z Troop ashore. The mine on an obstacle exploded under Y Troop's LCI before a tank landing craft came alongside and took off the Troop. Those who tried to swim ashore were caught in a strong current, but Y Troop's commander, Major D.R.W. de Stacpoole, managed to swim to the beach. Lieutenant Yates was drowned trying to swim with a line, and casualties were high. Sensibly, the Heavy Weapons Troop's mortars were spread between the craft; and although one crew were killed on the beach, Marine Thornton made several trips around a dangerously exposed position to bring their mortar to the assembly area. Jim Moulton too, was wounded, spattered by mortar fragments, but he continued to move along the beach, directing his men towards the assembly area.

The pre-assault bombardment had destroyed only a couple of houses in St Aubin, and the Canadians who landed at H-hour were battling around a major strongpoint undamaged by the bombardment on the esplanade. But there was no firing from Langrune village, where the Commando after establishing their base in a stone farmhouse on the eastern and landward side of this village 1,000 yards (900m) from the beach, would begin clearing the houses along the shore. Two Troops worked their way through the beach houses, finding little opposition until they were under fire from the Langrune strongpoint on the sea-front road. As they cleared the houses, an officer and a marine were killed by fire from their support craft, impatient perhaps at the slow progress, but by this point in the plan the craft were only supposed to fire into the houses on request. At a crossroads in the streets and houses behind the strongpoint the Troops were held, although some men broke into a house near the corner. Most of these had been fortified with bricked-up doors and windows, and inside there were booby traps. Time was passing quickly, and the patrol sent eastwards to contact 41(RM) Commando at the planned inland meeting-point found they were not there. Two RM Armoured Support Regiment Centaurs helped B Troop break into the south-east corner of the position, but a 5 foot 6 inch (nearly 2m) concrete wall, over a yard wide, blocked the road to the sea and a tank was lost on the minefield inland of the road barrier. Captain J.L. Perry leading B Troop was killed early in this attack.

As dusk came about 2100 hours, the Commando were withdrawn from house-clearing, for an armoured counter-attack was expected and they took up positions to hold Langrune.

The leading three companies of the 2nd Rangers were to land at H-hour, 0630 on the Omaha American beaches, below the cliffs of the Pointe du Hoc battery. The naval bombardment had opened 40 minutes earlier with the battleship USS *Texas's* 14-inch (355mm) guns shelling the battery before a strike by 19 medium bombers of the US Ninth Air Force went in at 0610. The Rangers, who had trained at Swanage, Dorset, for this 85- to 100-foot climb, came ashore in 12 British-manned LCAs that put them on the narrow beach only 30 yards wide below the cliff. Eight craft were each fitted with three pairs of rockets that could lift a ¾-inch (7mm diameter) rope or a toggle-rope attached to a grapnel. They carried 112 feet (34m) of light tubular ladder in sections (see Appendix 3) and two DUKWs came in with 100-foot (30m) London Fire Brigade turntable ladders carrying a pair of Lewis guns where the fire-hose normally fits. The rangers themselves carried a minimum of gear, their rations and demolition charges being in two supply craft. LCA 860 sank during the three-hour run to

The 100 foot (30m) Pointe du Hoc cliff-top view looking towards headland to the east beyond which lay Omaha beach.

Amphibious truck (DUKW) fitted with fire-brigade extension ladder, note rocket grapnel in foreground. Although satisfactory in training, these DUKWs could not get near the cliffs on D-day.

the beach. Four-foot waves were breaking over the heavily laden supply craft and one also sank but, as with 860, most men were rescued. Then, 10 minutes later, the second supply craft foundered with only one survivor. By now, the rangers were baling with their helmets, and although the control craft should have clearly seen *Texas's* shells falling on the point, she headed for a landfall three miles (4.8km) eastward; 30 minutes were lost while this distance was recovered. At 0710 hours the companies of the 2nd and the 5th Battalion following in received the message 'Tilt' sending them to their alternative landing at Vierville.

There would be no quick climb or major perimeter formed as the leading rangers'

nine LCAs ran a gauntlet of fire 100 yards offshore while heading back to the east side of the Pointe. The destroyers HMS *Talybont* and USS *Satterlee*, seeing their plight, both closed the point and shelled enemy troops moving to defences around the battery.

The LCAs got ashore on a 500-yard (450m) strip of narrow beach accompanied by the Rangers' commando instructor, but the DUKWs with their great ladders could not cross the cratered beach. Three or four Germans at the top of the cliff were chased off by the stern gunners in LCA 861 before the rangers fired her first pair of rockets aft. Heavy with sea-water, the line refused to lift, as did the second and third grapnel's rockets fired in succession; none pulled enough line out to lift the rope ladders with the climbing ropes. The rangers then ran ashore across the sliver of beach and, as 'potato-masher' stick-grenades were tossed and rolled down on them, fired the first of their hand-rocket lines a mere 15 yards from the cliff. Pfc (Private first class) Harry W. Roberts climbed some 25 feet up this rope against a near perpendicular cliff when it slipped or was cut. He went back up the second hand-rocket line and in 40 seconds - his estimate - he was in a crater forming a niche just below the clifftop. As he scrambled for a foothold, the line was cut above him, and his attempt to fix the free end to a picket failed when the next man's weight pulled it out. His team managed to negotiate a great mound of clay and throw him a third line which he anchored by spread-eagling himself across it as they climbed up to the niche. They then went over the clifftop for their objective, a heavily fortified OP at the inland (eastern) tip of this fortified area.

The other eight landing teams had equally gripping moments. Some heard a massive explosion above their heads, as probably one of the German 200mm (8in) shells was dropped from the wires suspending it over the beach in - as far as I can trace - a unique form of cliff defence. Others fell over their head into water-filled craters as they stepped off the landing craft ramps, but they got ropes and the sections of ladder - the ranger climbing the lower section to pass the next one over his head before securing it -

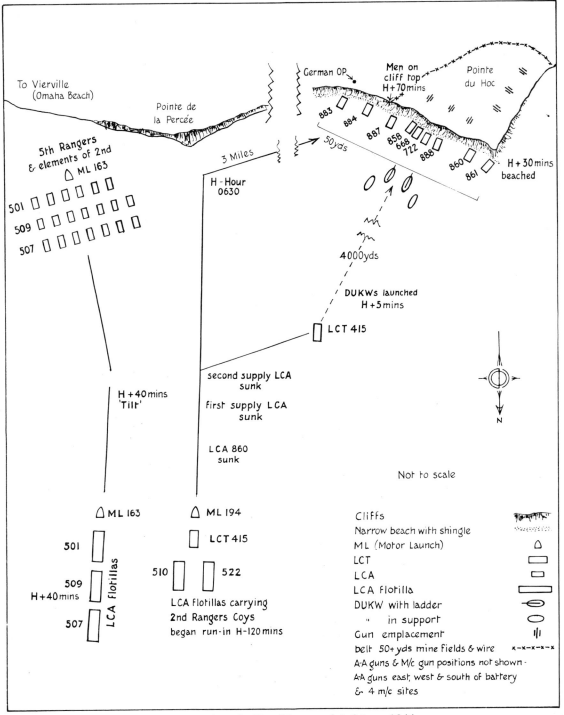

Landing of 2nd Ranger companies, Pointe du Hoc (Normandy), 6 June 1944.

up the cliff. They were hardly aware of the support fire, although Colonel James Rudder, leading these companies, had a great slab of cliff brought down on him by a naval shell. Again - as with 'No.48(RM)' - the naval gunners were over-keen in their willingness to help those ashore. Despite the complexity of the operation the rangers made progress. The rockets and line manhandled ashore from LCA 887, had to be fired by Tech Sergeant John I. Cripps using his hot-box three feet (1m) from each rocket's base with the result that they blinded him temporarily and covered him in mud. Sergeant William L. Petty came ashore over LCA 887's ramp, falling with his BAR into a crater, and later slipping down the cliff on his first climb. But the automatic fired when he needed it, despite the buffetting and the mud.

The rangers lost between 40 and 50 men of the 200 who were intended to land on the point. Many slipped on the wet, muddy ropes or lost their footing, if there was one, for in places they had to climb up vertical ropes away from the cliff face. But 30 minutes after landing they had enough men on the clifftop to launch an attack over a 'no-man's land of incredible destruction'. The big shells from *Texas* had made this a moonscape in which men had difficulty in keeping contact, and barely three yards apart a man might lose touch with his neighbour. Across this surface the squads drove the Germans to the ruins of the gun emplacements, but no big guns had been installed. These they found later, still in their coverings, waiting installation. The rangers pressed on 800 yards (720m) to their second objective astride the road from Vierville to Grandcamp. Two men scouting from this position found a German battery with five cleverly concealed guns and large stocks of shells ready to fire on Utah or Omaha beaches. No gun crews were there and the battery was disabled. However, the enemy were now beginning to recover, and one strongpoint on the cliff remained in action until it was blown into the sea, along with part of the clifftop hit by naval fire later that morning. Several rangers had been killed or captured in trying to take an anti-aircraft battery west of the Pointe in a couple of

separate sub-Section attacks, there being too few men to mount anything stronger for the rangers were virtually cut off for the rest of D-day. Understandably, therefore, their only message to reach V Corps caused some concern: Located Pointe du Hoe (Hoc) - mission accomplished - need ammunition and reinforcements - many casualties. The anxiety at Corps was not misplaced, for these three Ranger companies were down to 70 men and had fought off two counter-attacks from the direction of St Pierre du Mont while awaiting the advance of the 5th Rangers with the US 116th Infantry Regiment.

After 'Tilt', the 5th Rangers 10-mile (16km) approach run from HMS *Prince Baudouin* and HMS *Prince Leopold* swung towards Vierville, Lieutenant West RNVR, 'leaning over the side of the craft . . . directing (the LCAs) progress by hand signals . . . through an intricate system of mine-laden obstacles' - an appreciation from the ranger Major R.P. Sullivan of the crew of HMS *Prince Baudouin* who 'gave a magnificent performance'. The sea was rough, and the tide at H+75 minutes (0745) covered most of the anti-boat obstacles. One LCA was awash so she transhipped her cargo of rangers to an LCT before they were halfway inshore, and Lieutenant-Colonel Max Schneider got the flotilla commander to land east of the target beaches, which were under heavy fire. As a result of the scrub and grass being set afire by the bombardment, a pall of smoke hung over the shoreline obscuring targets on shore, although the Germans had a clear enough view of the Omaha beach approaches. Small-arms fire rattled against the armour plate and mortar bombs burst nearby as the landing craft threaded their way slowly through the obstacles.

As the rangers came over the LCA ramps, they could see a low wall 75 yards up the beach and dashed to its shelter. The first wave - part of Battalion HQ with A, B, and E companies - were soon joined by the rest of HQ with C,D, and a platoon of F Company in the second wave. They had suffered few casualties, although all along this beach there were many units caught in indecision under crossfire, not knowing whether to seek cover behind beach obstacles or make a dangerous dash for the wall. With his battalion organised behind the four-foot wall, Max Schneider sent his leading platoon forward through the wire with the thickening smoke giving them cover. They 'advanced unhesitatingly to a point near the top of the hill' beyond this beach, but its crest was clear of smoke and swept by machine-gun fire. 1st Lieutenant Francis W. Dawson led his platoon of D Company over the crest and cleared these guns from the strongpoint beyond; the battalion followed, the many minefields forcing them to advance in a column. Nevertheless, they dislodged a number of German infantry from well-sited weapon pits among the hedgerows before reaching a point on the road 1,050 yards (1km) east of Vierville.

Turning west, the battalion fought their way into the town, but the companies trying to probe south were blocked and that evening the rangers held the western outskirts of Vierville. A platoon of A Company, however, had been separated from the rest at the sea-wall, and fighting their way to the rendezvous point south-west of the town, where the 5th should have met the rangers from Pointe du Hoc, this platoon got through to the Pointe.

All day Colonel Rudder's men held Pointe du Hoc, with the help of naval support fire called in by signal lamp or the reliable SCR-284 radio. There were no means of evacuating the wounded, and that night the rangers were yet again counter-attacked at five past midnight (0005), by men yelling loudly as they walked forward after a long but inaccurate barrage of mortar and machine-gun fire on the American positions. This attack was repulsed, as was a second attack and a third put in about 0130, when the Americans had been shelled, but E Company was overrun and the situation was saved by F Company - mere handfuls of men by this time with fewer than 50 rangers in the perimeter. They held on through D+1 (Wednesday), sending volunteers to explode a store of German ammunition and making

Lieutenant-Colonel Moulton, 48 (RM) Commando, directing the fire of tanks supporting the attack on Langrune strong-point, D+1, 7 June 1944.

several aggressive - if small - patrols. Major Street, from the 11 Amphibious Force, came in twice during the day, bringing ammunition and rations, and with them came another platoon of 5th Rangers as reinforcements.

At 1700 hours that evening (Wednesday) the men on the Pointe were told to fight their way the 1,000 yards (.9km) to the relief force approaching from Vierville, but they were unable to break through the German cordon. This mixed force of 2nd Ranger companies and the 5th Battalion, joined by 150 men from 116th Infantry and some tanks, had reached Au Guay when heavy enemy artillery concentrations drove them back. However, the leading sub-Section - seven scouts (pointmen) - did not receive the recall and took one of four mutually supporting machine-gun posts, despite two of these scouts being killed and three wounded. The force then took up defensive positions around St Pierre du Mont, and during the night they had to go back into this town to clear it of German infiltrators.

Next morning, Thursday, D+2, the Rangers and two battalions of the 116th moved forward from St Pierre and Vierville, relieving the men at Pointe du Hoc. Even in this last hour of their brave stand, the rangers on Pointe du Hoc took a further buffeting when several men were killed in their own tank gunners' fire supporting the infantry relief column's attack on the last German positions round the Pointe. Hidden among the devastation of its defences were several severely wounded rangers who were rescued before the two Ranger battalions moved into Grandcamp - captured earlier by B and E Companies of the 5th - where they bivouacked: bed rolls, C-rations, and drinking water being brought up from the beaches.

During and since D-day, the build-up of reserves had brought in men and supplies, for even as the tide ebbed on D-day morning, the sappers in the Jig landing gaps - among others - began clearing wider landing-beaches. One sapper platoon commander took an obstacle mine to pieces in a

Colonel Peter Young briefs two snipers in the Orne river area, 17 June 1944.

quiet shell-hole, and found that beneath the heavy coating of pitch, this Teller mine had a simple push igniter - when struck, it would explode the mine. But this igniter, like the igniters on old shells attached to many obstacles, could be unscrewed, and the explosive was then safe to handle. This discovery speeded up the clearing of obstacles, which were made up into bundles of six or so for AVREs to tow to large stacks; by nightfall on D-day 2,000 yards (1.8km) of the Jig landing-area had been cleared.

That night the American command considered the position around Vierville their most critical, although the Germans had not been able to mount as sharp a counter-attack as the Rangers expected. In the gap between 'No.41(RM)' and 'No.48(RM)' German armour made an advance, their leading tanks being stopped by British anti-tank guns at Bieville, four to five miles (6km to 8km) inland from the Commandos, although some elements of this German Division got as far as Luc-sur-Mer, opposite 48(RM) Commando's positions, before turning back. 'Next morning the scene was transformed', Jim Moulton found as Allied vehicles streamed inland, and he led the Commando back through Langrune to renew the assault on its shore-road strongpoint. With the help of two Canadian M10 self-propelled anti-tank guns, the marines cleared these defences, working a way through the minefields to allow the guns a shot at the concrete roadblock. The M10s solid shot made a start, but the job was finished by an RM Sherman whose high-explosive lowered the wall to a height of two and a half feet, although it was still a tank obstacle after an hour and a half's hammering. Troops then rushed and cleared the houses on the far side of the street and were able to use picks and shovels to clear a way for the tanks to get around the beach houses. This push was paralleled by Troops working their way through houses until the garrison - two officers and 33 men of the 736 Grenadier Regiment - surrendered. Some 10 others had been killed.

46(RM) Commando, Lieutenant-Colonel Campbell R. Hardy, landed on D+1, and although trained for amphibious assault they would fight an essentially land battle during the next few days. The Canadians helped to re-equip the Commando, replacing the demolition charges and light arms they had carried for an intended cliff assault on either the Houlgate or Benerville coastal batteries - an operation that was cancelled on the night of D-day. Next morning (D+1) having taken the strongpoint at Petit Enfer, they gathered some enemy weapons. 47(RM) Commando did the same in their initial landings. 'No.46(RM)' then swung south of Jim Moulton's Commando at Langrune, and later had the task of clearing a narrow wooded valley running south from Putot en Bassin through Bretteville and Villons. This enemy salient along the Mue valley into the Canadian beach-head was cleared, with help from the Chauds (the Regiment de la Chaudière) of Canada. The Commando also sent two Troops to clear Douvres la Deliverande, beyond which village lay the heavily fortified radar station. During these actions, 'No.46(RM)' tangled with the 12 SS Hitler Jugend, who held their fire at one point as Y and S Troop advanced in line across the wheat-fields. The marines came steadily on when the enemy opened fire at point-blank range, and later the Commando worked with a squadron of Shermans, helping them to out-manoeuvre two Tiger tanks, before the inland strong points at Le Hamel and Rots at the head of the Mue valley were taken at 2000 hours on D+5, 11 June. Co-ordinated artillery shoots had enabled them to take these villages, but as they were without other support until early next morning the Brigadier doubted if the positions could be held. Even with the support of some Canadians' carriers and anti-tank guns, the positions were exposed and so the whole force was withdrawn before dawn.

When 47(RM) Commando came ashore on D-day, four of their 14 LCAs were sunk. They spent the whole day fighting their way inland and by evening had reached a hill behind their objective: the small harbour of Port en Bessin at the extreme western flank of Gold beach (see map p. 182). On the afternoon of D+1 they attacked this village with the support of HMS *Emerald* and a smokescreen laid by artillery, and had captured two of the three strongpoints before a German attack retook the hill that had been the marines' start line. However, Captain T.F. Cousins found a zigzag path leading into the third strongpoint, which was taken by 50 commandos as darkness fell. The German commander and 100 men surrendered, but a sniper killed Captain Cousins a few minutes later.

On the other flank of the British and Canadian sector, the 1SS (Commando) Brigade held their part of the line beyond the Orne. They had a quiet morning on Wednesday (D+1), but in the afternoon two Troops of 3 Commando attempted to clear the Merville battery (see map p. 182) which had been reoccupied by Germans after the British Airborne had drawn back to the Orne line. After breaking into the bunkers, the commandos were driven out by some self-propelled guns and lost half their Troops' strength, Major J.V.B. Pooley being killed by one of the last infantrymen in the battery. 45(RM) Commando attacked some villas beyond the gun positions on the outskirts of Franceville Plage, and might have been overwhelmed by counter-attacks but for the tenacity of C Troop enabling the Commando to form a tight perimeter near Merville. In the next few days the Germans were to make determined efforts to dislodge the Brigade from their positions, to which the high ground round Le Plein was the key. High ground, that is, in the geography of this coastal plain of the British sector, for nowhere else did the hills rise above a few hundred feet (100m) until the positions south of Gold beach around St Leger.

4 SS Brigade was to spend the next few days in the rear areas, although this was by no means a quiet time. On D+5 (Sunday), 'No.48(RM)', down to 223 all ranks after D-day, recced the radar station at Douvres but were moved before they could do more than harass these heavily fortified positions. They were taken a week later by 41(RM) Commando who had invested the strongpoints and, supported by artillery, were led on D+11 by four flail tanks across the

defences' minefields. The Commando lost only one man but captured five German officers and 221 men in a warren of strongpoints connected by underground passages.

Meanwhile, German attacks on 1 Brigade's positions had forced them into a tighter perimeter, and although commando casualties had been less than expected on D-day, now that they were frequently under mortar fire, they began to take casualties. German probes, with flares lighting up the woods at night, and the close country that enabled both armies to hold positions in places a mere 30 yards apart, gave the men little rest. By Friday (D+3) the commandos were red-eyed and tired, living in weapon pits that they defended with great skill, in the early days holding their fire so that their positions could not be located by any probing patrol: later, their fire caught strong counter-attacks when the Germans were unaware of the defence positions. 'The strange thing was . . . as an attack was seen to be coming . . . the more cheerful the troops became', and that night (D+3/4) German attacks in company strength overran some marine slit-trenches. A marine appeared in 4 Commando's positions calling 'Jerry's through', and Pat Porteous - recovered from his wounds at Dieppe - led D Troop of 'No.4' to recover the lost ground. Rising together, they stormed across the positions occupied by the Germans and drove them out of the marines' trenches, although there were two Germans for every commando. After this attack, D Troop - who had suffered many casualties around the Ouistreham tower four days earlier - were only 15 strong: two officers, the sergeant-major and 12 men.

Next morning, Saturday 10 June, men of 1 Brigade were nearly out on their feet, having had little sleep since reveille the previous Tuesday. Men, lying back for a moment, dropped off to sleep in the middle of a conversation, even though mortar bombs might be bursting around their slit-trenches. These came in more quickly around 0930 hours on 4 Commando's front at Hauger, and half an hour later two Germans with a radio reconnoitred the effects of this bombardment. They were shot 20 yards in front of F Troop before they could get back to the German lines. Continuous mortar fire, growing in intensity fell around 4 Commando during the next five hours and was survived 'well below ground' by F Troop and others - as the Brigade-Major discovered when he came forward. He insisted the men should have a hot meal, but the Sergeant-Major explained they were not really hungry; moments later the Major himself had to jump for cover in a trench. Around 1700 hours an army Forward Officer Bombardment came into 'No.4's' positions and 'thought he could control the big guns of HMS *Ramillies*'. He ordered over his radio a shoot at the Germans massing on the edge of a wood opposite F Troop. The commandos waited. Suddenly the ground erupted in the middle of their positions, and the FOB was not given the opportunity for a second ranging shot from the battleship more than six miles away. The control of the counter-bombardment was then taken over by the Forward Observation Officer (FOO) - bombardment officers controlled naval gunfire, observation officers the army's. The FOO had been landed with the Airborne two evenings earlier, receiving a slightly frosty reception from the Troop, afraid of another shortfall, but now he ranged the army guns on the Germans with 12 rounds breaking up their attack. The FOO then left, for 12 rounds were half his guns' ration of ammunition for the day, whereas the German mortars could continue firing. The Brigade had lost many men, before a German attack came in that evening, yet the commandos hung on. Murdoch McDougall lay in an orchard under German machine-gun fire as he directed his two mortar men's fire, and Sergeant-Major McVeigh fired the bren. Several other NCOs, having used all their grenades against 25 Germans trapped in a ditch, lay 10 yards from this patrol and threw back their stick-grenades, following these with tommy-gun bursts, killing half the Germans and capturing the rest, The first waves of Germans approaching the commando lines faltered; they reformed, but then the attacks melted away.

A week after the landing, Lord Lovat was severely wounded when an attack on Breville

was launched through 6 Commando's positions. This village was at the base of the only German salient into the Brigade's lines, and the previous day the Black Watch - in their first action in Normandy - had 200 casualties trying to take the village. On 12 June the 12th Parachute Battalion 'sadly under strength', 60 men of an Independent Parachute Company, and a squadron of tanks from the 13th-18th Hussars overran two German companies, securing the village by midnight and so ending the long series of attacks and counter-attacks around the village during that week. The 160 men of the Parachute Battalion had 142 casualties, and German losses were severe: the 858th Regiment had more than 400 casualties from a strength of 564 all ranks after this final day's fighting for the village.

Derek Mills-Roberts took over 1 Brigade, although he had also been wounded in the Breville fighting, before the commandos could take up positions near the village overlooking the plain running inland to the south and east of Caen. 4 Brigade moved into the Orne line on 12 June, with 48(RM) Commando digging in at Sallenelles - a fashionable seaside resort village - at the coast end of the ridge with its eastward slopes running to the river Dive and the Orne marshes to the west. For the next two months the Brigades held these ridge positions, plagued by mosquitoes, short of kit - 'No.48(RM)'s' big packs with greatcoats and a change of clothing was all they received after landing, supposedly for one week. They fed on composite pack rations as they had no cooks, but improvised meals - a patrol from 4 Commando used a cart to whisk a few sheep from a farm in no-man's land - supplemented the monotony.

Night patrols, putting out pairs of snipers often in preference to daylight patrols, and with warning trip-wires flares in front of their lines were routine during the next two months. But two months in fox-holes always liable to mortar attack and making constant patrols wore down the commandos' exuberance of the early days, and 'the elastic spring of physical fitness' was gone - in the view of one officer returning to 4 Commando after a spell in hospital.

A radio patrol of the 5th Rangers with the US 29 Infantry Division in France, August 1944.

When the breakout was made after Caen fell on 9 July (D+33 days, not D-day when it was an optimistic objective), 1 Brigade made a night infiltration led by 4 Commando with fewer than 160 men of the 435 who had landed on D-day. Reinforcements were brought in - two officers and 30 marines joined 'No.48(RM)' on D+3 - but all Commandos were under-strength. The Brigade reached their objectives over a difficult route in 'Stygian darkness when it was impossible to see the man ahead'; going through thick hedges and woods as they crossed the bocage country, following the tape as they moved in single file. They reached and held a road junction and a bridge on high ground near Deauville, east of the Dives, throughout 22 August 1944. Surprise was complete, many of the Brigade breakfasting off the German rations before fighting off four counter-attacks during the day. 4 Brigade the previous night had made a similar approach-march through thick woods, over fences, and along the beds of streams, following a parachute brigade to capture a hill near the village of Dozule seven and a half miles (12km) south-east of Deauville and three miles (4.8km) ahead of the main Allied positions. In this close country a map reference objective could turn out to be screened by trees, as the leading Troop of 48(RM) Commando found on one hill where they had no view of the enemy. Moving forward down the slope, they came under brisk fire in one of many sudden flurries between the Brigades and the retreating Germans.

Attached to the US 29 Infantry Division in the way many Special Force units would be deployed in the advance across Europe, the 5th Ranger Battalion often fought in difficult stretches of country that the armoured thrusts by-passed. At other times, rangers and commandos worked with a few tanks, for the amphibious part of their role was now matched by their ability to infiltrate enemy positions, a difficult task, but not perhaps as tricky when the enemy were retreating as it had been against prepared defences at Anzio.

On 4 September the British took Antwerp. This was, for some weeks, the northern tip of their salient from the general advance that had carried the Canadians and British 200 to 300 miles (300 to 480 km) from the beaches to face the Germans northward across the Scheldt, and had taken the American armies eastward almost to the borders of southern Germany. Further advances by any of these armies - the British

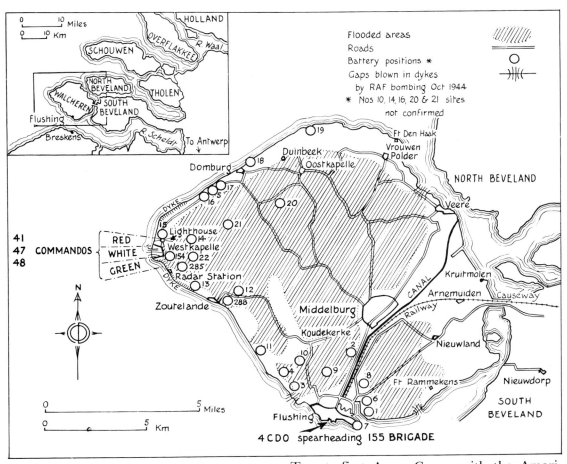

4 Commando Brigade's landings on Walcheren, 1 November 1944. Defences—Batteries 1–22 with code letter W housed about 40 guns from 75mm (3in) to 220mm (8.6in) including captured French and British guns. Typical batteries were: W13–4 155mm in concrete casemates, 2 75mm in casemates and 3 20mm; W15–4 3.7in A-A ex-British guns in concrete casemates and 2 3in A-A ex-British guns in open emplacements; and W17–4 220mm ex-French guns in concrete open emplacements.

The island was ringed by beach obstacles and had wire protected infantry defences for the heavy batteries. For example on the coast from Westkapelle to Zouteland, a 3 miles (4.8km) stretch, were 5 mortar positions, 5 infantry pill-boxes and several m/c gun posts. Mortar positions are exampled at 154, 285 and 288. Minefields protected landward approaches to batteries and access routes across dunes—behind W13, behind beach west of W13 and 900yds inland from this beach, further west near 48(RM) Cdo's landing, and on the road from the light-house, to name a few examples.

Twenty-first Army Group with the American Twelfth Army on their right and to the south where they joined the US Sixth Army - depended on some drastic improvement in their lines of supply. The British and Canadians were using 12,000 tons of stores a day; and, despite their overland petrol pipeline, organised airlifts, and ability to keep things rolling, the American tanks were stopped too often for lack of fuel: In mid-September General Eisenhower stressed the importance of clearing the Scheldt, for Antwerp docks 40 miles (65km) up-river from the sea could not be used until the island of Walcheren in the estuary (see map above) with its coastal batteries guarding the approaches, was overcome, and the river banks cleared of the enemy.

4 Commando replaced the 200 men of 46(RM) Commando in 4 Brigade, joining 41,

47 and 48(RM) Commandos training around Ostend in preparation for an assault on Walcheren. Meanwhile, the Canadians were becoming experts in amphibious operations as they cleared the flooded polders of the Breskens pocket, an area of coastal plain and reclaimed land. Under the protection of batteries across the estuary on Walcheren, the German 64 Infantry Division made a stubborn defence of these watery lands with their dykes and canals. The division had not been in action in Normandy, but their skill against the Canadian flame-throwing tanks and carriers, with massed Allied artillery, enabled the Germans to hold these defences until a seaward left-hook had outflanked the mile-wide isthmus to South Beveland, which was cleared of Germans. They would not now be able to interfere with the action on Walcheren, but efforts to cross the 1,200 yard (1.1km) causeway to Walcheren were blocked. Dead straight for its full length from South Beveland, this built-up strip of land was a mere 40 yards wide, the reed-grown flats either side giving no cover in the early winter cold when the Canadians put in a series of unsuccessful assaults against the Walcheren positions around the causeway's west end.

Both Walcheren and South Beveland are artificial islands recovered from the sea by the Dutch, Walcheren being a saucer's rim of dunes and dykes circling the flat island below sea-level. Around the village of West-kapelle is one of the oldest and strongest sea defences in Holland, 200 to 250 feet wide, rising to 30 feet (10m) and running for three miles (4.8km) along Walcheren's western rim (see map p. 198). In 1944 the Germans had W15 battery north of the village, one of 30 coastal and field-gun positions on the island, protecting its approaches and the gap in the Westkapelle dyke made by an RAF raid on the night of 2-3 October. Later in October this gap had been widened by further bombing, gaps made west and east of Flushing and on the north coast effectively flooding the whole island west of the Flushing-Veere canal and a large part of the land to the south-east of this waterway. After this inundation, the landing was set for 1 November after further bombing of the batteries.

4 Commando would land at 0545 hours while it was still dark at Flushing and 41, 47 and 48(RM) Commandos would land about 1000 hours around the gap in the dyke at Westkapelle. The marines were supported by 27 landing craft giving close fire support, including two LC Gun (Medium)s with 17-pounder anti-tank guns in two armoured turrets on each craft. The LCG(M)s would beach each side of the 380-yard (345m) gap while the other support craft came inshore with their 4-inch (100mm) guns, rockets, pom-pom 2-pounders, and 20mm to engage the batteries. One battleship and two monitors would provide heavier naval support. Air support was to include both heavy bombing and low-level attacks, but, to illustrate the complexities in the planning of such amphibious operations, the air strike requested by 4 Commando was misinterpreted by SHAEF (Supreme Headquarters Allied Expeditionary Force). The commandos wanted four pin-point targets knocked out, minimising the risk to Dutch civilians. These selected targets, however, were covered by the planners in area bombing, a flattening of houses and streets over several blocks. Understandably, senior officers at SHAEF then asked why the army wanted the town of Flushing devastated? In the event, the overcast weather and fog on English airports limited the air attacks immediately before the landings, although RAF Mosquitoes dropped some 500lb (227kg) bombs in spite of the bad weather just before the Flushing landing. Artillery on the southern shore of the estuary also covered the assault at various stages.

4 Commando, with a Dutch Troop from 'No.10', were roused from their billets in the shells of houses near Breskens and at 0400 hours the first pair of LCAs slipped from the rickety wooden jetty out into the river. Lieutenant Denny Rewcastle - known to wear a silk scarf in less ardous times - took his Section as the leading scouts for 4 Commando, and with them were a Tarbrush party, similar to those who found the Normandy beach obstacles the previous spring, plus the advanced party of Beach Commandos. These units (see Appendix 2) landed among the early waves in all major assaults

and larger raids, marking the positions of the two or three berths where larger craft could safely nose into the shore. The Beach Party were in contact with the major landing crafts' skippers by radio or loudhailer, and could adjust the sequence of landing from that planned if some change of priorities made, say, tanks more vital than bulldozers at a particular point in the build-up. They were also in touch with the salvage parties, whose bulldozers or other gear could clear a sunken minor craft from the shore or aid a larger one in backing out of her berth. Lieutenant Harry Hargreaves RNVR, who landed that night at Flushing, had controlled the beach for 4 Commando's landings at Dieppe and elsewhere in the early years of the war, and now, 90 minutes before dawn, he took his Beach Party across the Scheldt.

At 0530 hours the artillery opened a 10-minute bombardment while the two LCAs made for the beach near the mole. They identified the mole's position by a windmill's silhouette against the fires burning in the town. When the leading craft was caught on obstacles 30 yards out, the commandos swam ashore to a wooden jetty near the base of the mole. Scrambling up the wet stonework of a slipway in the sea wall, the leading couple of men forced a gap between two stakes, and just before 0545 hours they were on to the road which was covered with barbed wire. Behind them came two men laying the white tape the Commando would follow after this Section had cut a path through the wire. As the Beach Party's craft passed the end of the mole a shot was fired, but soon the leading commandos had overrun a 75mm (3in) gun position, and Harry Hargreaves, standing in the LCA, was signalling in the next pair of craft. Already the engineers were clearing mines either side of the two berths in a garbage tip, although the sappers had to swim ashore with their detectors. Men in the following LCAs lay out in the river. 'We felt like Aunt Sallies' as the German 20mm red tracer whipped over their heads, but the Germans were firing high for their only point of aim on LCAs low in the water was the small bow wave, and this was almost non-existent when the craft moved slowly. By 0635 the last Troops were ashore.

The Commando fanned out to form a 600-yard (540m) perimeter around the landing-area, with No.4 Troop passing through this to attack the German barracks of fortified houses overlooking the river half a mile (.8km) west of the landing beach. The Troop were ordered to avoid opposition, and in 10 minutes had entered the old town, skirting a machine-gun position as two men were hit. Working their way down the streets between houses and shops, shaken by some shells falling short from the Allied guns across the river, they came on the rear of the barracks. Nick Barrass, a tall, quiet-spoken ex-policeman, led his Section into a building and covered Sergeant Fraser's climb up a spiral staircase. As the Lieutenant crouched near a window he was killed by a shot from a house across the street. Murdoch McDougal's Section ran down an alleyway towards the barrack houses they were to clear, coming through a garage with its flimsy back door opening on to the blank wall of a bunker. In front of it were 15 or so Germans who reacted immediately; Murdoch McDougal called 'back this way' as he enlarged a hole in the thin garage wall. But a commando jumped into the doorway; feet firmly on the ground the stocky Private Donkin methodically swung his tommy-gun, firing left to right. His swing had reached the right-handed man in the group and he was still firing on the return swing when he was killed outright, shot through the throat by a man he had missed on the left when he began to spray bullets into the group. The Sergeant-Major shot this German before the Troop came back through the garage to find another way into the barrack houses. These they cleared in a running fight through the houses' three storeys and the long underground passage linking them to the strongpoints along the river front.

In the town they could hear the battle developing, for the Germans had recovered from their initial surprise and as the 4th King's Own Scottish Borderers (KOSB) began to land the German counter-barrage intensified, making impossible any further landings from across the river. The 5th KOSB were not able to get ashore until 1400 hours, by which time, with the help of rocket-firing Typhoon aircraft, some progress had been made. The commandos, mouseholing their way through buildings or swinging from gutters to reach upper rooms, fought their way street by street. One man, held by the legs, hung down from a roof and shot his way into an upper storey. Others took equal risks, and by the evening of 3 November (D+2) the town was cleared, the 155 Brigade's KOSB Battalions, a battalion of the Royal Scots, and support troops having fought their way into the town after passing through 4 Commando's beachhead.

At Westkapelle on 1 November, the three Royal Marine Commandos planned to land over three beaches: Tare Red, an 800-yard (760m) stretch north of the gap; Tare White, the 380-yard gap; and Tare Green, near the dunes about 450 yards south of the gap and 350 yards long for use in the later build-up. (For landing information, see diagram p. 202.) In addition to the medical units attached to each Commando were a platoon of Royal Engineers for clearing mines.

The support squadron of craft moved in two groups to get inside the shallows as the first German shells fell around the marker MTBs at 0809 hours. A few minutes later the battleship HMS *Warspite* opened fire, and as the gun-ships closed the beach some German batteries, untouched by this heavier bombardment, took a toll among the light support craft. A flak craft (LCF 37) went up in a sheet of flame, a rocket craft (LCT(R)) was hit, and firing her salvoes off-target misled her opposite number in the northern column who fired short. These northern group rockets fortunately fell between the craft of 41 and 48(RM) Commandos. An LCT hospital craft hit a mine, and a second flakker caught fire, but the leading LCG(M)s drew a lot of shot and shell that might have been directed at the commandos' craft. Both G(M)s beached although subsequently they were holed; one could not get off the beach and the other sank when it did so.

Four LCTs, carrying ten Flail tanks for mine-clearing, eight AVREs for crossing obstacles, four armoured bulldozers, and eight Sherman tanks of 30th Armoured Brigade, were heading for the left of the gap

where they were intended to help elements of 'No.41(RM)' clear the north dyke. The three Troops of this Commando, however, were in the wooden LCI(S) that 48(RM) Commando had found so costly at Normandy. The craft came in when there was sufficient water to cross the mud-flats, but the tide was not full, leaving some beach exposed below the high-water line at H-hour (0945). The sea was calm, but the intense anti-boat fire - two of the commandos' three LCIs were hit - delayed by half an hour the landing north of the gap. Once ashore the commandos were through the defences and had reached the outskirts of Westkapelle village in six minutes. The stones and cobbles of the dyke proved too slippery for the tracked vehicles, which had already taken some damage when an SGB - a tank carrying a swing-girder bridge - was blasted on to a Flail while still aboard their LCT. The fascine bundles on some tanks were also set on fire during the run-in, and the crews of these special vehicles on two of the LCTs could get only one Flail up the dyke, despite valiant efforts to tow the others with a bulldozer. The third and fourth LCTs then took their tracked vehicles south of the gap before beaching. The second wave of 41(RM) Commando landed in the amphibious Buffaloes (LVTs) with tracks that enabled the landing vehicles to swim as well as climb. These LVTs carried them through the gap and up the landward side of the dyke, out of the flooded fields. As they came in sight of a tower, Sergeant Ferguson's Flail tank put 11 75mm (3in) rounds into this observation post, and by 1115 hours the commandos had taken the village, where the two Dutch Troops covered the north flank.

On White Beach the first wave of 48(RM) Commando churned ashore in their Buffaloes, the amphibians' Polsten 20mm guns firing as these LVTs swam the 50-yard gap from their carrier LCTs to the shore before the tracks gripped firm ground and the first wave reached the dunes. Their Colonel, Jim Moulton, landed in his command Weasel, which he later described 'as the way to land, dry shod, plenty of fire-power, very few casualties, and my wireless set with me'. He was one of the first ashore at 1010 hours, 20

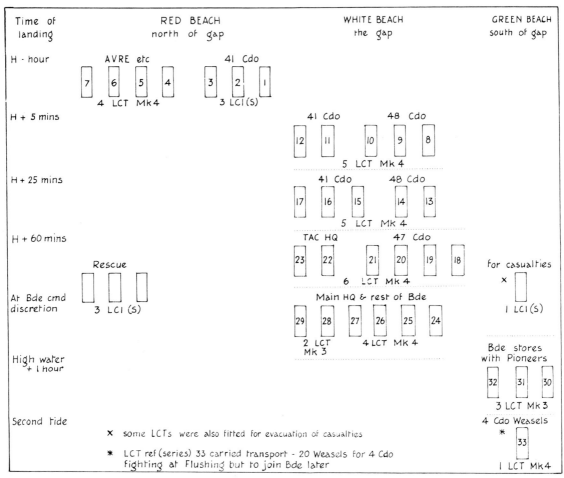

Landing plan 4 Commando Brigade and supporting units at Westkapelle (Walcheren), 1 November 1944.

minutes late. Dismounted from their LVTs, B Troop found that two low concrete pillboxes on the shoulder of the gap were wrecked and unoccupied; X Troop 'panted up the dune on their way to the radar station', which they found was also unoccupied but under small-arms fire. There was little small-arms fire on the beach, but shells burst among the craft and in the waters of the gap. The marines, consolidating their hold on the southern dyke and the sandhills running south of it, took battery W285 (see map p. 198) and Y Troop passed through to assault W13 to keep up the momentum of the advance, even though this battery's naval

gunners were firing at the assault ships and the Troop had no support. Their attack failed, and Major D.R.W. de Stacpoole RM was killed. The Commando held half a mile of dunes, but had no support because the FOO and FOB's Weasels had been sunk, the waves following in the first flights coming under heavy shelling and a landing craft sticking in one of the best landing-points for the LVTs. Heavy cratering around the dyke also made these vehicles difficult to manoeuvre. The Buffalo carrying 'No.48(RM)'s' Heavy Weapons Troop machine-guns was hit while still aboard its LCT, and although marines swam ashore with parts of these medium machine-guns, they found they had only two tripods and no barrels ashore. Other Buffaloes and Weasels moving along

Examples of loads by craft index references

| Unit | No. 1* | No. 4 | No. 8 | No. 17 | No. 20 | No. 22 | No. 31 |
|---|---|---|---|---|---|---|---|
| **numbers of men and** *vehicles*: | | | | | | | |
| 41(RM) Cdo | 50 | | | | | | |
| 47(RM) Cdo | | | | | 101 *5 LVT* *4 Wls* | | |
| 48(RM) Cdo | | | 68 *3 LVT* *3 Wls ** | | | | |
| 10(IA) Cdo | | 6 | | 84 *3 LVT* *4 Wls* | | | |
| 509 Fd Coy RE** | | | 2 *1 D7 ** | | 60 *1 LVT* | 2 *1 D7* *1 sledge* | |
| 510 Fd Coy RE | 5 | | 5 | 48 *1 LVT* | | | |
| 'A' LCOCU | 3 | | | | | | |
| 'A' Sqd 1st Lothians | | 2 *Flails* 15 *1 Sherman* | | | | | |
| 87 Sqd | | 1 *D7* | | | | | |
| Aslt Rgmt RE | | 15 *2 AVRE* | | | | | |
| 4 Cdo Bde Tac HQ | | | | | | 57 *5 LVT* *3 Wls* | |
| 4 Cdo Bde Sigs | | | 1 | | | 25 | |
| 2 Sec Beach Sigs RN | | | 5 | 6 | | | |
| 'L' RN Cdo | | | 5 | 10 | | | |
| 66 Unit FOB | | | 3 | | | | |
| 72 Unit FOB | | | | | 4 | | |
| IO (IA) Cdo | | | | | 6 | | |
| FDS** | | | | | | | |
| 4 Cdo Bde B Echelon HQ | | | | | | 9 | |
| 144 Coy Pioneers | | | | | | 3 | 37 (with Bde stores—200 tons) |
| II Cdn Corps sigs | | | | | | 3 | |
| Tcl 1 Cdn ASSU** | | | | | | 3 | |
| 191st Fd Rgmt RA | | | | | | 2 | |
| Aslt Rgmt RE*** | | | 15 | 20 | 30 | 25 | |

\*  All assault forces landed in amphibians except the personnel in craft Nos. 1 to 3.

\*\*  Fd Coy—Field Company; Wls—Weasels; D7—type of armoured bulldozer; FDS—Field Dressing Station, also landed were Canadian medical units 17th Light Field Ambulance, 5th Field Transport Unit and 8th & 9th Field Surgical Units; Tcl 1 Cdn ASSU—Technical party from Canadian Air Support Sigs Unit.

\*\*\*  Aslt Rgmt RE—LVT drivers from five sqds of 5th Assault Rgmt RE and detachments of 11th Royal Tank Rgmt.

---

the dunes were hit by shells or exploded on mines as the spade-like cleats on the tracks dug through the sand. One or two LVTs might safely cross a mine, but after the covering of four feet (1+m) of wind-carried sand had been scraped away, the third would blow it. These vehicles' 100-gallon (455 litre) fuel tanks then burned fiercely, exploding the ammunition cargoes.

The FOB, Captain Blunt RA, carried his 510-set forward on his own, his two naval telegraphists having been wounded, but only two LCG(L)s and an LCF from the close-support squadron were still in action - and they were almost out of ammunition. Three craft that had taken on W13's guns were sunk 300 yards from the shore. However,

the gunner officer kept in contact with the headquarters ship, and a couple of salvoes were ranged on the battery by the monitor HMS *Roberts*, her fire directed by Captain A.D. Davies RA, who came forward with his telegraphist.

Meanwhile, Jim Moulton gave his Commando in the dunes a breather to clean the wind-blown sand and salt from their automatic weapons and from the bolts of their rifles. About 1430 hours he walked back a few hundred yards to Brigade HQ in order to contact the gunners across the Scheldt, because the FOO's radio to these guns was not working. By this time, Dan Flunder had been sent with A Troop out on to a spit of sand running into the floodwater where they could give covering fire for an attack on W13. However, the Colonel wanted heavier support, and as well as artillery bombardment he arranged a low-level air attack for 1600 hours, five minutes before the commandos would put in their assault.

Going forward again, Jim Moulton found the commandos' positions had been heavily mortared - no one above the rank of corporal was unscathed in Z Troop and the Troop officer was believed killed. A junior officer, Brian Lindrea, was killed and two other officers were wounded. The FOB, Captain Davies, and his telegraphist were believed killed, and the doctor was missing from his aid post, before the bombardment was stopped when a long-range burst from one of A Troop's brens killed the German 81mm mortar crew. There were 30 minutes to the 1605 assault, and B Troop hurried forward to take over this job from Z Troop.

At 1545 hours the artillery 'started an intense and heartening bombardment', in the words of 'No.48(RM)'s' history. At 1600 came the cannon-firing Spitfires, each releasing a 500lb (227kg) bomb over the commandos' heads, hitting the battery in well-aimed trajectories. The dunes shook. The thud-thud-thud of A Troop's brens were joined by the delicate plop of X Troop's 2-inch mortars firing smoke-bombs, first indicating the target and then screening B Troop's assault. They ran forward over a minefield made harmless by drifting sand. Lieutenant P.H.Allbut RM came face to face with a German across the wire; both found their weapons were jammed with sand, and as the commando officer forced his way through the wire Sergeant Stringer shot the German. The Troop scrambled over the emplacements, finding one casement smashed by shells and bombs and all the crew killed, but as the commandos worked their way through the cratered sand and concrete, a 20mm fired in their direction from the far end of the battery. As it was getting dark by this time, and the Commando had collected 70 prisoners from their living-quarters below the dunes behind the battery, further advances were limited to a patrol by X Troop. After the excitement of the day, the commandos found they were cold and hungry on the open dunes. Moreover they had little ammunition, which, like their rations, had to be manhandled over the dunes, for most of the Buffaloes had been lost through shell-hits or mines and many Weasels had failed to survive in the strong current of the gap as the tide ebbed. The commandos made do with tins of self-heating soup, some chocolate, and sweets; ammunition was carried forward by men returning from the beach. They found the doctor's body alongside that of his dead orderly where they had been binding the wounds of Captain Davies and his telegraphist who had also been killed. Captain R.G. Mackenzie, who commanded Z Troop, was found alive but he died without regaining consciousness.

On the north of the gap, 41(RM) Commando, having taken W15 battery, came under fire from W17 at Domburg, which was not silenced until early in the afternoon after hits from the battleship HMS *Warspite* and low-level air attacks. The third Commando - 'No.47(RM)' - was ashore by then after a confusion that put three of their LVT carrying LCTs north of the gap; many of their amphibians could not cross the gap until the tide ebbed and there was only a 30-yard gutter to swim. By the time they were assembled in the dunes south of the gap, they had lost 17 of their 20 Weasels and three of their 20 Buffaloes.

On D+1 the Brigade developed their bridgeheads along the dykes and dunes, with 48(RM) Commando's leading Troop, having found little opposition, being pushed along the dunes into Zouteland, where the monitor HMS *Erebus* had been firing before she lifted her aim on to W11 battery. One garrison of 150 surrendered and Colonel Phillips came through with 47(RM) Commando, not over-pleased that 'No.48(RM)' had taken several of his objectives, although he soon had stiff opposition to overcome at battery W11, which was still firing on ships and which repulsed the first assault.

Allied casualties in this operation were about 7,700 including two out of every five commando Troop officers and one in four of the support craft's crews. The island was finally secured on 8 November (D 7), when 4

C Company of the 2nd Rangers on the march near Heimbach (Germany) on 3 March 1945

Commando took the barracks between Domburg and Veere at Vrouwenpolder. As they made the last 50 yards of their advance, bayonets fixed and carried at the high port, two old and scruffy Germans appeared with a white flag from the barracks. A patrol (from 48(RM) Commando) which had also moved across the island was travelling in two LVTs when the second one hit a buried sea mine. Lieutenant W.H. England, a South African seconded to the marines, was killed along with 18 men, and nine others, including the Royal Engineer crew of this LVT, were wounded. Such incidents would probably cause as many commando and ranger casualties as were suffered in set-piece battles during the winter and spring of 1944-45 in Europe.

The operations of the commandos and rangers that winter are shown in Appendix 7, but in a typical example the 5th Rangers were going forward during December 1944 with the Sixth Cavalry Group of General Patton's Third Army in a series of tank thrusts, supported by infantry, advancing from Diesen to Ludweiler. During these actions D Company broke in Ludweiler, but without artillery support they were driven back 500 yards (450m) from the town. Next day the battalion's F Company attacked Lauterbach, an action in which Pfc Leo Samboroski took his BAR down a forward slope to engage a strongpoint and 'then realised the greatest danger came from an emplacement on the left'. He ran further forward, giving covering fire from eight full clips that enabled F Company to advance before he was killed. The company reached the first few houses on the outskirts of the town, where a Tiger tank brought one house down on a squad who shook themselves free of the rubble, while Corporal Andrew Speir fired his bazooka from an upper storey at the tank. He fired several times, although once knocked from his perch by the Tiger's fire, but the tank did not retreat until rangers' mortar fire drove back the German infantry supporting it. That night A Company infiltrated past the German machine-gun posts into the town, but the mud prevented the tanks of the 6th Cavalry and the 602nd's tracked guns from moving forward, and without supporting fire no further advance was possible.

The unit histories in Appendix 7 tell a little of these many skirmishes and difficult raids as the Allies moved into Germany. There was a complex of rivers - the Maas (Meuse), the Rhine and its associated river the Waal - along which the British held positions facing north in the spring of 1945, while the Americans squeezed the Germans from the south-west banks of the Rhine. As were the 5th Rangers, the men of 3 Commando, commanded by Lieutenant-Colonel Arthur Komrower, were operating with the regular forces' advance, two Troops being forward without much support as the ice on the Montforterbeek canal would not carry tanks and all the bridges had been blown. Their only prisoner repeatedly wished to die for his Führer and might have done so when two German tanks came up. These blasted the forward Section's defended houses which were only 20 yards from the tanks' guns, with a dust-choking crash of bricks and roof rafters familiar to many rangers and commandos fighting in Europe. Holding a 2-inch mortar against his knee, Trooper Clinton launched a smoke-bomb while others flung phosphorous grenades out of the windows, giving the Section cover while they rejoined the Troop. Tanks of the 8th Hussars moved across a bridge over a gulley later that afternoon, but the Germans, although often drawn from many units including Luftwaffe aircrews fighting as infantry, were skilfully led. The tanks had to withdraw and 3 Commando spent an uncomfortable night in the snow-filled gulley as the engineers strove to replace the now-damaged bridge. Next morning, Nos.1 and 6 Troops went forward, riding on the Hussars' tanks, to find the Germans had left the town. In all these tank and infantry moves, the commandos and rangers would ride on the tanks until they reached a street of houses, thick cover, or other likely tank obstacles; then the infantry would dismount and probe forward, clearing any enemy waiting to ambush the tanks. In turn, the tanks would destroy concrete and other strongpoints that had held up the infantry's advance. This was more often a movement forward in fits and starts than a headlong charge in pursuit of the enemy.

The Rhine had been crossed, and was crossed again further west, on the night of 23-24 March 1945. The LVTs, making 100 yards a minute for the four-minute passage, carried over 'No.46(RM)', 6 Commando crossing in storm-boats just before a heavy raid by Lancaster bombers on the city of Wesel. The Commandos, supported by a machine-gun battalion of the Cheshires, won control of the city and linked up with the US 17 Airborne Division who had dropped north of Wesel as the commandos crossed the river. This was one of several major river crossings the commandos and rangers

undertook as the Allied armies crossed Germany, and on this occasion 1 Commando Brigade's Rhine crossing had spearheaded an army of 80,000. 45(RM) Commando crossed the Weser against fierce resistance before being joined by the rest of 1 Brigade in the bridgehead which was held with a battalion of the Rifle Brigade. From there they marched to the Aller, a river only 50 yards (45m) wide but one of the toughest crossings the Brigade experienced. It was crossed by the 11 Armoured Division west of Winsen, on 15 April and near here they found 40,000 starving men, women, and children, plus 10,000 unburied dead, in Belsen concentration camp. The same day, 1 Commando Brigade spearheaded the crossing at Rethem, 30 miles further west of Winsen. The road bridge at Essel was intact when 3 Commando rushed the railway bridge a mile downstream, getting a bridgehead established, although one span of this bridge was blown. They held German counter-attacks next morning, having secured the east bank of the road bridge with the help of 6 and 46(RM) Commandos. 'No.45' and '46(RM)' then passed through the bridgehead and into some woods where a battalion of German marines held the advance for several days although 53 Division moved around the town, crossing the river and moving on to high ground above it.

Jim Moulton now commanded 4 Commando Brigade, whose last action was by 48(RM) Commando in April, when this Commando's new colonel sent two Troops in daylight across the Maas river into the waterways of the Biesbosch to rescue a lost patrol. When they were safely across Jim Moulton thought the whole Brigade might follow and push up to the river Waal, but this was not allowed for - as he has written - 'the end was very near and those of us in responsible positions had to remember that a man could still be killed just as dead as on 6 June, but with infinitely less justification'.

Long before this stage in the War, however, when an enemy saw green berets opposing him, he usually took care to leave them in peace because of their reputation for ferocity.

# BURMA AND SOUTH-EAST ASIA, 1941 TO 1945

Swift Japanese victories in 1941-42 brought them to the gates of India when British and Indian troops fell back to the Assam hills north-west of Burma. The Chinese were fighting 25 Japanese divisions, and to aid their ally, the Americans, with British help, were flying in supplies over the Yunnan mountains (the Hump)

The British and Indian army had been repulsed in their first Arakan offensive of 1943, and they were harassed by Indian objectors to British rule who cut road and rail supply lines. But in February 1943, a special force marched 1,500 miles (2,400km) behind Japanese lines, cutting railways, making friends among the Burmese, and destroying the myth of Japanese invincibility. These 'Chindits' - British, Gurkha, and Burmese troops - may have inspired the Japanese attempt to restore their reputation after setbacks in the Pacific, but their attacks north up the Arakan were held, in part through Allied air superiority ensuring safe air delivery of supplies.

A second Chindit force successfully cut Japanese communications in the early summer of 1944. Over 100 miles to the east of their operations, the American 5307th Composite Unit (Provisional) - Merrill's Marauders - fought five major and many minor actions.

Commonwealth forces, including the Fourteenth Army - British, Indian, and African troops - fought on three parallel fronts during their campaigns in Burma: on the west (Arakan) coast; in central Burma; and alongside the Chinese in the north.

On 1-2 March 1945, the Japanese Fifteenth and Twenty-third Armies were trapped at Meiktila on the central front, cutting off their retreat to Rangoon. Other Japanese were surprised north of this pocket on 8 March at Mandalay, and by the end of the month the Japanese had been driven from central Burma. Early in April, the Fourteenth Army was struggling to cross the Pegu river after heavy rain had flooded airfields, and at the same time an amphibious landing against Rangoon was being mounted. This was hastened by a message painted on the Rangoon prison roof 'Japs gone, extract digit', and the port was taken in an unopposed landing on 3 May.

In Japan, the government had resigned on 4 April as their cities faced intensified incendiary attack, and the Americans' offensive, which had occupied Iwo Jima the previous February surged nearer.

# 12 BURMA AND THE SMALL OPERATIONS GROUP

Some success on land against the Japanese in 1942 and early 1943 did much to reduce the Allied soldiers' initial fears of this enemy as the supposed natural fighter among the jungles of Asia. The Japanese owed their early victories to good discipline and what might be called a light diet, for the men landing in Malaya came ashore in December 1941 with a month's supply of ammunition but only a week's rations: they were expected to gather the rest of their food off the country.

In the early months of 1942, some hundred Royal Marines of Force Viper, with Burma Commando II, formed a patrol on the Irrawaddy river and later a rearguard for General Slim's Burma Corps, who were withdrawing north from Burma over the high mountains to Imphal and Dimapur in Assam. The USMC Raider Battalions were fighting in the Solomons that summer, when liaison between the American and the British amphibious forces was developing with exchanges of experience between the Pacific and European theatres. On the formation of the Ranger Battalions, the US Army was directly concerned in these exchanges, although no Rangers fought in the Pacific until the 6th Ranger Battalion landed ahead of the American Sixth Army in the Philippines during mid-October 1944.

A body of advisers on amphibious operations, including a number of officers who had served in Combined Operations Headquarters, were established in India during 1942, setting up the Combined Training Centre on Lake Kharakvasia, 2,000 feet (610m) up in the hills near Poona. However, there were no landing craft for major operations, for at the time Lord Mountbatten came to India in the summer of 1943 - as Supreme Commander in South-East Asia - landing craft and ships intended for operations in Burma were held in the Mediterranean for the Anzio operations, among others. Plans to land on the Andaman Islands and on the Mayu peninsula running south from the Naf river, were therefore abandoned.

No.7 COPP, Geoff Hall (later Admiral G. Hall, DSC) and his number one Ruari McLean, arrived in India in the autumn of 1943, and within the next 12 months were joined by other reconnaissance and raiding units. Eventually on 12 June 1944, they formed the Small Operations Group (SOG, Appendix 7) 'to provide small parties of uniformed troops trained and equipped to operate against enemy coastal, river and lake areas . . . trained in reconnaissance of enemy beaches' seaward approaches . . . small-scale attacks . . . provision of guides for assaults . . . landing agents . . . providing diversions . . . seizing intelligence data and enemy equipment'. They would carry out some 170 operations, in which not only COPP teams and the Special Boat Section were used but also the Sea Reconnaissance Unit and Royal Marine Detachment 385 (for organisation see Appendix 2).

No.7 COPP did a reconnaissance in the Arakan, the strip of jungle-covered hills on the Burmese coast lying along the Bay of

Bengal, with the yellow Irrawaddy forming its eastern boundary. By this stage in the war the COPPist was a skilled navigator and canoeist, carrying 'the vector triangles in the back of his head'. Consequently a rough note on the navigator's lap-board sufficed to show the compass course to steer when making a true course across an inshore current for a pin-point landing. In measuring distances the paddler counted his strokes, from which the navigator-swimmer could tell when they had reached 2,000 yards or whatever the calculated distance along a course to the rendezvous. COPPists could also use their personal buoyancy, 'trimming down to chin level', in calm waters or inflating their life-jackets to carry their heads high when the sea was rough. In the steamy heat ashore, many did not like to wear their tropical swimsuit with its flapping kapok lining, and at least one swimmer from Detachment 385 landed without a life-jacket.

They were all good swimmers, but few could equal the men of the Sea Reconnaissance Units who were trained to swim many miles on their paddleboards before landing through surf. Other equipment of the SOG was designed for use in these rough waters on exposed beaches, where even with special gear they needed every ounce of skill and some luck to survive. Landing in surf one night, Geoff Hall became entangled in the line he was using to measure a beach's incline. The heavy waves tumbled him over as the line wound round his legs, and when Ruari McLean came in to look for him, Geoff Hall was under water his torch lit, but semi-conscious. Good training and flicker of a torch brought Ruari McLean near his skipper. At other times, COPPs, brought to the mouth of a tidal *chaung* (river), would paddle through the murky waters, taking soundings or looking for suitable beaches where a couple of landing craft might touch down on a raid against the Japanese lines of communication. Both Ruari McLean and Geoff Hall were awarded the DSC for their part in these reconnaissances in Burma that paved the way for later Commando raids.

3 Commando Brigade had been formed in November 1943 to spearhead these landings

in force. 1 Commando, after their actions in North Africa, 5 Commando, who had fought in Madagascar, and 42(RM) with 44(RM) Commando made up the brigade but they would not be all together in India until September 1944, although they sailed together from Scotland in November 1943.

Two Commandos were deployed during March to dominate a strip of coast west of the foothills of the Mayu Range. Operating south from the XV Corps' main offensive against the Maungdaw-Buthidaug road, 44(RM) Commando landed in three flights of leaky old assault craft. They came ashore at 2330 hours on 11 March 1944 near a village of bamboo-mat huts called Alethangyaw. Despite a confused fire-fight near the beach, with Japanese riflemen lying along the limbs of mangrove trees where they were nearly impossible to see, the marines held most of the village by dawn and pushed two bridgeheads across a *chaung* next day. A patrol moving further inland that day came under heavy fire and a wounded marine was dragged by the Japanese to an open paddy field as bait for possible rescue by his comrades. They had to leave him where he was until natives brought him in after nightfall. Throughout this and later actions the commandos and other Allied troops learnt to cope with these deceptions. They had also to be cautious in their use of radio messages. Lieutenant-Colonel F.C. Horton RM was once interrupted by a call on his 44(RM) Headquarters radio 'to pass a short message'. The Commando's Colonel said he had more important things to do, only to hear a 'Thank you, I know your voice'. This might be used later in passing false orders, apparently in the CO's voice, for the commandos' now-reliable communications were monitored by Japanese.

That night (D+1), the Commando moved inland north-east of the village towards a hill, the Colonel himself having given some bogus 'we are staying in the village' messages. They waded waist-deep up a *chaung* for most of the way, as this was the only route through thick jungle, and next morning they set up a box on the hill. This was common jungle practice - the Chindits used great boxes in their forays into Burma the

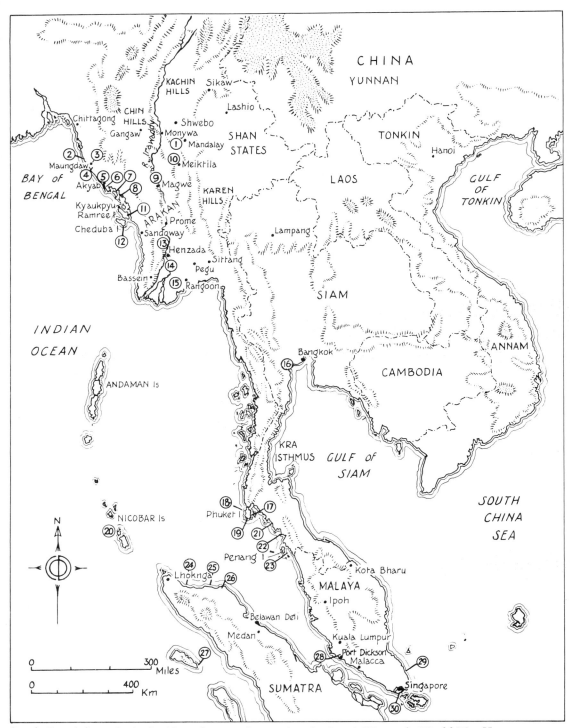

South-East Asia - principal raids and areas of operations by Special Forces in World War II.

Location of some operations of Special Forces in south-east Asia, showing large forces' actions in capitals (date and *code name*) in alphabetical order by year. Numbered locations run from north to south or follow stretches of coast line.

**1941**

| | |
|---|---|
| Irrawaddy patrols (Feb/Mar, Force Viper) | 13 |
| Myanaung (17 Mar, Burma II Cdo) | 14 |

**1943**

| | |
|---|---|
| Singapore (26/7 Sept, *Jaywick*) | 30 |
| Tek Naf | 2 |

**1944**

| | |
|---|---|
| ALETHANGYAW | 4 |
| Elizabeth Isl (Nov, COPP & others) | 6 |
| INDAW AREA (Feb/June, Chindits) 145 miles north-west of Lashio - not on map | |
| Irrawaddy crossings (Nov/Dec, SBS) | 9 |
| Law's Isl (Dec, SBS) | 11 |
| MAUNGDAW (Mar, 5 Cdo) | 3 |
| Pente Radja (17/23 Aug, *Frippery*) - approx. | 24 |
| Pente Radja (11 Sept, *Sprat Able*) - approx. | 24 |
| Peudada River (17/23 Aug, *Frippery*) - approx. | 25 |
| Peudada River (11 Sept, *Sprat Able*) - approx. | 25 |
| SHADUZUP (Mar, Merrill's Maurauders) 250 miles north-west of Lashio - not on map | |
| Singapore (11 Sept, *Rimau*) | 30 |
| WALAWBUM (24 Feb to 2 Mar, Merrill's Maurauders 300 miles north of Lashio - not on map | |

**1945**

| | |
|---|---|
| AKYAB (2/3 Jan, 3 Cdo Bed) | 5 |
| CHEDUBA (23 Jan, RMs from fleet) | 12 |
| Djoeli River (15 Apr, *Cattle*) | 26 |
| Hin Luk (8 Mar, *Baboon*) | 19 |
| Irrawaddy crossings & recces (Feb/May, SBS and SRU) | 1 |
| Kamorta Isl (18/9 Apr, *Defraud*) | 20 |
| KANGAW (Jan/Feb, 3 Cdo Bde) | 8 |
| Kaula Bahra (12 Apr, *Clearance Baker*) | 22 |
| Lasia (28/9 June, *Slumber*) | 27 |
| Mai Kha Bay (8 Mar, *Baboon*) | 17 |
| Maungmagan (West of, 19 Apr, *Fairy*) - approx. | 16 |
| MEIKTILA (Mar, RAF Svg Cdo) | 10 |
| Morib beaches (9 June, *Confidence*) | 28 |
| MYEBON PENINSULA (12 Jan, 3 Cdo Bde) | 7 |
| Pak Meng (South of, 19 June, *Graph*) | 21 |
| Palau Rawi Isl (25/6 July, *Subtract*) | 23 |
| Phuket Isl (8 Mar, *Baboon*) also see above | 18 |
| Phuket Isl (9 Mar, *Copyright*) also see above | 18 |
| RANGOON (3 May, British & Indian infantry) | 15 |
| Sungei Klesa (near mouth, 30 May, *Carpenter III*) - approx. | 29 |

Note: Many operations by COPPs, SBS and Detachment 385 were made in support of local forces throughout the area and are not all included above.

same spring - a square being formed with pickets in a few slit-trenches at each corner of the square making a defended base for patrols. There was little that could be seen through the jungle, even on a hilltop, and patrols had to go out to find the Japanese. One, led by Captain R.M. Sturges RM, had several 'spirited engagements in the late afternoon' when they matched the Japanese, who called out in English, or made a noise from one direction before attacking from another through the jungle. The Commando then withdrew, hearing the Japanese attack the empty positions on the hill. The marines later re-embarked, having possibly distracted some Japanese who might otherwise have stiffened their main defence line, and were replaced by 5 Commando in the Alethangyaw area.

Later that March both Commandos carried out similar operations on this coastal strip. They were then moved to Silchar where, with part of the IV Corps' Indian Army troops, they blocked any possible attempt by the Japanese to break into the Bengal plain.

No. 8 COPP, Lieut Freddy Ponsonby, had joined No.7 in south-east Asia, and their third raid was to Elizabeth Island in the wide mouth of the Kaladan river (see map p. 210) and south of Chittagong, where the COP-Pists transferred their canoes from a destroyer to an ML. They could see village fires ashore and sentries' huts - possibly the lavatories Japanese soldiers built at the end of small wooden jetties over the seashore. The night was bright enough for Michael Peacock to see Alex Colson clambering over the sand at the back of the beach, where he was fired on without any warning challenge - the Japanese must have known anyone on these beaches was against them if he wandered around at night. Michael Peacock who had dysentery swam clear of the beach but passed out, coming to while drifting across the bay with no one in sight. He struggled back ashore but three days later three islanders took no notice of the waterproofed packet of letters offering rewards for his safe conduct - although there were several versions of text in different dialects - and he was handed over to the Japanese. He was taken to Rangoon, later surviving a three-day march as the Japanese tried to evacuate 600 POWs in the retreat.

The ML and the rest of the party had returned to their forward base at Tek Naf (see map p. 211). Two days later, on 3 November, Lieutenant Ponsonby went back to the island with Peter Young - now deputy commander of 3 SS (Commando) Brigade - and 32 marines of 'No.42(RM)' with their CO, Lieutenant-Colonel Douglas Drysdale. One marine was lost when a Burmese in the pay of the Japanese gave away the commando's position, but he shot several of the enemy before he was hit. The raiders had intended to take a prisoner but were unable to find one, and coming off their LCVP fouled her propeller on the kedge warp. This was freed by 'a gallant Indian seaman who worked for 40 minutes in the water'.

Nigel Clogstoun-Willmott has compared this tour of duty for COPPs 'as not unlike those of crews in bomber command', and so Nos. 7 and 8 were replaced in south-east Asia by Nos. 1, 3, 4 and 9. The unhealthy waters of the Arakan - plagued by disease and Japanese ambushes - took their toll of boating parties. In daylight a canoe might be easily ambushed and this limited almost all intrusion to night raids. It was on a night recce that the neat device of COPP design, to measure the rise and fall of tides over a 12-hour period, was set. Cork floats between small poles allowed the high tide to push the top cork up, where it stuck on its inverted pins, while at low water the bottom cork fell to a position where its pins held it against the rising tide. The tide height could then be checked the following night. By such ingenuity, the parties added details to the otherwise scant information on the tidal conditions and terrain of the Burma coasts. The intelligence gathered in these difficult conditions was used in the Fourteenth Army's campaigns in the Arakan, and canoeists would provide similar information for the major river crossings.

The Fourteenth Army's advance south and east through Burma was in two main directions: operation 'Capital' the advance to gain central Burma and so relieve Japanese pres-sure on the supply roads to China; and 'Dracula' the recapture of Rangoon. These campaigns were largely possible because the 20 Chindit battalions, with a few guns (a battery of 25-pounders each and a light anti-aircraft battery) and four squadrons of British and Indian Engineers, had prevented the Japanese from using their inland communications routes: had the Japanese been able to do so, they might have gathered superior forces to defeat in turn the Allied advances moving into Burma in 1944. That spring the men of Bernard Ferguson's Chindits, the 16th (Long Range Penetration) Brigade, marched 360 miles to prepare the 'box' near Indaw in north-east Burma. Here, they and other Chindit forces aided General Stilwell's Chinese divisions. As the campaigns developed, the Chindit boxes - defended camps sited where enemy artillery concentrations would be difficult to bring together - were overtaxed by Army commanders who kept them in the field long after senior Chindit officers considered the men had more than done their duty. In June, a medical survey revealed 'all ranks both British and Gurkha were physically and mentally worn out' and the brigades were withdrawn. Also in the early summer of that year (1944), the American long-range penetration group - some 3,000 men of 5307th Composite Unit, Merrill's Marauders - fought a series of battles in these hills of north-east Burma, supporting the Chinese. But the Marauders were kept in action far longer than the three months expected of troops in such an unhealthy climate, and by the end of May they had lost half their number through disease and casualties, while those still on their feet had lost an average of some 35 pounds (12kg). This unit was disbanded, as were the Chindits, but the American special force was given no encouragement by authority: they did not have a unit badge; nor were their administrative arrangements adequate for the men's rehabilitation after months in the jungle. Yet this superb effort by Chindits and Marauders paved the way for more than a flow of oil along the Ledo road pipeline to China.

The Arakan coastline was marked for the commando forces by several key features:

Stan Weatherall, one of the SBS corporals in 1941 served in cross-Channel raids, in the Mediterranean, as CSM of No. 2 SBS and as a Lieutenant with the SBS in Burma.

the island of Akyab west of the Kaladan river delta; the Myebon peninsula to its east with the Kangaw track junctions just inland; Ramree island with its port of Kyaukpyu on the island's northern tip; and Rangoon. Further south by 600 miles (965km) lay Phuket island on the Malayan coast, and another 400 miles (480km) into the Malacca Straits were the Morib beaches in the Port Dickson area (see map p. 210). The Small Operations Group made reconnaissance raids and diversions along these coasts and in the neighbouring major islands.

A typical reconnaissance was made in December 1944 when canoeists of C Group of the Special Boat Section (SBS), while under the command of 26 Indian Division, visited Law's Island. They had made a number of forays during the previous weeks, as had A Group (see Appendix 7), going into the tunnel of mangroves where river outlets were hard to find even on a moonlit night and Japanese motor sampans patrolled with searchlights. Much of their information was obtained by their guides from V Forces talking to the local natives, this Force having volunteer officers from the police or army, with each group organised in the Arakan around a platoon of the Tripura Rifles who were joined by locally raised forces. Three

successful landings had already been made on Ramree before C Group came to Law's Island a mile from Kyaukpyu's jetty. They could see the Japanese sentries and noted their routines. On the day after they landed a local fisherman was found living on the island, and Stan Weatherall, now a lieutenant in C Group, beckoned him into the cover of some scrub bushes. The native was not allowed to leave, but he seemed happy enough when the commandos treated some of his body sores. Captain Livingstone - who had also made the raid more than a year earlier on the Italian railway tunnel - went across by canoe to contact a village headman on Ramree. While he was away the fisherman's father-in-law (with their family) came to Law's Island, where he agreed to go back to Kyaukpyu and mark the Japanese defence positions on a large-scale map. This English-speaking Burmese then provided the SBS with much of the data they needed and was rewarded by a visit to Calcutta, later returning to Ramree on the bridge of a battleship, HMS *Queen Elizabeth*. By then the Japanese had withdrawn, the island was secured on 21 January 1945.

Earlier that month 3 Commando Brigade, commanded by Brigadier Campbell Hardy, had landed on Akyab in the van of the 26 Indian Division, an airborne artillery observer having realised that the Japanese had quit this island, landed to confirm their going. The advance of XV Corps was accelerated as they continued to embroil Japanese who might otherwise have been evacuated.

General Christison's objective on the Arakan coast early in 1945 was to prevent the Japanese 54 Division's 5,000 men, including the well-led Matsu Detachment, with their guns and transport, escaping through An and the An river delta. Nor did he want the Japanese armies from central Burma to escape through the An Pass for evacuation by sea. However, before their escape route could be cut, the small Japanese force on the Myebon Peninsula had to be isolated so they could not interfere with a major amphibious landing nearer Kangaw. Here the motorable track, after coming out of the hills, followed the Kangaw river into

Marine commandos land on the Myebon peninsula, Arakan, January 1945. Along this coast were wide estuaries but many creeks were only a few yards wide between the great mangrove tree roots, these could be over the men's heads when the tide was out. Crocodiles and water snakes infested these waters in the oppressive heat.

the coastal plain. A second track went south from Kangaw through Kyweguseik to Dalet and on to An. There was also a track that bypassed Kangaw before rejoining the An road at Kyweguseik. If these routes were cut, the Japanese 54 Division would be caught by the West Africans of XV Corps driving down the coast from the north.

The Brigadier made a personal recce of the beaches where his 3 Commando Brigade would land on the tip of the Myebon Peninsula, borrowing a launch from the Royal Indian Navy.

The launch returned with some casualties, but the Brigadier had personal knowledge of the beaches to amplify the canoeists' reports from earlier recces. These had shown there were heavy coconut stakes set just above the low-water line and 300 yards (270m) from the proposed landing-points. On the morning of Friday, 12 January 1945, a COPP party blasted a 25-yard gap in these stakes and at 0830 hours HMIS *Narbada* and her companion sloop HMIS *Jumna* began a bombardment, while further offshore a destroyer and cruiser (HMS *Napier* and HMS *Phoebe*) protected the assault force - 3 LCIs, 5 LCTs, 12 LCMs, and 25 other minor craft and motor boats. The bombardment and a strafe by fighter-bombers reduced the

village of Agnu to ruins before aircraft dropped smoke to cover the leading craft, with 42(RM) Commando, coming ashore.

The craft found the gap in the stakes and only one was hit by a Japanese 75mm (3in), although several other casualties were caused by mines on the beach before a beach-head was established. Attempts to land some tanks failed as the quickly ebbing tide exposed a wide stretch of mud. However, 5 Commando was ashore and passed through 'No.42(RM)'s' beach-head. The units following - including 1 and 44(RM) Commandos - were taken to the wrong beach and, in following 42(RM) Commando, took three hours to get ashore through three feet or more of 'thick slime, grey mud covered by about a foot of water' - in the words of SQMS Henry Brown. Many men stripped off their clothes, and all their weapons needed cleaning. The plans for developing the beach-head had not been cut and dried, as little was known of the Japanese dispositions, but 'elaborate loading tables' had been worked out by Douglas Drysdale and Tony Pigot. These provided, in Peter Young's view, an example of excellent staff work. Peter Young came ashore on a rocky little beach west of the promontory, getting ashore dry shod on what would become the vehicle landing beach. Elements of 50 Brigade of the 25 Indian Division followed the commandos into both beaches, while 5 Commando advanced through thick jungle to a point some 800 yards (.7km) south-west of Myebon village. They were held by machine-gun fire from a hill they code-named 'Rose', and the rest of the day was spent getting the Brigade's ashore. In four hours, Madras Sappers, with a company of Gurkha porters, humped material by muscle power to build a road from the vehicle beach to the main landing-point, enabling three Shermans - a fourth had bogged down on the main beach mud - to join the Commando Brigades advance next morning.

After a dawn air strafe, 5 Commando, with the support of these 19th Indian Lancers' tanks, took hill 'Rose'. Without long-range anti-tank guns the Japanese could not prevent the tanks wreaking havoc among their defence positions. As 1 Commando advanced along the main ridge, 42(RM) Commando passed through Myebon village, which was unoccupied although they met stiff fire from three hills to the north. The tanks came forward, helping to clear these defences, but Lieutenant-Colonel H. David Fellowes, commanding the marines, was wounded and several of his men became casualties. After refuelling and re-arming, the tanks came back on to a pagoda-topped hill to help 1 Commando clear another hilltop bunker. In advancing with great dash, one tank turned turtle on the steep hillside, rolling over and over but without serious injury to the Sherman's crew. The Brigade then moved into Kantha, straddling a *chaung*. The Japanese had abandoned this village, although they kept the Commandos under sniper fire for the next three days. The Commando Brigade had lost four killed and 38 wounded in driving a path for 74 Brigade, who passed over the Kantha *chaung* to establish a defended area north of the peninsula. The assault on Kangaw could now begin.

Kangaw lies only eight miles (13km) from Myebon up the Myebon river, but this was covered by Japanese artillery, and a surprise approach was planned up the tortuous waterways of the Thegyan river and Daingbon *chaung*. This 27-mile (43km) approach route reached the target beaches where the *chaung* was only 100 yards wide, about half a mile (800+m) from the key defence hill to

the village, which lay a further mile from the river. The ridge of this wooded hill ran north-south above paddy fields surrounded by seemingly endless swamps. Spot height(?) '170' on the Brigade's maps, it overlooked Kangaw from the west. The plan was to land 1 Commando about noon on Monday, 22 January, to seize the hill, while 'No.42(RM)' held both banks of the Daingbon *chaung*. 5 Commando would follow 'No.1', consolidating the hold on the hill and so enabling 44(RM) Commando to advance against the village on D+1. The support for the landing included the by now usual air strafes, shelling from the two Indian sloops, with *Jumna* in the Myebon river and *Narbada* in the Thegyn river, artillery support from the Myebon peninsula, and field guns on Z lighters - 134-foot (40m) lighters designed for off-loading ships in harbour, but used on Burmese rivers as floating platforms for a troop of 25-pounders.

On the morning of 22 January the long convoys of assault craft, led by minesweepers, small support craft and motor boats, moved up the river and into the *chaung*. They were not seen. The route was not mined, although the line of boats 'stretched as far as the eye could see'. The leading craft of 1 Commando touched down at 1300 hours under a smokescreen laid by aircraft, and the commandos moved quickly between two small streams towards the hill. There had been some shelling as they neared the landing-point, but Allied air attacks, synchronised with the Commando's advance, enabled them to clear much of the hill with only three killed and nine wounded. By nightfall they more or less held this Hill 170, with 1 Commando on all but the hill's northern end, and 5 Commando with Brigade HQ on its southern slopes. 42(RM) and 44(RM) Commandos found their positions deep in mud and so waterlogged that the only way to build roads was by scooping out mud which, when partially dry, formed bunds - embankments above the tide levels. Moreover, because the beaches were no more than gaps in the mangroves, through which vehicles could not be used, the stores had to be manhandled. Even more serious was the lack of fresh water. The marines

Commandos move for cover when shelled during an attack on Hill 170, Kangaw.

moved forward on to Milford and Pinner, the hills east of '170', but for some unexplained reason three Troops of 44(RM) Commando did not properly dig in on Pinner.

The Japanese reaction came that night in an unsuccessful attack on Pinner. Next morning, Tuesday (D+1) at about 1000 hours, a fierce attack on '170' was beaten off, but the marines on Pinner fared badly. Their slit-trenches were only a few feet deep for the marines had not used the Japanese trenches 'as the enemy knew the position of these', despite the fact that they provided good cover. When a Japanese 75-gun came within close range, with great calmness Lieutenant-Colonel A. Stockley walked among his men before he withdrew them to Hill 170 - they had more than 60 casualties. Later 1 Commando, with artillery support, cleared the northern end of the ridge, getting a Troop in defensive positions beyond the saddle that divided this northerly point from the main positions. In the following days many of the shells falling on commandos' positions were dud - 19 out of one stream of 21 shots - possibly due to their storage in tropical conditions, or to the poor quality of Japanese munitions at this stage of the war.

Certainly the Japanese were heavily engaged in many theatres. In the Philippines, the Americans had overwhelmed them on Leyte and were closing in on the 80,000 Japanese defending a pocket in the more northerly Philippine island of Luzon, 1,000 miles (1,600km) east of Kangkaw. Still further east the US Marines would land on Iwo Jima in February, bringing them within 650 miles of Tokyo. In Burma, the Four-teenth Army's corps on the central front were poised to cross the Irrawaddy. The Japanese Imperial General Headquarters prepared for a war of attrition against Japan, believing that victory would go to the nations that accepted the increasing hardships when the war dragged on. They were, therefore, trying to extricate their forces where possible to build up the home defences, and in pursuit of this Lieutenant-General Miyazaki ordered the Matsu Detachment to keep the Kangaw route open. Therefore, although the 51 Indian Brigade had been brought ashore and held Melrose (a hill to the east of the Kangaw track), and there were a troop of the 19th Indian Lancers' Shermans ashore despite the difficulties in landing them, the Japanese began to mount attacks on Hill 170. If these succeeded, the already difficult supply of the 51 Brigade would become impossible.

On 31 January, the heaviest barrage for some time fell on No.4 Troop of 1 Commando who were beyond the saddle at the north end of the '170' ridge. Following the barrage came a determined infantry attack up the thickly wooded northern slope, breaking over No.4 Troop's positions. Counter-attacks by elements of 1 and 42 Commando failed to relieve the pressure, but in the afternoon two Troops of 5 Commando restored the position. By this time three of the 19th Lancer's tanks were on the western slope of the ridge but were stopped by marshy ground. By nightfall, the Commando Brigade's position was serious but more or less stable. For the Japanese, the tanks posed a serious problem and next morning they infiltrated 70 engineers to hunt them. Getting behind the Commando Brigade HQ they set their charges against two tanks, despite the efforts of a platoon of

Bombay Grenadiers who killed one Japanese officer on a tank and saw another killed in the blast of his own pole-charge. The rest of this suicide party were killed during the morning.

Men of the Matsu Detachment put in a series of equally desperate attacks on the positions of No.4 Troop. Their long French-style bayonets, dumpy figures, and mediaeval helmets made them appear like men from another world to one English commander. They overran nine three-man slit-trenches but were held by No.4 Troop. The Troop Officer, Lieutenant George A. Knowland, rallied his men and with the 24 commandos of his forward Section set up a defence, into which a few reinforcements came forward from the rear Section. George Knowland moved from slit-trench to slit-trench firing his rifle and throwing grenades, bringing forward ammunition at one moment, firing a bren the next until its wounded crew could be replaced. Firing this bren from the hip he distracted the Japanese long enough for stretcher bearers to bring out the wounded, including the new team for the bren, all hit as they tried to get forward. He was seen firing a 2-inch (51mm) mortar, its base against a tree as he launched the bombs into the teeth of another Japanese attack. When all the mortar bombs were used he picked up a tommy-gun but was killed around 0830 when the positions were overrun. However, the Japanese never dislodged the rest of 1 Commando from the higher ground behind the saddle, and George Knowland was posthumously awarded the Victoria Cross.

The Japanese placed machine-guns on the spurs of the ridge and beat back three separate attacks - two by No.6 Troop of 1 Commando, who lost half the Troop, and one by a Troop from 'No.42(RM)'. Twelve men were hit in succession at one bren position covering these assaults before the last Sherman still in action, its periscope shot away, got near the saddle in the afternoon and put shells fifty yards ahead of the exhausted remnants of No.4 Troop. At dusk, in the short tropic twilight, Thunderbolt fighter-bombers attacked the Japanese positions. These were deserted the next day

when 5 Commando cleared the hill. The Commando Brigade lost 45 men killed and 90 wounded in what Lieutenant-General Christison described as their 'magnificent courage on Hill 170'. The divisions of XV Corps were moving in, and the Matsu Detachment with the Japanese 154th Regiment Group withdrew, having prevented the destruction of their Division, which still held An Pass. But 300 Japanese dead were counted around No.4 Troop's positions.

3 Commando Brigade were withdrawn to India where they prepared to spearhead further landings in Malaya. Peter Young left them about this time to take command of 1 Commando Brigade in the United Kingdom. In preparation for these further landings, the Small Operations Group carried out a number of recces and diversions, the most ambitious of these reconnasisances being made on Phuket island near the narrow neck of land joining Thailand to Malaya. After the Allies entered Rangoon in an unopposed landing this was to be the next stage in the containment of Japanese forces in south-east Asia. Plans for the invasion of Malaya were being prepared while the Arakan was being cleared, and as the reconnaissances for the Malayan operations would possibly reveal Allied intentions too precisely, a series of diversionary raids were mounted by Detachment 385 under the command of the Small Operations Group. Other teams from SOG had already put ashore 'jitter' parties to keep the Japanese guessing where the next river crossing might be. B Group of the SBS had reconnoitred the Chindwin river crossing among other chores for the 11 (East African) Division between 11 November and 13 December of 1944. Men of the SBS and Sea Reconnaissance Unit (SRU) had carried out similar work for Indian divisions' crossings of the Irrawaddy in February 1945, when the canoeists also acted as guides to the craft approaching enemy riverbanks. And later that spring SBS and SRU parties on the Irrawaddy worked with 7 Indian Division, who held the right (west) flank of the 120-mile (190km) front after XXXIII Corps crossed this great river at four points. But by May, when monsoon rains made the river

unnavigable for their small craft, the canoeists and swimmers were withdrawn.

The SOG's teams visiting Phuket island were led by Major Ian Mackenzie RE, who had been in the Normandy landings the previous summer when he guided ashore the 13/18 Hussars' DD-swimming tanks on to Sword beach. The recce was intended to locate and assess air landing strips, so two RAF officers went with the teams of canoeists and engineers. After a 1,200-mile (1,900km) voyage in the submarines HMS *Torbay* and HMS *Thrasher*, No.3 COPP (Alex Hughes) made a periscope reconnaissance on the afternoon of 8 March, seeing some tents and huts near the beach. Nevertheless, they paddled in that night from *Torbay* but the three-man canoe carrying Flight-Lieutenant Guthrie RAF, Captain Johns RE, and Sergeant Camidge RE became separated from the pair of two-man canoes. Alex Hughes lost touch with Captain Alcock, a Canadian, but both these canoes made their way back to the submarine. They had seen lights and activity in the Papra Channel, no doubt when the Japanese were passing supply lighters up the coast. Next night, when the two canoes came back, all these lights and others along the coast were out. Sentries no longer flashed their torches but the Thai garrison - nominally allied to the Japanese - had men on the beach who were heard thudding over the sand. The swimmers completed their survey and came out.

What happened to the three men in the larger canoe was learnt after the war. She capsized and was pushed ashore, Captain Johns and Sergeant Camidge being shot as they dived for the cover of the jungle when some sentries came up. Flight-Lieutenant Guthrie managed to hide for a day, but the next night he was spent and walked into a Thai village where he was captured.

Ian Mackenzie had taken ashore his three canoes of Detachment 385 from HMS *Thrasher* intending to stay on shore for three days. His party left four men with Major J. Maxwell RM to guard the canoes and had made a recce of the airstrip, taking photographs and gathering soil samples, when on their first night ashore they were questioned by Thai police. Fishermen had seen the canoe camp where the raiders were spending the night. While Ian Mackenzie parleyed with the police as he was made to strip, a fire-fight developed and the Major skipped naked into the scrub. For the next 17 days the party made a series of attempts to reach the safety of several pre-arranged rendezvous off both north and south coasts of the island, but in brushes with Japanese patrols all were killed or captured. Marine B.P. Brownlie died when caught between two patrols after being ashore nearly three weeks. Major Maxwell and Colour-Sergeant Smith were executed in Singapore, along with another officer from SOG teams, in July 1945. Ian Mackenzie, Flight-Lieutenant B. Brown, and Corporal R.A. Atkinson were more fortunate: being prisoners of the Thais they survived captivity. This major disaster for SOG teams has been attributed by one expert to their attempt to land too large a party, for 20 men ashore were bound to attract the attention of local people. Although the submarines kept three rendezvous, the last nine days after the landing, and Alex Hughes and Captain Alcock paddled along the shore one night, the alternative evacuations failed probably because the men ashore were unable to find the correct rendezvous.

At times the SOG teams courted local attention, and on the night of 18 April canoeists from '385' landed on Kamorta island in the Nicobars, over 300 miles (480 km) west of Phuket island. In the bright moonlight they steered a course towards Expedition Harbour to deceive any coast watchers who might have seen them as they came in from the submarine about an hour after midnight. They were in canoes and an Intruder inflatable with a spare Intruder that was 'inflated on the way in - hell of a noise made by valves'. No one was on the beach, although they found many footprints and their CO records 'I . . . smelt natives (you've no idea how it smelt) . . .' They moved west along the jungle edge, with the men in two canoes ready to give covering fire from their Stens as the patrol from the Intruder made their way along the soft sand shore, but as they were in a confined area they did not stay ashore. Their CO, having

A submersible canoe developed by Camper & Nicholsons' boat yard and the RMBPD, used in only one south-east Asian operation.

sent the men back to the Intruder, fired several shots inland, but as no one came to investigate, after 15 minutes he moved back to the boat. There he fired more shots and 'threw a grenade which failed to explode (bad maintenance!) . . .'. They left the spare Intruder ashore with a rip in its bottom, a copy of an intelligence questionnaire, a chart trace of the island, and some small items of stores. In all this detachment made some 17 raids, including their visit with No.3 COPP to Phuket island. They frequently landed from a specially designed 20-foot (6m) surf-boat with low freeboard and a 5hp petrol engine that was 'quite easy to handle'. They were also landed from Catalina flying boats - a method pioneered in the Mediterranean - fitted with a platform from which quick release Mark III** canoes or inflatables were launched. On one of their raids they brought off a British officer and 20 Chins (of Force V?) who had made a 28-day patrol, having not eaten for the last five days. They were some 150 miles (240km) south of Akyab on the Bassein coast, the marines of '385' on this occasion working with MLs of the Bengal Auxiliary Flotilla.

In June 1945 Alex Hughes took No.3 COPP ashore with eight men in four canoes, landing on Morib beaches near Port Dickson where an amphibious assault by XXXIV Corps was planned to land over three beaches. The COPP obtained a detailed cross-section of the beach, including underwater gradients at several points, notes on the bearing surface of the beach with samples from above and below the waterline, and notes on the runnels above the water level. Details of underwater runnels and of a spit off the beach, tide heights and rates were recorded. A periscope photograph showing the beach silhouette was taken, and

information was gathered on enemy coast watchers. When the canoes returned to their submarine, HMS *Seadog*, two were missing, a search failed to find them. But after some weeks with their new Allies, a ruthless crowd who burnt suspected spies with logs during interrogation before beheading them, the four COPPists reached home.

By the time the war ended - the Japanese signed an armistice on 14 August 1945 after the atom bombs had dropped - the commando boating parties had perfected a submersible canoe, but so far as I can trace this was used in only one operation, in the South China Sea by COPP or SOE in September 1944. Airborne canoeists were also trained in the use of a folding canoe parachuted with them into the sea or a lake as the starting point for a raid.

Summarising the Burma campaigns in the British official history - *The War Against Japan* Volume IV, p.430, HMSO - the authors point to the relatively few large formations of Special Forces employed in late 1944 and 1945 by comparison with those in the field in the spring and early summer of 1944. They feel this bears out General Sir Claude Auchinleck and General Sir George Giffard's contention that 'a well-trained standard division could carry out any operational task with little special training, and underlines the waste of manpower in forming forces fitted for particular tasks which, as opportunities for their use in the role for which they are designed are likely to be limited, may spend the greater part of the period of hostilities in inactivity'. I will come back to these arguments in the final chapter, but before considering them, the exploits of the 6th Rangers in the Philippines illustrate the value of Special Forces, albeit created from a regular unit.

# THE PHILIPPINES, 1944 TO 1945

Although the last few headhunters were still practising their rites until just after World War II, the people of the Philippine islands 600 miles (960km) from China, had been in contact with Europeans since at least the 16th century. Among these diverse people, some Americans escaped from Bataan in 1942, and led guerrilla bands over the vast mountain ranges and 7,100 islands that abound in the 114,830 square miles covered by the Philippines.

The Japanese, ruling through the Philippine government, had some success in restraining guerrilla activity, but the insurgents' attacks on informers and spies in part obliged the population to support the guerrillas; when the Americans landed, there were 20,000 on Luzon alone.

Liberating the Philippines would place the Americans across the Japanese supply routes for oil and other raw materials from Indonesia. Therefore, after securing their approaches from possible air attack, American forces from the central Pacific joined with General MacArthur's men from the south-west in landings at Leyte Gulf on 20 October 1944. They advanced rapidly. At sea, a few nights after the landing, the Americans drove off Japanese warships in the last major action between surface ships during World War II. The Japanese kamikaze pilots, however, attacked both fleet and transports with some success.

Belatedly the Japanese decided to fight the decisive battle for the Philippines on Leyte and brought in reinforcements through Ormoc. For a time the Americans were held by difficult and easily defended terrain, but on 7 December the US 77 Division landed four miles (6km) south of this major base and Ormoc fell on 10 December, the island being secured by the end of the month.

Mindoro (262 air miles, 420km north of Leyte) was captured on 15 December as an airbase to cover the landings to be made in Lingayen Gulf on Luzon. Little resistance was met on Mindoro, nor on 9 January 1945 were the initial Lingayen Gulf landings seriously opposed, for on Luzon the Japanese had insufficient troops to defend the central plain - let alone the whole island - after reinforcing Leyte. Kamikaze planes and 70 small suicide boats made the only attacks on the transports in the Gulf.

The Japanese withdrew to strongholds in the mountains north, east and south of the plain. Manila fell to the Americans in mid-March, but the island was not completely cleared of defenders, despite some 50,000 Japanese being killed by guerrillas, in addition to those killed by regular forces. On Luzon, as elsewhere, many Japanese defences were either taken at leisure or left to surrender after the August atom bombing of Japan and the Japanese capitulation on 14 August 1945.

Men of the 6th Rangers on the move towards Cabantuan prison camp, January 1945.

# 13 PHILIPPINE ADVENTURE

Three minesweepers headed through rough seas into Leyte Gulf on the morning of 17 October 1944. They were followed by five APDs, the assault destroyers carrying companies of the 6th Rangers, their attached field hospital, and the 10th Signal Platoon. The gales of the previous few days had abated and as the naval task force began their bombardment in clear weather at 0900 hours, the assault craft were already running in towards the north-west shore of Dinagat island south of Leyte 43 miles (69km) long and some 8 miles (14km) wide with a wooded north-south ridge rising to 3,000 feet (1,000m) in the north. The beaches appeared ideal for a landing as these first Allied ground troops redeemed General MacArthur's promise to 'come back to the Philippines'. But as they neared the shore the craft, probing their way slowly through narrow channels in a coral reef, grounded 100 yards from the beach. The rangers waded ashore, some being tumbled over by the heavy surf, others falling into deep holes probably made by the earlier bombardment, and at least one man advanced into the jungle with only his trench-knife and hand-grenades.

By 1230 hours all the companies were ashore and the Battalion command-post established. A Company and an attached B Company of the US 21st Infantry Battalion formed a beach-head perimeter while C, E, and F' Companies moved north along the coast towards Desolation Point. Within half an hour they came on an enemy camp near Kanamong Point, some two miles (3km) north of the landing-beach, and found the bivouac had been abandoned in great haste. The Japanese - as they did in most retreats - had left scattered about many papers, from which the unit was identified as the island's garrison; its two roles were reporting air and sea activity, and attempting to secure the island against guerrillas. There was no opposition, except from Japanese aircraft, the rangers in the beach-head were able next day to continue unloading stores.

They had landed three days before A-day (the American equivalent of their Allies' D-day). Dinaget was 50 miles (80km) from the main Japanese base on Leyte, and although the Battalion had no anti-aircraft guns ashore, and were uncertain of the enemy's strength, 'there was no evidence . . . of undue concern among the men'. They had waited two years for action and under Colonel Henry Mucci were 'old soldiers', for the 6th Rangers were formed initially from men of the 98th Field Artillery Battalion.

That afternoon, Wednesday (A-2, 18 October), the companies came back from Desolation Point, having found the pill-boxes abandoned on this northern tip of the island. Repassing the empty camp at Kanamong Point, they had time to search it thoroughly, and a folded American flag was found in a Japanese officer's locker. His souvenir was the first Old Glory recovered in these islands.

During the two days of Tuesday and Wednesday (A-3 and A-2), other rangers had been on Homonhon island (to east) where B Company landed, and some 12 miles (19km) further east, on Suluan island, D Company were ashore. Both companies destroyed enemy radar and observation posts, and were looking for plans that might show that land-fired sea mines were expected in Leyte Gulf. However, there were no such mines. The detached companies rejoining the Battalion, the company of the 21st Infantry re-embarked. That same Wednesday afternoon, C Company returned to Desolation Point to guard naval personnel setting up navigation aids for the main fleet of transports. In the early evening, about 1800 hours, Captain Hemingway, an American Air Force officer at the time of the Bataan surrender in April 1942, came into the beach-head with 36 of his men. The rangers were the first Americans he had seen in more than two years as a Filipino guerrilla leader. He confirmed that the Japanese garrison force was the only one on the island, although from time to time others came across in small boats from the mainland. However, apparently only the garrison force infiltrated the position of C Company around the Point that night before being driven off, leaving one man dead.

On Thursday morning (A-1) both A and D Companies were taken on the USS *Crosby*, APD-17, six miles (10km) down the coast to the village port of Loreto. They received a friendly reception, spending a couple of hours in the area, and learnt that the Japanese had not been there for about eight weeks.

On 20 October landings began on Leyte's eastern shore where the US X Corps landed at 1000 hours south of Tacloban at the head of the gulf. Air raids over the rangers' beach-head stopped for a few days as the Japanese concentrated their efforts on the main assault force, drawing off the American carrier fleet. A second Japanese naval force came up the Surigao Straits between Dinagat and Leyte, but the battleship *Yamashiro* was lost with almost all her crew in an action with American battleships. Many Japanese sailors struggled ashore near Loreto, where C Company were stationed to prevent Japanese reinforcements joining the Dinagat garrison which had taken to the hills, and the company spent a couple of days rounding up the shipwrecked sailors, many of whom, once ashore were armed and ready to fight. Some escaped into the jungle, but 10 were captured. While they were being shipped to Leyte, two Japanese planes attacked the LCI transport and almost half the crew were killed or wounded, Ranger Technician Fifth Starkovich was also wounded and his fellow prisoners' guard, Technician Third Roth, manned one of the craft's .50in (13mm) machine-guns.

The weather in the Philippines was constantly wet through October when the 6th Battalion was patrolling from Loreto, the men being supplied by dugout canoes sailing from the original beach-head. Patrolling through deep swamps, in heavy jungle, and on steep mountainsides led to most of the men having skin infected with fungus; many had worn through the soles of their boots. Nevertheless, morale was high, and the first issue of candy and tobacco came in on 31 October when a supply of ten-in-one rations also made a welcome change from C rations. Fresh medical supplies for the 10th Portable Hospital, who had landed with the rangers, were parachuted in on 12 November.

Throughout the rest of the winter campaign in the Philippines the 6th Rangers were involved in various patrols and a further amphibious landing (see Appendix 7). One significant raid during this period sums up much of the concept of Special Forces, with their commando-style training for rapid movement over difficult and defended country, and their ability to work with irregular forces. The American Sixth Army had reached Guimba in its drive south-east across Luzon's central plain, having landed on the west coast at the head of the Lingayen Gulf on 9 January 1945. It was across these beaches of this northern island of the group that, almost four years earlier, the Japanese had landed in their invasion of the Philippines. The Japanese in 1945 had insufficient forces to hold the plain, but they planned to delay the American advance, while at the same time withdrawing into prepared mountain strongholds, one of which was north of the American thrust. As

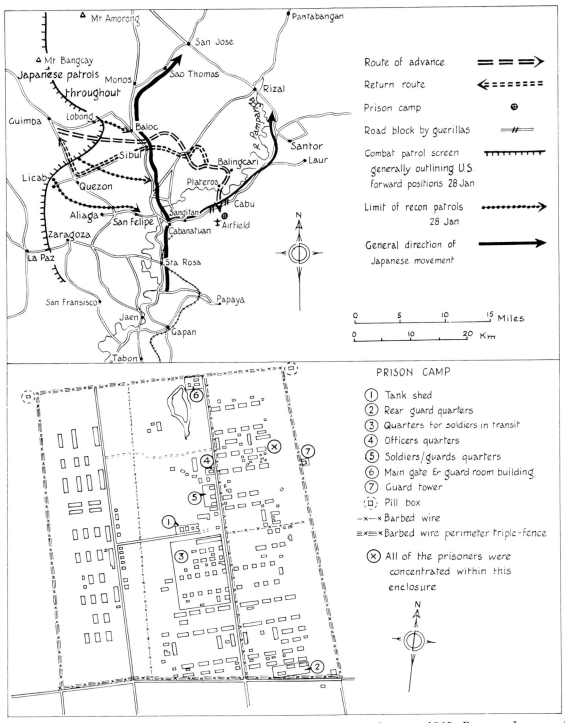

Top: 6th Rangers' route to Japanese Cabanatuan prison camp, January 1945. Bottom: Layout of Cabanatuan prison camp, January 1945.

these and other Japanese forces moved across their front, the Americans learnt of a prisoner-of-war camp near Cabanatuan in the eastern part of the plain, and the 6th Rangers were detailed to rescue the prisoners before they could be evacuated or worse.

Henry Mucci chose C Company, commanded by his 'wonderful Captain' Robert W. Prince. How often a particular Company or Troop appears throughout this history doing key jobs, frequently for the very good reason that their captain had created an extremely reliable unit. The Colonel went with C Company, reinforced by the 2nd Platoon of F Company - 121 men in all - with some borrowed bazookas and anti-tank grenades from the US 6 Infantry Division. By January 1945, Special Forces found no great difficulty in acquiring the tools they needed for a particular job, although they were still essentially light infantry. The reinforced Company set out at 0500 hours on Sunday, 28 January, in trucks that took them to the guerrilla headquarters of Captain Joson near Lobong, where his 80 men joined the force before they moved into enemy territory about three miles (5km) south of Baloc. Fording the Talavera river at midnight, they reached the Rizal road by 0400 hours next morning (Monday). American combat patrols covered five or so miles (about 8km) into the area, while on Sunday 28 January two reconnaissance patrols had probed a further 10 miles (16km) into the flanks of the Japanese withdrawal through guerrilla country.

During Monday, 29 January, the rangers bivouacked after reaching Balingcari at 0600 hours. They were given a meal by the villagers - roast chicken served in banana leaves. Captain Pajota commanded the guerrillas in this area, and 90 of his armed men, with 160 others who would act as porters, joined the force. However, they did not have all the information Henry Mucci needed to know about the prison stockade, and so he decided to wait until the return of the Alamo Scouts - American soldiers specially trained for reconnaissance often behind enemy lines. In the evening, about 1800 hours, these two scouts came into Plateros, where the raiders were now concentrated, and

reported that 500 Japanese were guarding the camp. They had also discovered a Japanese division moving up the road through Cabu, so no raid could be made until these troops had passed to the north. The action was put off until next day. In the morning, Tuesday 30 January, the Alamo Scouts and Lieutenant Tombo of the guerrillas made a detailed recce of the prison defences and, with the help of local civilians, were able to bring back details for a sketch plan of the camp. The Colonel made his plans that afternoon, knowing that the prisoners were in a fenced enclosure at the north-eastern part of the camp; its pill-boxes covered the north-east and north-west corners of the stockade around all the camp buildings, and there was a guarded main northern gate, plus guards at the rear gate and a guard tower on the eastern stockade perimeter.

To seal off the raiders from interference, two roadblocks would go in, with Captain Joson's guerrillas and a six-man ranger bazooka team under Sergeant White blocking the road 800 yards (.8km) south-west of the camp. It would be their job to stop any Japanese traffic moving north from Cabanatuan a town of some 9,000 people. While Captain Pajota's guerrillas blocked the road near Cabu bridge, a mile (1.6km) north of the camp, from where they could hold off the 800 Japanese in Cabu, F Company's 2nd Platoon (Lieutenant John F. Murphy), coming from the south, were to invest the guards' quarters behind the enclosure just west of the inner wire, with Staff-Sergeant Millican and six men taking the north-west pill-box. Lieutenant William J. O'Connell's 1st Platoon (C Company) would attack the front entrance, one Section attacking the gate and guardroom while the second Section gave covering fire through the stockade to the right (west). Other details were worked out so that each man knew exactly which enemy building he was specifically to attack or fire into. Such careful planning made in the field without the aid of a large staff had become a feature of Special Forces, but it was not the everyday practice of regular forces, although they certainly had officers capable of such feats. However, with the commandos and rangers, *every* officer was trained to plan in the field for out-of-the-ordinary roles.

In developing the Company's attack, the 1st Platoon's Weapon Section would follow the rifle Section through the gate to fire bazooka rockets into the tank sheds, corrugated buildings which also held trucks in which Japanese reinforcements might - and did - use to reach their alarm stations. As the bazooka teams moved forward, the covering fire for the gate party would lift, and the covering Section would move quickly into the camp to prevent any guards breaking through from the west into the prisoners' enclosure. The 2nd Platoon (Lieutenant Melville D. Schmidt) was to pass through the gate, break open the enclosure, and fire into the buildings already under fire from the platoon to the south. The 2nd Platoon's Weapon Section would bring out the POWs. The whole operation demanded a stealthy approach to ensure surprise, but once John Murphy's platoon opened fire from the rear (south) of the camp, saving the prisoners depended on speed. This difficult stealthy approach, followed by an action too quickly brought off for the enemy to react, epitomises the commando-style operation when *every* man had to be fit enough and skilled enough to play his part. Had one group of rangers failed, the Japanese could have killed their prisoners, or most of them in moments.

With the guerrillas protecting their flanks, the rangers began to move into position around the camp stockade at about 1800 hours that Tuesday evening. The going was slow for the ground was open, but in the gathering darkness C Company reached the ditch about 20 yards across a road in front of the main gate and were ready to go by 1925 hours. They had 20 minutes of tense waiting under cover until John Murphy's platoon opened fire. Guerrillas cut the camp telephone wires at this moment.

The Japanese in the north-west pill-box were killed, as were those on the main gate, in the living-quarters, and on the watch-tower. The tower sentry remained upright for a split second after he was hit, then he crumpled backwards flinging his rifle

involuntarily from the tower. The assault platoons broke through the main gate. Four tanks and two trucks - loading with men at the time - were knocked out. Everything went to plan, the prisoners being guided down to the main entrance while several rangers destroyed the radios they had been detailed to find. Many of the prisoners were extremely ill and had to be carried pickaback from the camp; most were silent when the rangers first arrived - years of Japanese camp life had taken its effect - but freedom quickly revived the fitter men. Although the rangers' dress was unfamiliar to those who had been prisoners since 1942, the gentleness of their rescuers revived memories of a happier life and soon the prisoners shouted 'They're Americans'. The buildings had been searched before Bob Prince (CO of C Company) fired the first red flare signalling the start of the withdrawal at 2015. The raid had been completed in 30 minutes.

When the column was a mile from the camp, Bob Prince fired the second red flare, telling the guerrillas the roadblocks could withdraw. Captain Joson brought his men out of the southern block, coming in behind the rangers, but to the north Captain Pajota's men were fighting off a strong force - not 800 but 2,000 by one report. This was held for another hour till the column was clear of the Cabu road, then the guerrillas formed a second flank rearguard. Local civilian *caraboa* carts were ready for the disabled ex-prisoners across the Pampanga river, but first the rangers and their guerrilla helpers had to get these men across the waist-deep, swift-flowing river. The invalids survived this crossing but two men died of heart attacks on the journey to safety, despite the care of the guerrilla Doctor Layug and his teams' medical treatment in the school building at Plateros.

At 2100 hours, the first 115 ex-prisoners were on the move to Balingcari, many in carts: in all there were 513 ex-prisoners to be brought the 25 miles (40km) from their old camp to the American lines. By 0200 hours as the column passed through Matasna Kahog, there were 51 carts in a one and a half mile (2.4km) column winding its way towards the Rizal road. The column's route

A ranger and one of the ex-prisoners of war rescued at Cabanatuan, Luzon, January 1945.

took them for half a mile down this highway, which the 1st Platoon sealed off with road-blocks 800 yards each side of the crossing and one 400 yards (365m) south of the point where the column left the road. Through this defence screen the carts took an hour and a half to clear the road, the last man coming through at 0430 hours. An hour later a short halt was made in a small village area *(bario)* but several attempts to establish radio contact with the Sixth Army units failed. This was not achieved until after the column reached Sibul at 0800 (Wednesday, 31 January), and then a fleet of ambulances was brought up the dusty road to evacuate the rescued. When the ex-POWs were safe, the rangers were the first to pay tribute to the Filipino guerrillas who had enabled them to reach and leave the camp, and to the local population who fed them and gave other help. The Ranger Platoons had lost one man killed at the camp, and another 26 - including guerrillas and the Rangers' doctor, the very popular Captain Fisher - were killed in the withdrawal.

Six months later the war ended and commandos and rangers began to be demobilised; the first 139 men left the 6th Rangers on 20 August within a week of the Japanese surrender, and in the United Kingdom the Commando Demobilisation Centre had been set up at Wrexham. For the 6th Rangers there was a spell in Japan; they loaded their gear - typically under pouring rain - on 15 September, leaving Luzon a few days later, and landing near Honshu in Japan, wet shod over the Wakayama beach, in the late afternoon of 25 September. Their victory was not contested during the follow-ing weeks: the 'people are very docile and cooperative', the 6th Battalion's unit history records. Although the barracks allocated to them were 'lousy with fleas and rats', these were soon cleaned up to be renamed Camp Fisher after their late medical officer. Near the end of November, the 6th Rangers had their final parade before General Krueger and General Eddleman, and were stood down - became inactive - on 30 December. The Army's Commando Brigades were dis-banded, the last, 1/5 Commando, during January 1947 in Hong Kong - but the Royal Marines carry on the commando tradition to this day.

# ONE ENEMY'S REACTION TO THE COURAGE OF RAIDERS

Ten canoeists, including survivors of a fighting retreat after an SBS raid attempted to sink Singapore shipping, were sentenced to death on 5 July 1945. Among them were Australian and British soldiers, sailors and marines of whom the Japanese prosecutor said:

'With such fine determination they infiltrated into the Japanese area. We do not hesitate to call them real heroes of a forlorn hope ... when we fathom their intention and share their feelings we cannot but spare a tear for them. The valorous spirit of these men reminds us of the daring enterprise of our heroes of the Naval Special Attack Corps. The respect ... the Australian people showed to those heroes we must return to these heroes in our presence. When the deed is so heroic, its sublime spirit must be respected, and its success or failure becomes a secondary matter ...'

The prisoners were executed on 7 July and 'every member of the party went to his death calmly and composedly and there was not a single person there who was not inspired by their fine attitude.'

# 14 ACHIEVEMENTS AND LIMITATIONS

There is no doubt of the commandos', rangers' and other Special Forces' great courage. The doubts expressed in 1940 and in some quarters today (1977) are whether this wealth of human valour should be concentrated in elite units or spread more evenly through *conscript* battalions. The judgement must be made, I believe, in the context of wartime campaigns and not in comparisons with peace-time regiments able to select recruits to 'carry out any operational task with little special training' and be 'raiders organised as a standard infantry regiment' suiting operational planners. The wartime battalions included - as they do in all global wars - some reluctant soldiers, some not fully fit, and men over forty years of age. But when every man has to keep up in a speed march, every rifleman react quickly and correctly to counter enemy fire, then the disinterested, the unfit and the old are weak links that can break a chain around enemy positions. This may not be important when other battalions are close by, but is vital in independent actions. Special Forces also spurred on many a unit to adopt commando training methods in preparation to emulate their feats for the Normandy invasion. While the Ranger Battalions' example was followed by so-called ranger squads trained within infantry battalions for the more difficult parts of infantry actions.

Commandos also provided opportunities for individuals to use their initiative, while in the necessarily more hidebound battalions such independence of mind may have to be discouraged. The conscripts' training and fighting is to tight rules suited to those without imagination, but creating an atmosphere of regulations the independent spirits find stifling. Yet in a major war you need every man to give of his best, and forming commando-type units is one of the few ways some men with imagination and an independent mind may be drawn into infantry service. There is also the advantage of their special units providing a source of specialists for small units like COPPs, the SBS and other small-scale raiding forces. But there are obvious limitations to the extent to which you can denude conscript battalions of men with initiative, who are the main source of junior leaders.

The criticisms of the commando idea of elite troops trained for special roles all turn on matters of degree: the numbers you bring together as commandos or rangers in one operational unit. While larger formations, like the 18,000 or so Chindits, can - as Field Marshall Slim has written - encourage 'the idea that certain operations of war were so difficult that only a specially equipped *corps d'élite* could be expected to undertake them ... [yet] armies do not win wars by means of a few bodies of super-soldiers but by the average quality of the standard unit'. That said, the Field Marshal made no criticism of the independent operations of a Commando with less than 500 although he considered that 'any single operation in which more than a handful of men were engaged should be regarded as [a] normal

The sophisticated weapons for the planned assault on Japan included the LVTs with six 4.5in (115mm) electrically fired rockets, in the 34th Amphibian Support Regiment, RM.

[operation]', in this regard he appears to have considered a 'handful' to be a few hundred men as at St Nazaire, Dieppe coast batteries, Port en Bessin, Brac, Alethangyaw, at Pointe du Hoc and Cabanatuan. Each was an operation needing skills a conscript battalion would have found hard to learn well enough for success in the time available to mount the operations. While the limited number of Commando units and Ranger Battalions in World War II - never more than the equivalent of 20 infantry battalions at any one time - can hardly be said to have impaired the officer corps in the Allied armies of several millions.

Taking the Commando-type operation as one of a special nature in night infiltration, perhaps, or with difficult cliff climbing routes, or unexpected political complications, the men engaged need more than the run-of-the-mill leadership found in most conscript battalions. For most men may be trained to shoot straight and many can learn to react quickly in a given situation, but there are special qualities of leadership needed to ensure every man holds his fire for the certain kill, or to plan an unexpected foray in something more than a conventional raid. Qualities some officers in every regiment possess, but not found in conscript battalions with the consistency essential for

commando operations. Since the war, the British solution has been happily found in Royal Marine commandos with both a Corps and commando tradition.

The Royal Marines also have the advantage of manning their own landing craft as they did in many minor craft flotillas of World War II, but at that time there was no practical way of providing the commandos with their own craft nor with their own air support. They did not have organic artillery - a battery of guns integrated with a Commando. At first they were expected to capture enemy guns, but this was only partially successful when at Vaagso, for example, a captured 75mm (3in) gun was turned against German trawlers. Brigadier D. W. O'Flaherty, CBE, DSO, in a letter to the author has traced the development of light artillery support as an integral part of a Commando Brigade. The Brigadier as a junior officer was wounded at Vaagso, served in north-west Europe, in Korea in the 1950s and elsewhere in post-War Commando operations. The Raiding Support Regiment provided one of the first integrated fire support units during the Adriatic operations of 1944, but in the invasion of Normandy and elsewhere the commandos' fire support was only part of a general fire plan for the parent formation of which they were part. However, in 1945 'the 1st Mountain Regiment supplied B.C. and OPs to 1 Commando Brigade for the Rhine crossing', with a battery commander attached to the brigade's staff. After the war the Brigadier was a leading advocate of organic artillery for commando brigades, especially for the defence of beach-heads, bridges, or air fields they had seized ahead of the main forces. In the summer of 1962 he commanded 29 Commando Light Regiment RA on its formation, and set down 'a simple rule: wherever the Commando Brigade went, by whatever means, so too should its affiliated regiment'. Trained as commandos this Regiment could 'move their guns by helicopter, sea, air, or even its own flat feet'. In 1963, 95 Commando Light Regiment RA was incorporated into the RM Commando Brigade, for the modern commando no longer dodges the issue of landing guns.

Without artillery the Commando targets were limited in World War II, although a shortage of landing craft was an even greater handicap. However, the smaller operations needing no major fire support and few craft were successfully continued through 1942 to 1944 in the search for military intelligence, the Twenty-first Army Group having curbed the habits of raiding for raiding's sake. The co-ordination of the intelligence-seeking COPP and other small party raids had been informal, but was closer than may appear in official records, because each group had a representative on the commit-

tee responsible for canoe designs. Through this and similar contacts most of the small raiding groups had kept in touch, but in 1944 they were formally put under the command of HMS *Rodent* a stone-frigate (base camp) at Liss in Hampshire. Raiding became more effective when it was co-ordinated with the operations of main forces, along the lines envisaged by Major Holland when he was with the General Staff's research section in 1938. In south-east Asia the Small Operations Group provided this co-ordination with the main campaigns, although one official history of the SOG units' actions stresses the difficulties in finding suitable targets for these raiders.

The records clearly show the difficulties, not only in south-east Asia, that senior staffs found in making use of the quick silver nature of Special Forces with their ability to take on unusual tasks. Yet commanders with the flair to see these commando-style actions as nothing out of the ordinary for men selected and trained to perform them, did emerge - more often through the political

Officers and men who attended the presentation of silver commando statute by the Commando Association to the Parachute Regiment's officers at Aldershot, including: second row, fifth from left, Colonel Charles Vaughan, eleventh from left, Mr. Henry Brown; front row - extreme left, Colonel A. C. Newman; fourth from left, Major-General T. B. L. Churchill; sixth from left, Lord Mountbatten; seventh, Field-Marshal Lord Montgomery; eighth, General Sir R. Laycock; tenth, Brigadier D. Mills-Roberts; and twelfth, Brigadier J. S. Durnford-Slater.

imagination of Prime Minister Churchill and President Roosevelt than through military channels. Such political influences were not always popular but were effective in forging links with established command circles. Lower down the scale the involvement of Special Forces with agents, guerrillas and other clandestine forces has been cited as a reason for avoiding their future recruitment, whether for action in uniform or out of it.

The history of Special Forces briefly outlined in Appendix 7, read in conjunction with a knowledge of the techniques described earlier, shows the serious approach of these commandos and rangers to their military roles as being far more efficient than some popular legends suggest. By the late 1940s amphibious warfare had become highly sophisticated, with such complex units as the 34th Amphibian Support Regiment RM equipped with flame-thrower and rocket amphibians (LVT(F)s, LVT(R)s). Yet the effectiveness of small-scale raiding remained essentially based on the canoe or inflatable, the mere threat of raids providing a means of forcing an enemy to overextend his defences as the German armies did in Norway - where the coastal army might have been better used in fighting the Russians on the Finnish border, if the Germans had dared to leave the west coast undefended. The Japanese might have concentrated their defences instead of being stretched over more islands than their resources could defend, as the raiders created the impression of moves first towards this island group and then towards that.

The achievement of sabotage raids must be set in the context of the overall war effort, when the loss of a bomber represented between £50,000 and £75,000 of effort, a submarine represented over £350,000, and a large armour-piercing bomb took £100 of work and materials. An estimate of the conventional forces needed to attack Bordeaux in the winter of 1942 was put at two divisions, yet the RMBPD canoes successfully damaged 6 ships, although all but one of the five canoe teams were killed or captured. Their canoes and explosives probably each represented less than £100 of

time and materials, while training a canoeist cost less than training their counterparts in aircraft crews. Such equations of effective effort are something of a guessing game, but there is no doubt of the necessity for COPP navigators to guide in landing craft, for there was no way the average standard of achievement in these flotillas might be brought to an adequate pitch for the job in hand, within the politically acceptable period of time for mounting a second front in Europe. But there is no formula by which to measure the undoubted success of commando and ranger exploits in raising their fellow countrymen's morale.

As individuals - proud, confident, and among them many with strong religious convictions - these Special Forces walked tall, with a quiet consideration among the majority for lesser mortals. A few were brash and boastful but in the author's experience these were men who had not been in battle or carried out a raid. A handful did not match up to the strain of continuous commando action, or as raiders failed to react quickly enough in confused situations, and were relieved of their commands. But the great majority achieved deeds of daring beyond their own expectations. Inevitably among such a group of individualists and unconventional military thinkers, there was some jockeying for position in the reorganisations from time to time, but none of the pettiness of position-seeking was ever apparent on the field of action.

After the war the Commando and Ranger traditions were carried on. In October 1950 a newly raised Royal Marine Commando fought alongside the US 1 Division in Korea, losing half their strength the Commando was awarded a Presidential Unit Citation. In Vietnam the American Special Force, wearers of the green beret, was expanded from a primary role of infiltrators to raise guerrillas, their designated role in Europe in the 1950s, to a counter insurgency unit 'what it was never intended to be and what it had not trained for'.* Now, however, the old ranger qualities are being taught at the 75th Infantry (Ranger) School in Fort Benning, Georgia. A ranger tradition which in the words of

*Robert B. Asprey: *War In The Shadows.* Macdonald and Jane's, London, 1976.

the veteran ranger Peter Deep 'reflect the American Indian's way of life . . . the Rangers made more versatile in their use of new methods, when through their knowledge of military history they created new tactics . . . their leaders did the scouting as well as the planning . . . and in combat the rangers sought to be among the first to challenge the enemy's strongholds'.

The British army's Commandos established their glorious reputation in only five years during World War II. Their mystique was enhanced by others but undoubtedly was a feature of their success, as it is with

The Commando Memorial, Spean Bridge, Inverness-shire, at the western end of the Great Glen not far from Achnacarry where commandos trained.

any military unit carrying through a succession of difficult operations. But the Commandos' success was built on more than the shadows of reputation, their example of courage, personal initiative and flair for daring operations can be seen in a succession of military feats of arms few units can equal. They will inspire others for generations to come in seeking the lasting peace for which the commandos and rangers fought.

# APPENDICES

## 1 ABBREVIATIONS

| | |
|---|---|
| AB | Able seaman |
| AO | Administrative Officer |
| AOP | Air Observation Post |
| APD | Auxiliary Personnel Destroyer |
| BC | Battery Commander |
| BCP | Boom Clearance Party |
| Bde | Brigade |
| Bn | Battalion |
| CCO | Chief of Combined Operations |
| Cdo | Commando |
| CO | Combined Operations *or* Commanding Officer |
| COPP | Combined Operations Assault Pilotage Party |
| COSU | Combined Operations Scout Unit |
| CSM | Company Sergeant Major |
| DCO | Director of Combined Operations |
| EO | Executive Officer |
| FOB | Forward Officer Bombardment |
| FOO | Forward Officer Observation/Forward Observation Officer |
| GS(R) | General Staff research section |
| HE | High explosive |
| HQ | Headquarters |
| IO | Intelligence Officer |
| ISTDC | Inter-service Training and Development Centre |
| LAD | Light Aid Detachment |
| LCA | Landing Craft, Assault |
| LCI(L) | Landing Craft, Infantry (Large) |
| LCI(S) | Landing Craft, Infantry (Small) |
| LCM | Landing Craft, Mechanised |
| LCN | Landing Craft, Navigation |
| LCOCU | Landing Craft Obstruction Clearance Unit |
| LCP(L) | Landing Craft, Personnel (Large) |
| LCP(R) | Landing Craft, Personnel (Ramped) |
| LCT | Landing Craft, Tank |
| LCVP | Landing Craft, Vehicle Personnel |
| LCR | Landing Craft, Rubber |
| LMG | Light Machine Gun |
| LO | Liaison Officer |
| LRDG | Long Range Desert Group |
| LSI(H) | Landing Ship, Infantry (Hand-Hoisting) |
| LSI(L) | Landing Ship, Infantry (Large) |
| LSI(M) | Landing Ship, Infantry (Medium) |
| LSI(S) | Landing Ship, Infantry (Small) |
| LVT | Landing Vehicle, Tracked |
| LVT(A) | Landing Vehicle, Tracked (Armoured) |
| LVT(F) | Landing Vehicle, Tracked (Flame Thrower) |
| LVT(R) | Landing Vehicle, Tracked (Rocket) |
| MGB | Motor Gun Boat |
| MI R | Military Intelligence Research |
| ML | Motor Launch |
| MNBDO | Mobile Naval Base Defence Organisation |
| MO 9 | Section of the War Office, military operations |
| MTB | Motor Torpedo Boat |
| OP | Observation Post |
| ORs | Other Ranks (enlisted men) |
| OSS | Office of Strategic Services |
| Pfc | Private first class |
| PO | Petty Officer |
| Plt | Platoon |
| QM | Quartermaster |
| RA | Royal Artillery |
| RAMC | Royal Army Medical Corps |
| RCT | Regimental Combat Team |
| RE | Royal Engineers |
| Recce | Reconnaissance |
| Recon | Reconnaissance |
| REME | Royal Electrical and Medical Engineers |
| RM | Royal Marine |
| RMBPD | Royal Marine Boom Patrol Detachment |

| | |
|---|---|
| RSM | Regimental Sergeant Major |
| SAS | Special Air Service |
| SBS | Special Boat Section |
| SEAC | South East Asia Command |
| SEU | Special Engineering Unit |
| SGB | Steam Gun Boat |
| SIS | Secret Intelligence Service |
| SO | Signals Officer |
| SOE | Special Operations Executive |
| SOG | Small Operations Group |
| Sp | Self-propelled |
| SRU | Sea Reconnaissance Unit |
| SS | Special Service |
| SSRF | Small Scale Raiding Force |
| ST | Signal Troop |
| Tp | Troop |
| Trp | Troop |
| TLO | Tank Liaison Officer |
| TSM | Troop Sergeant Major |
| USMC | United States Marine Corps |

# 2  ORGANISATION

## Special Service Brigade - 1940

Responsible to Director of Combined Operations (DCO).
Five battalions each of two Commandos with a battalion headquarters.

## Special Service Brigade - spring 1943

HQ SS Bde
- Bde Signal Troop
- Group HQ
  1 Cdo
  3 Cdo
  6 Cdo
- 2 Cdo
  4 Cdo
  5 Cdo
  9 Cdo
  12 Cdo
  Attached 2nd Bn US Rangers
- 40 (RM) Cdo
  41 (RM) Cdo
- 10 (IA [Inter-Allied]) Cdo
- 14 Cdo
  30 Cdo
  62 Cdo
  Special Boat Section and COPP
- Cdo Depot Mountain and Snow Warfare Camp

## Special Service Group - March 1944

SS Group HQ
- 1 SS Bde (UK)
  Bde Sig. Trp
  *L.A.D. Type A
  3 Cdo
  4 Cdo
  6 Cdo
  45 (RM) Cdo
- 2 SS Bde (Med)
  Bde Sig. Trp
  L.A.D. Type A
  2 Cdo
  9 Cdo
  40 (RM) Cdo
  43 (RM) Cdo
- 3 SS Bde (India)
  Bde Sig. Trp
  L.A.D. Type A
  1 Cdo
  5 Cdo
  42 (RM) Cdo
  44 (RM) Cdo
- 4 SS Bde (UK)
  Bde Sig. Trp
  L.A.D. Type A
  41 (RM) Cdo
  46 (RM) Cdo
  47 (RM) Cdo
  **10 (IA) Cdo
- Group Signals.
  Group 2nd Echelon (RM
    Personnel only)
  Sect. Field Security Police.
  Sect. Postal Unit
  Sect. Provost
  Repair Sect. L.A.D.
  Special Boat Unit (All Arms) HMS
    Rodent, Liss, Hants.
  RM Engineer Cdo.
  Holding Commando, Hermitage
    Camp, Wrexham.
  Cdo Basic Training Centre,
    Achnacarry.
  Cdo Mountain Warfare Training
    Centre, St. Ives, Cornwall.

Notes:
* L.A.D.—Light Aid Detachment from REME.
** 48 (RM) Cdo formed March 1944, replace 10 (Inter-Allied) Cdo in 4 SS Bde in April 1944. Medical teams attached to Brigades for particular operations.

## Army Commando - Mediterranean, August 1943

(461 all ranks)

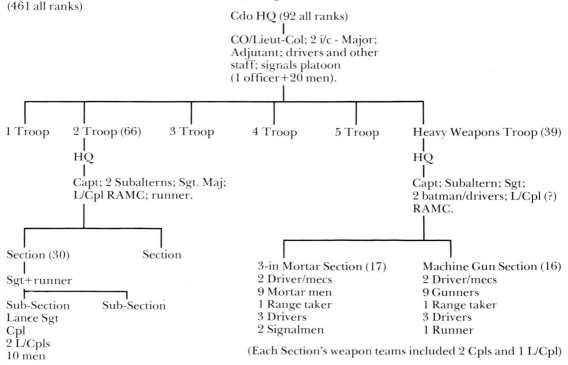

Cdo HQ (92 all ranks)

CO/Lieut-Col; 2 i/c - Major;
Adjutant; drivers and other
staff; signals platoon
(1 officer + 20 men).

| 1 Troop | 2 Troop (66) | 3 Troop | 4 Troop | 5 Troop | Heavy Weapons Troop (39) |

2 Troop (66) — HQ
Capt; 2 Subalterns; Sgt. Maj;
L/Cpl RAMC; runner.

Heavy Weapons Troop (39) — HQ
Capt; Subaltern; Sgt;
2 batman/drivers; L/Cpl (?)
RAMC.

Section (30) — Sgt + runner
Section

Sub-Section
Lance Sgt
Cpl
2 L/Cpls
10 men

Sub-Section

3-in Mortar Section (17)
2 Driver/mecs
9 Mortar men
1 Range taker
3 Drivers
2 Signalmen

Machine Gun Section (16)
2 Driver/mecs
9 Gunners
1 Range taker
3 Drivers
1 Runner

(Each Section's weapon teams included 2 Cpls and 1 L/Cpl)

Transport—35 bicycles; one 4-seater car; 18 5-cwt (Jeep-type) trucks—12 for heavy weapons; 8 15-cwt trucks; 3 3-ton trucks; one 15-cwt water carrier.

---

## British Independent Company Norway 1940

(290 all ranks)

Twenty officers and 270 other ranks in platoons with Sections, weapons mainly rifles and some brens. Carried 100,000 rounds small arms ammunition, £4000 in Norwegian and British money, and rations for five days (chiefly pemmican dried meat).

## British Army Commando Troop-1940

(50 all ranks)

HQ—Captain, Troop Sergeant Major and 2(?) runners; with two Sections of 23 men each commanded by Lieutenant or Sergeant. Sections probably divided into rifle and bren sub-Sections as Corporal's commands. Specialist medics, signallers, etc. attached as required.

Note:
Ten 50-man Troops made a Commando at this time. (Over the years the identification of Troops was by number No. 1 Troop, No. 2 Troop etc. or by letters A Troop, B Troop, etc.)

## RM Commando Troop-Normandy 1944

(60 all ranks)

Troop HQ: Commander—Captain; 1 or 2 Lieutenants; Troop Sergeant Major; orderly. Colt pistol carried by commander, *all* others in HQ carried rifles, the officers and TSM also carried Very pistols.

The Assault, Support and No. 2 Sub-Sections, 27 all ranks, made a Section with two Sections to a Troop:

Assault Sub-Section (11) including Bren Group:
Leader—Sergeant with tommy gun+5 magazines, 2 grenades, notebook and maps. Rifle Group—Corporal with tommy gun+5 magazines, 2 grenades, toggle rope and shovel; Nos. 1, 2 and 3 riflemen each with rifle+50 rounds, miner's pick, 2 bren magazines, 2 grenades and toggle rope; Nos. 4 and 5 riflemen as for No. 1 but shovels replaced picks.

Bren Group
Corporal with rifle+50 rounds, 4 bren magazines, pick and entrenching tool; No. 1—bren+4 bren magazines, pick and entrenching tool; No. 2—rifle+50 rounds, spare parts wallet, 4 bren magazines; No. 3—rifle+50 rounds, 4 bren magazines and shovel.

Support Sub-Section (5):
Corporal as for Rifle Group but carried binoculars and compass not wire cutters; Mortar L/Corporal—rifle+50 rounds; 3 2-in mortar bombs HE and 9 of smoke in/with 2 utility pouches; No. 1 mortarman—2-in mortar, 3 bombs HE, 3 smoke, Colt pistol and 3 magazines; No. 2 mortarman—rifle+50 rounds, 6 bombs HE and 6 smoke. Sniper—rifle with telescopic sights+50 rounds and 2 bren magazines.

No. 2 Sub-Section (11):
As for Assault Sub-Section but carried 40 lbs (18kg) explosives divided equally among men.

Bombs for Heavy Weapons Troop—3-inch (75mm) mortars were carried: 2 by each Lieutenant, 2 by HQ Orderlies; 2 by snipers; 4 by Sgt Asslt Sub-Sec; 18 by rifle Groups (except No. 2 Sub-Section carrying explosives); 5 by No. 3 of bren Group. Sixty bombs per Troop.

## Commando Depot - Achnacarry 1944
(later Commando Basic Training Centre)

See text p. 168. Came under Commando Group, but CO also responsible to Combined Ops HQ, North Highland District of Scottish Command, Royal Marine Adjutant General and Admiralty for various aspects of training and discipline. Colonel Vaughan, the Commandant, knew how to make the most of this variety of masters he skilfully played along to the Depot's advantage.

## 1st Ranger Battalion - June 1942
(488 all ranks)

Small HQ (Lieut-Colonel's command) with 6 companies (A to F) one with 81mm mortars as Heavy Weapons Coy. Each company about 80 strong in 2 30-man rifle platoons with a support HQ section. Each platoon had two 12-man Sections and a 5-man mortar Section with 60mm(?) mortars. The assault Sections were divided into 2 sub-Sections or Squads.

Note:
No establishment lists were available for a Ranger Battalion but an established strength of 538 all ranks was agreed about 1943 although in the field the strength was flexible.

## 4th Ranger Battalion - June 1943
(419 all ranks)

Small HQ (Major's command) with Executive captain and lieutenants as Adjutant, S-4, S-2, assistant S-3, communications officer, and medical officer. Each of the 6 companies commanded by a lieut or 2nd-lieut with two other junior officers in the coy. A company usually had 2 platoons each with about 30 riflemen and a support Section.

## Divisional 'Rangers' - 1944/5

These special patrol squads were initiated by some divisional commanders but were not authorised to use the title nor the insignia of Rangers.

### 1st Special Service Force - 1942
(The North Americans) (approx 1,250 all ranks)

The Force's three regiments each had 407 all ranks in a colonel's command of two battalions. There were three companies to a battalion. Each company had three two-Section platoons. The 108 Sections of the Force were each intended to have 4 Weasel carriers as were HQs in the original organisation.

### June 1944
(2,400 all ranks)

No longer based on carrier Sections, the Force had two-Section platoons commanded by a lieutenant with a staff sergeant, each Section of 12 men being led by a sergeant.

### British Army Rifle Battalion - 1943
(786 all ranks)

For comparison only: Bn HQ 5 officers+29 (approx.). HQ Coy (256) with Signals Plt, Carrier Plt, AA Plt, Pioneer Plt, Mortar Plt, Admin Plt; four Rifle Companies each of 124 all ranks in HQ and three platoons; each platoon (37 or 38) with HQ including anti-tank rifle and 2-in mortar, and three 10-man Sections.

### US Army Regimental Combat Teams of 81 (Wildcat) Division 1943/6

For comparison only: 321, 322, 323 RCT; with 321 RCT made up from 321 Inf Regmt, 316 Field Artillery Bn, 306 Engineer Coy and Medical Collection Coy.

321 Inf Regmt—HQ Coy, Service Coy, Medical Detachment, Anti-tank Coy, Cannon Coy and three infantry battalions.

Each infantry battalion had five companies—HQ Coy, three Rifle Coys, and Heavy Weapons Coy. Each Rifle Coy had four platoons (one a weapons plt) and each rifle platoon had three squads with *one* BAR automatic per squad (although more issued from time to time).

## USMC Battalion - 1944

For comparison only: the three rifle coys in a battalion each had three platoons of three rifle squads. These squads differed from US Army rifle squads, the marines working with three 4-man fire-teams and a squad leader, 13 in all. Each team had one BAR-man and three riflemen, spreading the responsibility of leadership between four men—the squad leader and three fire-team leaders. (This organisation developed in line with Raider Battalion concepts, apparently.)

## Small Operations Group November 1944

Colonel commanded with HQ staff, the Group's maximum strength was reached at this date with four COPPs, RM Detachment 385's three Troops, three SBS Groups, and SRU's four Sections.

## Special Boat Section - March 1942

(47 all ranks)

Major commanded—HQ (included captain instructor, CSM, clerks and storemen, 18 all ranks); four operating Groups each of 7 canoeists—a captain OC, lieutenant 2i/c, with 2 sergeants, 2 corporals, and a driver.

## June 1944    (72 all ranks)

Divided into three Groups—A with 7 officers; B 4 officers and 32 ORs; C 16 all ORs; and Z 7 officers with 6 ORs. (Administrative personnel provided by SOG).

## USMC Raider Battalion - September 1942
(901 all ranks)

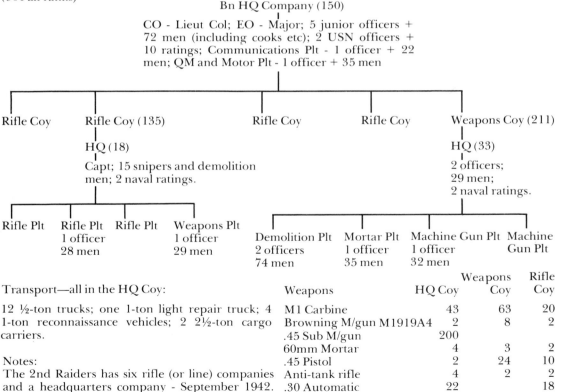

Transport—all in the HQ Coy:

12 ½-ton trucks; one 1-ton light repair truck; 4 1-ton reconnaissance vehicles; 2 2½-ton cargo carriers.

Notes:
The 2nd Raiders has six rifle (or line) companies and a headquarters company - September 1942. See main text for details of squads in platoons. Naval personnel included chaplains and medics.

| Weapons | HQ Coy | Weapons Coy | Rifle Coy |
|---|---|---|---|
| M1 Carbine | 43 | 63 | 20 |
| Browning M/gun M1919A4 | 2 | 8 | 2 |
| .45 Sub M/gun | 200 | | |
| 60mm Mortar | 4 | 3 | 2 |
| .45 Pistol | 2 | 24 | 10 |
| Anti-tank rifle | 4 | 2 | 2 |
| .30 Automatic | 22 | | 18 |
| M1 | 89 | 123 | 76 |
| M1903 (for snipers) | 4 | | 9 |

## January 1945

C Group was commanded by a major with a captain 2 i/c, two lieutenants, 4 sergeants, 8 corporals, a corporal storeman and a corporal driver.

## Sea Reconnaissance Unit - June 1944
(48 all ranks)

Lieut-Commander commanded—HQ (8 all ranks) with four Sections of which Nos. 1–3 had 10 officers and men, and No. 4 had 9.

## RM Boom Patrol Detachment - June 1944
(73 all ranks)

HQ and Administration (34 all ranks) with three Groups—A 16 officers and men; B with 6; and C with 17. (The HQ figures probably included men on experimental work.)

## Combined Operations Assault Pilotage Parties (COPPs) - June 1944
(174 all ranks)

HQ, training and administrative personnel 57 all ranks with ten Parties of which Nos. 1–6 and No. 10 each had 12 officers and men, and Nos. 7–9 had 11 each.

## Combined Operations Scout Units - June 1944
(40 +, all ranks)

Formerly called 'Camouflage B' there were four (?) Units each of 1 officer, 1 petty officer and 8 ratings (qualified wireless, RDF or radio mechanics).

## Boom Commando
- see LCOCU

## RM Detachment 385 - March 1945
(100+, all ranks)

Small HQ with 3 Troops each of 6 officers and 25 men divided into three Sections, their composition and numbers varied to suit specific operations.

## Special Engineering Unit
(formerly called 30 Commando) - c1943 (not known all ranks)

Personnel of all three services in teams of approximately 15.

## Royal Marine Engineer Commando - February 1945
(141 all ranks)

Two Troops—one with 1 Cdo Bde, second with 3 Cdo Bde—and third Troop being formed; 2 subalterns, 18 general duties marines, 6 carpenters, 1 concretor, 1 electrician, 2 masons, 3 miners, 2 painters, 2 plumbers, 2 driver/mecs, 2 men for vehicle maintenance. Established 61 all ranks but two Troops over strength in February 1945—3 officers+65, 2 officers+71.

## Landing Craft Obstruction Clearance Units - August 1943
(438+, all ranks)

Six Units with some administration (details not known) each Unit (or Section) of 73 all ranks—7 officers, 11 PO riggers, 16 leading seamen riggers mates, 13 leading seamen, 9 ABs, 7 signalmen. (These hands included swimmers).

## Spring 1945

For operations against Japan LCOCUs were deployed with Army bomb disposal teams in groups attached to each assault brigade for clearing 400 yards (360m) gap in defences.

## Naval Beach Party - Spring 1942
(55 all ranks)

Lieutenant RN as Principal Beachmaster commanded; 3 Lieutenants or Sub-Lieutenants as Beach Masters; 3 Lieutenants or Sub-Lieutenants as Assistant Beach Masters; and 48 ratings.

## Raiding Support Regiment - Mediterranean, December 1943
(600 all ranks)

HQ and five batteries manned by paratroops with mountain guns, anti-tank and anti-aircraft guns, 3-in (75mm) mortars and medium machine guns.

## Small Scale Raiding Force - Summer 1942

Operationally under CCO, jointly controlled by CCO and SOE this Force provided small parties of 8 to 10 men, sometimes fewer, for raids. Total strength not known but probably never more than sixty.

## 1st Special Raiding Squadron - Mediterranean 1943
(254 all ranks)

16 officers and 238 ORs in four(?) Troops all from 2nd SAS Regiment.

## Other small units of Special Forces Mediterranean, December 1943

(as shown in official reports)

OSS Operational Group 200 all ranks, Bataillon de Choc 500 (Corsican), Demolition Squad 75, 'Kalpak' guides and saboteurs 20, Long Range Desert Group 240 (in island ops), and 'Special Boat Squadron' 180—probably refers to Major the Earl Jellicoe's raiding force including SBS. Elements of these units including the LRDG formed the 1st Special Reconnaissance Squadron.

## Australian Independent Company Spring 1942 (267 all ranks)

Company HQ (69 all ranks) with CO (Major), 2 i/c, CSM, and 13 QM, drivers etc. Sapper Section: 1 officer, 17 men. Medical staff: captain & 4ORs. One armourer.
Three 66-man platoons each with HQ (capt, sgt & 7 ORs). The platoons had three 18-man sections each commanded by a lieutenant, with two runners and a rifle squad. Weapons: Mauser 15; .45 pistol 52; .303 rifles 140; bren gun 18; sub m/c gun 36; sniper rifle 9. 4 m/cycles, car, 30-cwt.

## 1st Commando Fiji Guerrilla Pacific 1943

(164 all ranks)

Commanded by a captain with HQ (CO+22) and two 75-man companies with lieutenants commanding. Each company was of three platoons led by a sergeant and had three sections of seven (corporal+6).

## American Air Command, Burma 1944

13 Dakota (C47) transport aircraft, 225 WACO gliders, 100 L5 light aircraft, 12 B25 medium bombers, 30 Mustang (P51) fighters and 6 experimental helicopters.

## RAF Servicing Commando North Africa 1942

(199 all ranks)

Divided into six parties A1, A2, B1, B2, C1 and C2 each with two sections usually of 10 to 16 men including aircraft and/or engine fitters, with smaller parties of armourers and a 3-man rear party.

Note:
Some other units' organisation mentioned in Unit Histories Appendix 7.

# 3 WEAPONS

## Close combat

Fighting Knife: 1940—Wilkinson Sword made 500 knives to specifications of first commando instructors in unarmed combat (Capts Fairburn and Sykes of Shanghai Intl. Police). The 7in (178mm) blades were of carbon (sword) steel with a ⅞in (22mm) diamond cross-section. The brass knurled grip had an oval cross guard 2¼in (57mm) by ½in (13mm) with its ends curved up and down. These 500 can be identified by the manufacturer cross-sword logo and a small 'FS' embossed on the opposite blade side. Some 250,000 similar knives without identification marks were made between 1941 and 1945, they had a black nickel finish and some design changes after mid-1941: the sharp edges were continued to crossguard and flat blade shoulders removed; a smaller crossguard was used; and the brass knurled grip replaced by a moulding—to improve balance. (Post-war knives include 10,000 with cross-sword logo and Royal Warrant embossing and a few for the Admiralty with 'F.R.693' on crossguard.)

American fighting knives were slightly shorter with a wider blade and some had a knuckle-duster hand-grip.

Cheese wire: length of strong wire between two wooden toggles, as used by grocers to cut cheese in 1940s.

Coshes: these could be as simple as a sock full of sand or more elaborate with large nuts on heavy springs from handles. One report suggests use was made of London Underground railway spring-designed 'straps' for standing passengers.

## Conventional infantry weapons

Special Forces' success depended more on their skill with conventional infantry weapons than in the men's ability to use non-standard equipment. Some points made by these forces on standard weapons are shown below:

Lee-Enfield No. 4 Mk I and Mk III—standard British .303in rifles with bolt action and 10-round magazine could be fired at the rate of 15 rounds a minute, muzzle velocity (mv) 2,400 ft per second for an effective range of 600 to 1,000 yards.

M1 Carbine—.300in with 15- or 30-round magazine—although only weighing 5.5lb (2.5kg) its low muzzle velocity at 1,970 ft per second limited its stopping power against a charging enemy.

Garand—.300in semi-automatic rifle with 8-round magazine weighed 9.5lb (4kg), a mv of 2,805 fps firing M2 ball ammunition of 152 grains for maximum range of 3,500 yards. Could be used with M2 ball to 'search' reverse slopes of hills at 2,000 yards. The somewhat complex mechanism with gases operating the reloading could nevertheless be taken apart and reassembled using only the point of a bullet. Big aperture backsight gave clear aim in pre-dawn and similar half-light.

Sniper's British and American rifles fitted with telescopic sights were used extensively by Special Forces, but their snipers had other jobs as well.

Thompson .45in Model 1928 1 sub machine gun fired 600 to 725 rounds per minute (rpm) from 20- or 30-round magazines, but low mv at 920 fps limited the effective range to 50 yards.

Sten Gun Mk II 9mm Mk II fired 500 to 550 rpm from 32-round magazine, mv 1,280 fps giving 80 yards (72m) effective range.

Browning Automatic Rifle (BAR) Model 1918A2 (introduced in 1941) .300in fired 550 rpm from 20-round magazine, mv 2,700 fps giving 650 yards effective range, weighed 19.4lb with bipod legs. This model could be set on 'slow auto' for 350 rpm. Gases operated reloading and the size of magazine made this almost a light machine gun.

Bren LMG Mk I .303in fired up to 450 rpm from 30-round—advisable to load 26—box magazine (100-round drum magazines also), mv 2,440 fps for effective range of 600 to 800 yards (540 to 720m) when fired from bipod legs, maximum range 2,000 yards (1.8km). Commandos fired this 23lb (10.4kg) gun from the hip on occasions.

Johnson M1906 .300in LMG fired up to 900rpm from 20-round box magazine that could be reloaded while on the gun by insert 5-round charges or single rounds, mv 2,800 fps. This 14lb 5oz LMG was flimsy and prone to jam.

Browning M1919A4 .300in fired up to 500 rpm from 250 rounds on belt, mv 2,800 fps, issued in fixed and flexible forms and fired by USMC Raiders and others from a tripod.

Boys .55in anti-tank rifle had 5-round magazine of 930-grain armour-piercing bullet, mv about 3,000fps for 200 yards (180m) range.

Piat fired a nose-fused 2½lb bomb that had a special head drawing explosion into armour plate. Weighing 34½lb, its maximum range was 100 yards (115 yards in some pamphlets) against tanks but with legs fully extended a 350-yard range was possible in house breaking.

Bazooka US anti-tank rocket launcher, an early mark fired the 2.37in rocket, the M9 fired a 2.56in rocket with a 0.5lb (227 grams) HE charge over 100- to 150-yard effective range (maximum 700 yards), mv 270 fps at 70°F but greater at higher temperatures and vice versa. Bazookas used by Commandos for house clearing.

Special Forces—commandos, rangers and US marines—used mortars at close quarters although the minimum 'range' of the 60mm mortar, for example, was 75 yards.

Vickers K-gun .303 gas-operated, developed from aircraft machine gun for use as light-weight gun firing 950 rpm from 100- or 60-round magazines. Had simple mechanism. The commandos used their K-guns and brens to supplement LC fire before landing with Heavy Weapons Troop.

Vickers K-gun

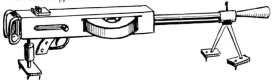

Lifebuoy back pack flamethrower weighed 64lb, range 30–40yds with 10 secs duration, carried in place of a rifle and rucksack by one man in some assault sub-sections after spring of 1944.

Grenades—the fragmentation anti-personnel and other infantry grenades—the birdlime coated sticky bomb, phosphorous smoke/incendiary grenades, etc.—were used by Special Forces who adapted all grenade fuses when appropriate to suit shorter or longer time intervals before detonation.

## Cliff climbing

Pairs of rocket grapnels attached to ropes laid with care for easy run-out from open boxes, could put a line up a 200ft cliff, when fired from LC in favourable conditions.

Hand-held rocket with small grapnel fired a line up 100 ft or more of cliff provided line was dry and wind conditions moderate.

Tubular scaling ladders in 4-foot (1+m) sections weighing 4lb were assembled by slotting sections together and in Normandy 2nd Rangers preassembled 16-foot lengths, carrying 112ft of ladder in each LCA going to Pointe du Hoc.

Toggle rope—varied in length but usually 4ft (1+m) with wooden toggle spliced into one end and an eye spliced at the other end. Linked together these not only provided climbing ropes but also could be used for V-shaped rope bridges.

## Demolitions etc.

Guncotton wet slabs were of dirty white fibrous appearance 6×3×1½in, weighed 19oz including 3oz of water and dangerous if dry (ie: flaky). The slab's tapered hole took a 1oz dry guncotton or CE primer (a cylinder of Composition Explosive that did not deteriorate as did a dry guncotton primer if its acetone coating was chipped).

The '808' plastic explosive supplied in 4oz cartridges of 3×1¼in (diam.) also fired by 1oz primer. This explosive could be moulded like plasticine, used underwater, and set off by rifle fire.

The standard No. 27 Mk I detonator was a 1¾in metal tube (of fulminate of mercury) explosive that slid into a hole in the centre of the primer. The open end of the detonator took either safety or 'instant' fuses that was crimped by special pliers to ensure fuse did not slip from detonator.

Safety fuse No. 11 of black powder in a waterproof cover burned at 2ft a minute (+ or − 7 seconds). Cordtex was a white flexible ¼in diameter fuse burning at *200 miles* a second and therefore virtually instantaneous over short lengths. Three turns of Cordtex around a No. 75 grenade would fire it (and its primer). Safety fuse could be fired by a percussion igniter. Pencil time fuses, 7 day (at 65°F) lead break delay fuses and celluloid-acetone fuses were used as well as press-, pull- and release-switch fuses.

The permutations of explosive charges, instantaneous fuse, safety fuse and other fuses are endless (see diagram opposite).

Pole charges had a timber frame 2ft by 1ft with four Hawkins No. 75 grenades at each corner linked by cordtex etc., the frame positioned by stout timber at angle to hold it against a wall in mouseholing between adjoining houses etc.

Bangalore torpedos were made up of 1½in or 2in diameter tubes 8ft long and packed with 10 to 12lb of explosive. Sections could be slotted together by an integral spring-clip ring and an initiating set of Terryl igniter etc. fitted to one end. The resulting explosion cut wire and set off some types of mines to give a cleared lane through obstacles.

Limpet Mk II held by six magnets to a ship's side or metal frame of piers etc. exploded a set time—several hours—after butterfly nuts were used to break chemical-fuse glass when raider had positioned limpet mine. Its 2lb of plastic explosive could blow a 6ft diameter hole in the plates of most merchant ships' hulls.

## Beach reconnaissance gear etc.

Details of these are shown in the diagram on page 62.

RG equipment: RG was a code name for a system of infra-red signals sent by a special lamp and received on a screen in a camera-like box. The receiving equipment included components capable of forming pictures and indicating the Allied line of development for a gunnery night-sight, therefore the equipment was 'top secret' until March 1944.

Beach marks: these ranged from simple triangular and diamond shapes of wood to 10-foot (3+m) canvas sheets of differing colour and patterns to mark the limits of beach landing points.

Sonic buoy: emitting underwater pulses of known frequency, the buoy could be identified with its range and direction shown by Asdic (sonar) equipment.

Swimming gear: SRU equipment included the back breathing gear developed for CCO, swim fins, dive masks, light diving dress with Type 'A' open-mouth helmets, bathing caps and trunks and special shoes made by Dunlop Rubber Co.

## Other weapons

Flower-pot bomb, a home-made incendiary device probably cast from a mixture of available ingredients to make sandpie-shaped bombs.

The variety of petrol bombs and do-it-yourself explosive devices appears to have been more a matter of improvisation with standard equipment than any radically original inventions.

## Miscellaneous

Commandos used tracer (1-in-5 probably) for automatic weapons with a higher proportion than normal used by 3 Cdo for the demoralising effect of fire you can see is aimed at you. The Rangers had armour piercing bullets not effective, however, against tanks.

The commando's SV boot had a composition sole with a pattern of ridges for better grip on rock etc. But most equipment was of standard issue: like the heavy-framed bicycle; and tins of self-heating soup 'boiled in a minute by lighting the wick at the top of the tin' according to one report—although others found these tins less efficient.

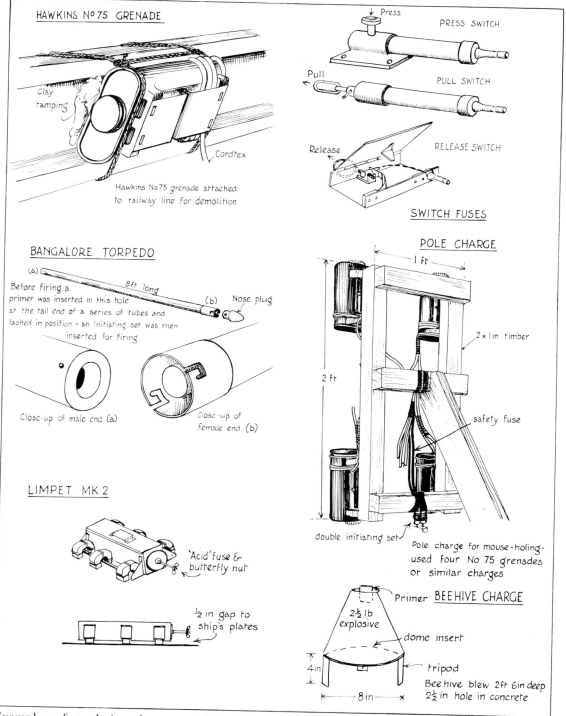

HAWKINS Nº75 GRENADE

Clay tamping

Cordtex

Hawkins No75 grenade attached to railway line for demolition

Press

PRESS SWITCH

Pull

PULL SWITCH

Release

RELEASE SWITCH

SWITCH FUSES

BANGALORE TORPEDO

(a)

8ft long

Before firing a primer was inserted in this hole at the tail end of a series of tubes and lashed in position – an initiating set was then inserted for firing

(b) Nose plug

Close-up of male end (a)

Close-up of female end (b)

POLE CHARGE

1 ft

2 ft

2 × 1in timber

safety fuse

double initiating set

Pole charge for mouse-holing used four No 75 grenades or similar charges

LIMPET MK 2

'Acid' fuse & butterfly nut

½ in gap to ship's plates

Primer  BEEHIVE CHARGE

2½ lb explosive

dome insert

tripod

4in

8in

Beehive blew 2ft 6in deep 2½in hole in concrete

Examples of explosive charges used by commandos.

RM commandos' kit: 1. bicycle; 2. camouflage net; 3. basic pouches, webbing and water bottle; 4. hand signal flares; 5. packet of Craven A cigarettes; 6. gym shoes; 7. lifejacket; 8. small smoke generator; 9. mug above mess-tins; 10. Thompson sub-machine gun; 11. gas mask (respirator); 12. clasp knife and lanyard; 13. 'housewife' sewing kit; 14. holdall with toilet items.

# 4 LANDING SHIPS, CRAFT, AMPHIBIANS AND OTHER VEHICLES

## Assault carrier ships, examples

HM LSI(H) *Royal Ulsterman* (4,200 gross tons)
Assault force 40 officers and 450 ORs (865 all ranks on a short voyage); range—4,000 miles (7,400+km) at 10 knots (18kph); LC carried—6 LCAs or similar, launched from hand-operated davits. This 340ft (103m) ship had a crew of 230 including those manning minor craft, she also carried 150 tons of cargo or 6 bren carriers. She was formerly an Irish Sea ferry.

HM LSI(L) *Glengyle* (13,000+ gross tons)
Assault force 34 officers and 663 ORs; range—12,000 miles (22,200km) at 14.5 knots (26kph) or 10,000 miles at 18 knots; LC carried—24 LCAs etc on davits (some minor support craft with LCAs) and 3 LCM launched by 30-ton or 50-ton derricks. This 500ft (152m) ship had a crew of over 500. She and her sister ships HMS *Glenearn* and HMS *Glenroy* were former fast cargo liners and were remodified late in 1943 to carry an increased number of minor craft as shown above.

APD No. 9 USS *Dent* (1,700 tons loaded displacement)
Assault force—140+ all ranks (200+ on short passages); range—varied as fuel reduced for increased assault force, maximum speed 23 knots (32kph): LC carried—4 LCP(L)/LCP(R) and inflatable rubber boats. This 314+ft (95m) ship had a crew of 112, four 3in/50s, 5 20mm guns and 6 depth charge projectors. Formerly she was a flush-deck destroyer and one of 32 converted to APDs.

## Shore-to-shore landing craft

LC Infantry (Large), the LCI(L) designed as 'a giant raiding craft' of 387 short tons loaded displacement: assault force 9 officers and 196 troops (early craft carried 7 less); after beaching, her force landed down two 36-foot (12m) bow gangways; range—8,000 miles (nearly 15,000km) at 12 knots (22kph) when loaded with fuel for ocean passages, when loaded for beaching the range was 500 miles (900+km) at 15 knots (27kph). This steel craft of 158+ft (47m) had a crew of 28, and 5 20mm guns but added weapons in various theatres.

LC Infantry (Small), the LCI(S) designed for long distance raids and of 110 long tons displacement: assault force 6 officers and 96 ORs (with 18 bicycles); after beaching, her force landed down two bow gangways; range—700 miles (1,200km) at 12½ knots (22kph). This *wooden* craft of 105ft (33m) had a crew of 17 and petrol engines fitted with silencers, 2 20mm and 2 Lewis guns. Armour was fitted over sides and some other vital parts.

LC Tank—a steel shore-to-shore craft of various marks designed to land tanks over a ramp onto a beach, the early marks carried 250/350 tons; but the smaller Marks 5 and 6 carried 150 tons and were often used in beach areas as ferries.

## Minor landing craft carrying men etc. from ship to shore

LC Assault (LCA) of 13 tons displacement when loaded
Assault force 35 troops with 800lb (360+kg) of equipment landed over ramp; range 50–80 miles (say 90–150km) depending on sea conditions, operational speed 7 knots (13kph), could make 2–3 knots on one of her two engines. This wooden craft of 41ft (12.5m) had a crew of 4 protected—as were the cargo personnel—by armour to the craft's well sides and to side decking but this protection did not extend to the engine compartment aft. An LCA(OC) was fitted out for use by LCOCU.

LC Personnel (Large), the LCP(L) of 9 short tons displacement
Assault force—25 on craft in RN, 30 to 36 on USN craft (loads of up to 8,100kg (3,700kg) could be carried depending on fuel load); range varied with type of single engine fitted but RN craft on tank of 200 US galls covered 120 miles (192km) at 9 to 11 knots, one USN type with a diesel engine did 130 miles (208km) on tank of 120 US galls at 8 knots (15kph). This wooden craft of 36ft 8in (11m) had a crew of 3 and one or two medium machine guns. The craft in RN service for raiding had a cockpit forward of the troop well and a canvas cover over this well giving protection from the weather. The craft in US service had two ring mountings forward for machine guns and capacity for use in mass landings. Men landed by jumping down from high prow. Armour only fitted to a few of these craft.

LC Personnel (Ramped), the LCP(R)
Similar to LCP(L) in American service but fitted with a bow ramp.

LC Vehicle Personnel, the LCVP of 9 short tons (unladen)
Assault forces 36 men or 3-ton truck or 8,100lb (3,270+kg) cargo; range between 68 miles (116km) at 9 knots (16kph) and 120 miles at 7

knots according to engine type. This wooden craft of 36ft (10.8m) had a crew of 3, armour plating to the ramp and two medium machine guns.

LC Mechanised, the LCM, of several types designed to land a single tank on to a beach, these steel craft had the capacity to lift 32,000lb (14,500+kg) in British design Mk 1 or up to 60,000lb (27,200+kg) in the Mk 3 American design.

LC Navigation, the LCN, was a LCP(L) with superstructure covering a wireless room and control position. Equipment included—WS Radar, Loran or Decca navigation aids to fix craft's position, echo sounder and a reel of 9 miles (14+km) of wire for 'taut wire' measurement.

## Dories and surf boats

Camper and Nicholsons Ltd of Gosport (Hampshire) carried out the design work and prototype development of several series of dories and canoes. Working in 1941 with Maj. March-Phillips, DSO, OBE of the Small Scale Raiding Force, this famous yacht builders' Southampton yard built the 18-ft CN1 Dory (see below), later developments included the submersible canoe on which the RMBPD did experimental work.

CN1 18ft (5.4m) multiple-hard-chine dory of West African type with moulded plywood frame: prototype built June 1941; between 1941 and 1943 some 200 of these (or similar) dories were built; brief specifications—18ft overall, 5ft 8in beam, depth 2ft 4½in, weight 4½cwt (504lb), capacity 1 long ton+5 men, crew of coxswain+2 or 4. Dry and buoyant but lifted too quickly in surf sometimes becoming 'uninhabitable' before oarsmen could get offshore.

CN3 22ft (6.6m) multiple-hard-chine surf boat of West African type, constructed in marine plywood: brief specifications—22ft overall, 6ft beam, depth 2ft 8½in, weight 9(?) cwt, capacity 2 long tons, crew of coxswain (?)+4.

PD1 13ft 6in (3.4m) modified Dutch pram dingy of clench (wood) construction: brief specifications—13ft 6in overall, beam 5ft 2in, depth 2ft 1in, weight 280lb, capacity ½ long ton+4 men, crew coxswain+1 or 2. Being single-ended (with flat transom stern) could only land safely bow-to-sea in surf and no great weight could be loaded in the bow but a manoeuvrable oared boat able to land five men in moderate surf. Oars 8ft 6in.

SN6 20ft (6m) dory of carvel double diagonal (wood) construction with 8hp Stuart Turner 2-cylinder engine giving 6 knots speed, brief specification—20ft overall, 5ft 4in beam, depth 2ft 2in, weight 6(?) cwt, capacity estimated at 1.9 long tons (8 to 10 men), crew coxswain+4. Oars 9ft 6in (see diagram p. 54).

Note:
Oars for these boats landing in surf were long, narrow and tapered. A specially designed rowlock 7⅛in height from base to tips and with 'arms' tapered and shaped to hold oar when knocked by surf.

16-foot (4.8m) wooden dories were designed in varying Marks mainly distinguished by the increased beam (Mk I 4ft 6in and Mk III 5ft 3in) the wider beam requiring a special launching technique from carrier (MTBs etc) using a steadying line. The Mk III had modified 'end' buoyancy tanks for stowage space to take Seagull or British Anzani outboard. A Mk IV design introduced in March 1945 incorporated improvements on Mk III.

Other dories and modifications—a two-engined dory was built for 2nd SAS Regmt; and a 4-engined dory designed for Norwegian operations by Forfar force in summer of 1943—no details of numbers built or specifications traced.

Some SN6 dories had Austin engines (100lbs heavier than the Stuart Turner and with some difficulties in adjusting gearbox to disengage prop). Experiments with a 'silent' outboard were in hand in March 1945 but none appear to have been used operationally. Other experiments led to a variety of small craft being tested, only those described above appear to have been used operationally but from time to time local boats were requisitioned for raids.

## Canoes

Folbot 16ft (5m) of rubberised canvas on wooden frame: brief specifications—overall length 16ft, beam 2ft 6in, depth 1ft, capacity 2 men, folded into pack 4ft 8in× 1ft× 1ft when frame rods etc. dismantled, weight approx 50lb. 'Handling quickly learnt, very fragile, very fast and silent. Prone to turn turtle'—report of 6 Commando's trials. Described in official documents as 'Cockell Mk I' and a peacetime sports canoe designed by the Folbot Company.

Cockle Mk II 16½ft. (3+m) rigid canvas and wood design to suit launching from submarine. (S and T submarines could swing canoe outboard by special fitting in forward gun.) Weight 80–100lb fitted with bow, stern and longitudinal air-filled buoyancy bags the canoe carried up to 1cwt of gear and two 13-stone men (total 480lb), drawing

6in. Designed paddling speed 3½ knots with designed max speed of tow 5½ knots. Watertight cover over cockpit fitted around crew, the canvas skin reinforced to withstand pounding on shingle. This replaced the Mk I Folboat but was too wide to pass easily through some submarine hatches.

Cockle Mk I** a modified Folbot-type incorporating a rigid frame with adjustable cross-member, allowing the beam to be reduced by 2in (to pass through smaller hatches) before refixing for launching with a 1ft 11in beam.

Three-man canoe—modified Cockell Mk IIs and an experimental type designed with solid wooden floor and collapsible canvas side.

Three-man canoe with wooden floor and sides, 21(?)ft (7m) overall used by SBS.

Rob Roy—no records traced for this but probably a 2-man rigid 16-footer by description of its use in operations.

Motorised canoe with two outriggers that lifted and slid inboard through a 'torpedo' hatch: engine electric self-starter ½hp motor for lorry, driving tiny 3-bladed prop; knife contact plates to battery disconnected readily on capsize. Canoeist in prone position had chin on sorbo rest. The prototype exceeded 5 knots in calm water but Camper and Nicholsons designed this canoe for 6 hours endurance at 5 knots.

Parachute pack canoe dropped with paracanoeist on line to hit water before he landed.

Submersible canoe of about 15ft (4.5m) driven by lone canoeist in diving gear, appears to be a development of motorised canoe. One used in operation in South China Sea September 1944 probably by SOE, an abortive operation by Norwegians using this canoe was also reported.

## Other small boats and buoyancy aids

Goatley collapsible boat 17ft 6in (5+m) with wooden bottom and green canvas sides: brief specification—11ft 6in overall, 4ft 6in beam, depth 1ft 9in (collapsed depth 8in), carried 7 men (six paddling), weight 2 cwt. Two men could assemble in 1½ minutes and 'the best folding boat 6 Commando has been issued with'.

Inflatables included a variety of British and American designs eg: LCR(L) used by 8-men patrols could be fitted with an outboard but its noise destroyed any chance of surprise. The inflatable reached about 2mph when paddled but could reach 3½mph with an experienced crew over short distances.

Miscellaneous boats were tried out in a series of tests by 6 Commando—Canadian 2-man canoes 'light, fragile but more easily learnt [to handle] than Folboat', 19-foot collapsible 11-man canoe 'too slow'; 11ft 6in Assault boat with metal bottom carried 7 men 'easy to handle'; 23ft 6in plywood folding boat carried 14 men 'very heavy'—it weighed 8cwt.

Paddle board—a hollow marine plywood 10 foot (3m) surfboard-like buoyancy aid with pointed ends, paddled by man lying along rear three-quarters of board and using paddle (table-tennis like) bats strapped to each hand—arm strokes' cycle 1, 2, 3, and rest, repeated. Photographs of a post-WWII board show a compass mounted in its forward part. Paddlers wore heavy protective clothing and although self-contained underwater breathing apparatus (SCUBA) was not available they were trained in use of Davis submarine escape apparatus breathing oxygen below 30 feet depths—known in 1970s to be dangerous.

## Special carriers

X-craft modified small submarines -Vickers design originally for releasing two 2-ton explosive charges under enemy ships in harbour - to carry COPP recce personnel: brief specifications—overall length 51ft 7in, beam 5ft 9½in, displacement on surface 27 long tons, submerged 29.7 tons, diving depth 300ft, range on surface at 4 knots 1,860 miles, human endurance 7 to 10 days, main engine 42hp at 1,800rpm driven by batteries with 112 cells. Fitted with gyro compass, oxygen supply, $CO_2$ absorption, 9ft day periscope, short fixed night periscope with small directional hydrophone fitted, R/T equipment, Cher/Chernikeef log, etc.—towing gear enabled submerged passage speed of 10½ knots (max 12(?) knots) reducing endurance of T-class submarine by 5½ per cent at 10 knots (30 per cent reduction for S-Class). See text for details of COPP personnel carried but designed crew 3 to 4 for hand-operated hydroplanes and steering but also carried electric steering 'with automatic helmsman'.

Welman midget craft designed by ISRB to carry an external charge with 560lb of explosive: brief specifications—overall length including charge 20ft 2in, height 5ft 9in, beam at saddle 3ft 6in, surface displacement 4,600lb, propulsion by 2½hp electric motor, normal operating depth 75ft (max 300ft), endurance 10 hours at 2.5 knots, 20 hours at 1.7 knots. One man crew had forward vision armoured glass in conning tower and 4 portholes, steered by joystick, tanks trimmed and bilges pumped out by foot or hand pumps, compass etc. fitted, course keeping 'gyro direction indicator set by eye'. The British Army developed these craft at Welwyn (Herts)—hence Welman—for attaching limpet mines from the craft's nose to enemy ships, but the only operational references traced suggest there were several anti-shipping raids in Norway by these craft. Norwegians certainly trained to use them as did the SBS.

**Country craft** - converted cutter carrying and launching RMBPD canoes.

## Amphibious vehicles

Landing Vehicles Tracked, the LVT, were designed with tracks that paddled these armoured troop carriers across water and over mud. The earlier Marks had no ramp but the Mark 4 (26ft 1in×10ft 8in×8ft 2½in(ht)) had a ramp at the back for quickly offloading the cargo/personnel, maximum weight carried 23,350lb. The Mk 4's aircooled 200hp engine gave a land range of 150 miles with max speed of 25 mph, over water the range was 75 miles with a max speed of 5.4 knots.

LVT (Armoured), the LVT(A)s, were various marks of LVT fitted with field guns etc.: LVT(A) Mk I with a 37mm M-6 gun and coaxial machine gun and 2 .30 machine guns in ring mountings behind turret; Mk 4 with 75mm M-8 howitzer and single .50 mg in mounting behind turret.

Weasel, a tracked amphibian designed for use over snow, mud, water and hard ground, was developed from the T15 prototype. Several marks were manufactured, the M29 with a 6-cylinder 65hp Studebaker Champion front engine was modified to achieve 3.3 mph over water carrying three passengers and with the rear half of the watertight hull clear for cargo. In 1944 a field conversion kit—bow and stern cells, track side panels, sponson air tanks and cable-controlled twin rudders—was issued to modify the MC29 Cargo Carrier into the MC29C amphibian. Manufactured by Studebaker, the M29C had a land speed of 36 mph and over water made 4 mph, land cruising range 175 miles on 35 US galls of fuel (no figures traced for ranges over water but probably under 50 miles). The carrier needed a driver only and carried 1,200lb cargo.

## Land Vehicles

The ubiquitous Jeep was used to carry some commando mortar teams in 1944/5 and by Ranger radio recon patrols in Europe. Other commando and ranger vehicles were of standard service types, although in 1944/5—as with many Allied units—German vehicles were acquired.

# 5 COMMUNICATIONS

## Developments

The first signals Troop under Capt. (later Colonel) A. J. Leahy Royal Signals was formed in 1940, for brigade communications on the intended Pantelleria (Mediterranean) operation. The unit later provided signallers for raids including the Vaagsö landing and carried out experimental work to establish by the summer of 1941 'the use of man-pack radio as a practical primary means of communications at all times during an operation . . . and therefore relied almost entirely on radios carried on our backs, our chests or on handcarts'. In 1942 Combined Operations HQ developed a number of techniques for communications in amphibious landings. Commander Paul RN pointed out that a ship should be designed around the radio sets for invasions rather than attempt to build these into existing warships; and this suggestion among others led to the commissioning of the Headquarters Ship HMS *Bulolo*, formerly a cargo ship built in the 1930s. Major Cole, Royal Signals (later Major-General E. C. Cole, CB, CBE) devised the No. 46 set with crystal control eliminating the tuning necessary on other sets when finding a given frequency. Most of the Combined Operations HQ signals developments affected all forces, not only Commandos, and ranged from waterproofed canvas bags keeping sets dry after several hours submersion, handcarts – devised by Major Cole with the Triang toy firm – for heavy sets, and air-to-ground communications for forward units.

In the same year (1942) the original brigade signals Troop was expanded to a force of 100+ providing signallers to accompany single dory raids or for brigade-sized battles. Each Commando had its own signals Section from early in 1941, and in 1943 the Army Commando's 100+ brigade signals force combined with the RM Division's signallers to form four SS Brigade Signal Sections. The Group Signals unit attached to the Commando Group HQ in 1944 was purely administrative. After the Normandy landings, by 29 August 1944 there were two army signal detachments with two RM Signals Troops at the Tactical HQ of the SS Group. Five army commando signal detachments were on standby for raids and small operations, and two cable detachments were available for HQ communications when Commandos were deployed in infantry roles.

# Radios' characteristics:

| Type | Range in miles Voice | *CW | Weight |
|---|---|---|---|
| No. 18 Set | | | |
| Mobile | 2 | 6 | up to 3 5lb |
| Stationary | 5 | 8 | |
| for infantry patrols | | | |
| No. 38 Set | 4 (max) | | 12lb |
| developed from No. 18 | | | ex. batteries |
| No. 68 Set | | | |
| further development in this series | | | |
| No. 11 Set | | | |
| Mobile | 4 | 10 | 47lb |
| Stationary | 6 | 15 | |
| for information to guns | | | |
| No. 21 Set | | | as for No. 11 Set |
| development of No. 11 | | | |
| with additional frequency band | | | |
| No. 22 Set | 20/40 | 50 | 3 packs each |
| for division to | | | of 30lb |
| brigade | | | |
| and fitted in some support craft | | | |
| No. 46 Set | 3/4 | | |
| Crystal control | | | |

| | | | |
|---|---|---|---|
| 510-Set Naval† | 40+ | | |
| TBX (American)† | | 15 | 30 | 29lb |
| SCR-284 (American)† | 40+ | | |

109-Set (used by Australians)
  performance appears to have
  been more powerful than No. 22 Set

Dry battery portable (New Zealand)
  performance appears to have
  been similar to No. 38 Set

*CW (continuous wave) corresponds to US A-1 transmission.
†performance estimated from action reports.

Wireless networks' links to 48(RM) Commando during Walcheren landings, 1 November 1944.
The Commando network (net) linked all Troops with the CO's signaller moving (roving) with him. On this net 68-sets were backed by 38-sets as alternatives (circled figures show set types). The FOO was linked to the Commander Royal Artillery's net through a separate channel to the Cdo's rear HQ. Other links through the rear HQ and direct to Bde mortars, support craft, etc are shown in the diagram.

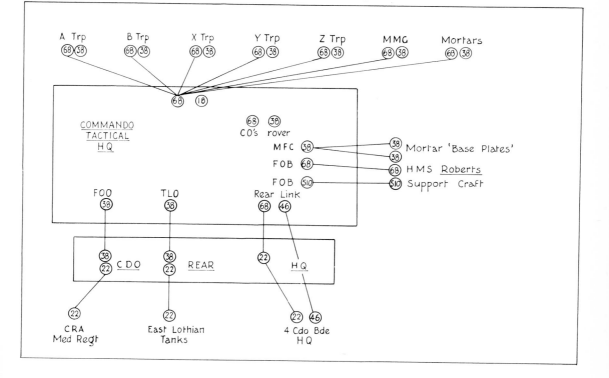

# 6 TRAINING PROGRAMME OF COMMANDO DEPOT 1942

Basic training in 3 months course (later cut to 5 weeks) with advanced courses of 2 weeks to a month for officers and NCOs training as instructors.

## Basic course

a. Offensive demolitions.
b. Close combat—unarmed; using fighting knife, pistol, Thompson, grenades; firing rifles and bren guns from hip; bayonet fighting; stalking; fighting in closely wooded country and streets.
c. Assault—opposed landings; field firing (using live ammunition on special firing ranges); surmounting obstacles; destroying anti-tank mines; elementary bridging; use of assault boats and scaling ladders.
d. Tactical schemes involving: endurance, living on concentrated rations, subordinate leadership, automatic battle drill, ambushes, night operations, road blocks, fieldcraft, quick reactions and necessity for rapid decisions,

## Instructors' courses

Close combat
Lectures and demonstrations over 9 periods of 55 minutes; practical—10 periods of PT, 14 of unarmed combat, 8 of sabre fencing to teach footwork, 12 of weapon training (grenade-throwing, etc.), 3 on assault course, 1 of boxing, 8

of stalking, 2 of field firing, 7 on scheme (tactical exercise), 8 on firing weapons etc., issuing equipment and free periods etc. took 13 periods of the 95 in a course of approximately 2 weeks.

Field craft
The 91 periods of this course included 15 of practical map reading, 28 on tactical schemes, 2 on mess-tin cooking, 2 on food values and 3 on constructing bivouacs. Map reading covered not only finding routes etc., but also panoramic drawing and field sketching.

Demolitions
Theory; technical appreciation; electrical circuits; destruction of railways, machinery, boilers, lock gates, petrol, etc.; practical in driving trains and placing charges, bore-holes, etc.

—extracts from *British Commandos*, Military Intelligence Dept. US War Department 9 August 1942

Note:
In January 1944 commando recruits to the Holding Operational Commando spent two weeks in preliminary weapon training, medicals, night-vision tests, etc. before a five-week course at the Commando Basic Training Centre (Achnacarry) followed by a week's leave. (For some months in 1943/4, the Basic Course was apparently cut to 4 weeks.) In preparation for war in the Far East, street-fighting and other practical skills only associated with European battles were substantially cut from the courses.

Close combat was taught to enable commandos to use every trick when opportunity offered, but if the advancing enemy was not intending to take a live prisoner, the man with a knife has no defence against a bullet. However a rifle is cumbersome at close quarters and if the enemy can be enticed close enough, a knife thrust or kick in the crotch proves effective.

# 7 UNIT HISTORIES

*Note: Decorations and awards include those awarded after the operations named.*

## BRITISH SPECIAL FORCES

### Special Service Brigade - 1940

The first parent organisation for the commandos was disguised as a Charity Committee and met in the private house of Sir Horace Rumbold but before the end of 1940 the Brigade was formed under Brigadier J. C. Haydon DSO, OBE and by March 1941 it had eleven Commandos. The Brigadier reorganised the commandos' formations, co-ordinated their training and established their roles in conjunction with Combined Operations Headquarters *et al*. In October 1943 the Brigade was replaced by the Special Service Group that would co-ordinate the activities of numbered brigades.

### Special Service Group

Formed in October 1943 under Major-General Sir R. G. Sturges KBE, CB, DSO the Group co-ordinated the work of the commandos and the transfer of men on the disbanding of the Royal Marine Division. In January 1944 the Group's deputy commander, Brigadier J. F. Durnford-Slater DSO, set up a planning headquarters alongside the British Second Army's HQ as part of the preparations for the Normandy landings.

The group and its successors administered Commando Brigades until these became totally an RM commitment in 1946.

### 1 Special Service Brigade
(renamed from SS to Commando)

Formed for the Normandy operations, this Brigade was raised by Brigadier the Lord Lovat DSO, MC with 3, 4, 6 and 45(RM) Commandos. (Officially it was the only SS Bde with an ordinal number as 1st SS Bde.) Landed in Normandy on 6 June 1944, the Brigade took their initial beach objectives and moved to their main task of holding the east flank with airborne troops along the Orne line. Holding these positions with only minor changes along the front, the Brigade withstood many German attacks. Lord Lovat was wounded on D+6 and Brigadier D. Mills-Roberts DSO, MC took command. During August the Brigade moved forward - 19 August they attacked high ground east of Dives and held it. They were withdrawn from France on 7 September 1944 after 83 days, and returned to the UK to prepare for campaigns in the Far East.

But after the German Ardennes offensive opened they returned to mainland Europe with 3, 6, 45(RM) and 46(RM) Commandos in January 1945, first at Asten on the Maas, where the Commandos were deployed in various operations including the penetration of the Siegfried Line at several points. In the February thaw they patrolled where tanks bogged in mud. Early in March the Brigade was brought by train to the Rhine where its primary task was the capture of Wesel taken after crossing the river on 23/4 March. During April under the command of 6 Airborne Division the Brigade took Osnabruck on 3/4 April. Three days later reinforcing a weak British company's bridgehead across the Weser, the Brigade had a fierce fight with German defenders of Leese, the commando advance guard being checked until the whole Brigade could cross the river on 7/8 April.

Transferred to the 11 Armoured Division's command for the Aller river crossing, the Brigade secured the rail bridge crossing on 12 April forcing a passage for the armour to cross by the Essel road bridge secured after two days fighting. A week later, under command of 15 Scottish Division and on their right flank, the Brigade prepared to cross the Elbe - 300 yards (270m) wide with a 150 foot (135m) eastern cliff bank near Lauenburg - low cloud preventing parachute drops and bombing. In a night crossing by Buffaloes under fire the Brigade stormed the cliffs and seized high ground north of the town. This was cleared and a patrol seized intact the main bridge of the Elbe-Trave Canal in the Brigade's last action. Early in May they were on the Baltic, having crossed five large rivers. After service with the Allied Army of occupation the Brigade was disbanded in 1946.

### 2 Special Service Brigade
(renamed from SS to Commando)

Formed in Italy November (?) 1943 under Brigadier T. B. L. Churchill MC from 2, 9, 40(RM) and 43(RM) Commandos with Belgian and Polish Troops of 10 Commando. Reconnoitred two enemy-free islands in Adriatic while based at Molfetta on Italian east coast under command of General Dempsey's XIII Corps. Sent 9 Commando to assist X Corps on west coast December 1943, the remainder of the Brigade followed and were concentrated at Naples under Fifth Army, 9 and 40(RM) Commandos went into the line for two months. The Brigade (less 2 Commando sent back to the Adriatic's Dalmatian coast) landed virtually unopposed at Anzio on 22 January 1944 and were withdrawn three days later.

Early in February 1944 they were in the line attacking three mountains - including Monte Faito of 3000+ft (1000+m) - overlooking the British 46 Division's positions on several lower peaks. On the night of 2/3 February in the bitter cold of the high Appenines, the Brigade captured Monte Ornito and a second peak, Point 711, but concentrated enemy mortar fire causing heavy commando casualties - the brigade lost 183 all ranks - prevented them reaching Monte Faito. On 2 March 9 and 40(RM) Commandos returned to Anzio (see their unit histories) where these elements of the Brigade distinguished themselves in several assaults culminating in their attack on one of the German's favourite start-lines among hillocks and ravines outside the perimeter. Although driven back at first, the Brigade regained the ravines before being withdrawn. April was spent resting back at Molfetta on the east cost.

There 2 Commando had been operating with Yugoslav partisans from the Island of Viz since February, their administration provided by the Brigade. Late in February other Commandos were moved to Viz. Brigade Headquarters landed there on 5 March and became part of Force 226 with British infantry, artillery and specialists. RAF Regiment units were also landed to protect the airfield built on the island in May when 'No. 40(RM)' also landed from Italy. In raiding from Viz ·the Brigade had much success until early June when they lost 127 all ranks on the island of Brac. After a meeting with Marshal Tito, standing patrols were placed on several islands and their supporting artillery successfully bombarded German positions on two occasions - once using a decoy LC making flashes beyond range of enemy guns to cloak the fact that the 25-pounders were ashore on a nearby island.

Commandos of the Brigade were patrolling Brac's north shore when partisans retook the island on 19 September. 2, 9 and 40(RM) had returned to Italy from where they operated in Albania (2 Commando), and in the north Adriatic (9 Commando).

In September the Brigade's advanced headquarters with 2 and 40(RM) Commandos were landed six miles from the port of Sarande on the Albanian mainland opposite Corfu. Here in monsoon-like rain, often on open mountainside studded with closely packed sharp small rocks, the Brigade spent a couple of weeks before putting in an assault on 8 October. Then in fine weather they attacked at three points assisted by the RAF Parachute Levies, partisans and artillery put ashore seven miles up the coast. 2 Commando had a difficult approach march for their dawn attack which succeeded in taking a German

battery of captured 25-pounders. The Levies, put ashore to isolate a German hill position, had taken their objective by noon, partisans took all their objectives but one. This was taken next day, 2 Commando using the recaptured 25-pounders. The Germans had mined the town but this was discovered by an RE officer and the town evacuated before the explosion (two days later). The Brigadier and his staff landed next day on Corfu when white flags were reported. A garrison was left on the island. The Brigadier, unable to get transport to chase the retreating Germans, resigned in protest but was given command of an infantry battalion on his return to the UK. The individual Commandos served as peacemakers and police among Greek and Albanian factions during the rest of the winter but in February 1945 were concentrated in Ravenna.

The Brigade then spent 6 weeks in the line to gain experience of German tactics before making an assault cross the Comacchio lagoon (see page 162). They next seized a large tract of land south of the Valetta canal before being relieved on 4 April. On 16 April 9 Commando was with the Guards Brigade forcing the passage of the Fossa Maxima north east of Agenta; the rest of the Brigade cleared the watery flats south-west of this town and took the bridge north of Menate. A series of actions that took the German commander (General-Lieutenant Graf von Schwern) by surprise, and opened the way for the main Allied thrust by V Corps coming through the Agenta gap before the Germans in North Italy surrendered on 2 May. Next day General McCreery told the Brigade commander that their successes on Agenta mud flats had been a decisive phase in the battle.

After service with the occupation forces and some reorganisation in September 1945 the Brigade was disbanded in 1946.

# 3 Special Service Brigade
(renamed from SS to Commando)

Formed in November 1943 under Brigadier W. I. Nonweiler with 1, 5, 42(RM) and 44(RM) Commandos for operations in south-east Asia, the Brigade sailed from the UK on 15 November 1943. A near-miss from enemy bombs in the Mediterranean loosened one transport's plates but caused only one casualty. However the ship took weeks to repair in Alexandria, causing delays for 'No. 1' and 'No. 42(RM)' so the whole Brigade was not together in the Far East until November 1944. Before then 'Nos. 5 and 44(RM)' were in action in Burma, but the Brigade did not land as a unit until January 1945 when led by Brigadier

Campbell Hardy DSO, landing unopposed on Akyab island off the Arakan coast.

Landing on 12 January they cleared a path for 74 Brigade to secure the Myebon peninsula, before the 22 January landings near Kangaw - see page 214. Despite heavy Japanese pressure to dislodge them from the key ridge position on 'Hill 170' the Commando Brigade held fast during the initial development of the battle and again when the Japanese final attacks were made on D+10. The Brigade was withdrawn to India to prepare for operations in Malaya and were ready to sail on 5 August when the landings were cancelled, the first atom bomb being dropped next day on Hiroshima.

The Brigade moved to Hong Kong later that summer and was reorganised in October 1946 when the Army 1 and 5 Commando were disbanded. A new *40 Commando RM* was formed from 'No. 44(RM)' and 45 Commando RM joined them from the UK. All commandos by this time were Royal Marines and their units designated Cdo RM with 40, 42 and 45 Commandos RM in the Brigade.

## 4 Special Service Brigade
(renamed from SS to Commando)

Formed in the late summer of 1943 under Brigadier B. W. Leicester DSO for operations in Normandy, the four Royal Marine Commandos of the Brigade (nos. 41, 46, 47 and 48) were landed on D-day and D+1, June 6/7 1944 with flank force roles. Although 46(RM) Commando's intended early D-day landing against a battery was cancelled and they landed on D+1. (See Chapter 11 for Brigade dispositions 6 June 1944). The Brigade joined 1 SS Bde in the defence of the east flank of the Allied beach-head, and were in this Orne line for two months until 19 August when they made a night infiltration moving south of 1 SS Bde to capture Dozulé in the heavily wooded country east of the Dives river.

Moving towards the Seine advanced elements of the Brigade reached the river Toucoques on 21 August, and in pouring rain were shelled by self-propelled guns across the river and Le Havre's big guns. 3 Parachute Brigade were trying to break into the burning Pont l'Evêque and on 23 August, in conjunction with 1 SS Bde, the commandos prepared to force a night crossing of the river to aid the paras. The operation was cancelled when the Germans withdrew after destroying their ammunition dumps. The following day (25 August) the Brigade set out to outflank the Germans holding the paras. They succeeded in making a 1,000 yard penetration south of

Beuzville, and on 26 August completed the 70 miles (110+km) of a 6 day advance with a night infiltration to St Maclou. The Brigade then passed from 6 Airborne Division's command to I Corps - Major-General Gale commanding the Airborne in an order of the day said '. . . the Green and the Red berets have fought as one'.

Crossing the Seine on 31 August at Duclair, in the next 5 days the Brigade liberated Pavilly, Yerville, Motteville, Yvêtot, Bermonville and Valmont. During the rest of September, after a spell policing Le Havre, the Brigade contained the German forces isolated in Dunkirk taking over from 2 Canadian Division. The port's surroundings were actively patrolled by the commandos before they in turn passed these duties to a composite force with carriers, and prepared for the Walcheren landings.

Training near Ostend during October when 'No. 4' replaced 'No. 46(RM)', the Brigade rehearsed landings in their amphibious vehicles and trained drivers for the Weasels allocated to them. They were joined by two Troops of 10 (Inter-Allied) Commando, a squadron of the Lothian Tank Regiment with Flails, an Assault Regiment with AVREs, two Field Companies RE, 144th Pioneer Company, and the 10th Canadian Field Dressing Station. Their landings on Walcheren are described in Chapter 11.

The Brigade left Walcheren on 12 November and after a rest period near Breskens they moved at the end of the month to defend the Scheldt islands. They were stationed around Goes on South Beveland during December, with some redeployment when the German offensive opened later that month. In February active patrolling began in a series of raids against Schouwen, Overflakkee and Tiengemeten islands (north of the Beveland islands) with the intention of moving north across the channels of the estuary if the Germans had evacuated the islands. Several raids over 2 miles (3+km) from their bases showed little German activity, but the Brigade actions further east on the Maas, when 47(RM) Commando had already been detached to join 1 Cdo Bde, was more active. Here south-east of Rotterdam and running east to west the Waal with the Maas 5 to 10 miles (8-16km) further south, forms part of the Rhine estuary rivers. 'No. 41(RM)' and later 'No. 48(RM)' were detached for a time on the Maas front, serving under command of 116 Infantry Bde.

The Brigade provided mobile reserves behind a Belgian battalion and 600 Dutch resistance fighters, while raiding into the Biesbosch complex of islands in the Maas/Merwede triangle of waters. The last raid was made on 22 April finding little opposition. Firing ceased on 1 May except for defensive and counter battery fire against definite targets, for the Allies were airdropping food to the starving population of north-west Holland.

The Brigade moved to Minden (Germany) late in May, here some reinforcements for 1 Commando Bde were drawn from 4 Bde in June expecting to see service in the Far East. After various guard duties the Brigade returned to the UK and was disbanded early in 1946.

## 1 Commando

First formed in the summer of 1940, some men transferred as parachute volunteers to the airborne. 90 men raiding Pointe de Saire (Courselles) from a small LSI were mistakenly landed at St Aubin on night 27/8 September 1941, the eastern force was driven off by machine gun fire but the western force ambushed a German cycle patrol and brought off an enemy body after 25 minutes ashore. The following April they sailed to the River Adour south of Bayonne but did not land due to estuary sandbars. In June 1942 they landed in the Boulogne/Le Touquet area penetrating 500 yards. The Commando in the Torch landings (North Africa) with attached American troops, came ashore on 8 November 1942 in the Algiers area, see Chapter 8.

During December 1942 the Commando were in the Allied line and in the next few months took part in overland raids and patrols based for part of the time in the area of Sedjenane. Returning to the UK on 24 April 1943, they prepared for operations in the Far East with 3 Commando Brigade. Delayed when their ship was bombed in the Mediterranean they did not reach Ceylon until September 1944, joining 3 Commando Brigade two months later.

Landing in Burma early in November 1944 they spent a short period with the XV India Corps carrying out eight patrols and experiencing the Japanese tactics in jungle warfare.

In early January they landed on the Myebon peninsula. Eight days later, 22 January, they came ashore as the assault Troops in taking Hill 170 when the Brigade landed near Kangaw. Moving in single file they secured the southern slopes but were held by enemy fire, however later that day they took the rest of this ridge-hill. On 31 January they beat off a major counter-attack, and in heavy fighting next day succeeded in holding nearly all the ridge against a series of attacks that lasted all day. The Commando moved with 3 Brigade to Hong Kong and was merged in the 1/5 Cdo before being disbanded in 1946.

## 2 Commando

Intended as a parachute unit on formation in July 1940, this Commando was later reformed for amphibious operations. The major part of two Troops went to Vaagsö with 3 Cdo (see page 34) in late December 1941. Drawn largely from 54 (East Anglian), 55 (Liverpool) and the London Divisions, the Cdo under Lieutenant Colonel A. C. Newman VC, TD, DL (Essex Regiment) provided the principal force for the successful St Nazaire raid in August 1942 (Chapter 2).

Reformed under Lieutenant-Colonel J. M. T. F. Churchill MC by the summer of 1943, the Commando arrived at Gibraltar (22 July 1943) and on 15 August they landed near Cap D'Ali (Sicily) as part of a force intended to cut off the German coast road retreat to Messina. They met little opposition spearheading the raiding force's drive into Messina, as the Germans had evacuated the area. In September they landed in Salerno Bay (Italy) and were virtually unopposed in coming ashore at Marina, but in the following week helped to hold the defile of La Molina against German counter-attacks.

After a spell of rest near Catania and a recruiting campaign among troops in the Mediterranean theatre, the Commando arrived at the island of Vis (Dalmatian coast) on 16 January 1944. From here they raided - often in company with Yugoslav partisans - first attacking the German outpost near Milna (a port on the island of Hvar) taking five German prisoners on 27 January. On 28 and 30 January further reconnaissance patrols landed on Hvar, on 3/4 February No. 2 Troop landed against a German platoon outpost at Grablje (Hvar) and captured the Germans' two fortified houses. Lieutenant Barton landed on the island of Brac, staying several days on a recce in mid-February. Posing as a shepherd, he infiltrated the German HQ area in the village of Nerejisce and with two partisans broke into the German CO's billet where the Lieutenant - using his Sten gun - shot the German in his bedroom. Escaping with the partisans, Barton was safely returned by them to Vis. The Lieutenant went back to Brac on 27 February and his small recce patrol captured a German outpost. Seven Americans of the Special Operations Group landed the same day on Hvar and outshot the only German patrol they met. Several recces were made on Solta during the next few weeks in preparation for a major raid.

The Solta landings were made on 17 March by two Troops of 2 Commando, 'No. 43 (RM)'s' Heavy Weapons Troop, two units of the American Special Operations Group (100 all ranks) and

3 captured Italian 47mm (1.7in) mountain guns manned by anti-aircraft gunners - a force of 43 officers and 450 ORs. They landed successfully and with their partisan guides made a night approach through steep hillside vineyards. The enemy had been alerted before the Commandos' support fire and a well-timed air attack enabled the raiders to break into the small garrison town of Grohote. The German CO was captured in the street fighting and persuaded his men to surrender, 104 prisoners were taken and four Germans killed. The Commando and Americans lost two men killed and 14 wounded. On 10 May a force of partisans with Commando support accounted for most of the other garrisons on this island.

The Commando helped the partisans in further reconnaissance raids on Korcula, Mljet and other islands during this spring (1944). On 23 May 2 Commando, with 'No. 43 RM', made an unsuccessful raid to Mljet where the expected German garrison could not be cornered and the commandos withdrew having taken some casualties from enemy fire. Early in June the Cdo landed on Brac (page 157) as part of a force including 1,300 partisans and Colonel Jack Churchill was captured. The Commando returned to Vis where they were later inspected by Marshal Tito before returning to Italy to rest and refit under Lieutenant-Colonel F. W. Fynn MC who had been Colonel Jack Churchill's 2i/c. In July he led them ashore 4 miles (6km) south of Spilje near the village of Himara in Albania, as part of a force of 12 officers and 700 men he commanded, including C Company of the 2nd Highland Light Infantry, the LRDG, a medical detachment and a press unit. The Germans had been warned of the landing and were ready to defend their four strong points. After repeated attacks on so stoutly defended a position, the Force withdrew and two days later partisans took the Spilje garrison when the German defenders were down to 32 tired men. In September the Commando landed at Sarande to support Albanian - and later Greek - partisans, see 2 SS Brigade's history.

After their return to Italy they were concentrated with 2 SS Bde near Ravenna in February 1945. Their part in the March 1945 assault across Lake Comacchio is described in Chapter 9. After this action the Cdo with 'no. 43 (RM)' operated in the flats south of Argenta as part of V Corps drive through the Argenta gap.

After the German surrender in Italy the Commando served with the occupation forces during the winter of 1945 and were disbanded the following year.

# 3 Commando

Formed at Plymouth early in July 1940 under Lieutenant-Colonel J. F. Durnford-Slater DSO who was appointed one of the first Commando COs on 28 June. He led 40 men of the 150-strong force raiding Guernsey some three weeks later. Ten of the first 35 officers were regulars and until the reorganisation early in 1941, the Commando - like others formed in 1940 - trained independently. In March 1941 they landed unopposed in the Lofoten Islands, the following December they made the first opposed major raid to Vaagsö - both actions are described in Chapter 2.

The Commando's target at Dieppe in August 1942 was the Berneval battery because - their CO has written - they were good at climbing cliffs. Enemy action at sea led to only a few men getting ashore but they successfully disrupted the battery's fire (see Chapter 5).

Brought up to strength in the autumn of 1942, the Commando relieved 'No. 9' at Gibraltar in February 1943. Here they were available for raids should Spain enter the war to help Germany. They were relieved by 2 Commando after several weeks and went to North Africa to train for the Sicily landings, these and their actions in Italy are described in Chapters 8 and 9 - the landing near Cassibile (Sicily) to take the battery north-west of this town; the outflanking landing to Malati bridge, their last operation in Sicily marked by a memorial stone inscribed 'No. 3 Commando bridge'; patrols landed to recce Bova Marina 27/8 August 1943; the early September landing at San Venere in the Toe of Italy; and the action at Termoli in a landing to outflank the German positions on the Biferno river.

Returning to the UK, in the winter of 1943/4 they prepared for the Normandy landings under Lieutenant-Colonel Peter Young DSO, MC. On 6 June 1944 they followed 'No. 45(RM)' and 'No. 6' across the beaches at La Breche west of Ouistreham. The Commando took their place in the Orne line, from here on the afternoon of D+1 (7 June) they put in a two-Troop attack on the Merville battery but after an initial success they were driven back by SP guns, one patrol led by Lieutenant H. T. Williams were all killed or wounded while stalking these guns. In the following weeks the Commando showed their excellent fire discipline, often waiting until an enemy patrol was almost on top of their positions before opening fire to destroy the enemy. They made the advance with 1 SS Bde east of the Dives.

In September they returned to the UK, but were back in the Allied line on 16 January 1945 at

Asten. Their first action was 10 miles west of the Siegfried Line at Linne (Holland).

The Commando crossed the Rhine in LVTs on the night of 23/4 March, passing through the leading commandos of 1 Cdo Bde into Wesel they cleared an area of the north and north-west suburbs with 46 (RM) and 45(RM) Commandos on their left cutting off the town's garrison from reinforcements. On 3 April in heavy spring rain showers they were 19 hours on the move, before putting in a night attack on Osnabruck from high ground north-west of the town. They met little resistance although others found serious opposition. The town fell to the Brigade next day. The Commando then found good billets with their HQ in a mansion and many men in a brewery.

After following 'No. 6' across the Weser, the Commando moved through woods on 8 April to attack a V-2 rocket factory a mile north of Leese. Capt. J. Alderson MC was killed and the CO - Lieutenant-Colonel Bartholomew - climbed on a tank in an exposed position, while he directed its fire and other tanks' shots until resistance ceased.

Taking the lead for the Brigade's crossing of the Aller on 12 April, No. 6 Troop in the van crossed the demolished first span of the railway bridge lying in fields a mile down river from Essel. While silently crossing the still intact river spans, 5 men were wounded but the bridge was taken and demolition charges removed.

The Commando's last action was in clearing Lauenburg with the Brigade on 29 April. After service with the occupation force, the Commando was disbanded in 1946.

# 4 Commando

Formed in July 1940, the Commando's medical teams were among the first to see action at Vaagsö in December 1941. From time to time the Commando provided men for raids, and in August they made a perfect flank guard's assault on the coastal battery west of Dieppe - see Chapter 5.

Their next major action was the Normandy landings of 6 June 1944 when, commanded by Lieutenant-Colonel R. W. P. Dawson, the Commando took the Ouistreham battery before moving to the Orne river line and two months active patrolling.

A detachment was sent (with some men of 6 Commando) to guard General Montgomery's Headquarters for several weeks.

On 18 August the Commando made a 3-hour march, having by-passed the wood on their front, to reach Bavent village evacuated by the Germans that morning. At 2000 hours on 20 August,

Troop leaders were briefed for the night march to L'Epine, their starting point for the assault on the road crossing near Deauville on the plateau beyond the Dives river. The light was fading as the men were briefed for the complicated route to follow, passing over a duckboard bridge across the River Dives to a difficult scramble up the far bank. They reached the start line after a nightmare march although no enemy opposed them until they came to a strip of road some 400 yards from their crossroads objective. Next day they marched on to the plateau and a welcome lack of mosquitoes. They passed through the burning Pont L'Eveque, prepared for another infiltration, but the Germans had withdrawn and in bright sunshine they marched to Beuzeville. Three miles beyond the town each Troop was given an area with barns where they slept on straw 15 hours a day from 28-31 August.

After returning to the UK they came back to mainland Europe in October joining 4 SS Bde to prepare for the Walcheren assault. Their landing at Flushing (see page 199) was a fine example of the exploitation of opportunity, for no detailed landing point could be fixed before they crossed the Scheldt. After the actions on Walcheren and a short rest at Ostend, the Commando raided a German HQ on Schouwen getting ashore unopposed on this island in the Maas. They killed four pairs of sentries but were driven off the island by superior numbers.

The Commando was disbanded on 1 July 1946.

# 5 Commando

Formed in July 1940 largely from regulars and reservists who had escaped from Dunkirk. On 30/31 August 1941 30 men of the Commando landed at Merlimont Plage (south of Hardelot) and got ashore at two points but found no enemy. Four of the Commando were killed at St Nazaire, Sergeant F. A. Carr RE was awarded the DCM and Lieut S. W. Chant the MC, for their part in this raid. Two months later the Commando landed on Madagascar with the 5 Division to secure this French colony from possible Japanese invasion. After the men had 'a run ashore' in Durban the fast and slow convoys sailed north to meet at dusk on 4 May off Diego Suarez, before a destroyer led them through the reefs into this naval base's outer anchorage where the landing craft were launched at 0620. The Commando reached the town without serious loss but the artillery could not be landed until nightfall as their LST HMS *Bachequero* could not find a steep enough shore and when she did so there was no road inland from this beach. At Antsirane 50

Royal Marines got into the town by determination and good fortune, after landing from a destroyer under fire, and 'took the Frenchmen's eyes off the ball'. By daybreak the Vichy forces surrendered. They had lost 150 killed and 500 wounded in these actions and two more landings - by 29 Brigade - were made during the next 5 months before the island was secured. By then the Commando was back in the UK where under Lieutenant-Colonel Shaw they became part of 3 SS Bde. Colonel Shaw was 'a first rate officer' in the opinion of a fellow CO.

They reached Bombay with 44(RM) Commando on 22 January 1944 and early in March landed at Alethangyaw where they were ashore several days near this Arakan village before returning to the main XV Corps' positions. On 23 March they were again in this coastal strip and in a series of patrols they took machine-gun posts on several hills near Maungdaw (120 miles south of Chittagong). Withdrawn to Silchar with other forces waiting a possible Japanese advance through north-west Burma, before the Commando was withdrawn to Ceylon joining the rest of 3 Cdo Bde.

Their part in the landings at Myebon and Kangaw during January 1945 is described in Chapter 12. They were withdrawn with the Brigade to Poona (India) and disbanded from Hong Kong in 1946 as 1/5 Cdo.

## 6 Commando

Formed at Scarborough in the summer of 1940 under Lieutenant-Colonel T. E. Fetherstonhaugh OBE, this Commando - like several others - spent some months standing by for possible raids to the Atlantic islands, and in December 1941 they embarked for a raid with half of 12 Commando against Floss (Norway). The raid was called off due to navigational difficulties but there were 17 casualties, including 6 men killed when a press camera-man moved some grenades and a 36 grenade went off before it could be hurled clear of a hatchway. Sailing to River Ardour estuary with 1 Commando in April 1942, they did not land. On 3/4 June 250 of the Commando landed north of Plage St Cecily, but their radar station target was heavily defended. The raiders nevertheless got ashore although their approach was detected.

They boarded transports in October for the Torch (North African) landings and came ashore under Lieutenant-Colonel I. F. MacAlpine on 8 November 1942 with Americans near Algiers - see Chapter 8. On 22 November they had 43 casualties (11 killed) when their train was strafed.

On later reaching the Maizelia Valley they made several patrols. During one of these Nos. 1 and 3 Troops found the reported enemy tanks were clever dummies with track marks leading to them. In a series of such patrols the Commando killed or captured 28 Germans before leaving the Valley. On 26 November they made their base in the mine at Sedjenane. Among other forays they attacked the flat-topped 'Green' hill. Here No. 5 Troop's feint attack at 0400 hours on 30 November merely awakened the Germans to the pending assault by Nos. 3, 4 and 6 Troops who were caught in fire from the hilltop's diamond-shaped defences. Artillery support that afternoon failed against rock-hewn defences, and in the wet and misty weather No. 5 Troop was ambushed with only 5 survivors, No. 6 Troop was held and Nos. 3 and 4 forced back from their penetration of the defences. Lack of ammunition prevented further artillery support, Capt. J. Murray Scott was killed and the attack died away with 80 casualties.

When the CO was invalided home, Lieutenant-Colonel Derek Mills-Roberts took command. On 5 January 1943 three and a half Troops returned to the Green hill - as Mano force under Captain J. R. D. Mayne. Two Troops made a 10 mile (16km) march to seize high ground while one and a half Troops held Point 227 protecting 36 Brigade's left flank. Next day Mano force covered the Brigade's withdrawal.

Late in February 1943 the Commando with a depleted Recce Regiment covered the plain of Goubellat east of the 11 Brigade's mountain positions. On 26 February a dawn patrol surprised a strong enemy force and the Commando lost 55 all ranks in the next 5 hours but extricated themselves from encirclement. In the following three weeks of heavy rain interspersed with fiercely hot days, they patrolled the plain - the Green Patch. After a spell of rest they were withdrawn from North Africa in April 1943 to prepare for Normandy.

On 6 June 1944 they landed to pass through the assault infantry and make a rapid advance to support the airborne holding bridges over the Caen Canal and Orne River - see Chapter 11. They dug-in above Le Plein and on 12 June took heavy casualties from shelling during the capture of Breville, Lieutenant-Colonel Lewis taking over from Brigadier D. Mills-Roberts, DSO, MC who now commanded 1 SS Bde. The Commando took part on 19 August in the night infiltration of high ground beyond the Dives River. The Commando were withdrawn with 1 SS Bde to the UK.

The first major action on returning to Europe was on 23/4 January 1945, crossing the Juliana

Canal to occupy Maasbracht they held off counter-attacks and next day took crossroads beyond the town in an advance with a squadron of 8th Hussars' tanks. In the next fortnight, often riding on the Hussars' tanks, the Commando lost 106 all ranks in penetrations of the Siegfried Line. But the February thaw halted the armour.

Crossing the Rhine at Wesel (see Chapter 11) on 23/4 March, the Commando was in storm boats under fire and with many outboards breaking down. Several men were drowned when one boat drove under the river current, and RSM Woodcock had three boats sunk under him before he got across.

To reinforce 'No. 45(RM)' and a Rifle Bde company in Leese, the Commando collected sufficient boats to cross the Weser at midnight on 7/8 April and led the Brigade's march across ditches, marshland and embankments to be behind the town at dawn. No. 2 Troop then captured a position of four 20mm guns and the town was taken by 0700 hours. Four days later the Commando charged the road bridge across the Aller, their hunting horns and cries 'must have curdled the blood of the German marines' that mid-morning, for the Commando reached positions 400yds (350+m) into the heavily defended woods beyond the bridge and the Germans never retook these defences.

In their last river crossing the Commando stormed the far bank of the Elbe 2 miles (3km) downstream from Lauenburg landing in LVTs at 0200 hours on 29 April. The leading Troops, Nos. 1 and 2, drove the enemy from the low cliff tops before their 1 Cdo Bde passed through the bridgehead. The assault was covered by guns of the Mountain Regiment whose FOO, Captain R. Marshall, was killed in the cliff assault. Later that day they helped to clear Lauenburg in their last action before disbandment in 1946.

## 7 Commando ·

Formed in August 1940 the Commando sailed with Layforce arriving in Egypt on 10 March 1940. As 'A' Battalion of a brigade in 6 Division they raided Bardia on 19/20 April meeting little opposition - see Chapter 8. In May they went to Crete as part of the British reserves. Here in a bayonet charge Captain F. R. J. Nicholls' G Troop dislodged Germans from a hill enfilading the Commando, in one of many of their rearguard actions in Crete during four days 27-31 May 1941. Many were captured when the British evacuation foundered and the remainder were dispersed - some to the Middle East Commando - when the Commando was disbanded that summer.

## 8 Commando

Formed in June 1940 under Lieutenant-Colonel R. E. Laycock (later Major-General R. E. Laycock, CB, DSO) with many men from the Household Cavalry, the Foot Guards, the Somerset Light Infantry and some Royal Marines. Their actions as part of Layforce and 'B' Battalion of the Brigade attached to 6 Division in the Mediterranean are described in Chapter 8 - the rearguard skirmishes in May on Crete, and the attack on Twin Pimples near Tobruk. The Commando was disbanded in July 1941.

## 9 Commando

Formed in the summer(?) of 1940. A Troop of the Commando landed on 22/3 November 1941 east of Houlgate to attack a 4-gun position, but coming ashore ¼ mile (400m) from their intended landing point, they were unable to cross a clay cliff in time to put in a final attack. Private J. Davidson, a bren gunner in the cover party that stayed aboard the two LCAs has written: '. . . after a couple of weeks aboard *Princess Beatrix,* we sailed on a suitable night . . . before boarding the LCAs we were issued with 1,000 Fr francs and "pills" for escape rations . . . one LCA broached-too in the rough landing and was towed off (with difficulty) . . . but no enemy were about . . . we realised that the returning party would have to swim for it . . . suddenly Very lights were shot into the air . . . searchlights beamed on us . . . I could see trucks on the coast road, they would have 3 or 4 miles to cover before they reached the embarkation point.' After an exchange of torch signals between those ashore and the LCA crews, the raiders swam out. The LCA gunners holding their fire, for any stream of tracer from the craft would reveal their position. One party of raiders had called at a farmhouse and on being told of an expected 2-man cycle patrol they set a rope across the road to dismount these riders, but no sooner was the ambush set than 'the balloon went up'. The commandos always assumed they were given away by the woman who told them of the patrol, but there is no evidence of this betrayal. Private Davidson's LCA 'half-full of water and with only one engine working' was attacked by a Stuka. This plane was almost certainly shot down on its second strafing run when Private Davidson got two bren gun bursts into its fuselage.

This accurate personal account has interesting differences from the official record, but as Mr Davidson has pointed out: it is only a part of the story.

The Commando went to Gibraltar where their CO (later Brigadier R. J. F. Tod DSO) prepared plans for possible raids. In November, with men of 'No. 40 (RM)', they visited Tremeti and Pianos finding these Adriatic islands free of enemy. In December they moved to the west coast of Italy carrying out the successful diversion raid north of the Garigliano river - described in Chapter 9. On 22 January 1944 they landed unopposed at 0530 hours in the Allied Anzio outflanking move against Rome. A plan was abandoned for Special Forces to seize the city in a separate action, as they could not be put ashore nearer than 21 miles from Rome before 0200 hours, and, as no transport was available, dawn would break before even Commandos could be expected to march this distance and cross defences.

Within the week they were withdrawn and in the Allied mountain line reconnoitring the Monte Ornito area in front of the British 46 Division. Colonel Tod was hit, six officers and the RSM were killed and with casualties mounting the Commando were drawn back on to the forward slopes of Monte Ornito. With the Brigade they held these positions until relieved that night.

After two weeks' rest they were back at Anzio early in March, when 9 Commando made eleven patrols. On 19 March, led by Colonel Tod recovered from his wounds, they made a night sally from the perimeter against the German area of ravines where attacks were often formed up. A determined German attack reached the Commando HQ in an hour-long battle. Colonel Tod and the mess cook, Douglas Brown, manned a bren before the Commando surged forward. They were, however, ordered to withdraw under the cover of artillery fire.

April 1944 was spent in rest and reorganisation at Molfetta. In May a Troop was landed 30 miles south of Ancona and some 100 miles north of Rome, rescuing 120 prisoners of war from 70 miles bechind the German lines. A raid by 109 of the Commando on the bridge joining Cherso and Lussino Island, and Fascist HQ at Nerezine (40 miles NE of Zadar) was successful against 'no real opposition'. The Commando occupied the island of Kithera a few miles from the southern tip of the Greek mainland. They protected the island naval base at Kapsali and were brigaded with several Greek units including 350 men of the Greek Sacred Regiment, as Foxforce. The commandos worked to help the new Greek government avoid factional fights between opposing Greeks, and negotiated the surrender of the German garrison of Kalamata (on the southern Greek coast). The whole Force moved to Poros in the Aegean, on 1 October, where they threatened the Germans still on Crete, Cos, and Leros, although the Germans still held Corinth, Athens and its port. Over-estimating Foxforce's strength,

the Germans withdrew and on 14 October the Force landed at Piraeus (the port of Athens) seizing the airfield nearby. That afternoon the Commando made a ceremonial entry into Athens, before going to Salonika for garrison duties and returning to Italy in February 1945.

Their actions around Comacchio are described in Chapter 9. On 16 April 1945 they fought their last action when they and the Guards' brigade forced the passage of the Fossa Maxima. The following year they were disbanded.

## 10 (Inter-Allied) Commando

Formed in January 1942 under Lieutenant-Colonel Dudley S. Lister MC with Major Peter Laycock as 2 i/c, by 31 October 1942 was 9 officers and 96 ORs with attached French marines and Dutch soldiers: 3 officers and 64 marines of the French Navy and 4 Dutch officers with 75 ORs. Troops of various nationalities joined the Commando or were attached to it, and a brief history cannot do justice to the range of operations carried out by these Commando Allies many having escaped from German-occupied territories.

The French under the marine Captain Philippe Kieffer provided Nos. 1 and 8 Troops and a K-gun Section of No. 9 Troop. Their first action was at Dieppe, where 15 officers fought as interpreters and guides. A dozen or so were casualties in later small-scale raids of 1943/4, described in Chapter 10; by the summer of 1944 there were about 180 Frenchmen attached to the Commando, and on 6 June 1944 two Troops landed with 4 Commando, they had captured the Casino at Ouistreham by 1100 hours. From this D-day afternoon until 26 July they were in the Orne line near Amfreville, then they moved to south-west of Bavent on the right of the line. They advanced from Bavent on 19 August across flooded fields of the Dives Valley, attacking the high ground beyond as part of 1 SS Bde. Their first contacts in the field with French resistance forces was near Beuzeville on 26 August and by 6 September they were making recces towards Honfleur and Paris before returning with the Brigade to the UK. They came back to Europe in October and landed with 4 Commando at Flushing, later raiding Scheldt river islands, their last Unit operation being a raid on Overflakkee in January 1945. Over 400 men had served with these Commando Troops (the 1er Bataillon Fusilier Marin) by the end of the War, when a detachment served in Berlin (1945/6) and others trained the new French army's Commandos.

The Dutch Troop under the giant Captain P. Milders landed with 4 Cdo Bde at Westkapelle in

November 1944, and provided raiding forces before then. The Belgian Troop under the cheerful Captain G. Danloy served in Italy and Yugoslavia with 2 Cdo Bde. The Polish Troop was also with this Brigade and vied with the Belgians in the fierceness of their patrolling high in the Apenines, on one occasion with men of X Troop (see below) they carried out guerrilla operations near Monte Rotondo successfully disrupting German communications.

The Norwegian Troop provided men for raids during 1942/4 with some raiders spending days at a time on the occupied Norwegian coast. The Yugoslav Troop, never more than 2 officers and 14 men, worked on SOE-type operations, apparently. A Czech group parachuted in one of these operations to curb the outrages of Reinhard Heydrich in Prague. X Troop, under Captain Bryan Hilton-Jones was mainly recruited from Germans and Austrians, with some Hungarians and Greeks.

The eight 'Hardtack' dory raids in December 1943 and the 'Tarbrush' series the following May (described in Chapter 10) are typical of the actions in which 10 Commando provided men for a series of diversions and reconaissances. On 24/5 February 1944, 7 men landed north of Schevneningen in Holland to reconnoitre as far as the Aakver Canal but in the laconic report, typical of several about these raids, the 'party landed 0200, dory waited but nothing more was seen of the party'. At other times these commandos worked with regular forces, as in the 17 June 1944 landings at Elba, when a small party of French commandos landed at 0100 (H - 1 hour) taking many casualties but destroying the guns covering Campo Bay.

After the war many of the records of their operations were wisely destroyed, but there is no doubt that this Unit provided an opportunity for many different nationalities to fight for freedom.

## 11 Commando

Formed before the end of 1940, this Commando - sometimes known as the 'Scottish Commando' - sailed with Layforce to the Middle East, where in May 1941 they provided the Cyprus garrison. On 7/8 June 1941 they landed against French defences on the north bank of the Litani River in Syria, the CO Lieutenant-Colonel R. R. H. Pedder was killed and the Commando lost 25% of its strength - see Chapter 8.

They returned to Cyprus and were disbanded in the late summer when some joined the Middle East Commando and others returned to their regiments.

## 12 Commando

Known as the Irish and Welsh Commando, the unit was formed mainly from men of North of Ireland and Welsh regiments early in 1941 and 16 men in two LCAs made the cross-Channel raid to Ambleteuse - a partial success - in July 1941. In December that year they sailed but did not land in abandoned Floss (Norway) raid but on 26 December 223 (all ranks) of the Commando, under their CO Lieutenant-Colonel S. S. Harrison MC with attached Norwegian forces (78 soldiers and 65 sailors), landed unopposed in the Lofoten Islands. Their supporting force of 23 ships had to withdraw due to enemy bombing and the raiders did not stay as long as planned. In February 1942 they provided the recovery force of 32 men for the Bruneval parachute raid. In March three were killed at St. Nazaire, and Lieutenants Gerard Brett and C. W. Purdon of the Royal Ulster Rifles were awarded the MC for their part in this raid, Sergeants S. Deery (Royal Inniskilling Fusiliers) and James Johnson (Gordons) were awarded the MM. From 11-14 April a detachment visited Deviken Fjord (Norway) in operation *Carey*. Later in 1942 four of the Commando landed on Sark with the SSRF in October.

During 1943 the Commando provided men for several raids including: Stord Island (Norway) where 50 men including guides from 10 Commando destroyed mine installations on 23/4 January; 8 men of a 10-man cross-Channel raid to Eletot 3/5 August, visited again 1-4 September when the raiders stayed ashore 2 nights; and on 3/4 Sept another party - 18 men from 'No. 12' and 2 Rangers - raided the Porz/Ahech enemy post on Ushant killing two enemy (probably) but were unable to identify the German unit, in the last recorded operation of the Commando.

## 14 Commando

Raised early in 1943 for raids over long distances into the Arctic Circle, where German bases supported their armies on the Finnish border and their bombers attacked Allied convoys to Murmansk, the Commando trained in Arctic warfare planning to destroy torpedoes and bombs in these northern Luftwaffe bases. A number of Canadians and Red Indians served with this Unit.

The severe weather conditions and turbulent northern seas made their raids extremely hazardous but in April 1943 six men of the Commando crossed to Norway in an MTB towing a cobble carrying canoes. They sailed the fishing boat into Haugesund on 27 April but nothing was heard of them after they left the MTB. Unconfirmed reports suggest they used their limpets to do some damage to shipping near Bergen. The Commando was disbanded probably before the end of 1943.

## 30 Commando

(Special Engineering Unit and later 30th Assault Unit)

Trained as free divers to collect papers from sunken ships and including specialists in intelligence who collected papers from enemy headquarters, the Unit operated as near to - if not ahead of - the vanguard of invading forces. Formed by the summer of 1941, this small unit made searches of enemy HQs in Sicily and Italy during 1942/3. In February 1944 they became an Admiralty Intelligence Unit, the 30th Assault Unit. They were unable to get into the radar station at Douvres when the planned capture of this strong-hold failed, but maintained a patrol 200 yards from its perimeter until 17 June when - before the station fell - they were moved to join a second party (A and B Troops with most of the Unit's HQ). On 22 June they fought their way into Cherbourg and found 'masses of material as well as an excellent wine cellar'.

They searched the safes, files, dustbins of burnt paper, desks and lockers during the next two days. The Unit wore Green Berets but after June 1944 ceased to wear Commando flashes.

In July 1944 began a series of races '... towards Rennes ... after 4 days searching [files] ... towards Brest' and in August they followed the French Forces into Paris, moving ahead of T Force, the Army Intelligence counterpart to the 30th Assault Unit. In September they worked along the Channel coast ports as these were captured. The Unit was redesignated 30 Advanced Unit in the winter of 1944/5 and disbanded in December(?) 1945.

## Royal Marine Commandos

These commandos' operations are part of their Corps' history in WWII when many marines from ships' detachments as well as their Commando units carried out amphibious operations. Although the RM Commandos were not individual volunteers, they were all volunteers for RM service. However, in the opinion of one of their senior officers, some of the best men had been posted from the RM Division when its battalions of 1940/1 were reorganised as Commandos: 8th Bn-41(RM) on 10 October 1942; 1st Bn-42 (RM) on 10 October 1942; 2nd Bn-43(RM), 3rd Bn-

44(RM), 5th Bn-45(RM), all during 1943; 9th Bn-46(RM), 10th Bn-47(RM) both in August 1943; and 7th Bn-48(RM) on 2 March 1944. (A full history of the Royal Marines in World War II is in the course of preparation in October 1977.)

Many of their senior commando officers later rose to high rank in the Corps, including: General Sir Campbell R. Hardy, KCB, CBE, DSO** (46(RM) Commando); General Sir Ian H. Riches, KCB, DSO (43(RM) Commando); Major-General G. C. Horton CB, OBE (44(RM) Commando); Major-General H. D. Fellowes (42(RM) Commando); and Major-General J. L. Moulton CB, DSO, OBE (48(RM) Commando).

## 40(RM) Commando

Raised at Deal on 14 February 1942 and designated RM 'A' Cdo for a short period until 29 October 1942, the Commando took heavy casualties in the Dieppe landings of August 1942 when the CO, Lieutenant P. Picton-Phillipps RM, was killed. Brought up to strength they served in Sicily, Italy and the Adriatic where their CO, Lieutenant-Colonel J. C. Manners RM, died of wounds. Lieutenant-Colonel R. W. Sankey DSC, RM led the Commando during their later operations in Corfu and north Italy.

This Commando absorbed 43(RM) Commando on 10 September 1945 and typically of all post-WWII British Commandos, after disbandment in 1946, the unit was reformed as 40 Commando RM from 44(RM) Commando in March 1947.

## 41(RM) Commando

Briefly designated RM 'B' Commando in October 1942 the Commando landed in Sicily, at Salerno (Italy), in Normandy (June 1944) and at Walcheren (November 1944) serving with distinction in all these operations.

## 42(RM) Commando

Served in Burma 1944/5 landing at Myebon and Kangaw, their CO Lieutenant-Colonel H. D. Fellowes DSO was wounded in these actions.

## 43(RM) Commando

Their first operation was the January 1944 landing at Anzio in Italy, where later they fought on the Garigliano front before transfer to the Adriatic and subsequent return to North Italy.

## 44(RM) Commando

Landed in March 1944 on their first raid into the Arakan, and subsequently took part in the Myebon and Kangaw landings of January 1945.

## 45(RM) Commando

Landed 6 June 1944 in Normandy where their CO Lieut-Col N. C. Ries, RM was wounded, and Lieutenant-Colonel W. N. Gray (later CMG, DSO*) took over command for the rest of the War. While attacking Linne (Germany) in bitterly cold weather the Commando was heavily engaged on 23 January 1943, when L/Cpl Eric Harden RAMC was killed rescuing the third of the casualties he brought out from A Troop's isolated position. An action for which he was awarded the VC.

## 46(RM) Commando

Landed D+1 (7 June 1944) in Normandy and took heavy casualties in subsequent fighting in support of Canadians. Took part in German river crossings, commanded by Lieutenant-Colonel T. M. Gray, DSO, MC, RM.

## 47(RM) Commando

Landed D-day 6 June 1944 in Normandy taking Port en Bessin by D+1 in an independent action. After further action in France and a spell of rest, they landed at Walcheren in November 1944. Served in Holland January-April 1945.

## 48(RM) Commando

Landed D-day 6 June 1944 and after action in France took part in Walcheren landings (November 1944). Served in Holland January-April 1945.

## 50 and 52 Commandos

Raised in the Middle East early in 1941 these small units were amalgamated as the Combined (Middle East) Commando and became D Battalion of the Commando force with 6 Division. They wore the knuckle-duster cap badge and included Royal Marines apparently, but after service in Crete presumably - for no detailed Unit History is in the Public Record Office - the unit was disbanded that summer (1941). See also Middle East Commando. One reference to 51 Commando suggests it may have been planned but not created.

## 62 Commando

Formed in July 1941, later joined by former members of the 1 Small Scale Raiding Force, and under Lieutenant A. David Stirling, Scots Guards, served as 'L Detachment' in Egypt. David Stirling believed that a major strike against one target behind enemy lines was wasteful and resources were better employed in a series of small simultaneous raids by determined men. During operations with the Long Range Desert Group against Axis communications in North Africa, the unit developed its own heavily armed jeep with a Browning machine-gun firing forward and twin Lewis or Vickers K-guns firing to the rear. They did parachute training but their only air drop at this stage of the war (on 16 November 1941) failed to destroy fighters on five enemy airfields before an Allied offensive.

For a short period the unit was designated 'No. 1 Small Scale Raiding Force' but in February 1943 they became the 1st Special Air Service (the SAS). From a strength of 10 officers and 40 ORs in February 1943, their establishment rose to 400 all ranks with five squadrons. (See SAS brief history below.)

## Middle East Commando

On disbanding Layforce (7, 8, 11, 50 and 52 Commandos) after their actions in Crete and Syria, a Commando force attached to the Eighth Army was sometimes known as the Middle East Commando. 6 officers and 53 ORs of this force made the November 1941 raid on what was thought to be Rommel's desert HQ (see Chapter 8). The force was disbanded early in 1942.

## The Chindits

Brigadier (later Major-General) Orde Wingate in 1943 led seven columns of his 77th Infantry Brigade in a 4 months' raid behind the Japanese lines in Burma. They were supplied by air having marched in. The following year Orde Wingate and his Brigadiers - including Mike Calvert and Bernard Fergusson - took six brigades, now called 'Chindits', into the Indaw area. But Mike Calvert has written that the Chindits' long range penetration warfare 'was never meant to be "guerrilla warfare" ... these columns would operate independently ... and then come together forming a fist ... [as] an outflanking movement from the air'. Their use almost as troops in the line led to their near destruction before the last Chindit Brigade was withdrawn in August 1944.

# AMERICAN SPECIAL FORCES

## 1st Marine Raider Regiment

Formed 15 March 1943 in Espiritu Santo (an Allied Pacific base in the New Hebrides) as part of the First Marine Amphibious Corps (IMAC) from existing 1st, 2nd, 3rd and 4th Raider Bns who were later detached from time to time. After moving to Guadalcanal, the Regiment's CO, Colonel Harry B. Liversedge, commanded the Northern Landing Group originally planned as a Raider operation against New Georgia but made up of 1st Raiders, US Army's 3rd Bn (45th Infantry) and 3rd Bn (48th Infantry). The unopposed 5 July 1943 landings were on a narrow front as only 4 craft could beach at one time. The Force advanced south-west from Rice Anchorage to block Japanese reinforcement of their south coast Munda air-base's defences, or their later withdrawal from this area attacked by US Army Units that July after a series of landings.

The Force divided with one army battalion moving to block the southern trail to Munda while the remainder cleared the area of Dragon Point between Enogai village and Bairoko Harbour further west. The Force was held on 9 July by the Enogai defences despite air support, but without artillery. The Princeton University study of USMC amphibious warfare in the Pacific, points out the limitations in conventional battles for Raider Regiments without heavy guns. Although well led and determined men, the Raiders did not take Enogai until next day, when over 300 Japanese dead were counted - 47 raiders had been lost. The failure of close air support on this occasion led to later improvements in ground-to-air cooperation but in 1943 bombers were not an adequate substitute for artillery.

The Regiment - joined by its 4th Raiders - in aggressive patrols scouted the defences of Bairoko meeting fierce opposition. This village was bombed by B-17s and shelled by light naval forces but held out. The Munda airbase was taken on 3 August and the Northern Force moved south to cut off the Japanese retreat in a series of scattered actions during the following three weeks, before the Japanese evacuated the village of Bairoko on 24 August.

The Raiders were withdrawn and not brought up to strength before the Regiment was disbanded on 1 February 1944, when most of the men had been transferred to the 4th Marines.

## 2nd Marine Raider Regiment (Provisional)

Formed 12 September 1943 under Lieutenant-Colonel Alan Shapley to coordinate 2nd and 3rd Raiders' operations on Bougainville when these battalions were attached to 3 Marine Division - the 2nd with the 3rd Marines Regiment and the 3rd with the 9th Marines. Bougainville is 125 miles (200km) long and 30 miles (48km) wide, lying across the channel (the 'Slot') separating the two chains of Solomon Islands running south east from Bougainville (the largest of these islands). The island's northern mountains fall away to a southern plain where the Japanese had several airfields. These were part of the defence system protecting the major Japanese base at Rabaul (New Britain) and in turn would provide Allied fighter bases to block Japanese air raids from that base.

The Raider battalions on Bougainville, after the 1 November 1943 south-west coast landings, took part in a number of offensive patrols and had their share of defensive work on the perimeter, but the Japanese could not bring together their full strength of two divisions for a counter attack until January 1944. By this time the Marines had been withdrawn in a sensible use of amphibious forces - having taken the beach-head, and enlarged it so that enemy artillery fire could not reach the airfield, the 3 Marine Division handed over a prepared perimeter to an army corps, who in turn passed the defences to Australians when the American army later moved against the Philippines, bypassing Rabaul.

The 2nd Raider Regiment were withdrawn from Bougainville on 11 January 1944 and disbanded on 26 January.

## 1st Marine Raider Battalion

Formed 16 February 1942 under Lieutenant-Colonel Merrill A. Edson, these raiders landed at Tulagi in August 1942, and later that summer were in action on Guadalcanal in the Solomon Islands - see Chapter 6 - where they held Bloody Ridge against frenzied Japanese attacks. They left Guadalcanal on 16 October for rest and reorganisation at Nouméa (New Caledonia) 800 miles south of Guadalcanal. On 5 July 1943, as part of the Northern Landing Force at New Georgia, the Battalion was in a series of actions. Their heaviest fighting, on 20 July (D+15), began at 1015 hours when moving towards Bairoka, they came on Japanese machine-gun and sniper positions. In minutes they were pinned down, as the enemy's log and coral bunkers under sprawling banyan roots made a series of well camouflaged defences along a ridge. The thick jungle cover exploded mortar bombs before they reached the bunkers, and without flamethrowers the marines had only demolition charges and small arms to reduce these defences. The 1st Raiders were joined by the 4th Battalion but progress was slow despite the Raiders' determination. The Raiders therefore withdrew that night to their positions around Enogai.

The 1st Raiders had lost 74 killed and 139 wounded before finally leaving New Georgia on 28/29 August 1943. The Battalion had fought their last action and was disbanded on 1 February 1944. They received a Presidential Unit Citation for their operations in the Solomons.

## 2nd Marine Raider Battalion

Formed on 16 February 1942 under Lieutenant-Colonel Evans F. Carlson the 2nd Raiders raided Makin Island on 17 and 18 August 1942, and made a month-long raid on November 1942 behind Japanese lines on Guadalcanal - see Chapter 6. In November 1943 under Lieutenant-Colonel Joseph P. McCaffrey USMC, they landed west of Cape Torokina (in the Empress Augusta Bay Area, Bougainville) on 1 November 1943. Coming ashore on Green 2 beach, they moved east to a mission station, and on D+8 (9 November) they fought a stubborn battle for a trail junction they took that afternoon. For the rest of the month and into December they fought in support of the 3rd Marine Regiment before being withdrawn to Guadalcanal on 11 January 1944.

The Battalion received a Presidential Unit Citation for their operations in the Solomons before being disbanded on 31 January 1944.

## 3rd Marine Raider Battalion

Formed under Lieutenant-Colonel Harry B. Liversedge on 20 September 1942 in American Samoa. (Harry-the-Horse Liversedge was an international athlete). On the night 20/1 February 1944 led his Battalion ashore unopposed on Pavuvu (in Russell Islands north-west of Guadalcanal), an operation supporting the US Army's landing the same night on nearby Banika island. No enemy were on the Rangers' island which they garrisoned for a month. In the 1 November landings west of Cape Torokina, the Battalion was commanded by Lt-Colonel Fred D. Beans They took the small offshore Puruata Island and by 1800 hours had overcome a reinforced Japanese rifle company. Meanwhile M company, detached for this landing, came ashore over the

main Green 2 beach and set up a road block 1,000yds (0.9km) inland. Later that month the 1st Parachute Bn (temporarily attached to the 2nd Raider Regiment) with M Company and a forward observation team of the 12th Marines, landed by sea on 29 November at Koiari an hour's voyage south of Cape Torokina. Put ashore by mistake in the middle of a Japanese supply base, they fought all day and were only extricated that evening by destroyers and the 155mm guns at the Cape laying a three-sided box of fire.

They were withdrawn from Bougainville on the 11 January 1944 and disbanded at the end of the month.

## 4th Raider Battalion

Formed at Camp Linda Vista (California) on 23 October 1942, the Battalion trained at the Raider Training Company's Camp Pendleton base. In late February 1943 they arrived at Espiritu Santo, the base in the New Hebrides. Their first CO, Major James Roosevelt, trained them and in May command passed to Lieutenant-Colonel Michael S. Currin.

The Battalion's first action was on New Georgia near Segi Point when the Colonel led O and P Companies with half the HQ, to pre-empt any Japanese occupation of this eastern tip of the island. A week later, after paddling their boats 8 miles (13km), they landed at Regi at 0100 hours on a patrol in strength that would take them through jungle and swamp, often waist deep in muddy water. On this first day they set up a rearguard 2 miles inland protecting the swing west to their first bivouac. From here they needed two days in terrible terrain to work their way around the Viru inlet, a distance of some 12 miles. Several attacks by Japanese patrols were brushed off before the two platoons east of the inlet took Tombe village on 1 July, and the same morning the main body took Teterma with its 3in gun overlooking the narrow harbour entrance. An attempted forcing of this passage by a naval force had been blocked, and the raiders had to fight off a final suicide attack after six hours' battle before the village was taken, and the anchorage secured that evening.

The day before, 30 June, N and Q Companies with the rest of HQ landed at Oloana Bay on Vangunu Island, a staging point for New Georgia which it adjoins. The raiders contacted a scouting party ashore and established a beach-head for the 103rd Infantry, despite the landing parties being scattered in the rough weather. The marine and army companies became separated in the subsequent fighting but had taken the main enemy positions by nightfall. Next night a Japanese barge convoy attempted to land stores and was sunk, other mopping up was completed before these companies rejoined the Battalion for the move to New Georgia's north coast on 18 July. After their action at Bairoko during their six weeks in northern New Georgia, with the 1st Raiders, the Battalion's effective strength was only 154 - 54 had been killed, 139 wounded and others were sick.

The Battalion was not brought up to strength before being disbanded on 1 February 1944.

# 1st Ranger Battalion and Darby's Rangers

The formation in June 1942 and subsequent actions of this Battalion are described in Chapter 6. In the spring of 1943 they provided the cadres for new battalions: A and B companies for the 3rd; C and D for the 4th; and E and F the new 1st. All three battalions became known as Darby's Rangers although from time to time battalions operated independently.

The 'new' 1st Battalion landed at Gela in the early hours of D-day, 10 July, and held part of the town for 36 hours despite Axis tank attacks. On D+3 they and the 4th Battalion - Darby's Force in Sicily - attacked the Mount Delta Lapa positions of the Italians which were supported by two batteries of heavy artillery. With tank support and bayonet charges, the Rangers cleared these defences taking 600 prisoners, and next day made contact with the US 3 Division advancing on their left. Darby's Force became a self-contained unit on 13 July with the addition of 18 SP howitzers from an armoured field artillery battalion. However, they took the old fortress mountain city of Butera, without bombardment when a 50-man patrol gained the centre of the city after outflanking road defences and charging the old walls' gate.

While training replacements during the next weeks several rangers were killed when mortar rounds fell short, also at this time the Ranger Cannon Company was formed with six SP 105mm (4.1in) guns under Captain Chuck Shundstrom.

Three Battalions - 1st, 3rd and 4th Rangers - landed at Salerno, see Chapter 9. During October these battalions were in the Allied line overlooking the Venafro valley some 40 miles from Naples. The mountain peaks changed hands several times while the Rangers were 45 days in the line, taking some 40 per cent casualties.

Reorganised for the Anzio landings all three Battalions came ashore in the cold early morning of 22 January 1944, taking a battery of 100mm guns, three armoured cars and two machine-gun posts. They dug-in on the perimeter and on 25-8 January held the salient near the Carrocetra-Aprilla factory area. Relieved by British troops on 29 January, they marched through the night to positions for a spearhead attack leading the US 3 Division's assault on Cisterna, See Chapter 9.

The 1st and 3rd Battalions lost 60 per cent of their numbers killed or wounded, and only 18 of the survivors escaped capture, the 4th Battalion lost 60 men killed and 120 wounded with five company commanders being killed. The remainder of the 4th Battalion fought on in the beach-head for 60 days attached to the US 4th Paras. Then 190 survivors of the original 1st Battalion were sent home to train others, and those who had joined in North Africa transferred to the 1st Special Service Force (the North Americans).

# 2nd Ranger Battalion

Formed in the USA during April 1943 when 500 men were selected from 2,000 volunteers, the Battalion completed training in the States that November - having established a US army record of 15 miles (24km) in a 2-hour speed march. They crossed the Atlantic in the liner *Queen Elizabeth* and were based at Bude (Cornwall) in the spring of 1944, with a spell in civilian billets on the Isle of Wight where their allowance was US $4(£1) a day. They completed their cliff-climbing exercises at Swanage (Dorset) and sailed for Normandy on 5 June 1944.

D, E and F Companies landed from the carriers HMS *Amsterdam* and HMS *Ben My Chree*, at the base of Pointe du Hoc cliffs, these they climbed with some difficulty when the rocket fired ropes were waterlogged - see Chapter 11. The companies drove the enemy from the battery positions and established a perimeter for aggressive patrolling, some Sections reaching the main road beyond the battery's inland defences. Here D Company on the right, E in the centre and F on the left set up a semi-circle of defence positions, destroying four unmounted 155mm guns before accurate 88mm fire stopped any movement in the forward positions. The Germans got behind them, cutting these forward Sections from the command post on the point. Nevertheless they withstood these attacks and a patrol re-established contact with the rear Sections about 2200 hours.

Before dawn on D+1 the second of two strong German attacks overran D Company, and the Companies shortened their perimeter by falling back on the reserve Sections at the point. Naval gun fire and accurate small arms fire from the rangers broke up further enemy attacks during the rest of D+1, and in the evening strong patrols went out to successfully destroy an ammunition dump and a German OP. On D+2 when the companies were relieved, they were down virtually to the strength of single Sections, E Company having one officer and 19 enlisted men.

Replacements were trained during July and August before the Battalion's next action: protecting the US 29 Divsion's right flank in the attack on Brest (Brittany). This pocket of 20,000 Germans included many of General Ramcke's parachute division who made good use of the long-established defences. The Rangers' patrol were in contact with these defenders from 20 August, and in two days of stiff fighting on 1 and 2 September. The Battalion advanced some 1,000 yards (0.5km) on the 5 September but were under heavy artillery fire for several days before reaching the area of the Lochrist (Graf Spee) battery on 8 September. Next day Lieutenant-Colonel James Rudder led his 2nd Rangers in a successful attack, the Battalion securing the battery by mid-day. 1,800 prisoners were taken at the battery and in mopping up Le Conquet peninsula. Before the port was finally taken on the 18 September, however, the American assault divisions of the Ninth Army lost almost 10,000 killed, but the port installations were destroyed by Allied shells and bombs covering the attacks.

The 2nd Rangers moved east to Paris and on through Luxembourg. They were camped deep in the Huertgen forest of Germany on 6 December. Snow had fallen earlier in the day, but the log huts were warm if dimly lit by 'No. 10 can' heaters filled with dirt soaked in petrol - like desert cookers. That evening the Battalion moved at 15 minutes notice, trucks and a final approach march bringing them through Brandenberg to the outskirts of Bergstein at 0430 hours (7 December). A, B and C Companies deployed south and west of the town, while D, E and F moved through it to prepare for an assault on a hill beyond the town. Several units had failed to capture this high ground overlooking the Germans at Schmidt and the Roer dams.

E Company opened the road to the hill at 0730, and D and F passed through to seize the hill by 0830. Withering fire pinned down all three companies who had lost half their strength by 1100 hours before a slight easing in the bombardment enabled them to improve their positions. E Company went forward to reinforce the men on the hill and the following morning a second major attack was repulsed, evacuating the wounded to the forward aid station at the church was difficult - some wounded had lain on the hill all night - but they were at last got out when American artillery fire at 0808 hours cut the road from the north, the German attacks dying away.

The battle reopened in the afternoon when for three hours German 88mm and SP guns and 150 infantry tried to retake the hill, getting within 100 yards of the aid-post church at its foot. Their last attack was stopped by artillery at 1800 hours, although General Model offered special awards to any unit retaking the hill. The rangers held on and were relieved on 9 March.

Later that spring they moved further east - Leipzig, Meresburg, and into Czechoslovakia where the Battalion was stood down at Pilsen and disbanded about June 1945.

## 3rd Ranger Battalion

Formed in North Africa from volunteers around a nucleus of 1st Rangers, Major Herman W. Dammer led them ashore near Licata in Sicily on 10 July - see Chapter 8.

A radio patrol of the Battalion Signals Officer and two NCOs went further west on the night of 16/7 July, with vehicles of the 3rd Reece Troop. Two miles south of Agrigento they were caught by 15 light tanks, but the ranger sergeant got a grenade into the open turret of the leading Renault tank which then ran out of control into the crater of a blown bridge. Two other tank crews were captured. The skill of the rangers' patrols and their daring, kept down casualties to 12 in their first eight days on Sicily.

The Battalion served in Italy with the 3rd and 4th Rangers (see above) and in the fateful infiltration to Cisterna on 30/1 January 1944.

## 4th Ranger Battalion

Activated on 29 May 1943 by Fifth Army Special order of 19 April, 31 officers were transferred from the 1st Rangers, and Lieutenant-Colonel Roy Murray was promoted from captain to command this Battalion. Their landings at Gela are described in Chapter 8, and their service later in Sicily and in Italy as part of Darby's ranger force is briefly described above. In attempting to breakthrough to the 1st and 3rd Battalion on the Cisterna road (30/1 January 1944), they - the 4th Battalion - were at first checked by machine-gun fire. Then A and B Companies put in an attack to the west of the road but were again held by heavy machine-guns' fire, E Company managed to take two of these positions and some houses overlooking other Germans 150 yards away. They were within 200 yards of the German defences but could not break through. At 1100 hours that morning two Ranger Cannon Company 75mm SP guns and 4.2in mortars supported an attack on enemy buildings, but mud and mines limited the two half-tracks' movement. Nevertheless, with the support of E Company's machine guns, F and C Companies got along the ditch east of the road and by mid-day had taken buildings on both sides of the road 'after heavy fighting'. Mines lying on top of the road were quickly cleared, and the half-tracks' fire prevented the enemy leaving the cover of ditches and buildings beyond the rangers' advance. Two light tanks came up to help D Company consolidate the position, the action report concluding 'our casualties were high'.

During February and March in the Anzio beach-head, the Battalion reports include many references 'intermittent artillery fire laid on our positions all day'. After leaving Anzio the battalion was disbanded.

## 5th Ranger Battalion

Activated on 1 September 1943 at Camp Forrest, Tennessee, the Battalion's 34 officers and 563 enlisted men arrived in the UK in March. Major Max F. Schneider was appointed CO while the Battalion was in training, first in Scotland, then at Braughton (Devon) before going to Swanage.

They boarded their British carrier ships on D-5 for the Normandy landings on 6 June 1944 described in Chapter 11. They had some 60 casualties on this D-day. On the night of D+1 Sergeants Moody and McKissick got a field telephone line to the 2nd Rangers on Point du Hoc - Moody was later killed and McKissick severely wounded. The Battalion relieved the 2nd Rangers on the Pointe on D+2; and with two half-tracks (from the 2nd) A, C, and F companies captured the 105mm howitzers at Maisy; on D+4 C, D and F Coys took the coastal defences from Grandchamp les Baines to Isigny, meeting little resistance. The Battalion received a Presidential citation for their actions on 6 June.

At Brest the Battalion captured Le Conquet in a 2-hour assault and La Mon Blanche with less opposition. On 17 September, attacking pill boxes defending Fort du Portzic, a 40lb (18kg) charge failed to break open one steel-and-concrete strong point. So that night at 2140 an 11-man patrol placed two 40lb and two 50lb charges of C-2 explosive on the concrete and covered these Beehive-type charges with 20 gallons of a petrol-and-oil mix. Half an hour later the pyre went up burning for 40 minutes. The Germans then placed machine guns outside other posts to prevent further demolitions, but the defenders were demoralised by the great explosion and were relieved to surrender next day.

During October and November the Battalion provided the security guard for Twelfth Army Group's HQ in Belgium. In December they were attached to the Sixth Cavalry Group of General

Patton's Third Army, with many individual companies working with particular troops of tanks.

On 9 February, attached to the US 94 Infantry Division, they took over an 11,000 yard (10km) front near Wehingen and attacked north-west towards Oberleuken across 'another tank ditch'. F Company's leading sections found themselves in an electrically controlled mine field under heavy enfilade machine-gun and mortar fire, but were extracted by other companies' assaults. On 23 February the Battalion was sent into 9 Division's bridgehead across the Roer, which had been in spate after the Germans blew the discharge apparatus of two reservoirs creating a long-term flood of water that delayed the Americans two weeks. The Battalion, under shell fire, crossed the only bridge - a jitter-bugging footbridge over the strong current - and were infiltrated through the enemy lines for a 48-hour operation. They marched for 9 hours through the winter night taking great care to make no noise. At 0735 hours, dawn on 24 February, they halted.

A patrol recced the route forward, before the Battalion advanced in a T-formation with D, E, C Companies from left to right across the top and F, B and A forming the column. Every few hundred yards there was a skirmish. That night they held defensive posts in and around some houses 1300 yards (1.2km) from the Irsch-Zerf road, and by 0830 on 25 February the Battalion was covering the road; they got their mines out; caught some German vehicles and walking wounded evacuating down the road. Two strong counter-attacks in the late afternoon were held although two tanks supported the German infantry. The American 294th Field Artillery provided invaluable support, their FOO calling down fire to break up further attacks being made by the German 136th Regiment of the Second Mountain Division. On the morning of 28 February the Rangers attacked the high ground to the south, being checked once on its heavily wooded slopes by rockets, they were finally held near the hilltop. Over 1,100 rockets and large shells fell on the Battalion's position that night but the signal log for 1 March begins '0015 ... 3 AAA guns knocked out and the other hit but can still fire the one. CO. ... 0805 HQ personnel - cooks, mechanics, etc - for combat and send them to my forward CP. CO. ... 0905 initial contact (with relieving force) has not been reported ... 1525 1st Bn 302nd Inf (relieving force) back at line of departure ... 2105 no artillery in last hour.' They had held ground dominating the German supply route west of Zerf, easing the passage of the American armour's breakthrough. The Battalion was finally relieved on 3 March some 9 days after they set out on their infiltration.

During April they took 1,000 Germans to see Buchenwald on General Patton's orders. On 21 April they rode on the 3rd Cavalry's tanks and took a bridge across the Danube, against minor resistance. On VE day they were in Ried (Austria), the Battalion being disbanded early in June (last Unit diary entry 31 May).

## 6th Ranger Battalion

The six rifle companies, HQ, HQ company and medical detachment of this Battalion were formed from the 98th Field Artillery Battalion on 20 August 1944 in New Guinea. They came ashore on Dinagat on 17 October, three days before the main forces' first Philippine landings - see Chapter 13. On 14 November they were relieved and spent the next two weeks near Tanuan, beside the Leyte HQ of the US Sixth Army, acting as a guard force they moved with this HQ to Tolosa and also guarded a 'Sea Bee' naval construction force building an airstrip at Tanuan (the former HQ site).

In the Lingayen Gulf landings on Luzon, 9 January 1945, the Battalion came ashore at White beach. XIV Corps bore the brunt of the drive on Manila. During this the 6th Rangers made their well organised rescue of American prisoners from behind the Japanese lines - see Chapter 13. For this action their CO, Colonel Henry A. Mucci, was awarded the DSC, every officer received the Silver Star and every enlisted man the Bronze Star. Later that spring B Company trekked 250 miles (400km) behind the Japanese lines in a 28-day recce of Aparri, and prepared the landing zones for paras to drop in the final Philippine operation.

The Battalion was disbanded at Kyoto (Japan) on 30 December 1945. But the Ranger tradition is carried on in the 1970s at Fort Benning, Georgia.

## 1st Special- Service Force
(The North Americans)

In an order of 16 June 1942 General Marshall, Chief of the American Staff, assigned Lieutenant-Colonel Robert T. Frederick to the Plough Project - the use of snow vehicles for raids, suggested by COHQ, and Americans and Canadians volunteered. The Unit's name 'was picked out of the air' and a hunt began for suitable equipment, as in July 1942 there was no standardised Arctic equipment - reindeer suits were on a 2-year delivery!

Three Regiments were raised from volunteers. The snow warfare project was dropped - see Chapter 9 - and the Regiments reorganised for combat rather than sabotage raids. In August

1943 they landed in the Aleutians where the Service battalion was organised with companies of cooks, bakers and parachute packers etc.

The Force landed in Italy in the early winter of 1943 and in December fought in the Naples-Foggia campaign - Monte La Difensa 3-6 December, Monte La Rementanea 6-9 December, Monte Sammucro (Height 720) on Christmas Day. Early in January they fought at Radicose, Monte Majo, Monte Vischiataro and on 2 February moved into the Anzio beach-head (see Chapter 9) where the Force held the right-hand sector for nearly 4 months. On 2 June they moved to Colle Ferro and two days later entered Rome, the Force was by now 2,400 strong.

In August they were in the so-called 'champagne landings' of Southern France coming ashore on Iles d'Hyeres on 14 August and moved north - Vence 1 September, Mentone 7 September - before they were disbanded in the Mentone area. By this date they had suffered 2,300 casualties, mainly in the Italian mountains. During January 1945, 74 officers and 612 enlisted men along with 7 Ranger officers and 427 rangers who had survived Anzio, transferred to the 474th Infantry Regiment (Separate).

## American Air Commando

Led by Colonel Cochran USAAF, these fliers took the Chindits into Burma in 1944, supplied them by air, flew out the wounded and gave air-to-ground support. Flying from jungle airstrips with their single-engined high wing Vultee L-5 light planes, there were occasions when these planes were caught on the ground as Japanese fighters strafed the Chindits' defensive boxes. The Air Commando were given protection by Spitfires of the 81st and other RAF Squadrons, however the withdrawal of part of this cover led to much of the light aircraft stores being destroyed outside *Broadway* box in March 1944. A few days later Mustangs of the Commando shot up an attacking ground force, after an RAF pilot had made a ground recce from the box before being flown out to brief them. The Japanese withdrew from the perimeter and the box was later evacuated on 13 May before they could mount a fresh assault.

The success of this integration of ground and air forces contributed to the development of such techniques, a feature of World War II.

## Merrill's Marauders

Brigadier-General (later Major-General) Frank D. Merrill raised this 5307th Composite Unit (Provisional) from volunteers in the South-west and South Pacific theatres, they trained in India under the overall supervision of Major-General Wingate, for long-range penetration. From February to May 1944 they carried out five major and thirty minor engagements mostly against the Japanese 18 Division, as these 3,000 raiders penetrated the Japanese controlled areas from the Hukawng Valley in northern Burma to Myitkyina on the Irrawaddy, taking the airfield at Myitkyina with its all-weather strip. Their Distinguished Unit Citation reads, '. . . the United States first ground combat force to meet the enemy on the continent of Asia . . . after a brilliant operation on 17 May 1944 [they] seized the airfield . . . an objective of great tactical importance . . .' The raiders' operations had been co-ordinated with the advance of Chinese divisions under the American General Stilwell's command, clearing north-east Burma mountains and jungles of Japanese to open the supply road from Ledo to China.

They were disbanded on 10 August 1944 but immediately reformed as an infantry regiment of Mars Force fighting in Burma till July 1945. In 1953 the Marauders were reformed as the 75th Infantry Regiment with colours carrying a Burma/India streamer.

# ALLIED SPECIAL FORCES—SMALL OPERATIONS UNITS

## British Independent Companies

Nos. 1 to 11 formed in late spring 1940 for ship-based raiding operations to harass possible German supply routes in Norway. Four companies landed between 4 and 9 May 1940 in the Mo/Bodö area protecting the southern flank of the Allied landings near Narvik (North Norway).

The Companies provided the nucleus of several Commandos formed later that summer. One record shows a No. 12 Independent Company but this does not appear to have been operational.

## Australian Independent Companies

The first four Companies were raised in Australia in the winter of 1940/1. Detachments from 2/1 Company provided the Australians' most northerly line of watchers in island posts along more than 1,000 miles (1,600+km) of the Pacific Ocean from Manus (Admiralty Islands) through Kavieng and Namatanai on New Ireland, Buka (Bougainville), Villa (New Hebrides) to Tulagi in the Solomons. These men gave warning of the Japanese advances in December/January of 1941/2. There were only 2 survivors of the detachment on Amboina, 500 miles north of Darwin, for those not killed in Japanese attacks were massacred while prisoners of war. The Sections at Manus and Buka, however, managed to get into the hills where they continued to watch and report. Survivors of 2/1 Company joined 2/3 as the first Company was not reformed.

2/2 Company spent 11 months on Timor harassing the Japanese to such good effect that the enemy thought this island would be the likely point of an Allied counter thrust - see Chapter 4.

2/3 Company garrisoned New Caledonia for 8 months until the Americans took over this island's defence, and the Company was flown into Wau (New Guinea). As they landed they came under fire but later joined up with 2/5 Company already in the area.

2/4 Company were landed on Timor in the summer of 1942 to support 2/1 Company, but in January 1943 the 2/4 Company was withdrawn. A further four companies completed their training during 1942.

2/5 Company spent 13 months shadowing and reporting on Japanese build-up of the bases at Lal and Salamaua on the northern shores of eastern New Guinea. Their first raid during 1942 was a model operation: Sections of the Company got into the centre of the Salamaua base, killed 123 Japanese, and came out without a casualty.

On their return from Timor 2/2 and 2/4 Companies became Australian Command Squadrons. They were with 2/6 and 2/7 Companies in the advances along the Ramu Valley spearheading the Americans.

## First Commando Fiji Guerrillas
(South Pacific Scouts)

Led by 44 New Zealand officers and NCOs with approximately 200 Fijians, later joined by 24 Tongans and some Solomon Islanders, the Unit was formed from the 'Southern Independent Commando Company', one of three commando-styled defence forces with some mounted patrols on Fiji in April 1942.

On 23 December 1942 30 officers and men landed on Guadalcanal for patrol duties, the first 7-man patrol moving up the Lunga river on 24 December for three days outside the Henderson field perimeter. After other patrols, often working with District Officers from the Solomon Islands, in the early summer of 1943 they were reorganised as independent 15-man patrols the Americans named South Pacific Scouts. On 2 July they landed on New Georgia's small islands in Roviana lagoon. They cleared these, travelling in native canoes. But the capture of Munda airfield took 30 days, almost 3 weeks longer than planned. Working with Western Force - while the 1st Raider Regiment was in the north - the Scouts were led by their CO, Captain (later Major) C. W. H. Tripp DSO who had raised them in Fiji.

The plan had been for two RCTs of US 43 Division to sweep to the airfield on a 4,000 yard front from the Bariki river with the Scouts patrolling the right flank. Moving to establish an advanced HQ and OP on high ground in the upper reaches of the river, the Scouts ran into an enemy force. In the next three hours the patrol advanced 2 miles yet fired only 500 rounds. Despite the bewildering noises in their first battle, the Fijians followed their six New Zealand NCOs and later came out of the jungle with only one casualty. On 6 July a Scout patrol established a base 5 miles inland.

A week later Captain Tripp with 28 Scouts while leading the US 172nd Regiment overland towards Laiana beach was suddenly caught round the waist by a Japanese leaping up from a slit trench, a second Japanese shot at Tripp as he killed the first one. The bullet was deflected as the Captain fell and he was quick enough to shoot this second enemy. 40 per cent of the Scouts' officers and 30 per cent of the NCOs had been killed, many were wounded. But the Scouts operated on Vella Lavella later that year and were not disbanded until May 1944.

## Second Commando Fiji Guerrillas

Formed from three Independent Commando companies on Fiji, these Scouts patrolled outside the American perimeter in the Empress Augusta Bay area of Bougainville. They were commanded by Major P. G. Ellis during their relatively short period of operations before being disbanded on 31 May 1944.

## Landing Craft Obstruction Clearance Units

(LCOCUs)

These 'Locku' parties of clearance divers originated as Boom Commandos: naval ratings trained to clear floating obstructions expected across the entrances to Mediterranean harbours, and which they would defend once Allied ships had passed through into a port. In November 1942 they were transferred from the Admiralty to CCO's command, doing experimental work at Appledore which became the LCOCU base. By August 1943 there were six 73-man units and they were joined in February 1944 by 3 officers and 69 marines of the RM Engineers.

## Special Boat Section

101 Troop carried out a number of cross-Channel raids including: a limpet attack on shipping in Boulogne on 11/2 April 1942; a raid on Dunkirk pier, the 4-man team being forced to withdraw when picked up by a searchlight; and some of the 'Hardtack', December 1943, recces of French coast, in one of which Lieutenant Phil Ayton was severely wounded and died after his team brought him back to the UK. In the Mediterranean during 1941 Z Group made a limpet attack on Benghazi ships when the 2-man team was captured after a successful raid; five successful attacks were also made on railways in the summer of 1941 but two in September were thwarted by enemy patrols. In 1942 their raids included: Kastelli Airfield where 7 planes were destroyed on 9/10 June by three canoeists with three agents as guides; 13/4 June one canoeist with four Frenchmen and a guide were betrayed raiding Herakleion (Crete) airfield with partial success, but some escaped; on Rhodes in September eight canoeists with their guides destroyed some aircraft but only two escaped capture.

In 1944/5 the SBS Groups A, B and C operated under the command of SOG (see below): in September 1944 one Group landed in Northern Sumatra but was unable to find their target bridge at Pente Radja; on the same day - 11 September - Group B blew the Peudada river bridge in Northern Sumatra. Group A reconnoitred the Chindwin river during this period in November/December while Group B reconnoitred the Chindwin river during this period in 1944, and Group C operated in the Arakan during the winter of 1944/5 and landed at Rangoon. SBS canoeists worked on the Irrawaddy during February and again from 15 April to 28 May 1945. (See also SOG history).

There was a group operating from Australia, which in September 1943 sank 7 ships in Singapore harbour. Their next visit a year later, however, failed to penetrate Japanese defences, the party was two-thirds Australian and led by Lieutenant-Colonel I. Lyon, DSO, (Gordons). On 6 October 1944 their captured junk was challenged by a police boat off Puloe Samboe, as they waited their opportunity to enter Singapore. In the ensuing escape by four parties in rubber boats, the raiders were all killed or captured during a month of island hopping, one officer reaching Timor in a journey of over 2,000 miles (3,200 +km). He, with others, was shot while a prisoner.

The work of the SBS passed to the Royal Marines after the war.

# Combined Operations Assault Pilotage Parties (COPPs)

See Chapter 3 for origins. The Parties served in Europe, and the Mediterranean and for 18-month tours in south-east Asia, with changes of personnel from time to time as men were assigned to less arduous duties. In the summer of 1945 the Parties in north-west Europe were regrouped in lettered units A, S, M and E.

No. 1 made Normandy beach surveys in the winter of 1943/4 and in southern France later in 1944. On 6 June navigator/pilots of this COPP led in the British I Corps to Sword and Juno and crewed X-craft markers.

In 1945, under Lieutenant Peter Wild RN, they were attached to the Small Operations Group (SOG) in south-east Asia. Canoeists with other COPPists set the timed demolition charges to blow a gap in the anti-boat stakes for the Myebon landings. In the busy waterways canoes collided on at least one occasion with a Jap boat during a night recce, the paddlers escaping, probably being mistaken for natives. At other times they escaped the probing lights of enemy sampans, while carrying out their share of the 15 COPP operations in the Arakan. They were in Madras waiting for their next operation when the war ended.

No. 2 manned LCNs for the Normandy surveys of late 1943. Moved to the Mediterranean and under the command of Lieutenant Richard Fyson RN they worked with raiding forces in the Aegean and Adriatic.

No. 3 made the February recces of Sicily where 3 of the Party were lost, see Chapter 3. Joining the SOG in July 1944 they made recces in the Arakan, and on 8 March landed on Phuket Isl for the unsuccessful recce described in Chapter 12. Later that year they surveyed the Morib beaches for the planned Malaya landings.

No. 4 lost several swimmers on 26 February and 9 March 1943 in recces of the Sicily beaches. In the summer of 1944, attached to SOG, they made a number of Arakan recces - once taking soundings on a bright night in view of a Japanese battery but were not attacked.

No. 5 surveyed the Syracuse (Sicily) beaches in late June 1943, finding batteries tunnelled into the cliffs and not visible from the air. Their submarine was picked up on radar the third night but the canoeists were recovered. They laid three beacon buoys on D-1 timed to surface just before H-hour on 10 July, canoes were launched despite the storm and these markers along with the other COPPists in MLs (homing on the buoys' radio signals) led in the British assault force on Sicily.

At the end of July they surveyed Italian beaches in the Gulf of Gioia but these were not used and on 30 August they began a survey of the Salerno beaches. The SBS team with them on these surveys was caught at the waters' edge in the light of Allied bombers' flares but escaped attention. The survey data was radioed in code from the submarine and the Party transferred at sea to later guide in assault forces including the Rangers.

After returning to the U.K. they were called at 24-hours notice to recce the Rhine at Wesel the night before the 23/4 March crossing. No artillery cover was available as the guns were moving forward, but despite this and bright moonlight they surveyed the enemy bank for minefields. They reached Asia 'too late to take part in any operations'.

No. 6 arrived in the Med in April 1943 and surveyed Sicilian beaches late in June. Among later operations, after returning to the UK, they guided in AVREs in Normandy landings.

No. 7, the first COPP to reach India, reccied Akyab Isl in October and the following March visited an island off northern Sumatra. After returning to the UK they were deployed in river recces in north-west Europe, swimming the Elbe in April 1945 to recce its crossing.

No. 8 followed No. 7 to India, made a recce north-west of Akyab and to northern Sumatra early in 1944. In Sumatra their submarine escaped damage when attacked while submerged near - if not in - an enemy harbour.

No. 9 provided personnel for X23 marker boat off Sword beach on 6 June 1944. In 1945, while attached to the SOG, their OC climbed ashore from a river jetty to find 40 Japanese in defence positions, but the canoeists escaped by paddling close to the protecting river bank. On another occasion their LC was fired on as the canoes were being launched, but her answering fire enabled the COPPists to withdraw. In April they attacked an enemy OP and took a prisoner in one of their last actions of the War.

No. 10 carried out 31 operations between 1 June and 30 November 1944 in the Mediterranean. They recced the Anzio beaches and on Adriatic islands, providing data for partisans, LSIs bringing in raiders. On Mljet they saw two Germans making a COPP-type survey from a canoe. Later No. 10 operated in the Piraeus and the Salonika areas.

They moved to India in 1945.

Note: COPP No. 7 among others were due to return to south-east Asia or had actually reached India in preparation for the invasion of Japan but the War ended before they carried out any operations in this theatre.

## Sea Reconnaissance Unit

(SRU)

Lieutenant-Commander Bruce Wright, CD, RCN (R) in January 1941 put forward the idea for these long distance swimmers, while he was serving as a junior officer in a corvette. The proposal was not accepted for nearly 2 years, then in December 1942 Lord Mountbatten arranged for the Unit's training at USMC's Camp Pendleton. Here white sharks and cold water limited the 5 to 10 miles (8-16km) paddle board swims, and the Unit moved to Nassau (Bahamas). They were followed there by an American team of swimmers later that summer (1943).

Sea training was completed by March 1944, but the previous winter the back-breathing apparatus developed technical faults for this SCUBA (self-contained underwater breathing) apparatus had only been invented during 1943. The Unit and other British frogmen therefore used the Davis Submerged Escape Apparatus breathing oxygen. Operations proposed for the Aegean, Adriatic, Black Sea and Danube were not carried through, but these powerful swimmers with a low silhouette on fast and manoeuvrable boards might have had a seaborne role in Asia.

A proposal to split the Unit was resisted on the grounds that at least 40 men were required for successful operations in any one theatre. By comparison - 'the Japanese swimmers in Burma . . . were used in several hundreds at a time . . . the Italians had 2,000 men in training [as swimmers] at La Spezia'. The whole Unit was, therefore, sent to Asia after training as parachutists and further practice in landing through heavy surf. But the Unit was deployed - as part of the Small Operations Group - in recces across the Irrawaddy, where the SBS teams had been working. Typically, an SRU 10-man team had their paddle boards portered across three miles of no-man's jungle in the dark, before crossing the 6-knot river current on the next night 11/12 February 1945. The 20 Indian Division's patrols should have guided the swimmers to their launching place but they were brought 3 miles short of the intended point. The team - as others were to do elsewhere - got to the far bank and successfully checked the narrow beach. This No. 1 Section operated with 20 Division near Myinmu, further downstream on 13 February No. 2 Section (with 7 Indian Division) made recces near Nyaungu and ten days later 4 Section was further north reconnoitring the beaches near Ngazun. In the crossings the SRU Sections guided in assault boats and/or set up beach markers at the four crossing points along the 120 miles of river, and for two feints made either side of the southern (Nyaungu) crossing. At this end of the front No. 2 Section worked also with 28 (East African) Division. In all these operations the Unit had no casualties. Three Sections moved to the An Pass area operating with COPPs and clearing routes around the barriers the Japanese set across chaungs, as they retreated into the swamps.

The Unit was disbanded at the end of the War.

## RM Boom Patrol Detachment

These marine canoeists made the 'Cockleshell' raid on shipping in Bordeaux during December 1942. An operation that would have required two infantry divisions if this port was to be raided in force. The Detachment's *Earthworm* Section was preparing for a raid on Norway in the winter of 1942 when they were transferred to the Raiding Forces Middle East. This 12 man (all ranks) Section did further demolition training near Haifa (Palestine). Some were trained as radio operators and parachuted on to islands, their attache-case radios had a 1,000-mile range and enabled them to report to Cairo HQ on Axis movements. The Section's raids included one on Leros, staging through the Raiding Force advance HQ in a caique off the Turkish coast. On this coast their MLs lay-up under camouflage nets by day. Around midnight on 17 June 1944 three canoes entered the naval base at Laki, crossed three booms and were undetected despite the calm sea and starlight. Although the canoe *Shrimp* was challenged, her crew answered in Italian and called out '*Brandenburger*', the name of a German small boat patrol. *Shark* and *Salmon* successfully placed their limpets and all three withdrew.

In the UK during 1944 this Detachment did experimental work on explosive motor boats designed to destroy beach obstacles, and the motor submersible canoe, the marines developing techniques to parachute both these boats and canoes into operations. The RM Special Boat Section of the 1970s is a direct descendant of the RMBPD.

## Small Scale Raiding Force

(SSRF)

Members of this force operated from Poole (Dorset) in the trawler *Maid of Honour*. There is a record of a cutting out expedition with this ship capturing a liner (unnamed) during 1941 before they took the trawler to West Africa. During 1942 the SSRF was formally set up with responsibilities to CCO and SOE. The founders - Major G. March-Phillips DSO, OBE; Major J. G. Appleyard DSO, MC*; and Captain G. Hayes MC - were all killed in action with SSRF or similar units. The Force trained along commando lines but did parachute training as well as small boat work. Much of their work was of a clandestine nature but typical of their early raids were those in the two weeks to 14 February 1942: 2 men in canoe to recce Anse de St. Martin (Cherbourg Peninsula); 10 men raiding for prisoners near Omonville; and 10 men raiding Herm and Jethou in Channel Islands.

In the summer of 1942 they made several raids including: north-west of Pointe de Saire killing 3 enemy; to the Casquet Light on the Channel Island rocks notorious for rough seas; and to Ste Horoniné near Cherbourg where the landing party was captured or killed. After January 1943 such raids were co-ordinated by an Auxiliary Operations Group or its equivalent and the SSRF's independent operations ceased in the Channel (but see 62 Cdo).

## 1st Special Raiding Squadron

The designation of 2nd SAS for operations in the Mediterranean - see Raiding Forces Middle East - on 3 September 1943. 243 all ranks landed unopposed at Bagnara Calabria (Italy) but were engaged by Axis forces in hills behind this port before XIII Corps linked up with them on 4 September.

## Raiding Forces Middle East

Under Brigadier D. J. T. Turnbull the operations of the LRDG including a New Zealand Squadron, Major the Earl Jellicoe's 100-strong units of the Special Boat Section, 30 Commando, some American medics and the 1st Special Raiding Squadron, were brought into a co-ordinate series of operations from 11 November 1943. Before this date these units had carried out independent raiding, some of their units reached Cos (north of Rhodes) before the end of September, and other parties set up observation posts on Leros, Calino, Simi and Stampalia. But on 12 October the SBS party withdrew from Simi after being in action with advancing German troops. They were replacing Italian garrisons and when the LRDG attempted that month to capture Levinthos they lost 43 of the 50-strong raiding party.

The raiding forces continued to operate in the Aegean and Adriatic islands with the three caiques of the Levant Schooner Squadron, an RAF launch, and naval coastal forces. They landed on 13 islands in the Aegean, on 22 in the Cyclades (between the Aegean and the Sea of Crete) and on 7 in the Dodecanese Islands running north

from Rhodes, with over 380 separate small and large operations. In April 1944 a party of nine (British and Cretans) captured the German General commanding Crete bringing him out on 14 May. Some units of this force later operated in North Italy at Comacchio where SBS and other raiding units worked with 2 Commando Brigade.

## RM Detachment 385

This Royal Marine Detachment was formed in the UK during summer of 1944 and completed their training with SOG becoming operational in January 1945 in south east Asia. In their first operation Nos. 1 and 2 Troops both lost their commanders and 4 marines were killed, No. 1 were landed by inflatables from a Catalina flying boat to create a diversion on Biluyen Island but strong tides caused casualties. A section of No. 2 Troop landed on Phuket Island with COPP No. 3 in the unsuccessful operation described in Chapter 12, but most of '385's' 14 independent operations were successful during the early summer of 1945. These included deception raids to the Thailand coast and the Nicobars, elsewhere they landed agents and stores for guerrillas.

In August 1945 Nos. 1 and 3 Troops were aboard HMS *Princess Beatrix* and No. 2 Troop at Madras, preparing for further raids that were cancelled when the War ended.

## Small Operations Group
(SOG)

Lieutenant-Colonel H. G. Hasler, DSO, OBE, RM of the RMBPD had co-ordinated and trained the small-scale raiding forces in south-east Asia during the spring of 1944, when Detachment 385 was formed to strengthen these forces. Officially SOG was not formed until 12 June with a base staff and training unit. Commanded by Colonel H. T. Tollemache the Group carried out 19 independent operations mounted by SOG and 154 on the Arakan coast and Burma rivers by the Group's units attached to specific forces - known as Force Commanders' Operations.

The Group's maximum strength was four COPPs (several parties being relieved by others), Group A, B and C of the SBS, the three Troops of Detachment 385, and the SRU's four Sections. The organisation of these units with a parent base and adequate staff to provide back-up facilities and intelligence, proved successful. In over 170 operations they had only 27 casualties, a remarkable record in such hazardous work.

## RN Beach Commandos

In December 1941 eight Beach Parties were planned and during the next few months they trained with Army Beach Groups. The name Beach Parties was changed to RN Commandos, with their training school on Loch Long (HMS *Armadillo*). The Beach Commandos came in early in any operation, for example: the Principal Beach Masters landing in the 5th Wave (H+25) at Normandy, at Flushing in 1944 the Beach Master landed in the first flight of LCAs.

## Combined Operations Scout Units
(COSUs)

These Units, formerly known as 'Camouflage B', created 'some diversions at the time of assault, simulating a landing away from the main assault'. Their training began in October 1943 at the Army's Light Scout Car Training Centre (Ballantrae, Ayrshire). Diversions of this type were used in Sicily, Salerno and Comacchio operations, but in Normandy the naval units were not apparently used. They trained for the Far East, where not only diversion noises were to be used but also cover and terror noises.

Four Combined Operations units had the equivalent capacity to one army (land) unit and by 6 April 1944 four COSUs had been trained. However, American developments in this field led to the suspension of further work although units' equipment had been tested in various craft of which coastal forces' vessels proved most suitable.

## RAF Servicing Commandos

These commandos serviced aircraft on advanced airfields often taking over fields still under artillery or even small arms fire. They brought in petrol, ammunition and replacement parts, and serviced engines, guns and airframes from the roll of tools for their trades that each man carried in an assault landing. The units had one mobile workshop that was brought ashore as early as practical, their other vehicles and tankers usually landing late on D-date when vehicle-carrying convoys arrived for the build-up of a beach-head.

They wore Combined Operations flashes (AMO-29 October 1942).

Their unit histories are full of such comments as those for '3207' at Meiktila (200 miles due east of Maungdaw, Burma) in March 1945: '23 March 1130 hours - Beachcraft lands . . . immediately takes off with battle casualties . . . 1400 hours two Dakotas of No. 238 Squadron land to take off casualties . . . port engine of second aircraft refused to start . . . Sergeant Brown promptly ran

to the strip . . . shells were falling extremely close . . . one or two within 50ft of him . . . the aircraft was hit . . . another Beachcraft, attempting to land, was hit . . . and completely burnt out. Sergeant Brown . . . warned [other] aircraft to take off immediately . . . 1730 hours: CO and Sergeant Brown . . . removed equipment from damaged Dakota'. Throughout the day the men were under fire and held 50 yards (45m) of the perimeter of the defensive box that night. Next day the CO rescued a wounded soldier from outside the wire, in fighting at one corner of the box. The CO of the RAF Regiment's defence force was killed at this time.

3201 Commando was formed in 1942, landed in North Africa on D-day at about H+60 mins, and reached Maison Blanch airfield at 0910. They served in North Africa and like many Service Commando operated with aircraft recovery units when not required for assault landings. They were in Sicily in 1943 and moved to Corsica in January 1944. Their CO for the 2½ years was Flight-Lieutenant E. H. Webster who has written: 'the Unit was misused after Sicily because no-one on the staff knew its capabilities.'

3202 Commando served in North Africa and southern Italy disbanded at Taranto December 1943.

3203 Commando served in North Africa, Sicily, and at Salerno where they serviced Taylorcraft of Air OP etc. Disbanded at Portici (Italy) February 1944.

3204 Commando landed Sicily July 1943, disbanded at Catania 3 February 1944.

3205 Commando landed D+1 (7 June 1944) Normandy, two men were killed as one vehicle hit a mine on leaving their LCT; the Unit serviced Spitfires during June - each Commando had fitters trained to work on the types of planes likely to use their airstrips. They arrived in India 5 December 1944 and from LCMs on Akyab in January 1945; and operated in Arakan, Malaya, and Java before being disbanded in February 1946.

3206 Commando landed D+10 in Normandy, June 1944, and operated through France to Belgium spending December under canvas. Returned to UK and disbanded in April 1945.

3207 Commando arrived in India in December 1944 and after helping No. 3 R & SU with major rebuilding, flown into Meiktila - see above. They were withdrawn on 29 April and later serviced planes including those repatriating ex-prisoners until disbanded in April 1946.

3208 Commando landed in Normandy on D+10, servicing Mustangs among other aircraft, they moved forward to advanced airfields including those flying off Mosquitoes covering the Rhine crossing. Disbanded in March 1945.

3209 Commando landed in Bombay, January 1945, intended for airfields captured/built on Phuket Island they worked mainly on recovery. Disbanded about December 1946 when A Squadron was serving in Bangkok and B Squadron in Saigon.

3210 Commando landed in India in spring of 1945 and in Malaya over Morib beaches on 17 September, for work on Kuala Lumpur's Kelanang airfield. Disbanded about October 1945 in Java.

3225 Commando formed in UK in July 1942, served in Egypt before being disbanded in December (?) 1943.

3226 Commando formed in July 1942, served in Sicily, and at Salerno where strip under fire but petrol brought up from beach area. After further service in Italy, disbanded January 1944.

3230 and 3231 Commandos formed in Egypt in March/April 1943, landed in Sicily and Toe of Italy before being disbanded in November 1943 and January 1944 respectively.

## Various

A number of other units had Commando titles or were forces made up of Commandos. The Burma II Commando of 30 men under Mike Calvert destroyed installations at Henzada on the Irrawaddy in March 1942. 142 Commando formed from men of the Burma Rifles, served with parachutist Brigadier Wingate's forces on their 1943 march into Burma. The Raiding Support Regiment's gunners firing anti-aircraft, and support weapons, used great ingenuity in getting these weapons on to Adriatic islands. They provide one of many examples of artillery support the Special Forces of all nationalities enjoyed in later years of the War. The 34th Amphibian Support Regiment typifies many of the units whose personnel had special skills used in support of commandos, although the same individuals might be formed into different units from time to time - most of the marines of the 34th Regiment had served in the tanks of the RM Armoured Support Regiment, landing in the assault waves at Normandy.

There were many units especially among airborne forces that from time to time carried out commando-style raids while acting as ground troops, most notable of the British Units in this role was the SAS.

## Special Air Service

The 1st SAS was formed from 62 Commando in February 1943, under Lieutenant-Colonel A. David Stirling (who had formed 'No. 62'). He was captured in the Sfax-Gabes area and later Lieutenant-Colonel R. B. (Paddy) Mayne - credited with more aircraft destroyed than any fighter pilot in the desert war - became CO of the 1st SAS. The 2nd SAS was formed as a unit of the First Army and served among the Mediterranean Islands as the 1st Special Raiding Squadron.

The work of the SAS involved more clandestine activities than in commando work; parachuting into Sicily, for example, ahead of the Allied advance on D+2 (12 July), 12 men dropped but Major Geoffrey Appleyard's plane was lost with his party and its crew. By January 1944 there were five SAS regiments - 2 British, 2 French and 1 Belgian, who played an undercover role on many occasions in their 42 operations in North West Europe.

## Force code names

The grouping of British commandos in various forces from time to time included the following:
Layforce - 7, 8 and 11 Commandos sailed to Middle East early in 1942 and joined by 50 and 52 Commandos to form a brigade of the Eighth Army, disbanded after Crete operations in May 1942.
Northforce - drew on men of 12 and 14 Commandos for operations in Norway, including the long reconnaissance at the end of February 1943 to Sognefjord.
Timberforce - formed in late summer of 1943 but by February and March 1944 found raiders could seldom surprise German defenders in Norway.
Fynnforce - men of 12 Commando serving in Northforce.
Forfarforce - parties of about 10 men raiding across the Channel to identify enemy coastal units and capture technical information in the summer of 1943. Men drawn from 12 Commando, SBS, etc.
Layforce II - took over cross-Channel raiding from Forfarforce in November 1943, men from 10(I-A) Commando, 4 Commando and an airborne Troop.
Hiltforce - men of 10(I-A) Commando and RE specialists for May 1944 reconnaissance across the Channel looking for element-C obstacles.

# BIBLIOGRAPHY

## Histories

*James Altieri, *The Spearheaders* (Bobbs-Merrill, 1960); *American Forces in Action*, series (US Army, Office of History) including: *Omaha Beach-head 6-13 June 1944;*

J. E. Appleyard, *Geoffrey: being the story of Apple of the Commandos* (Blandford, 1947);

*Robert B. Asprey, *War in the Shadows* (Macdonald & Jane's, 1976);

Alan Baker, *Merrill's Marauders* (Ballantine, 1972);

Roger A. Beaumont, *Military Elites* (Hale, 1976);

Christopher Buckley, *Norway - Commandos - Dieppe* (HMSO, 1951);

Robert D. Burhans, *The First Special Service Force: a History of the North Americans* (Washington Infantry Journal Press, 1947);

Bernard J. Callinan, DSO, MC, *Independent Company: the 2/2 and 2/4 Independent Companies in Portuguese Timor* (Heinemann, Melbourne, 1953);

*Michael Calvert, *Chindits: Long Range Penetration* (Ballantine, 1973);

Maurice Chauvet, *D-Day, 1er B.F.M. Commando* (Amicale des Anciens Parachutistes S.A.S. & Commando, 1974);

Joseph H. Devins, *The Vaagsö Raid; the Commando attack that changed the course of World War II* (Hale, 1967);

Eisenhower Foundation, *D-Day - the Normandy Invasion in Retrospect* (University Press of Kansas, 1971);

Sir Bernard Fergusson, *The Watery Maze* (Collins, 1961);

O. A. Gillespie, *The Pacific* (Owen, Wellington, 1952);

Henry S. Glassman, *Lead the Way Rangers: a history of the Fifth Ranger Battalion* (published privately, Bruckmann, 1945);

Harold W. Gunther, *'E' Company 2nd Ranger Battalion* (published privately, c.1946);

A. Cecil Hampshire, *On Hazardous Service* (Kimber, 1974);

*History of the Second World War* series and allied books (HMSO) including: L. F. Ellis, *Victory in the West* (1962); *M. R. D. Foot, *S.O.E. in France*; *S. W. Kirby, *The War Against Japan*; C. J. C. Molony, *The Mediterranean and Middle East* (Vol V, 1973);

Gordon Holman, *Commando Attack* (Hodder, 1942);

*Jeter A. Isley and Philip A. Crowl, *The US Marines and Amphibious War: its theory, and its practice in the Pacific* (Princeton University Press, 1951);

P. K. W. Johnson, *The Story of 46 Commando Royal Marines* (Gale & Polden, 1946);

Vincent Jones, *Operation Torch* (Ballantine, 1972);

John Laffin, *Anzacs at War* (Abelard Schuman, 1965);

Gordon Landsborough, *Tobruk Commando* (Cassell, 1956);

Colin R. Larsen, *Pacific Commando* (Reed, Wellington, 1946);

Sir Robert Bruce Lockhart, *The Marines Were There* (Putnam, 1950);

George Millar, *The Bruneval Raid* (Bodley Head, 1974);

*J. L. Moulton, *Haste to the Battle* (Cassell, 1963);

*Ross Munro, *Gauntlet to Overlord: The Story of the Canadian Army* (Macmillan, Toronto, 1946);

C. E. Lucas Phillips, *The Cockleshell Heroes* (Heinemann, 1957);

*C. E. Lucas Phillips, *The Greatest Raid of All: St Nazaire 1942* (Heinemann, 1958);

C. E. Lucas Phillips, *The Raiders of the Arakan* (Heinemann, 1976);

Hugh Pond, *Sicily* (Kimber, 1962);

Patrick Pringle, *Fighting Marines* (Evans, 1966);

*Raiding Forces, the Story of an Independent Command in the Aegean* (No. 1 Public Relations Service. M.E.F. 1945);

*Ranger - a short history* (US Army Infantry School, Fort Benning, Georgia, 1962);

*Hilary St George Saunders, *The Green Beret: the Story of the Commandos 1940-45* (Michael Joseph, 1949);

*Sir William Slim, *Defeat into Victory* (Cassell, 1956);

C. P. Stacey, *The Canadian Army 1939-45* (Ministry of Defence, Ottowa, 1948);

Bill Strutton and Michael Pearson, *The Secret Invaders* (Hodder, 1958);

R. W. Thompson, *The Eighty-Five Days, the story of the Battle of the Scheldt* (Hutchinson, 1957);

*The United States Army in World War II* series (United States Army Office of History) including: M. Hamlin Cannor, *Leyte the return to the Philippines;* R. Ross Smith, *Triumph in the Philippines;*

*Charles L. Updegraph, Jr, *Special Marine Corps Units of World War II* (Historical Division, USMC, 1972);

Peter Young, *Commando* (Macdonald, 1970);

*48 Royal Marine Commando, The Story 1944-6* (published privately, 1946) *The 81st Infantry (Wildcat) Division in World War II* (Washington Infantry Journal Press, 1948).

## Memoirs and biographies

*Michael Davie, editor, *The Evelyn Waugh Diaries* (Weidenfeld, 1976);

*John Durnford-Slater, *War Commando* (Kimber, 1953);

Donald Gilchrist, *Castle Commando* (Oliver & Boyd, 1960);

*Murdock C. McDougall, *Swiftly They Struck: story of No. 4 Commando* (Odhams, 1954);

*Derek Mills-Roberts, *Clash by Night* (Kimber, 1956);

*Suzanne Lassen, *Anders Lassen VC* (Muller, 1965);
Ralph Neville, *Survey by Starlight* (Hodder, 1949);
*Eric Newby, *Love and War in the Apennines* (Hodder, 1971);
George Talbot, COPPs Ten's Boxes (unpublished typescript in the care of the Imperial War Museum);
Bruce S. Wright, *The Frogmen of Burma* (Kimber, 1968);
Peter Young, *Storm from the Sea* (Kimber, 1956).

## Articles, references and other papers

*The Army Commandos* (Ranger Bn Association newsletter, 1971);
*The Arctic Front* (anon, Norseman Vol 1, No. 6, 1944);
*Army Training Memoranda (British) Nos. 34-7* (1940);
*British Commando* (Military Intelligence, Special Series 1, US War Dept, 1942);
*Evans F. Carlson, *Report of the Operations of this Battalion (2nd Raiders) on Guadalcanal 4 November to 4 December 1942* (operation report, 1942);
*Diary notes of a commando officer* (manuscript in the care of the Imperial War Museum);
*Dunlop Digest of Technical and Commercial Information for Dunlop Executives* (February, 1946);
John M. Haines, *Report of Marine-Submarine Raider Expedition* (operational report, 1942);
Julian S. Hatcher, *Book of the Garand Rifle* (National Rifle Association, USA, 1948);
*Fact Files* (Macdonald & Jane's, various dates in 1970s);
*The Independent Companies* (On Service, Vol III No. 8);
Sapper Jack, *Beach Clearance Party* (RE Journal Vol LXVI, No. 2);
*Sir Martin Lindsay Bt, *The Battery* (British Army Review No. 50, 1975);
Henry A. Mucci, *Rescue at Cabanatuan* (US Army press release, 1945);
Ranger Battalions - various action reports;
*Report on amphibious vehicles* (Borg Warner, 1957);
*Small Unit Actions* (United States War Dept, 1946);
J. P. O'Brien Twohig, *Are Commandos really necessary?* (Army Quarterly, 1948);
E. J. D. Turner—correspondence with RN Submarine museum, describing Welman one-man submarine;
T. J. Walden and James Gleeson, *The Frogman: the story of wartime underwater operations* (Evans, 1950);
*S. C. Waters, *Anzio* (Canadian Army Journal Vol 2 Nos. 5 & 6, 1948);
*30th Assault Unit* (notes in the care of the Royal Marines Museum);
*'385'* (diary notes in the care of the Royal Marines Museum).

*Note:
Permission to quote from these books on the following pages is gratefully acknowledged:

*The Spearheaders* - pp 108 rt. col. - 112, 131, 166 rt. col.;
*War in the Shadows* - p 232;
*Chindits* - pp 212, 262;
*S.O.E. in France* - p 163;
*The War against Japan* - p 219;
*The US Marines and Amphibious War* - p 100;
*Haste to the Battle* - pp 13, 187, 202, 208;
*Gauntlet to Overlord* - p 128;
*The Greatest Raid of All* - pp 48, 52;
*The Green Beret* - pp 52, 86, 89, 90, 91, 127, 158, 167 re friar, 187, 214;
*Defeat into Victory* - p 229;
*Special Marine Corps Units of World War II* - pp 95, 97;
*Waugh Diaries* - pp 119, 120;
*War Commando* - pp 36, 88, 93, 108 rt. col., 128, 133, 134, 135, 147-148;
*Swiftly they Struck* - pp 185, 195, 200;
*Clash by Night* - p 87;
*Anders Lassen VC* - p 163;
*Love and War in the Apennines* - pp 122, 123;
*The Battery* - p 88 rt. col;
*Guadalcanal Report 1942* - pp 102-103;
*Anzio* - p 153.

# INDEX